Heirs of the Pharisees

BROWN CLASSICS IN JUDAICA

Editorial Board

Jacob Neusner
Chairman

Dagmar Barnouw
Wendell S. Dietrich
Ernest S. Frerichs
Calvin Goldscheider

Sidney Goldstein
David Hirsch
Alan Zuckerman
Robert Warnock

BROWN CLASSICS IN J·U·D·A·I·C·A

HEIRS OF THE PHARISEES

BY

JAKOB J. PETUCHOWSKI

University Press of America, Inc.

Series Introduction © 1985
Copyright © 1986 by

University Press of America,® Inc.

4720 Boston Way
Lanham, MD 20706

3 Henrietta Street
London WC2E 8LU England

All rights reserved

Printed in the United States of America

Copyright © 1970 by Basic Books, Inc.

Library of Congress Cataloging in Publication Data

Petuchowski, Jakob Josef, 1925-
　Heirs of the Pharisees.

　(Brown classics in Judaica)
　Originally published: New York : Basic Books, 1970.
　Includes bibliographies and indexes.
　　1. Tradition (Judaism)　2. Judaism—20th century.
I. Title.　II. Series.
BM529.P363　1986　　296.1　　86-1496
ISBN 0-8191-5256-0 (pbk. : alk. paper)

All University Press of America books are produced on acid-free
paper which exceeds the minimum standards set by the National
Historical Publications and Records Commission.

In Memory of My Teachers

LEO BAECK, ISRAEL BETTAN, SAMUEL S. COHON,
BRUNO ITALIENER, BENNO JACOB,
ARTHUR LOEWENSTAMM, ISAAK MARKON.

"And they that are wise shall shine
as the brightness of the firmament."
(Daniel 12:3)

CONTENTS

	Brown Classics in Judaica	ix
	Introduction to Brown Classics in Judaica Series Edition	xi
	Introduction	3
CHAPTER 1	The Pharisaic Tradition Today	8
CHAPTER 2	The Bible of the Synagogue	20
CHAPTER 3	A Fence with Loopholes	39
CHAPTER 4	The Magnification of Hanukkah	57
CHAPTER 5	The Hero of the Isaac Story	68
CHAPTER 6	Reflections on a Title	76
CHAPTER 7	The Grip of the Past	84
CHAPTER 8	Not by Bread Alone	100
CHAPTER 9	Beyond Fundamentalism and Iconoclasm	110
CHAPTER 10	Revelation and the Modern Jew	116
CHAPTER 11	Reflections on Revelation	130
CHAPTER 12	The Christian-Jewish Dialogue	141
CHAPTER 13	Prayer in an Unredeemed World	160
CHAPTER 14	Criteria for Reform Jewish Observance	167
CHAPTER 15	The Holy Community	181
	Index of Scriptural References	191
	Index of Rabbinic Passages	193
	Name Index	195
	Subject Index	197

BROWN CLASSICS IN JUDAICA

Classics of scholarly exposition of important problems and themes in Judaism gain renewed life in the series at hand. The criterion for selection for reprint explains the purpose of the editors. We seek to place into the hands of a new generation the enduring intellectual achievements of an earlier time in our own century and in the one before. The issues of Judaism and the life of the Jewish people, analyzed in a rigorous and responsible way, retain perennial relevance. For what being a Jew meant in times past derived from the on-going imperatives of Judaism, on the one side, and the condition of eternal Israel, the Jewish people, on the other. The editors therefore maintain that scholars speaking to a broad audience in one age continue to address the lasting realities of ages to come. For scholars to begin with ask not what is current but what is true, not what presses today but what is urgent everyday, for all times.

The records of the past teach diverse lessons. The one we wish to impart is how first-rate minds confront the record of the past as an on-going encounter with an enduring condition and an on-going human reality. So we promise that the books of this series exemplified in this one, will speak to today's readers as much as it did to the ones who first received the works we now reprint. The series highlights modes of address we find exemplary. When scholars speak, they demand a hearing because they ask the tough questions and trouble to discover rigorous answers to them. Scholars are not always right. Time alone will sort things out. But scholars always take responsibility for knowing the requirements of truth and attempting in good faith to meet them. They do not make things up as they go along and declare new truth morning by morning.

This series proposes to renew the life of classics of Judaic learning because the editors deem an important task the on-going renewal of sustained learning in the realm of Judaic discourse. So this book is in this series because it shows, in one way or in another, how, when it comes to the study of Judaism and of the life of the Jewish people, we think people should carry on the labor of learning.

Jacob Neusner

In behalf of the board of editors

*Introduction to the
Brown Classics in Judaica
Series Edition*

The Pharisees formed an unimportant sect in the period before the destruction of Jerusalem in 70 C.E., but laid the foundations for the Judaism that took shape afterward. Most scholars concur that the Pharisees before 70 produced traditions carried on by the rabbis afterward. So here Petuchowski takes up that heritage and treats it as a challenge to contemporary Jews.

Petuchowski speaks lucidly and powerfully to "the heirs of the Pharisees," meaning to all Jews today, since he identifies Judaism as the outcome of "the teachings of the scribes and sages who began their activity during the days of the Second Temple." As an important theological figure in contemporary Judaism, Petuchowski, long-time professor at Hebrew Union College-Jewish Institute of Religion, Cincinnati, take up a position in the process of framing and handing on the tradition that Judaism inherited, through the Pharisees, from Sinai. The importance of this book, therefore, derives from the author's interpretation of that heritage of contemporary Jews. The urgency implicit in the pages of this book comes from the author's ability to render issues vital and arguments persuasive. This is a book that conveys an ancient message to an on-going generation, and that is why it demands for itself the audience of the twenty-first century that this Classics-series provides.

What makes Judaism the heir of Pharisaism in the most positive sense? That is the argument of Chapter One, which identifies with Pharisaism the power of exemplifies all that is good and attractive in the Judaic tradition. In particular Petuchowski finds in the address out of Pharisaism to the masses of Jewry the source of the power of the Pharisaic-rabbinic tradition. Petuchowski really refers to his own generation: the secret of the ancient Pharisees' success in winning over a whole people lay in their refusal to accept the lowest common denominator as the norm and the ideal.'' What he is saying pertains to Reform Judaism: do not settle for the lowest common denominator, aim at the highest. Do not serve as the movement demanding slight commitment, raise your sights, and with yours, the sights of all other Jews. That address, to Reform Judaism which Petuchowski serves as theologian, pertains as much to Conservatism, Orthodoxy, and Reconstructionism alike.

In the subsequent chapters Petuchowski proceeds to explain how the Pharisees and later rabbis received and inherited Scripture. They did not merely receive and paraphrase the teachings of the Written Torah. They entered a creative and innovative relationship with Scripture. Along these same lines, Petuchowski proceeds to explain how the Pharisees and rabbis dealt with Hanukkah, with Genesis 22, and other important topics.

The chapters the reader will find particularly suggestive come with Petuchowski's treatment of theological issues, particularly in connection with revelation. Without a well-framed doctrine of revelation, no Jew can explain the authority and value of the Torah. So here Petuchowski works out what he calls a "non-fundamentalist" approach to the document of Revelation. In a sequence of important chapters, Petuchowski as distinguished theologian works out

Introduction to the Brown Classics in Judaica Series Edition

a theory of revelation entirely credible to contemporary Jews. He reaches into our own experience to make sense of a difficult and alien idea. At the end he turns to the contemporary dialogue between Judaism and Christianity, another subject of intense concern to Jews living in Europe and North America.

Petuchowski addresses the issue of how Judaism, an age-old tradition, adapts to the movement of time and circumstance: "Thus far the adaptability of that tradition has been the key to its survival." He proposes to explain how that same tradition lives today. The strength of his writing is its clarity, capacity to take up serious questions and consider tough issues, and rigorous and thoughtful responses. His message, written nearly two decades ago, remains remarkably relevant:

> For only if the 'holy community' remains undivided on the basic level of its existence, only if there can be an unqualified acceptance of one another as fellow Jews, will there be hope for the flourishing growth of individual piety and the productive diversity in religious expression.

What draws people together, beyond the divisions of conviction and sentiment that divide, them? It is that power of rational discourse, careful argument, rigorous reasoning and vigorous and sustained result, that is exhibited by Petuchowski in this excellent classic of contemporary Judaic theology.

Jacob Neusner
Brown University
Providence, Rhode Island

Heirs of the Pharisees

Introduction

The modern Jew is the heir of the Pharisees. The two millennia which separate him from the last of the biblical books do not represent a vacuum. Modern Judaism does not take up the thread where the Bible left off—although, throughout Jewish history, there have been sectarian movements which have occasionally attempted to do so. For the majority of Jews, the biblical thread has never been interrupted. There is a direct connection between the Jew of today and his biblical ancestors.

The link which connects the modern Jew with the canonical literature of his Hebrew forebears is the religion of the Pharisees, the teachings of the scribes and sages who began their activity during the days of the Second Temple, and the result of whose monumental labors has been preserved in the vast literature of the Talmud and in the very fabric of Jewish life. Looking upon themselves as mere "interpreters" of the Torah, those scribes and sages, in fact, initiated a process of continuous reform, adapting the biblical provisions to the ever changing circumstances of life and laying the foundations of the whole post-biblical evolution of Judaism. Strictly guarding the heritage entrusted to them against the harmful influences emanating from the outside world, they nevertheless endowed Judaism with enough elasticity to be ever receptive to such environmental factors as would contribute to its own strength and survival.

The historian may indeed wish to limit the period of the "Pharisees" both in space and in time, considering this phenomenon in Jewish history to have been superseded by other forms of organization and structure to which, for clarity's sake, he might prefer to apply a different nomenclature. The fact remains that the contribution of the Pharisees has been a permanent one. It was included in, and became the basis for, all later reformulations of post-biblical Judaism. To the extent, therefore, to which the modern Jew is not an absolute literalist in interpreting the Bible, to the extent to which his religion includes elements not found in the Scriptures, and even to the extent to which his religious way of life excludes biblical provisions without doing harm to the over-all religious structure— to that extent the modern Jew is, and remains, an heir of the Pharisees.

His relation to that heritage may, of course, be negative as well as positive, or—and this seems to happen not infrequently —somewhat ambivalent. Yet even those Jews whose attitude toward the Pharisaic tradition is wholly positive are by no means unanimous in their understanding of it or in their plans for its further preservation and development. Some may wish to "freeze" it at one or another of the stages of its evolution, and to transmit it in the identical form and content in which they received it from their immediate predecessors. Others, again, may be so impressed by the very dynamics of change, which a historical analysis of the Pharisaic phenomenon reveals, that they, as heirs of the Pharisees, feel perfectly free to set little store by traditional sentiment and inherited custom, being ever ready to reshape their religion in terms of present and (estimated) future "needs." Still others may wish to retain the outward forms of the Tradition and yet let go of its doctrinal content; while yet a fourth group, both liberal *and* traditional in doctrine, lays claim to the right of changing outward forms where the absolute necessity of such a change has

Introduction

been clearly demonstrated and can be effected on the basis of traditional precedent.

To say that the Orthodox, Reform, Reconstructionist, and Conservative movements in American Judaism each cater to one of those four groups, while admissible as a rule of thumb, is not, strictly speaking, accurate. Major areas of agreement and disagreement frequently transcend "denominational" boundaries to such an extent that the ideological disagreements within one and the same camp have, on occasion, been known to exceed in gravity those disagreements which normally divide one camp from the other. At the same time, particularly within the ranks of the younger Jewish theologians in recent years, the bonds of agreement with colleagues in other "denominational" groupings have been strong enough to bridge the separation caused by "denominational" loyalties.

It is for this reason that the author, writing from what would generally be regarded as a "Reform" point of view, feels confident that the problems with which he is dealing in this book are problems of both interest and concern to all modern "heirs of the Pharisees," whatever their "denominational" commitments. It is also hoped that this "inside" view of the Pharisaic tradition will be of interest to Christian readers—particularly to those who are beginning to realize that there may have been more to the Pharisees than the authors of the New Testament have chosen to record.

Not unlike the Pharisaic-Rabbinic manner of Scripture interpretation, which was a constant shuttling backward and forward between the sacred text and the new problems which had to be solved, this book, too, is less concerned with all the details of the historical setting of the original Pharisees and far more concerned with the implicit dynamics of the Pharisaic phenomenon and with the relevance of Pharisaism to the religious problems facing the modern Jew. Our first chapter sets the tone for this. Here, the historical background of Pharisaism is very briefly examined in the light of modern scholarship, and an attempt is made to show how the Pharisaic pattern tends to repeat itself, and what its implications are for modern Judaism. But whatever the Pharisees and their successors, the early Rabbis, ultimately achieved, it was as interpreters of the Bible that they primarily looked upon themselves. Our second chapter, therefore, is devoted to a description of the Bible as it was read and understood by the Pharisees and the Rabbis. The next three chapters furnish concrete illustrations of Pharisaic-Rabbinic activity: in legislating, in dealing with a post-biblical festival, Hanukkah; and in the interpretation of a theologically significant chapter in the Bible, the twenty-second chapter of the Book of Genesis.

Since the immediate successors of the Pharisees, from the end of the first century of the Common Era on, were called "Rabbis," Chapter 6 is devoted to the implications of that title, both at the time of its origin and in modern Jewish usage. Progressive as Pharisaic-Rabbinic Judaism has always been, particularly when contrasted with such "fundamentalist" Jewish sects as the Sadducees and the Karaites, it has, nevertheless, always represented itself as the true guardian of the past. But this seems to be a characteristic of every reform movement in history; and Chapter 7 explores the psychology behind that phenomenon.

Basic and central to the whole Pharisaic enterprise was the belief in a God who reveals Himself, and in a Revelation which was not exhausted by the contents of any one written document. Although the Pharisees and the Rabbis could not have anticipated some of the philosophical and theological problems confronting the belief in Revelation in more modern times, their "non-fundamentalist" approach to the document of Revelation remains highly suggestive and instructive for the modern Jewish theologian, and enables him to remain aware of his indebtedness to Pharisaic Judaism. Aspects of that relationship are dealt with in Chapters 8, 9, 10, and 11.

The Pharisees erected their system upon the foundations of the Hebrew Bible. But they were not the only heirs of the biblical legacy. Nascent Christianity, too, laid claim to that heritage. Yet Judaism and Christianity, in spite of their common back-

Introduction

ground, developed into entirely different, and often conflicting, religious philosophies. However, for many centuries Rabbinic Judaism maintained itself within a Christian world. Confrontations were inevitable. For some nineteen centuries, those confrontations took the form of "disputations." Hopefully, we may now have reached the far more positive stage of "dialogue." Chapters 12 and 13 are devoted to aspects of that "dialogue."

Every age confronts the Pharisaic-Rabbinic tradition with a new set of questions and problems. Thus far, the adaptability of that tradition has been the key to its survival. But ours is a revolutionary age, both in its disappointments and in its promises. Can the tradition meet the new and unprecedented challenges? Can it survive the centrifugal tendencies of our secular age? What could be the basis of Jewish observance today? What the conditions of Jewish religious unity? Partial answers to such questions are attempted in the last two chapters of this book.

CHAPTER 1

✍ The Pharisaic Tradition Today

Scholarship, both Jewish and Christian, has done much during the last one hundred years to restore the reputation of the Pharisees. It is generally conceded now that the New Testament references to this sect were penned in the heat of controversy, and that the brief account given of them by the contemporary historian Flavius Josephus is not to be taken at face value, since it suffers from that historian's compulsion to fit Jewish religious ideas into the pattern of Hellenistic-Roman schools of thought.

Though no one denies that there were hypocrites among the Pharisees—the Talmud itself says as much—the pendulum has swung the other way, and it has now become fashionable to credit their sect with all that is of value and permanence in traditional Judaism. Jewish writers like Abraham Geiger and Jacob Z. Lauterbach and Christian writers like George Foot Moore and R. Travers Herford have represented the Pharisees

---

Reprinted, with revisions, from *Commentary* (February 1956), pp. 112–117. Copyright © 1956 by the American Jewish Committee. The author is grateful for permission to reprint this material.

The Pharisaic Tradition Today

as the party of religious progress. Opposed to the priestly monopoly on the interpretation of the Law, the Pharisees stressed scholarship to the exclusion of caste. In contrast to the Sadducean effort to keep religion within the narrow confines of the Written Law, the Pharisees infused the whole of life with religious idealism, and insisted that the Written Law must be supplemented by the Oral Law. Thus areas of life for which the earlier legislators could make no provision were subjected to the rule of law by the Pharisees. Thus also could moral progress be made, for the literal meaning of the biblical text had to give way before the more enlightened and humane interpretations of the Oral Law. The old rough and retaliatory justice, "an eye for an eye," for example, was understood in terms of *monetary* compensation for injuries inflicted, while the *patria potestas*, permitting the stoning of a rebellious son (Deut. 21: 18ff.), was hedged around with so many restrictive minutiae that a later Rabbinic generation found it impossible to believe that it had ever been put into operation at all.

Above all, by espousing synagogal worship, with its non-sacrificial and lay character, in contrast—though not in open opposition—to the priestly pomp and circumstance of Temple worship, the Pharisees, and they alone, are to be credited with the survival of Judaism after the destruction of Temple and State had invalidated the very basis of the Sadducean approach. Indeed, so firmly was the Pharisaic position established that, at various times in Jewish history, when sects arose who sought to go back to the plain and literal meaning of the Scriptures, thus bypassing the Oral Law, *they* were considered heretics and innovators, while the Pharisees stood forth as guardians of the authentic Revelation.

So thorough has this revaluation of the Pharisees been that even the deviationists from Rabbinic Judaism insist nowadays on seeing themselves as the modern heirs of Pharisaism. It used to be quite different. In seventeenth-century Amsterdam, when the ex-Marrano Uriel da Costa refused to submit to the rabbinical regimen, and thus came into conflict with the rabbinical authorities, he found it quite natural to invoke a New Testament characterization of the Pharisees in order to hurl abuse upon his opponents. Again, when Reform Judaism established its beachhead on American soil in the 1820's (in Charleston, South Carolina), some of its pronouncements took the form of conscious disaffiliation with the whole tradition of Pharisaic-Rabbinic Judaism. The same happened in England in the 1840's. But today all this has changed, and Reform Judaism, for one (Conservative Judaism as well), likes to see itself right at the heart of the Pharisaic tradition. After all, it is said, does not modern Reform endeavor to adapt the old faith to modern needs, very much as the Pharisees adapted religion to the needs of their own times? Does not the Orthodox quasi-deification of the sixteenth century code, *Shulchan Arukh*, smack much more of the Sadducees' unbending attitude toward the Written Law than of the Pharisees' courage in coming to terms with changed conditions?

Add to this the loose application of such epithets as "democratic" and "popular" to the Pharisaic phenomenon, and it becomes rather easy to combine enthusiasm for the Pharisees with attachment to the American Way of Life. Hence, while at one time Reform Judaism tended to ignore the post-biblical developments of Judaism, attempting to take up where the Prophets left off, the modern teacher of Reform is likely to echo the words of the Anglo-Jewish preacher, Morris Joseph, that Pharisaism, "far from setting a term to the growth of Judaism, in reality is the guarantee of its continuous evolution. It makes provision for that adaptation to environment which is the essential condition of development and life."

All this is undoubtedly true. But so also is another aspect of Pharisaism which is seldom attended to outside the academy and the scholar's study. In the first place, the conscientious scholar will point to the considerable gaps that still remain in our knowledge of ancient Jewish sects in general and of the Pharisees in particular. Recent controversies about the meaning and the provenance of the so-called Dead Sea Scrolls leave us

The Pharisaic Tradition Today

in no doubt as to the more or less hypothetical nature of any statement made about the early sectarian divisions in Judaism. However, we do know that the Pharisees, in spite of their reputation for being the "popular" party, aimed to set up a religious elite. In fact, the very name "Pharisees" in all likelihood means "those who have separated themselves [from the rest of the people]."

From the perspective of history, we are justified in holding the Pharisees responsible for religious progress and evolution. But in the context of their actual lives, and of the time and place in which they lived, the Pharisees represent those Jews who made the ritual laws more stringent for themselves, and became more particular and meticulous in the observance of the laws governing diet and Levitical purity than they thought the ordinary Jew to have been.

Vis-à-vis the priestly aristocracy, the Pharisees undoubtedly appear as democratic levelers. But we must not overlook the fact that the Pharisees developed an "aristocracy" of their own. Few expressions could be more contemptuous than those which the Pharisees employed in talking about the man who fell short of their standards of religious practice and learning—the *am ha-aretz*, or ignoramus, boor. Apart from warning their followers against marriage with the *am ha-aretz*, this bitter scorn could lead to such exclamations as the one recorded in the Talmud (b. *Pesachim* 49b) by Rabbi Eleazar: "It is permitted to stab an *am ha-aretz* on a Day of Atonement which coincides with the Sabbath." The hatred was mutual. The famous Rabbi Akiba, who obtained his education late in life, could reminisce about the days when he was an *am ha-aretz* himself, and when he was in the habit of saying: "Would that I had a scholar here, so that I could bite him like an ass!" (*ibid.*)

No doubt, the bark was fiercer than the bite. The very fact that Akiba could rise from the ranks of the *am ha-aretz* into the class of scholars would lead us to expect that membership in this aristocracy of piety and learning, unlike in that of the Saducean priesthood, was not restricted. Indeed, we even find the following sentiment in the Talmud: "Be careful with the sons of the *am ha-aretz*, for Torah may proceed from them!" (b. *Sanhedrin* 96a). Nevertheless, if we are to judge from the self-imposed legislation of the Pharisaic "brotherhoods" that has come down to us from Rabbinic sources, the Pharisees must have been a rather exclusive set. And if "Pharisee" does mean "Separatist," then it is not at all unlikely that the word was first used opprobriously in the mouth of an opponent.

These things are as true—though perhaps not quite so well known—as that other aspect of the Pharisees which has of late given them the reputation of having been a popular, democratic mass movement dedicated to religious progress and evolution. It is, in truth, a curious paradox that the Separatists should have won over the people as a whole, that their interpretation of the Law should have gained virtually universal acceptance, and that the very stringency of ritual observance that they adopted as a "badge" of their exclusivism should have become, in the course of the generations, the norm of Jewish piety for everyone alike.

But the paradox lies only on the surface. Psychologically. it is not hard to understand. If we jump across the centuries, we find the same psychology at work today. How many people belonging to exclusive golf and country clubs would really care for club membership if it were not so difficult to obtain, if it were not so exclusive? It is, in fact, the very exclusiveness which challenges the outsider to struggle to get in.

The Jews living at the time of the Pharisees seem to have worked on some such assumption. And not only the Jews of Palestine! From Hellenistic Jewish circles we have the so-called *Letter of Aristeas*, dated variously between 200 B.C.E. and post-33 C.E. While the *Letter* is a pseudo-historical work, purporting to describe the origin of the Greek version of the Bible, the Septuagint, it contains much else besides. The book is particularly emphatic on the point of Jewish separatism. It glories in the dietary laws by which "we have been distinctly separated from the rest of mankind"; and it is grateful to the lawgiver

The Pharisaic Tradition Today

(Moses) who "fenced us around with impregnable ramparts and walls of iron, that we might not mingle at all with any of the other nations." Yet withal, modern scholars have no trouble detecting in this tract one of the many propaganda attempts to convert Greek-speaking Gentiles to Judaism (*cf.* Robert Pfeiffer, *History of New Testament Times*, p. 225).

Far from soft-pedaling Jewish separatism and particularism, the Hellenistic Jewish writers emphasized them in their propaganda—even though the very existence of such propaganda literature was evidence enough of the universalistic Jewish "out-reach." They must have been guided by experience in what they were doing. Perhaps they even took a leaf out of the book of the Hellenistic mystery cults, which, in spite of all "mystery," must have constantly been on the lookout for new initiates, and which possibly just *because* of their mystery-making and secretiveness were never lacking in new applicants.

It may well be that this is also one of the reasons why so many thinkers and philosophers coming from an irreligious background today find shelter with that branch of Christianity which makes the greatest demands on them, both physically and intellectually, the Roman Catholic Church, and why they eschew liberal Protestantism or Unitarianism.

All these parallels may, or may not, be apposite. The fact remains that, while on the surface the Pharisaic phenomenon presents the paradox of having become a popular religion *in spite* of its inherent exclusiveness, a psychological approach would see its popularity *as a result* of that exclusiveness. Both the popularity and the exclusiveness of Pharisaism ought to be borne in mind when we try to identify a modern religious movement in Judaism as being in the Pharisaic tradition. To equate Pharisaism with religious "democracy" pure and simple means, on the one hand, to be untrue to the historical facts and, on the other, to deprive oneself of a very useful mechanism in the revitalization of modern religious life.

Pharisaism and its successor, Rabbinic Judaism, were at the opposite pole from abolishing the differences between scholar and ignoramus, between observance and laxity in observance, and from regarding the lowest common denominator of religious knowledge and practice as the norm of their "democratic" religion. The distinction between scholar and *am ha-aretz* was maintained with the utmost rigor right up to modern times. Its redeeming quality was that elevation into the ranks of the scholars was facilitated by an elaborate system of free education. Poverty was never regarded as barring one from the Pharisaic "aristocracy." Yet, while not so provided in theory, the practical exigencies of life occasionally made it impossible for large sections of Jewry to lift themselves out of the depths of *am ha-aratzuth*.

This was particularly so in seventeenth- and eighteenth-century Poland, with the result that the far more educated Jews of Lithuania began to look down on their Polish brethren with all the haughtiness which proud academicians could muster for the humble *am ha-aretz*. Out of this friction, Hasidism was born, that movement which has aptly been described as the "revolt of the *am ha-aretz*" who refused to be denied his share in the God of Israel. The intellectual element of religion receded, overshadowed by the emotional appeal, and serving the Lord in gladness took the place of arid Talmudic scholasticism. But in true Hegelian fashion, there was brought forth out of the thesis of Talmudism and the antithesis of Hasidism the synthesis of *Habad* Hasidism. Inscribing on its banner the words *chokhmah* (wisdom), *binah* (insight), and *da'ath* (knowledge), this offshoot of the Hasidic "revolt" restored the intellectual element to its customary exalted position in the Jewish scheme of things.

It is only when we come to very recent times that the old clear-cut distinctions tend to get blurred—particularly so on the American scene. Here, the predominantly Protestant environment, with its insistence on the "priesthood of all believers," reminded the Jew that, in origin at least, this ideal was his own. Since Judaism recognizes no intermediary between man and God, since it has no consecrated hierarchy, and since, tech-

The Pharisaic Tradition Today

nically, every ordinary Jew, in the company of at least nine others, can conduct formal public worship, Judaism could fit into the American pattern so well that Jews began to think of Judaism as the "democratic" religion par excellence.

In this connection it is worth noting that the "priesthood of all believers," Hebraic though it be in origin, is an ideal easier to attain under Protestantism. After all, Protestantism does not, like Judaism, judge a purely intellectual exercise like legal study as equal in value and significance to the observance of all the rest of the commandments. It does not, in its theology, share the synagogue's insistence on "works."

In Pharisaic-Rabbinic Judaism, where "works" and study do figure prominently, it is difficult to escape the creation of a religio-intellectual elite, and an emphasis on the difference between scholar and *am ha-aretz*. Yet it was precisely this dichotomy, rooted in the very *raison d'être* of Pharisaism, which was sacrificed to the dominant American culture pattern in the process of Jewish assimilation.

Though the parties involved may have hardly been conscious of this particular aspect of their struggle, it would seem that the last time the problem of the Pharisaic paradox was faced on American soil was during the third quarter of the nineteenth century, in the fierce controversies between Rabbis David Einhorn and Isaac M. Wise. Both of them were exponents of Reform Judaism, and while Einhorn was the more radical of the two, and Wise the champion of moderation, even the reforms sanctioned by the latter must have seemed revolutionary departures from tradition by contrast with what Reform Judaism became in its European birthplace.

From one point of view, the dispute between Einhorn and Wise can be regarded as reflecting the religious radicalism of the American East, represented by Einhorn, in opposition to the moderation of the Midwest, where Wise had his headquarters. And yet it was primarily a struggle between personalities and deep convictions. Einhorn did not see Reform Judaism as a popular mass movement. He was quite content, and he said as much, to have Reform appeal to the intellectual elite brought up on German *Kultur* and Enlightenment. He was not concerned about its effect on the remainder of Jewry. Wise, however, saw Reform as *the* American Judaism, on the platform of which American Jews of all backgrounds were ultimately to unite. Since the unity of Israel was Wise's prime object, he was always willing to compromise, and conviction may on occasion have played a lesser role in his case than expediency.

The issue at stake was basically this: is Reform Judaism to be the faith of a religious avant-garde and an intellectual elite, or is it to be the religion of the "people," giving approval to whatever departures from tradition may have become necessary, yet never going to logical extremes in disturbing the status quo? The paradox of Pharisaism was here broken up into its two apparently contradictory constituents, its exclusivism and its popularity; and each became the battle cry of an opposing faction.

It was inevitable that Wise's view would prevail in the long run. Einhorn's Reform was too heavily German in accent. He even insisted on the German language as a *sine qua non* of Reform Judaism. Wise, in contrast, never tired of preaching the "Americanization" of the Synagogue, and the realities of American Jewish life were in his favor.

But it took about half a century for the implications of Wise's victory to be fully realized; and it is not until fairly recently that we find American Reform Judaism preening itself on its appearance as a popular mass movement. The late Rabbi Solomon Goldman once quipped that Reform Judaism had now substituted a public relations department for the "Mission of Israel." This may not be quite true, but Goldman certainly caught the spirit of many of the changes and innovations in recent Reform Jewish thought and practice. The questionnaire has become a competitor of theology, and the hand raised in blessing might on occasion look like the "glad hand" (as described by David Riesman).

We are back where we started. Modern Judaism, claiming to

The Pharisaic Tradition Today

be the heir of the Pharisees, glorying in the "democracy" of the synagogue, is yet totally oblivious of that side of Pharisaism which, appearing "snobbish" on the surface, nevertheless provided the subtle appeal that attracted the mass of people. The problem of the relevance of Pharisaism is complex, for its example also offers dangers. Modern religion has no room for the "holier-than-thou" attitude to which a *misguided* Pharisaism might lead. There is a certain arbitrariness in setting up standards for a Jew to meet in order to be considered a "better" Jew than he was—and there is a concomitant danger that he will then not only consider himself better than *he* was, but also better than his fellow-Jews *are*.

We also lack the fundamentalist belief in the direct divine revelation of every single word of the Bible which enabled earlier generations to bow in humble submission to the undisputed will of God as manifested in the letter of the traditional codes.

For all these reasons one might deny the relevance of Pharisaism to modern Jewish life, and give up the occasionally hollow boast that we are the "heirs of the Pharisees." But, on the other hand, it can be argued that such a divorce from Pharisaism would ultimately deprive Judaism of any incentive it might give to its adherents to spiritual growth and endeavor. After all, Judaism, being what it is, remains irreconcilable with a *sancta simplicitas*; it is still true to say that the educated Jew realizes more of the inherent potentialities of Judaism than the ignorant one does. And to that extent, at least, the educated man will be a "better" Jew.

We cannot get away from the Pharisaic dichotomy of scholar and *am ha-aretz*. If this be denied, then the *am ha-aretz* may become not only the norm, but, in the end, the ideal, too. When this happens, Judaism will undoubtedly be popular, but it will also eventually lose whatever thinking people may be born into its midst.

In communities where facilities for adult education are made available to everyone, there would be nothing contrary to our basic democratic convictions in giving the intellectual elite its due recognition and in fostering the formation of an "aristocracy" of learning that would be learned though never, in actual practice, exclusive. In filling positions of community leadership, we could help to raise standards all around by sharing just a little of the ancient Pharisees' suspicion of the *am ha-aretz*.

As for religious observance, we shall have to be broad-minded enough to allow the individual to experiment according to his own needs and to grow at his own pace. There will have to be lanes and byways, to borrow Franz Rosenzweig's metaphor, rather than the one common highway on which Jews walked in the past. But those lanes and byways will all lead in the same general direction. To do more, not less or nothing at all, will be the Pharisaic criterion of "betterment." But it will be betterment measured by personal growth rather than by comparison with others. The Jew who observes more commandments than his fellow will not thereby be considered a "better" Jew. But the Jew who tries, the Jew who grapples with these problems as they present themselves to him, *will* be a better Jew than the one who does not even care to try. That such a growth in personal Jewish living will have to be envisaged in terms of "standards" rather than of "laws"—to use Jacob B. Agus's apt terminology—should need no further elaboration here. Indeed, standards which one is striving to meet may very well present the better incentive and the greater challenge than laws to the observance of which one is a priori obligated, and which carry the ominous implication of "All or Nothing."

The secret of the ancient Pharisees' success in winning over a whole people lay in their refusal to accept the lowest common denominator as the norm and the ideal. It lay in the very difficulty of the challenge they presented. The ancient Pharisees were undoubtedly "tradition-directed" in the contemporary sociological sense. Yet the problems they pose cut across all sociological lines and categories. The struggle between Einhorn and Wise can, for example, be described, if one so desires, as a contest between "inner-directed" and "other-directed" religious character types. But to those three categories, Pharisaism, as a spiritual force and as a historical phenomenon, has added a fourth: that of "upper-directedness." To cultivate this kind of religious character should be the preoccupation of all those who claim to be the modern "heirs of the Pharisees."

CHAPTER 2

✍ *The Bible of the Synagogue*

Thirty-nine books of ancient Hebrew literature—though Jewish tradition counts them as only twenty-four—have found their permanent place within the covers of a single volume. We call it the Bible, that is to say, the Book par excellence. Yet the modern Jew who reads this book, be it in the original Hebrew or in translation, has a choice not of one but of three different books.

There is first the Bible of modern scholarship. Here the "once-and-for-all-time" revelation at Mount Sinai, which is how the Law accounts for its own existence, is assumed to be a myth, a pious fraud, an attempt of later legislators to tie together the civil and cultic legislation which developed gradually through the centuries. What was once read as the "Law of Moses" turns out, on closer scholarly inspection, to be a mosaic of various codes and narrative traditions, having their provenance in many different times and places of Israel's history. The mixture of

---

Reprinted, with additions, from *Commentary* (February 1959), pp. 142–150. Copyright © 1959 by the American Jewish Committee. The author is grateful for permission to reprint this material.

The Bible of the Synagogue

comfort and admonition, of reproof and promise, which so many prophetic books contain, is also sorted out into precise components. The occasion for each utterance is found in the religious and political history of the people. And modern scholars feel confident that they are able to say exactly who was a "prophet of doom" and who was not. If, then, the promise of a glorious future is found in the writings of a Prophet who is known to have been prophesying doom, it can easily be labeled a "later gloss." The same goes, of course, for any reference to the cult which might indicate a positive attitude toward institutional religion on the part of the Prophet. Since modern scholarship is convinced that the Prophets, or at any rate the pre-Exilic ones, were the enemies of the priesthood, such references must obviously have been inserted into the text by a later "priestly" editor or glossator.

If the modern reader's interest in early Hebrew literature is comparable to his interest in early Greek or Roman literature—if, that is, he wants to be truly "scientific" about it—he cannot afford to ignore the findings of modern scholars, or to close his eyes to their reconstruction of biblical history. But this scholarly Bible is only *one* of the three Bibles available. Another Bible is that of individual piety and edification—the book read by the man looking for spiritual strength and comfort. To this Bible, modern scholarship is irrelevant. When, for example, a Jew feels inclined to recite the Twenty-third Psalm, either to express his gratitude for bounties received or at a funeral ceremony, he does not stop to consider whether King David was really its author. And when, in synagogue, the ethical monotheism of Judaism is presented to him in the words of Deuteronomy, the fact that modern scholars dismiss the authorship of Moses does not concern him. Or take the pun in Isaiah 7:9—*im lo ta-aminu ki lo te-amenu,* "If you will not believe, surely you shall not be established." What difference does it make to the man who turns to his Bible for inspiration and for edification if he is now told by modern scholarship that this text is corrupt, that the present wording has to be emended, and that the original actually went something like this: "If you will not believe, yes, if you will not believe, then ask a sign of the Lord your God"? After all, it is the so-called corruption which has been the source of inspiration for so many generations, and not the religiously inferior "original" reading.

Clearly, then, the man who goes to his Bible for spiritual meaning need not be preoccupied with problems of authorship, dating, and textual reconstruction. What should be noted, however, is that we are not dealing with a question of "either/or." The Bible read for inspiration and edification, and the Bible read as a source book for the history of ancient Israel, can both be enjoyed and appreciated by one and the same person—though not necessarily at the same time. To cite a comparable example: there need be no conflict between following a minute textual analysis of *Hamlet* and enjoying a complete performance of the play.

The very fact that there are hundreds of Christian Bible scholars who study the "Old Testament" scientifically without being converted to Judaism, and the fact that for the last nineteen hundred years Christians have been using the Hebrew Bible for inspirational purposes without thereby abandoning their Christian faith, should make it quite clear to us that there is no necessary bridge leading from either the Bible of modern scholarship or from the Bible of personal edification to Judaism as it has developed during the last two millennia. And yet, while it would be a mistake to assume that twentieth-century Judaism is coextensive with the "Old Testament," Judaism nevertheless claims that it is *based* upon the Hebrew Bible, that it is the "Religion of Torah," and that all its major beliefs and practices have evolved out of, or can be derived from, the teachings of biblical prophets, sages, and legislators.

To understand this claim, we have to understand the *third* Bible available to the modern Jew. I should like to call it the Bible of the Synagogue. But before describing this particular

The Bible of the Synagogue

Bible in greater detail, I want to glance at the position the Bible occupies in Protestant and Catholic Christianity respectively.

One of the great victories claimed by the Protestant Reformation was to have made the Bible available to the people at large. This was accomplished not only by providing vernacular translations, but also, and perhaps above all, by releasing the individual from dependence upon a Church authority for interpreting what the Bible says. The Roman Catholic Church, on the other hand, reasons as follows: without the agency of the Church, we would not today be in possession of the Bible. But if you trust the Church to transmit the Bible, you must likewise trust the Church to interpret it correctly, for without the Church you would not have a Bible to begin with.

Without pressing the analogy too far, it may be said that the Bible of the Synagogue is closer in conception to the Roman Catholic point of view, with its insistence upon an authoritative ecclesiastical—and yet ever readily adaptable—interpretation of the Scriptures, than to the Protestant outlook, with its tendency to culminate in fundamentalism. This is not to say that the fundamentalist view is completely unknown in Jewish history. On the contrary, there was the eighth-century schismatic movement of the Karaites who rebelled against Rabbinic Judaism with the battle cry: "Search ye the Scriptures!" But the Karaites, after all, remained schismatic. Moreover, even they were compelled in the long run to develop authoritative hermeneutics of their own to counter the chaos of religious observance in their community which resulted from a multiplicity of individual interpretations.

Rabbinic Judaism, by contrast, consistently maintained, and was in fact based upon, the doctrine of an authoritative exposition of the Written Word—an exposition which remained oral for a long time, and which was believed to have been as distinctly revealed by God to Moses as was the Written Law itself. But since the teachers who transmitted the "Oral Law" are the very ones to whom we owe our possession of the text of the Scriptures—and this is the analogy to the Roman

Catholic position—it follows (as the twelfth-century exegete Abraham Ibn Ezra maintained in the preface to his commentary on the Bible) that "there is no difference [in value] between the two Laws, for from the hands of our fathers have both of them been transmitted to us."[1]

While it is true that the Rabbis of the Talmud ascribed the origin of the Oral Law to the Mosaic Revelation, and while there is a statement in Rabbinic literature to the effect that "whatever a disciple of the wise may propound by way of explaining a law in the most distant future was already revealed to Moses on Mount Sinai,"[2] we would be wrong to ascribe to all the ancient Rabbis the belief that everything contained in the Talmud and other Rabbinic literature actually went back, in its present form, to Moses himself. The idea of religious evolution, or of "progressive revelation," was indeed unknown to the Rabbis, but they were very conscious of the fact that certain provisions of Jewish law had their origin in the need of meeting the particular requirements of specific times. They even admitted that some of their Scriptural exegesis was not so much aimed at eliciting the full implications of a text as at using the text to support a religious provision which they felt it necessary to enact.

Rabbinic literature contains a legend which tells how Moses was granted a last wish before his death—to sit in at a session of Rabbi Akiba's academy (second century C.E.). Akiba was expounding the Law in terms so completely unknown to Moses that the latter was stupefied. He only regained his composure when Akiba, asked by one of the students for the basis of his remarks, replied that he was teaching a tradition on the authority of Moses![3]

The sympathies of the modern reader are more likely to be enlisted by the veiled skepticism contained in this story than by the statement that any innovation in Scriptural exegesis likely to be made by a future scholar was already known to

Moses himself. Nevertheless, the traditional literature contains a number of arguments in support of the antiquity of the Oral Law which cannot simply be brushed off as being naïve.

Take, for example, the legal procedures of divorce. The only direct reference to those procedures in the Written Law is an incidental remark in the twenty-fourth chapter of Deuteronomy, where the law is found which prohibits one's remarriage to his divorced wife, after the latter has had a second husband. That law is introduced by the following "if-clauses": "When a man takes a wife, . . . if then she finds no favor in his eyes, . . . and he writes her a bill of divorcement and puts it in her hands and sends her out of his house. . . ." Apologetes for the Oral Law point out that the Written Law nowhere tells us what exactly a "bill of divorcement" is, what terminology is to be contained therein, and how the whole matter of divorce is to be handled. They argue that Moses must have given a full explanation of all the details involved, and that this explanation was transmitted by word of mouth until it was incorporated into the Talmud. If we did not assume this, the scant reference to divorce in Deuteronomy would make no sense.[4] Again, when we are enjoined in Leviticus 23:40 to take, on the Festival of Sukkoth, "the fruit of goodly trees, branches of palm trees, and boughs of leafy trees, and willows of the brook," and we find a universal consensus of opinion among Jews that the "fruit of goodly trees" is the *ethrog* (and no other kind of goodly fruit), and that "boughs of leafy trees" refer to the myrtle (and to no other kind of luxurious vegetation), we are, it is argued, forced to assume that Moses provided an oral interpretation that was preserved along with the written text.[5]

No doubt, other explanations besides the Oral Law hypothesis could be advanced to account for the traditional divorce procedure and for the choice of specific plants on the Festival of Sukkoth. But in a period like ours, when Bible scholars, particularly those associated with the Scandinavian school, have shifted their attention from the earliest *literary* strata of the Hebrew Bible to the tracing of *oral traditions* which preceded the literary repercussions, it should not be too hard to accept the view that what we have in front of us, black-on-white, in the pages of the Bible, is only a part (perhaps only a minute part) of the totality of biblical tradition which existed in oral form long before any of it was committed to writing. In other words, we can now maintain on scientific grounds that much of what is contained in the Hebrew Bible can be fully understood only in the light of the early *oral* traditions of Israel. But this is precisely what is implied by the doctrine of the Oral Law, which, as Ibn Ezra says, is of equal validity with the Written Law, "for from the hands of our fathers have both of them been transmitted to us."

To forestall any misunderstandings, it should be pointed out here that the phrase "Oral Law"—despite its wide currency in English—is not an adequate translation of the Hebrew *torah shebe'al peh*, the "Oral Torah." The word *torah* primarily means "teaching"—a word that embraces much else besides law. This distinction is important, for although the teachers of the "Oral Law" endeavored with all their might to achieve unanimity in the interpretation of the strictly legal passages of the Torah, the greatest leeway was allowed in the interpretation of the non-legal parts of the traditional "teaching." It was conceded, for example, that the words of the Torah lent themselves to seventy different interpretations. The verse spoken by Jeremiah in the name of God, "Is not My word like fire . . . and like a hammer which breaks the rock in pieces?" was understood as likening the divine word to the sparks resulting from the hammer's impact upon the rock—each spark contained part of the revelation, but no single spark its totality.[6]

It has already been pointed out that the ancient Rabbis did not share our modern concepts of religious evolution and "progressive revelation." They were, in fact, lacking in some of the most elementary notions of history which today we simply take for granted. What this implied in practice will be demonstrated here by a few illustrations.

The modern student of Judaism notes a distinct moral and

religious advance in the Pharisaic-Rabbinic substitution of monetary compensation for the literal application of the *lex talionis* in Exodus 21:24: "An eye for an eye, a tooth for a tooth." The Rabbis interpreted this verse to mean that the offender must compensate the victim for the loss of the eye or the tooth, rather than that the offender himself should be punished by having his own eye or tooth knocked out.[7] But the Rabbis would never have admitted that this interpretation highlighted their own moral advance over the rough provisions of a primitive law. They would not have admitted that their interpretation was an innovation. If the law in Exodus 21:24 is said to demand monetary compensation, then this is what the law has *always* meant—from the very day on which it was committed to writing, as they believed, by Moses himself.

In accounting for a number of chronological inconsistencies in the Pentateuchal narratives, the Rabbis maintained the principle, "There is no earlier and no later in the Torah,"[8] that is to say, it is not the intention of the Torah to teach us the precise chronological sequence of the events described. The Rabbis themselves were blissfully unconcerned with questions of "earlier" and "later" in their understanding of biblical history and of its characters. A charming anachronism is, therefore, an inevitable part of all their descriptions of biblical figures. It was, for example, inconceivable to them that the Patriarchs, Abraham, Isaac, and Jacob, who lived long before the Sinaitic Revelation, should have found such favor in the sight of God without having followed the dictates of the Torah. That they were pious men is both implied and explicitly stated in the Torah itself. But piety to the Rabbis could only mean piety as expressed in the forms known at the time of the Mishnah and the Gemara. Consequently, they taught that the Patriarchs observed the Torah even before it was revealed to their descendants at Sinai.[9] (Of course, an element of polemics and apologetics might have been involved in this particular case, since Paul and the early Church Fathers made much of the fact that Abraham was "saved" by "faith," and not by "works.")

This sort of thing can be laughed out of court by a sophisticated invocation of the canons of historical research. But such anachronisms sometimes serve as the vehicle for the transmission of profound spiritual insights. How much true Jewish sentiment, for example, is revealed in the Rabbis' view of King David! The wars which, according to the Bible, David so successfully fought are the "dialectics of Torah study." The armies he is said to have recruited are the bands of scholars and disciples with which he surrounded himself. And David never took a step without first consulting his *beth din*, his Rabbinical court of law.[10] In short, if King David was to merit the love and esteem in which he was held by Israel, if he was in truth to be the ancestor of the Messiah, it was surely not too much to believe that he conducted himself no less "Jewishly" than a recognized Jewish leader in third/fourth-century Sura and Pumbeditha!

But this soft-pedaling of what few military glories there were in early Jewish history is typical of the whole Rabbinic outlook on life. You can detect it in the studied silence which the Talmud preserves on the whole chain of events leading up to the institution of the Hanukkah festival. A victory of the Hasmoneans over the "Greeks" is indeed referred to, but only to set the stage for the "miracle of the oil" in a rededicated Temple.[11] Judah the Maccabee is not even mentioned by name!

You find it also in the story of the Rabbi who visited a Palestinian town and asked to see the "guardians of the city." When shown the local militia, he called them the "destroyers of the city," and pointed to the students in their school as the city's true "guardians."[12]

Thus, while the so-called Higher Critics of the "Old Testament" may tell us that early Israel adopted YHWH as a "war god," the Rabbis, for their part, know of the "Book and the Sword which came down from heaven together,"[13] and they also know that Israel opted for the Book. Characteristic of their whole attitude are the early Rabbinic comments on the law about the altar of stone: "And if you make an altar of stone,

The Bible of the Synagogue

you shall not build it of hewn stones; for if you wield your tool [lit. "sword"] upon it you profane it. And you shall not go up by steps to My altar, that your nakedness be not exposed on it." (Exodus 20:25ff.)

This is the biblical law—which may be of archeological interest to the reader of the Bible of modern scholarship, and which could hardly be said to contain much material for the edification of the reader of the second Bible we have mentioned, the Bible of inspiration and edification. But in the Bible of the Synagogue this is what we find: "The altar is made to prolong the years of man, and iron is made to shorten the years of man. It is not right for that which shortens life to be lifted up against that which prolongs life." Furthermore, "the stones of the altar do not see nor hear nor speak. Yet, because they serve to establish peace between Israel and their Father in Heaven, the Holy One, blessed be He, has said, 'You shall lift up no iron tool upon them.' How much the more, then, should he who establishes peace between man and his fellowman, between husband and wife, between city and city, between nation and nation, between family and family, between government and government, be protected so that no harm should come to him!" And again, "the stones of the altar have no sense of what is proper or improper. Yet God said that you should not treat them disrespectfully. It is, therefore, but logical that you must refrain from treating with disrespect your fellowman, who is made in the image of Him by whose word the world came into being."[14]

What should not be left out of sight, however, is the fact that, in addition to those spiritual implications, the Rabbis also recognized that the law about the altar of stone had a very real and concrete application in the sacrificial service of ancient Israel. This brings us to the question of how the Bible exegetes of the Synagogue looked upon their own work.

The Talmudic sages established the norm that "no verse of Scripture ever departs from its literal meaning."[15] That is to say, homiletical interpretations should be clearly taken for what they are, and not be allowed to encroach upon the literal application of the sacred text. Nevertheless, it is not too often that we find the sages abiding by this norm. The whole development of Rabbinic Judaism, in contrast to the early Sadducees and the later Karaites, necessitated a frequent disregard of the literal meaning of the biblical text. It was only in the thirteenth century, and then possibly under the influence of the scheme which Christians had earlier adopted for their exegesis, that we find in Jewish sources a systematization of the four different methods of exegesis through which the Bible of the Synagogue had come into being.

There is, first of all, the *peshat*, the literal meaning of the text. Then there is *derash*, the homiletical exposition. Then comes *remez*, the typological and allegorical sense of the text. And finally there is *sod*, the secret meaning, which is the sense given to a passage by the mystics.

Naturally, there were many commentators who were striving for the *peshat*, to get at the literal meaning of a text. But the *peshat* turns out to be a very elusive thing. What one generation may regard as the literal meaning of a text may be considered as homiletics pure and simple by a succeeding age. Even in the case of modern scholarship, which professes to be interested in *peshat* and nothing else, we can detect the traces of transient contemporary notions. If we think of the reconstruction of Israel's early religious history propounded by the Wellhausen school, with its clear-cut antagonism between the "prophetic" and the "priestly" elements, and with the supposed "synthesis" represented by such books as Deuteronomy, we shall not go far wrong in seeing behind this "scientific and objective" approach to the "Old Testament" a very obvious precipitation of the dialectic of Hegelian philosophy, which was the dominant view at that time in all German institutions of higher learning. It is at least suggestive that the Graf-Wellhausen hypothesis lost in popularity at the very time when Hegelian philosophy gave way to other philosophical constructions. That the latest fashions in Bible scholarship, associated with the name of Rudolf Bultmann, should go hand in hand with an Existential philosophy is also not surprising.

The Bible of the Synagogue

Of course, as long as the search for truth motivates human efforts, the search for *peshat* will always remain a significant aspect of the Synagogue's approach to the Bible, even as it is the one and only professed aim of modern biblical scholarship. But it should be clear that Judaism, as it has developed over the millennia, is not now, if it ever has been, coextensive with the literal meaning of the text of the Hebrew Bible.

That is why the Rabbis recognized the importance of *derash*, the derivation of the text's *implicit* meaning—as they understood it. Thus the comments quoted above on the law about the altar of stone would be considered *derash* on the text of which the *peshat* is merely concerned with the prohibition of the use of hewn stone for the erection of an altar. On the other hand, to refer to another illustration we have already mentioned, the interpretation of the biblical *lex talionis* in terms of monetary compensation (rather than of physical retaliation) would be considered the actual *peshat* of that text—notwithstanding the quite different *peshat* which ancient Sadducees and modern scholars would find here.

A *derash* interpretation may keep rather close to the wording of the biblical text, but it may also go to extremes. It may account for a grammatical irregularity, such as the mention of stones (in the plural) in Genesis 28:11 and the mention of only one single stone in Genesis 28:18, by telling us that all the stones at Beth-el were vying for the honor of having the Patriarch Jacob use them as a headrest, so that God united them all into one single stone.[16] But in addition to perpetuating such folkloristic elements, *derash* interpretation also served as a channel for the transmission of Platonic notions to the Jewish academy. Thus, in a comment on the first verse of the Bible, it is said that the Torah preceded the creation of the world. God is pictured as consulting the Torah in the act of creation just as an architect would consult his blueprints.[17] In fact, any attempt at systematizing Jewish theology is largely dependent on *derash* exegesis for source material on the Jewish outlook on life and Jewish dogmatics.

The method of *remez*, of finding an allegorical meaning in

the Scriptures, was the method largely followed by the Hellenistic Jews of Alexandria, of whom Philo Judaeus (first century C.E.) was the outstanding representative. It is extremely doubtful that the Alexandrian school of allegorical exegesis had any significant influence upon the master-builders of the Rabbinic tradition. But there is one book in the Hebrew Bible where the only interpretation the Rabbis would consider legitimate was the allegorical. And this was the Song of Songs. Instead of taking literally the references in that book to the young lover and his beloved, the Rabbis maintained that the whole book was an allegory of the love between God and Israel. Though the allegorical interpretation of the Song of Songs may have little to commend itself to the modern mind, it will still have to be conceded that we owe the canonization, and hence the very preservation, of this delightful book solely to this interpretation. Rabbi Akiba was thinking of the allegorical meaning when he exclaimed that, of all religious poetry, the Song of Songs was the "holy of holies."[18] What should also not be overlooked in assessing the merits of the *remez* interpretation is the role which the Song of Songs has played—and played just because of the allegorical interpretation—in the history of Jewish piety, liturgy, and mysticism. Nor should we forget that, in the hands of a Maimonides, the method of *remez* as applied to other parts of the Bible, to the "Wisdom Books" in particular, could be turned into an instrument of philosophical enlightenment.

The perspective of *sod* (lit. "secret") was that of the mystics, who maintained that every single word of the Torah had a deeper meaning than the obvious sense evident to those not initiated into the mysteries. As the Zohar puts it, to the ordinary bona fide Jew "we impart the revealed matters of the Torah. That is to say, we make known to him the general outlines, and we caution him about the strict observance of the commandments of the Torah. But no more—unless he rises to another level." And this "more" is understood as the "mysteries of the Torah, and the secrets of the Torah, which one need not reveal except to him who has reached a suitably higher level."[19] Indeed, the very function of the Zohar, that major work

The Bible of the Synagogue

of Jewish mysticism which, in its structure, represents a running commentary on the Torah, is to point out those "secret" meanings of the text. It is, moreover, sufficiently obscure in style and language to remain relatively inaccessible to the ordinary reader who comes to it without the requisite preparation.

Considering the doctrine of "emanation" and other neo-Platonic notions which play a major part in Jewish mysticism, it may be said that the method of *sod* provided another opportunity for philosophy to be assimilated to basic Jewish concepts (and vice versa). While, seen from a rationalist point of view, the *sod* method of interpretation may be said to have led to a number of far-reaching aberrations, it will still have to be admitted that the mystics' insistence that the "real" meaning of the Torah is not exhausted by the written words has been another factor responsible for preventing traditional Judaism from espousing a Protestant type of biblical literalism.

We must now turn to the question of *where* the Bible of the Synagogue can be found. There is no single book that contains it. The so-called "Rabbinic Bible" (*Miqra-oth Gedoloth*), which reproduces the original text surrounded by some thirty-two commentaries and paraphrases, does indeed give us a representative selection of the various methods of exegesis which we have discussed above. But it is a *selection* just the same.

In a sense, the Bible of the Synagogue is the *totality* of Rabbinic literature. The earliest part of that literature, the Tannaitic *midrashim*, took the form of running commentaries, mostly of a legal character, on the biblical text. The Mishnah, though not actually a running commentary like the Tannaitic *midrashim*, is nevertheless based on the Oral Law's understanding of biblical legislation. The Gemara, which, together with the Mishnah, makes up the Talmud, is, in a way, a commentary on the Mishnah, while a considerable part of Jewish literature through the ages also took the form of commentaries and super-commentaries on the Talmud.

The various legal codes, of which type of literature the sixteenth-century *Shulchan Arukh* is perhaps the best-known example, are basically an attempt to present the law of the Talmud in more accessible compendia; and, in their turn, they gave rise to a host of commentaries and super-commentaries. At their side there arose the literature of "Responsa," which, dealing with questions of the concrete application of the Law, again reflected the Synagogue's understanding of the provisions of the Torah.

That homiletical literature is by definition nothing but the application of the method of *derash* to the exegesis of the Bible goes without saying. And we have already seen that even the Zohar purports to be a commentary on the Torah. What may not be so well known is the fact that even the philosophical literature of Judaism is, in the last analysis, a form of Bible exegesis. It represents an attempt at reconciling current philosophical notions with the doctrines derived from the Bible, or, where that is not possible, at defending the Torah against philosophical attacks. For example, a considerable portion of the *Guide of the Perplexed* by Maimonides is given over to the interpretation of biblical expressions; and even the works of such moderns as Hermann Cohen and Franz Rosenzweig are to a very large extent concerned with a philosophical exegesis of the Hebrew Bible.

The various branches of Rabbinic literature are overwhelming in their sheer bulk. But perhaps we shall be able to understand why, in the academies of Eastern Europe, Talmud study was stressed at the expense of Bible reading. It used to be said, and not always without justification, that the *yeshivah* student of Eastern Europe knew his Bible only from biblical quotations which appear in the Talmud and other Rabbinic literature. And when *Time* magazine, on one occasion, identified the "Jewish Bible" with the Talmud, the mistake was more of a bibliographical than of a historical or existential nature. For the Bible of the Synagogue is not identical with the literal meaning of the "Old Testament" text, but it is that text as refracted through the lenses of Rabbinic literature.

The Bible of the Synagogue

It was inevitable that Reform Judaism, in its formative period, should have been somewhat antagonistic to the Talmud. After all, Reform Judaism was rebelling against Talmudic law as interpreted by the official rabbinate of the nineteenth century. There was also the obvious influence of Deism. Just as the Deists had claimed that there was a core of the true "Religion of Nature" in the Bible, which had become overlaid with the productions of fraudulent priestcraft, so *mutatis mutandis* the early Reformers argued that the Bible as a whole represented true religion, whereas Rabbinic literature was but an overgrowth of insipid accretions, which had to be cleared away in order to restore Judaism to its pristine purity.

The emphasis given to Bible studies in Reform rabbinical seminaries was, therefore, the logical consequence of the movement's original motivation. But whereas early Reform Judaism, by emphasizing the Bible at the expense of the Talmud, merely righted the balance which had been upset in the European *yeshivoth*, there is something incongruous in Reform's retaining this particular emphasis to the present day—while its theology has in the meantime changed by giving prominent expression to the doctrine of "progressive revelation."

"O Lord," we read in the latest edition of the *Union Prayer Book*, "open our eyes that we may see and welcome all truth, whether shining from the annals of ancient revelations or reaching us through the seers of our own time; for Thou hidest not Thy light from any generation of Thy children that yearn for Thee and seek Thy guidance."[20]

Now, the enthusiastic attempt of Reform Jewish scholars to get at the scientific *peshat*, at the original meaning of biblical texts freed from all glosses and corruptions, would be perfectly intelligible if Reform Judaism believed that Revelation was what the modern theologian would call *einmalig*, occurring only once and for all time. If such were the case, then it would be vitally important, would, in fact, be a *conditio sine qua non*, to determine the precise wording of what God had actually said when He made His one and only Revelation.

But this is precisely what Reform Judaism does *not* believe. Yet if Revelation is "progressive," if God does not hide His light from any generation of His children that seeks His guidance, then there is no compelling reason why the one thousand years of biblical literature should merit more attention than the two thousand years of Rabbinic literature. With all the importance which must duly be ascribed to the question of what a Moses or an Isaiah did or did not say, by the terms of reference provided by the doctrine of "progressive revelation" this question could not possibly be more important than a study of the teachings of Rabbis Akiba and Ishmael in the second century, of Rab and Samuel in the third century, or of Nachmanides in the thirteenth century. Ironically enough, the doctrine of "progressive revelation" makes the study of Rabbinic literature no less mandatory for Reform Judaism than the dogma of the "twofold Torah revealed at Sinai" makes it for Orthodoxy.

It is not being suggested here that the scientific study of the Hebrew Bible should be abandoned. The quest for "origins" will always retain its fascination for scholars of a certain bent of mind. It is also proper that the spokesmen of modern Judaism, and even the laity, should have some idea of what the Hebrew Bible looks like when viewed from the perspective of textual criticism. But due recognition should be given to the undeniable fact that Judaism as we know it—yes, even Reform Judaism—can be linked to the original documents of the Bible only by way of the chain of Rabbinic tradition. This fact, once it is fully grasped, will not only call for greater proficiency in Rabbinic literature on the part of the modern rabbi, but it will also make it incumbent upon the modern Synagogue to devise and provide the best possible means of transmitting this literary heritage to the twentieth-century Jew.

This Jew should still be able to study and enjoy the Bible of modern scholarship, and he can be as radical as he wishes in his historical and textual hypotheses. He should also be able to read the Bible for purposes of inspiration and edification, without anybody's telling him: "So-and-so says the verse means this. And so-and-so says the verse means that." But when it comes to that Bible which is the foundation of Judaism, the modern Jew must learn to rediscover the "Bible of the Synagogue," that repository of "progressive revelation" of which we have here tried to give a brief description.

There is something to be said, after all, for the old Rabbinic reconstruction of a dialogue said to have taken place between God and Moses. When God revealed the Torah, Moses wanted to write it all down—both that part of the Revelation which became known as the Written Law, and that part which was to be called the Oral Law. But God would not have it so. He said to Moses: "There will come a time when the nations of the world will take the Written Law away from you, and claim that *they* (not you) are Israel. Therefore I am giving you the Pentateuch in writing. But its true interpretation, the Mishnah, the Talmud, and the Aggadah, I am giving you orally. They will be what distinguishes Israel from the nations of the world."[21]

Perhaps that is why to this day the "Old Testament" may be read as the first part of the Christian Bible, whereas "*Chumash* with *Rashi*" is the Jew's real link to the event at Sinai.

NOTES

1. Abraham Ibn Ezra, Introduction to the Commentary on the Pentateuch.
2. J. *Pe-ah* II, 6 (ed. Krotoshin, p. 17a).
3. B. *Menachoth* 29b.
4. Cf. David Werner Amram, *The Jewish Law of Divorce* (Philadelphia, 1896), p. 12.
5. Cf. David Nieto, *Matteh Dan* II, 120 (ed. Jerusalem, 1958, pp. 41ff.).
6. B. *Sanhedrin* 34a.

7. B. *Baba Kamma* 83b–84a.
8. B. *Pesachim* 6b and parallels.
9. Cf. b. *Yoma* 28b.
10. B. *Berakhoth* 4a.
11. B. *Shabbath* 21b.
12. J. *Chagigah* I, 7 (ed. Krotoshin, p. 76c).
13. *Sifré, Eqebh*, par. 40 (ed. Friedmann, p. 79a).
14. *Mekilta, Bachodesh*, ch. XI (ed. Lauterbach, II, 209ff.).
15. B. *Shabbath* 63a.
16. Cf. Rashi's commentary on Genesis 28:11.
17. *Genesis Rabbah* 1:2.
18. *Mishnah Yadayim* 3:5.
19. *Zohar, Acharé Moth*, p. 73a.
20. *Union Prayer Book*, Newly Revised, I, 34.
21. *Exodus Rabbah* 47:1, and parallels.

CHAPTER 3

🕮 *A Fence with Loopholes*

PER GENUS ET DIFFERENTIAM

In the period when the religion of ancient Israel gave rise to a literature or, at any rate, that part of it known as the Bible, old Israel was not a people living in isolation. In fact, it is doubtful whether there ever was a time in history when the Israelites, or the later Jews, did live in isolation. The very location of Palestine, bridge between Africa and western Asia, made that quite impossible. So did the Diaspora existence of the Jews in the days of the Second Temple, to say nothing of the existence of the Jews in the four corners of the earth ever since. Even ethnically no claim to racial purity was made by biblical Israel, as witness the Prophet Ezekiel's address to his people: "Your origin and your birth are of the land of the Ca-

---

Reprinted, with additions, from *The Menorah Journal*, Valedictory Issue, XLIX, Nos. 1 & 2 (1962), 77–88. Copyright © 1962 by The Menorah Association, Inc. The author is grateful for permission to reprint this material.

naanites; your father was an Amorite, and your mother a Hittite" (Ezekiel 16:3).

The evolution of a distinctive Israelite-Jewish view of life, and of a distinctive mode of worship, is therefore all the more remarkable. Not that there were no influences from the environment. These we would expect, even without the proofs furnished by modern scholarship based on the myths of Babylonia and the cult of Canaan. Yet there developed something that could be recognized as uniquely Jewish by Jew and Gentile alike. What this distinctive thing was, and is, presents a problem to both scholar and believer, no less than to the apologists and polemicists in modern Jewish life.

Without purporting to provide a complete solution of this problem, the following pages are meant to indicate one of the avenues along which a part of the answer might be found. These pages are predicated on Aristotle's requirement that a complete definition be *per genus et differentiam*, that is, in terms of what the thing is in its own kind and in terms of its differences from others. Indeed, the Ten Commandments themselves follow this pattern when, after the statement, "I am the Lord, thy God," there follows the prohibition, "Thou shalt have no other gods before Me." Ever since that time, it has been found to be considerably easier to define those "other gods," which had to be rejected, than to know the essence of the Lord Himself—a fact which induced Erich Fromm to remark, "While it is not possible for man to make valid statements about the positive, about God, it is possible to make such statements about the negative, about idols. Is it not time to cease to argue about God and instead unite in the unmasking of contemporary forms of idolatry?"[1]

We might, therefore, say that a fairly good picture of Judaism could be obtained by examining what, in any given age, was deemed by Jews to have been "idolatry." As a matter of fact, the sources of both biblical and Rabbinic Judaism are quite outspoken on that score. But we have an even clearer indication than the somewhat broad concept of "idolatry." Rabbinic Judaism knows of a category called *chukkoth hagoyim*, the "statutes of the

A Fence with Loopholes

Gentiles," which designates something not necessarily "idolatrous," but sufficiently non-Jewish, or even "un-Jewish," to call forth the opposition of the legislators. The category itself is based on such biblical verses as Leviticus 18:3, "You shall not do as they do in the land of Egypt, where you dwelt, and you shall not do as they do in the land of Canaan, to which I am bringing you. You shall not walk in their statutes."

The concept of "walking in the statutes of the Gentiles" has had a long history. It was often invoked in periods of transition, when Jews were involved in the process of acclimatization to a new environment. It was last brought into the field with éclat by the Orthodox defenders of the old ways against the nineteenth-century Reformers who attempted to change the mode of synagogue worship along the lines of Western decorum and tastes. But the classical age of the formulation of this concept was the period of the Tannaim, roughly from the first century B.C.E. through the beginning of the third century C.E. This was the time of the crystallization of Rabbinic Judaism, a time of great change and transformation, when Judaism had to come to terms with the loss of Temple and State, and also a time when Palestinian Jewry was a part of the Roman-Hellenistic world. It will be our aim to show just what was considered to be "statutes of the Gentiles" at that time, and what, on the other hand, though of known Gentile usage, was considered to be permissible, and why. Finally, it will be our task to note a number of practices which, though of Gentile origin, managed to enter Judaism, as it were, by the back door.

SEXUAL MORES IN THE PAGAN WORLD

In interpreting the meaning of the biblical phrase, "statutes of the Gentiles," the Rabbinic sources are, of course, aware of the existence of idol worship. They also accuse the pagan nations of bloodshed. But the "statutes of the Gentiles" which specially stand out are the sexual mores of the non-Jewish world. The Gentiles are accused of adultery, sodomy, homosexuality, and polyandry.[2] That these accusations are not due merely to "Jewish animosity" toward the Gentiles is evidenced by the identical accusations which the Apostle Paul levels against them. He, too, speaks about the women who "did change the natural use," and about the men who, "leaving the natural use of the woman, burned in their lust one toward another."[3] Indeed, classical writers themselves, men like Dio Cassius and Juvenal, bear witness to this state of affairs.[4]

This view of the "statutes of the Gentiles" had its repercussions in the law. For example, animals must not be placed in inns kept by heathen, nor must a woman be alone with them, nor again may a father employ a heathen as a tutor for his son. And all of this is motivated by references to the moral untrustworthiness of the Gentiles.[5] Even before these laws were formulated in the sources of Rabbinic Judaism, we find as "enlightened" and "hellenized" a person as King Herod refusing to send his young brother-in-law, Aristobulus, to the Roman court at the request of Antony. Josephus reports: "He did not think it safe for him to send one so handsome as was Aristobulus, in the prime of his life, for he was sixteen years of age, and of so noble a family; and particularly not to Antony, the principal man among the Romans, and that would abuse him in his amours, and besides, one that freely indulged himself in such pleasures as his power allowed him without control."[6]

"STATUTES OF THE GENTILES" PAR EXCELLENCE

If sexual immorality was the most blatant aspect of pagan life from which Rabbinic Judaism endeavored to separate itself, another aspect of hardly less prominence was the favorite pastime of the Roman-Hellenistic world: the theater, the circus, and the arena. They are described as the "statutes of the Gentiles" par excellence.[7] Interestingly enough, the Synagogue and the early Church were at one, not only in their condemnation of this aspect of Gentile life, but even in their use of the identical "proof-texts" to justify their opposition. With the Rabbinic sources on this subject one can compare the treatises *De Spectaculis* and *De Idololatria* by the second/third-century Church Father, Tertullian, and the fourth-century *Constitutions of the Holy Apostles*.

In the opposition to theater and games, the primary consideration was, of course, that those events were dedicated to the gods, and that they, therefore, partook of the character of "idol worship." "Even if only one chariot is being driven," says Tertullian, "it is the chariot of Jupiter."[8] "One does not go to the theater and to the circus," says the Talmud, "because sacrifices are brought there to the idols."[9] This, however, is only a formal ground for the prohibition. It leaves open the possibility that participation in these events might be permissible if no overt idol worship were to take place. But the opposition of the Rabbis (and of the Church) to this aspect of pagan life was more thoroughgoing than that.

Recent films like *Ben Hur* have attempted to give us a picture of the Roman arena. It is one which is hard to reconcile with the ideal of piety which the Rabbis tried to foster. Consequently, we are not surprised to read in the Rabbinic sources that, even "if sacrifices are not brought there, it is still forbidden to attend on account of the Psalm verse (Psalm 1:1): 'Happy is the man who ... does not sit in the seat of the scorners.' "[10] Similarly, Tertullian, after telling us that the prohibition of going to the circus, the theater, the races, and the games is nowhere stated in such specific terms as the laws against idolatry, murder, and adultery, nevertheless stresses the fact that the very first pronouncement of David (i.e., the verse about the "seat of the scorners") refers also to our case.[11]

The contrast, in the Psalm, to the man who "sits in the seat of the scorners" is the man "whose delight is in the Law of the

Lord." Time spent at the circus is, therefore, so much time wasted, time which should have been used in the study of the Torah. This is specifically stated in the *Jerusalem Targum* to Deuteronomy 28:19. The verse, part of a threatened punishment for disobedience, reads: "Cursed shalt thou be in thy coming in, and cursed shalt thou be in thy going out." The *Targum* paraphrases it as follows: "Cursed shall ye be when ye go to your theaters and circuses, thereby wasting time belonging to the words of the Torah; and cursed shall ye be when ye come out again to attend to your businesses." (Let us note in passing that the *Targum* does seem to imply that Jews *were* to be found among the spectators.)

More forceful still are the words of the *Tosephta*: "He who sits in the arena is like one who sheds blood."[12] Here, perhaps, we have the clue to the whole antipathy. Cruelty to man and to beast—that was the law of the arena. And that could not be reconciled with the nature of Judaism! This very cruelty stamped those forms of entertainment as characteristic "statutes of the Gentiles."

But Jews were living in the Roman world, not only in the Diaspora but in Palestine itself. Much of the business affecting the welfare of the community was transacted in the public meeting places where the games took place. Rabbinic Judaism was, therefore, realistic enough to permit attendance at the theater and the circus in exceptional circumstances. One *may* go to the stadium in order to save lives, and one *may* go to the circus to deal with matters affecting the welfare of the community, provided only that the man who is going does not stand to gain by it financially as an individual.[13] The situation envisaged is one where a person, otherwise doomed to die in combat, could be ransomed; or, if that was no longer feasible, where the presence of Jewish witnesses at the time of his death would make it possible for his widow to remarry. This very permission is a sad commentary on the "statutes of the Gentiles" prevalent in those days, one, moreover, which is echoed in the Christian *Constitutions of the Holy Apostles*, which state: "You are also to avoid

A Fence with Loopholes

their public meetings, and those sports which are celebrated in them. For a believer ought not to go to any of those public meetings unless to purchase a slave and save a soul."[14]

While the lack of sexual morality and the events in theater and arena are among the more prominent "statutes of the Gentiles," the concept itself was applied to other areas of life as well. It was developed in such a way that the biblical commandment was made to refer to any kind of "imitation" whatsoever. This process was aided in no small measure by the etymology of the Hebrew phrase, *chukkoth hagoyim*, itself. Although the term *chukkoth* is derived from the root *chakak* ("to legislate"), it was also brought into relation with the verb *chakah*, which means "to imitate." Any imitation of non-Jewish ways could thus be brought under the biblical prohibition of the "statutes of the Gentiles."

"Do not say, 'Because they are going out in toga, purple, and helmet, I, too, shall go out in toga, purple, and helmet.'"[15] This statement in Rabbinic literature is likewise echoed by Tertullian, who takes pains in explaining that "the purple, or the other ensigns of dignities and powers, dedicated from the beginning to idolatry engrafted on the dignity and the powers, carry the stain of their own profanation."[16] Indeed, while the Rabbinic prohibition is part of an interpretation of the phrase, "that thou inquire not after their gods" (Deuteronomy 12:30), thus showing that the Rabbis' motivation had been identical with that of the Church Father, the prohibition of "imitating" the clothes of the Gentiles has been preserved—without any reference to idolatry—by the ultra-orthodox Jews of East European provenance to this day. (That their *caftan* and *streimel* are themselves of non-Jewish origin, representing the Polish garb of an earlier century, merely shows the curious ways in which the prohibition of the "statutes of the Gentiles" gets mocked by history.)

Even in speech nothing was to be done that would create the impression of one's acceptance of idolatry. The Rabbis warn: "Do not ask someone, 'Where do you live? In the place of such-

and-such an idol?' Do not say: 'Wait for me at the place of such-and-such an idol'!"[17] While again it is Tertullian who echoes the Rabbis by discussing the appropriateness of such phrases as "You will find me in the Temple of Aesculapius," or "I live on Isis Street."[18] (Tertullian takes a more lenient view than the Rabbis do of this manner of speaking.)

THE "WAYS OF THE AMORITE"

A special subdivision of the "statutes of the Gentiles" consists of the "ways of the Amorite."[19] The Amorites were among the original inhabitants of Canaan, and they were credited with all the customs and practices which, to the Rabbis, appeared as rank superstition. It would be quite wrong to claim that the Talmud itself is completely free from superstitious elements. But it is interesting to see how, within the limits of the then possible, the Rabbis did endeavor to root out superstition by crediting the "Amorites" with its origination. Magic cannot be reconciled with monotheistic faith. The biblical statement; "Thou shalt be whole-hearted with the Lord thy God" (Deuteronomy 18:3), is interpreted by the *Midrash Tannaim* to mean: "One is not allowed to make inquiries of astrologers."[20]

But every rule has its exceptions. Abaye and Rava both agree that "whatever is used for medical purposes cannot be included in the category of the 'ways of the Amorite.' "[21] The test, we may suppose, was a purely pragmatic one. Applications of folk medicine which "worked" were permitted. Those which did not "work" were mere superstition, and hence prohibited as "ways of the Amorite." This may be rather poor medicine, but it is characteristic of Rabbinic Judaism that human life is valued above all, and even the fight against superstition was halted where there was the slightest suspicion that a superstitious "medicine" might actually help to save a life.

A *Fence with Loopholes*

JEWISH "SEPARATISM"

We are now in a position to inquire into the *positive* character of Judaism or into what remains once the "statutes of the Gentiles" have been excluded. The three characteristics of the Jews, according to the Talmud, are that they are "merciful, modest, and charitable."[22] We can see how the rejection of the contemporary sexual mores, and of the bloody sports of circus and arena, contributed to this ethical ideal. Yet there was more involved in the rejection of the "statutes of the Gentiles." Jewish separatism was considered to be a value in its own right.

"Rab Hunnah said in the name of Bar Kappara: For the sake of four merits was Israel redeemed from Egypt—because they did not change their names, and because they did not change their language, and because they did not engage in tale-bearing, and because not a single one among them was guilty of immorality. They did not change their names: as Reuben and Simeon they went down [to Egypt], and as Reuben and Simeon they went up again. They did not call Reuben, Rufus; or Judah, Julian; or Joseph, Lestes; or Benjamin, Alexander."[23]

The conclusion of this passage shows its true intent. Rufus, Julian, and Alexander were not *Egyptian* names at the time of Moses. But they were common names in the Roman-Hellenistic world in which the Rabbis lived. And when sermons were preached about the merits for the sake of which Israel was redeemed from Egypt, such sermons were not essays in history and archeology. Rather must we understand them in terms of the contemporary situation of the Rabbis themselves. Just as Israel awaited redemption from Egyptian slavery, so the Jews at the time of the Rabbis were waiting for the messianic redemption. And the Rabbis utilized this longing by telling their listeners about the ways which proved to be effective in bring-

47

ing about the redemption from Egypt. In our particular passage they warned against immorality and tale-bearing, against the giving up of the Hebrew language, and against the substitution of Roman-Hellenistic names for the original Jewish ones. (Again, we may note in passing that, among the Rabbis themselves, there were those who answered to the names of Antigonos, Dosethai, Symmachus, and Eurydemus—to mention but a few.)

This last-ditch attempt to hang on to the traditional names and the traditional language was born out of the realization of Jewish minority status in a world, both pagan and Christian, which tried its best to induce the Jews to give up their Judaism. If Scripture, as part of the terrible curse threatened for nonobservance of the Covenant, makes God say, "I shall bring them into the land of their enemies" (Leviticus 26:41), Rabbinic literature was able to call this threat "a good dispensation for Israel." "Let not Israel say: 'Since we have been exiled among the nations of the world, we shall do according to their deeds.' I, God, will not let them do so, but I shall raise My prophets over them, and they will bring them back to improvement, under My wings."[24] In fact, it is only by the possession of the Torah that Israel can maintain its individuality. But "Torah," in Pharisaic-Rabbinic parlance, meant the totality of the inherited way of life.

Gone were the days when Hellenistic Jews took the initiative in the spiritual conquest of the pagan world for Judaism. Gone, too, were the days when Pharisaic Judaism was engaged in missionary activities—an endeavor, by the way, for which they earned the ridicule of Jesus. Now it was all a question of preventing the pagan world from encroaching on that which was saved from the destruction of Temple and State. But the lure of the pagan world was strong, and Judaism had to meet the Hellenistic appeal to the Good, the True, and the Beautiful. The Rabbis were very much aware of this. They reckoned with the "evil inclination" within the Jew, which would say: "The Gentiles' statutes are prettier [!] than ours."[25]

A Fence with Loopholes

The result was that form of separatism which rejected any kind of "imitation," and which considered the withdrawal from the "statutes of the Gentiles" as an important component of true "holiness."[26] It would, however, be wrong to regard this as making a virtue of a necessity. It was a necessity only for those who saw a virtue in the continuation of Judaism, and who desired it strongly enough to make the requisite sacrifices. The followers of the Rabbis did not *have* to remain Jews. The outside world was all too ready to see them assimilate completely; and there were always individuals who took the easy way out. For those who remained, the legislation dealing with the "statutes of the Gentiles" was a necessary defense mechanism.

This must also color our own judgment concerning separatism. It is not a question of whether we should like to see the same system rigorously maintained today. Instead, we must evaluate it within its historical setting. Here we should have to come to the conclusion that, if we regard the survival of Jews and Judaism as something positive, then we must allow that Jewish separatism in the Roman period was a necessary thing.

THE REJECTION OF EXTREMISM

This conclusion is all the more valid once we realize that the separatism was not nearly so stringent in actual practice as it appears to have been in theory. We can appeal here to the Rabbis themselves. There are two key passages to help us. The first is the consideration of an apparent self-contradiction of the Prophet Ezekiel. In Ezekiel 5:7, the Prophet castigates the people because, among other things, "ye have not done according to the ordinances of the nations that are round about you." But in Ezekiel 11:12, the people are called to task precisely because "ye have done according to the ordinances of the nations that are round about you." Now, some modern scholars solve this problem quite simply by omitting the little Hebrew word *lo* ("not") in the first passage, thereby making both passages mean the same: Israel is accused of doing "according to the ordinances of the nations." But this solution, involving a textual emendation, was not available to the teachers of the Talmud. They had to resolve this contradiction in some other way. And they did so by making the Prophet criticize the people for following the corrupt practices of the Gentiles, and for *not* following their *proper* practices! From this we learn that, in the view of the Talmud, there *were* practices among the Gentiles which were "proper," and which Israel should have followed.[27]

The other passage is a comment on the *locus classicus* of the whole concept of the "statutes of the Gentiles," the verse in Leviticus 18:3—"You shall not do as they do in the land of Egypt, . . . and you shall not do as they do in the land of Canaan." The question is raised: Does this mean that the Israelites cannot build buildings as the other nations do, or plant plants as the others do? The question is immediately answered in the negative. The only prohibited "statutes of the Gentiles" are those that have a bearing on sexual mores![28]

The question about buildings and plantations is not a purely hypothetical one. Throughout the pages of the Hebrew Bible we can trace the conflict between two ways of life: the nomadic and the urban. In many a Prophet's mind, the period of desert wanderings was the "honeymoon" of God and Israel. It was only contact with the land of Canaan, urbanization with its inevitable moral laxity, and the adoption of pagan forms of worship, which led to Israel's repeated "unfaithfulness." The Prophets, as a whole, did not, however, ask for the clock to be put back. They only pleaded for a return to the old morality. But some fringe groups never seem to have made their peace with the new conditions of life. In the days of the Prophet Jeremiah we hear of the sect of the Rechabites, who lived by their founder's commandment: "Ye shall drink no wine, neither ye, nor your sons, for ever; neither shall ye build house, nor sow seed, nor plant vineyard, nor have any; but all your days ye shall dwell in tents. . . ." (Jeremiah 35:6,7)

A Fence with Loopholes

It is conceivable that some of this "old-time religion" lived on, if somewhat subterraneously, until the time of the Rabbis, even as the formation of civilization-denying sects is not an uncommon phenomenon in the history of any religious system. For us it is important to realize that Judaism *could* be given such an interpretation. But it is even more important to know that Rabbinic Judaism rejected it. The Jews were not to become a people of Rechabites, the clock was not to be put back, and only those aspects of civilization were to be shunned which were irreconcilable with the moral standards of the Torah.

Obviously, such a broad approach is in conflict with some of the more wholesale condemnations of any "imitation" of the "statutes of the Gentiles" which we have encountered before. This is quite in keeping with the nature of Rabbinic literature, which is hospitable to a variety of views on any given subject. Moreover, we must make allowance for the differences in temperament and outlook between various teachers. Besides, the stringent and lenient application of laws of this kind will have been very much dependent upon external political conditions, and on outside pressures.

Take, for example, the case of Rabban Gamaliel, who was bathing in the Bath of Aphrodite, in Akko. When asked by a pagan how he could possibly do such a thing, in the light of the provisions of the Jewish Law, he replied: "The bath was not made as an adornment for Aphrodite, but Aphrodite was made as an adornment for the bath." He then went on to explain that only "that which is treated as divine is forbidden, but that which is not treated as divine (and the Aphrodite of the bath definitely was not) is allowed."[29]

We can easily imagine other teachers, at other times, and in a different place, who would have denied themselves the pleasure of the bath under such circumstances. But with Gamaliel, as with Rabbinic Judaism's rejection of the Rechabite point of view, common sense prevailed.

More striking, by reason of its direct contravention of the law's original intent, is the fact that, in the Jerusalem Temple, while it was still standing, modifications of the sacrificial ritual were introduced to bring it more in line with the forms of heathen sacrificial worship of the time. These modifications, according to Professor Saul Lieberman, were justified on two grounds. In the first place, it was argued that the heathen were following an originally Jewish practice, and not the other way about. Secondly, in matters of *external decorum* the Jews might imitate the Gentiles without feeling that they were breaking the law; after all, it was commendable "to adorn a religious act." There was a general pattern in the ancient world of temples and sacrifices in which the Jews shared.[30] (Much bad blood in the nineteenth century might have been avoided if the defenders of Tradition had borne this precedent in mind when confronted with the first Reform strivings for an aesthetic change in the worship service of the synagogue. But then, as we have already seen, the laws against the "statutes of the Gentiles" did not always develop in a straight line.)

Yet the awareness of similarities, of any sort, between Jewish and Gentile modes of worship could not but raise the question: "Seeing that the heathen bring sin-offerings and guilt-offerings, one could imagine that Israel should not be doing so." But the answer was given that the heathen were offering to their gods things which were abominable to God, whereas Israel's sacrifices consisted of things acceptable to God.[31]

That the question rested on more secure grounds than the answer is evident from Rabbi Levi's clear recognition that the Jewish sacrificial cult was indeed only a concession which God made to the Israelites. Previously they had been accustomed to bring their sacrifices to the gods of Egypt, and a continuation of this practice would have brought untold harm to the world. Whereupon God told them: "Bring your sacrifices to Me at any time in the Tent of Meeting." They were thus separated from idol worship, and they were saved.[32] In popular presentations it is usually Maimonides who receives credit for having propounded this explanation. He did indeed enlarge upon it; but, in and by itself, it goes back to the Midrash.

In the same way, we might look at the Rabbis' treatment of

the sacred pillar. The erection of such a pillar is expressly forbidden in Deuteronomy 16:22. Still, when the Bible, in Genesis 28:18, records that the Patriarch Jacob had set up just such a pillar, there is not the slightest hint of even an implied criticism. To the Rabbis this could only mean that the sacred pillar "was beloved in the days of the Patriarchs, but hateful in the days of their descendants."[33] This comes rather close to modern notions of "progressive revelation" and the evolution of religion. For the Rabbis, however, it was nothing of the sort. Maimonides is closer to the Rabbinic mind when he accounts for the prohibition of the sacred pillar by telling us that, in the meantime, it had become a pagan form of worship, and was thus prohibited to the later Israelites.[34]

Be that as it may, the interesting fact remains that just as non-Jewish practices, though to all intents and purposes "statutes of the Gentiles," could, on occasion, enter Judaism by the back door, so could practices that were originally authentically "Jewish" become prohibited as "statutes of the Gentiles," when Judaism itself outgrew them. The Rabbis may indeed have lacked the concept of progress and evolution, but they were certainly involved in the process. Perhaps this is not the least thing we can learn by studying the legislation against the "statutes of the Gentiles."

CONCLUSION

Summing up, we may say that the legislation against the "statutes of the Gentiles" was a fence which the Rabbis erected to protect Judaism against total assimilation and dissolution. But it was a fence with loopholes. It did not exclude, and it was not meant to exclude, the outside world altogether. Judaism is far too much of a "this-worldly" religion. Indeed, the very Prophet Ezekiel was understood to have been angry at his compatriots because they did *not* follow the *proper* ordinances of the Gentiles. And the circumstances of time and place always had their bearing on the extent to which this legislation was applied.

Though imitation of foreign ways, as such, was on occasion interdicted (including such diverse matters as coiffure and language, names and attire), in the final analysis it was recognized that what had to be guarded and protected were the Jewish characteristics of Mercy, Modesty, and Charity. When these came into conflict with the upholders of the Good, the True, and the Beautiful, the latter claim was not denied, but, in the absence of Mercy and Modesty, the claim to Goodness and Truth was not recognized.

It is tempting to speculate on the Rabbis' preoccupation with the "statutes of the Gentiles." It should be remembered that we have considered only the first stages in the evolution of this concept. There is much more of it in later Rabbinic literature—right down to our own times. Can we detect an ambivalent attitude, the sort of feeling which—according to Freud—a taboo prohibition inspires among taboo races? "In their unconscious they would like nothing better than to transgress them, but they are also afraid to do it: they are afraid just because they would like to transgress, and their fear is stronger than the pleasure."[35] Perhaps—for the Rabbis never denied the attractiveness of the "statutes of the Gentiles." At any rate, the *practical* significance of this legislation in terms of Jewish survival is indubitable. The Christian Church, at first sharing the Synagogue's aversion to the "statutes of the Gentiles," sooner or later made its peace with them. Many of the differences between Judaism and Christianity can be traced back to this "peace."

Finally, although this has been an investigation into an earlier stage of Jewish development, a word about the later application of the concept of the "statutes of the Gentiles" may not be out of place. Maimonides, writing in the twelfth century, had this to say about our subject: "All these prohibitions have one purpose in view: that the Israelite shall not make himself like unto the nations, but he should be distinct from them, recognizable in his dress and in his actions, just as he differs from them in his philosophy and in his moral qualities."[36] It is left to our modern age, when most of the traditional restrictions have fallen into oblivion, to demonstrate that the Jew *can* retain his distinctive convictions and his morality in spite of his endeavor to share his heritage with the world at large, and to assimilate outwardly (as in dress and in speech). To do so, he would require a profound sense of moral judgment, a close familiarity with the Tradition, and—let us never forget it—a taste, delicate in the extreme.

NOTES

1. Erich Fromm, *Psychoanalysis and Religion* (New Haven, 1950), p. 118.
2. *Sifra Acharé Moth*, parashah 9 and pereq 13 (ed. Weiss, pp. 85c, d, 86a); *Sifra Qedoshim*, pereq 11 (ed. Weiss, p. 93c).
3. Romans 1:26f.
4. For references, see I. H. Weiss, *Dor dor vedorshav*, II, 18ff.
5. *Mishnah Abhodah Zarah* 2:1; *Tosephta Abhodah Zarah* 3:2 (ed. Zuckermandel, p. 463).
6. Josephus, *Antiquities* XV, 2, 6.
7. *Sifra Acharé Moth*, pereq 13 (ed. Weiss, p. 86a); *Tosephta Abhodah Zarah* 2:5,6 (ed. Zuckermandel, p. 462); b. *Abhodah Zarah* 18b.
8. *De Spectaculis*, ch. 7.
9. *Tosephta Abhodah Zarah* 2:5f. (ed. Zuckermandel, p. 462); b. *Abhodah Zarah* 18b.
10. Ibid.
11. *De Spectaculis*, ch. 3.
12. *Tosephta Abhodah Zarah* 2:7 (ed. Zuckermandel, p. 462).
13. Ibid.
14. *Apostolic Constitutions*, Book II, ch. LXII.
15. *Sifré Re-eh*, pisqa 81 (ed. Friedmann, p. 91b).
16. *De Idololatria*, ch. 18.
17. *Mekilta Kaspa*, ch. 4 (ed. Lauterbach, III, 180).
18. *De Idololatria*, ch. 20. On the whole relationship between the Church Fathers and the Rabbis in terms of the rejection of the "statutes of the Gentiles," cf. Jakob J. Petuchowski, "Halakhah in the Church

Fathers," in *Essays in Honor of Solomon B. Freehof* (Pittsburgh, 1964), pp. 257–274.

19. Cf. *Tosephta Shabbath*, chs. 7 and 8 (ed. Zuckermandel, pp. 117–119); *Mishnah Shabbath* 6:10; *Mishnah Chullin* 4:7; *Sifra Acharé Moth*, pereq 13 (ed. Weiss, p. 86a); b. *Shabbath* 67a,b.

20. *Midrash Tannaim* (ed. Hoffmann, p. 110).

21. B. *Shabbath* 67a.

22. B. *Yebamoth* 79a.

23. *Leviticus Rabbah* 32:5; *Mekilta Pischa*, ch. 5 (ed. Lauterbach, I, 34).

24. *Sifra Bechuqothai*, ch. 8 (ed. Weiss, p. 112b).

25. *Sifra Acharé Moth*, ch. 13 (ed. Weiss, p. 86a).

26. *Mekilta Bachodesh*, ch. 2 (ed. Lauterbach, II, 206); *Sifra Qedoshim*, ch. 9 (ed. Weiss, p. 91d), and ch. 11 (ed. Weiss, p. 93d).

27. B. *Sanhedrin* 39b.

28. *Sifra Acharé Moth*, parashah 9 (ed. Weiss, p. 85c,d).

29. *Mishnah Abhodah Zarah* 3:4.

30. Saul Lieberman, *Hellenism in Jewish Palestine* (New York, 1950), pp. 129f.

31. *Sifré Re-eh*, pisqa 81 (ed. Friedmann, p. 91b).

32. *Leviticus Rabbah* 22:8.

33. *Sifré Shophetim*, pisqa 146 (ed. Friedmann, p. 103b).

34. *Yad, Hilkhoth Akkum* 6:6.

35. Sigmund Freud, "Totem and Taboo," in *The Basic Writings of Sigmund Freud*, ed. A. A. Brill (New York, 1938), p. 831.

36. *Yad, Hilkhoth Akkum* 11:1.

CHAPTER 4

✣ *The Magnification of Hanukkah*

Festivals, like books, have their fate. Changing times and environments can be either beneficial or detrimental to a festival's survival, and, in this connection, its position within the rubrics and definitions of canon law is relatively unimportant. Witness the observance of the New Moon. There can be no doubt that, in biblical times, the New Moon was an important festival. It is mentioned alongside the Sabbath; it seems to have been an occasion when people ceased from work and went back to listen to the teachings of the Prophets and other men of God. The vision of the future with which the Book of Isaiah concludes provides "that from one New Moon to another, and from one Sabbath to another, all flesh shall come to worship before Me, saith the Lord" (Isaiah 66:23).

Yet, in spite of the Rabbinic injunction that the New Moon be marked by an additional service (*Musaph*) and the recitation of the *Hallel* psalms, and also by special inserts in the statutory

---
Reprinted, with additions, from *Commentary* (January 1960), pp. 38–43. Copyright © 1960 by the American Jewish Committee. The author is grateful for permission to reprint this material.

57

prayer as well as in the Grace after Meals, the New Moon today has all but lost its festive character. A generation ago it was still possible to find pious women who would abstain from work on that day—somehow the New Moon had become especially a women's festival. But even that aspect of it has been lost. Observant Jews will, of course, still follow the Rabbinic provisions regarding the day's liturgy. This might mean that the daily morning service will have to be even more rushed than usual; the service must be over in time for the opening of offices and stores. The New Moon simply is no longer what it used to be in the days of the Bible!

But just as it is possible for an important festival to lose its importance, so it is possible for a minor festival to gain in esteem. Hanukkah is a case in point. For modern American Jews, Hanukkah ranks next in importance to the High Holy Days and the Passover. It was not always thus! In Jewish Law, Hanukkah is a minor festival. Work is forbidden only during the half hour or so when the candles are burning. There are indeed liturgical inserts for the daily services, similar to those of the New Moon, but they do not make Hanukkah any less workaday for all that. In some parts of the Jewish world there may have been the custom of providing the children with "Hanukkah money," but *the* annual occasion for the exchange of gifts was Purim—not Hanukkah.

As a matter of fact, the very reason for the observance was only dimly perceived. The Talmud records a victory of the Hasmoneans over the "Greeks," which led to the cleansing of the Temple. This, in turn, led to the "miracle of the oil"—a cruse of oil sufficient for one day lasted for eight. Yet Judah the Maccabee is not even mentioned by name. One simply lit candles for eight days to commemorate the miracle.

In the early collections of Rabbinic homilies—such as the *Pesikta de Rab Kahana*—the Hanukkah sermons do not contain a single reference to the historical events behind the festival. They all deal with the dedication of the Tabernacle in the wilderness, and with the values of institutional religion. They

The Magnification of Hanukkah

are based on the Torah readings for Hanukkah, and, naturally, the Torah could contain no reference to the events of the second century B.C.E. Hanukkah could, in fact, be nothing but a minor festival.

The nineteenth and twentieth centuries were the making of Hanukkah. On the one hand, rationalistic tendencies were unkind to the old festival. Nobody could believe in miracles any more, and the "miracle of the oil" was demoted to the rank of a legend—which is nothing to celebrate. Happily, some other forces were at work. The same rationalism which did away with the "miracle of the oil" worked to overcome the old Rabbinic ban on the reading of the "outside books," the Apocrypha. The Apocrypha contained the two Books of the Maccabees, where, in stirring language, the Maccabean battles and victories were described. If it was no longer possible to celebrate the "miracle of the oil," it now became possible to celebrate the "Feast of the Maccabees."

The first fight in history for the freedom of conscience and of worship! The victory of Jewish monotheism over Hellenistic paganism! The Jewish idea of the equality of all men triumphing over an economy based on slavery—for the latter was still maintained by as enlightened a Greek as Aristotle himself. Such were the motivations for the new celebration of Hanukkah. The oil miracle was a small price to pay for such a glorious new festival, a festival, moreover, which was so much in line with contemporary Jewish aspirations for political freedom and emancipation. "Restore my house of prayer," so ran the old Hanukkah hymn, *Ma'oz Tzur*, "and there I will sacrifice a thanksgiving offering." But the nineteenth century had a different language: "Yours the message cheering," the new hymn, *Rock of Ages*, proclaimed, "that the time is nearing, which will see all men free, tyrants disappearing!"

The Reform Jews who thus reinterpreted Hanukkah were usually quite antagonistic toward the rising movement of Jewish nationalism and Zionism. But both the opposing elements helped in the transformation of Hanukkah from a minor to a major festival. For the Zionists, too, had a great liking for this festival. Any nationalist movement is in need of heroes whose shining example can be held up to fire the imagination of a new generation. Nineteenth-century nationalist movements in Europe could point with pride to the freedom fighters of past ages. Jewish nationalism had only the "People of the Book." (The defenders of Massada did, indeed, die heroically. But the Romans won.) Jewish Garibaldis were not so easy to find—the glories of Israel have usually been of a spiritual nature. In a world of nations and of empires, Israel was, in the words of Balaam, "a people that shall dwell alone, and not be reckoned among the nations" (Numbers 23:9). Yet the Jews had their Maccabees—they could serve as an inspiration for the rising nationalist movement. Theodor Herzl wrote a moving piece about the Hanukkah candlestick. And the songs of the new movement helped the transformation of the festival. "Who can express the mighty acts of the *Lord*," thus sang the Psalmist of old, "or make all His praise to be heard?" (Psalm 106:2). But a modern Zionist Hanukkah song proclaims: "Who can express the mighty acts of *Israel?*" And it goes on to relate that "in those days, at this time, the Maccabee was the savior and redeemer. But in our days, the whole people of Israel will unite and arise to redeem itself."

Such reinterpretations in and by themselves would have been sufficient to make Hanukkah viable in the modern world. But in time a third factor came to strengthen it—one which might have borne the whole burden of the festival even if no reinterpretation had ever been attempted. Hanukkah may have been a minor festival in the Jewish calendar. But Christmas is a major festival in the Christian calendar. And the twenty-fifth day of the month of Kislev (the beginning of Hanukkah) has an uncanny habit of more or less coinciding with the twenty-fifth day of the month of December. (Woe unto the American Jewish parents in those years when it does not!)

The Magnification of Hanukkah

No doubt, the annual winter festival is older than either Hanukkah or Christmas, and both may have a common pagan ancestry. The kindling of lights is common to them, too. But here the resemblance ends—unless, of course, one were to claim that without the victory of the Maccabees in the second century B.C.E. there never would have been any Judaism left two centuries later for Jesus of Nazareth to transform into Christianity. (As a matter of fact, the festival calendar of the Roman Catholic Church does contain a "Feast of the Maccabees.") Yet all of this is neither here nor there. Yuletide, in Christian civilization, is the traditional season for "peace on earth, good will to men." And it is this Yuletide "spirit" which is made to live also in the American Jewish Hanukkah observance. From the exchange of gifts, to home decorations, to greeting cards, to specially imprinted gift wrapping paper, Hanukkah matches Christmas. If, because of religious scruples, the "Hanukkah bush" has as yet fallen short of universal acceptance, the candelabrum can be made to enter the competition against the Christmas tree; and cut-out paper Maccabees can console the Hebrew infant for the absence of a crèche. Moreover, if everything else fails, one is fortified by the knowledge that Hanukkah lasts for eight long days—with gifts every single night.

Festivals, like books, have their fate.

The kindling of the Hanukkah lights gave rise to a question of far-reaching consequences in the Babylonian Talmud. The Talmud establishes the rule that the kindling of the lights is to be preceded by the benediction: "Praised be Thou, O Lord our God, King of the universe, Who hast sanctified us by Thy commandments, and commanded us to kindle the lights of Hanukkah" (b. *Shabbath* 23a).

Immediately the question is raised: "Where did God command us to do that?" The underlying assumption here is that the revelation on Mount Sinai was a complete and perfect revelation, in which God had communicated to Israel all they had to know about their religious obligations. Yet one may search the Five Books of Moses from the beginning of Genesis to the end of Deuteronomy, and he will not come across the slightest hint of any "commandment" for the kindling of Hanukkah lights. Still, if God had really commanded us to kindle the Hanukkah lights, how could He have omitted this item in the official transcript of His commands, in the Torah?

Like so many other questions in the Talmud, this one was asked only to provide an excuse for a good answer. The good answer was given by Rab Iviya, a fourth-century Babylonian teacher, and was in the form of a reference to the seventeenth chapter of the Book of Deuteronomy. There we read that "if there arise a matter too hard for thee in judgment . . . then thou shalt come unto the priests the Levites, and unto the judge that shall be in those days; and thou shalt inquire; and they shall declare unto thee the sentence of judgment. And thou shalt do according to the tenor of the sentence which they shall declare unto thee. . . . According to the law which they shall teach thee . . . thou shalt do; thou shalt not turn aside from the sentence which they shall declare unto thee, to the right hand, nor to the left" (Deuteronomy 17:8-11).

In the evolution of Pharisaic-Rabbinic Judaism those were very important verses indeed. It is evident that here the Law was making provision for the eventuality that a matter might arise in the future which was not specifically covered in the codes of the sacred text. Naturally, in such a case, the priests would be the ones whose "lips should keep knowledge," and at whose "mouth one should seek the Law" (Malachi 2:7). This, indeed, seems to have been the procedure in the days of the First Temple, and at the beginning of the period of the Second Temple. But our text does not only speak about the Levitical priesthood. It also contains a reference to "the judge that shall be in those days"; and this was the basis seized on by the lay scholars in the days of the Second Temple, in their attempt to break the priestly monopoly. Not just the hereditary priesthood, so they claimed, but also the lay Israelite—to the extent

The Magnification of Hanukkah

to which his knowledge qualifies him for the office of judge—can act as an interpreter of Torah. Here was the origin of the Pharisaic movement.

Anything then which, though not contained in the Five Books of Moses, was ordained by a duly constituted authority—priestly or otherwise—could rely on the scriptural support furnished by the seventeenth chapter of the Book of Deuteronomy. And since the authority behind Deuteronomy was divine authority, was, in fact, God Himself, that authority carried over to the later enactments reached on the basis of Deuteronomy. Now Hanukkah, it was believed, was instituted by the duly constituted *beth din*, or Rabbinical court of law, of the Hasmoneans. Therefore Rab Iviya could invoke this chapter of Deuteronomy as the scriptural basis for the "commandment" of the Hanukkah lights.

A more sophisticated generation was unable to follow this chain of reasoning. Rabbi Isaac M. Wise, for example, the organizer of American Reform Judaism, seems to have been bothered by the same question that bothered the Talmud, but he was unable to accept Rab Iviya's answer. In his reformed prayer book, the *Minhag America*, Wise omitted the benediction about God's commanding us to kindle the Hanukkah lights. Instead, he made use of another benediction, one which the Tradition had prescribed for the first night of Hanukkah, thanking God for "keeping us alive, sustaining us, and letting us reach this season"; he simply tacked on the words: "to kindle the Hanukkah lights." Wise would not have done away with the Festival of Hanukkah, for the reasons we have discussed. But he was also too much of a rationalist to believe that God Himself had commanded its observance. (We have dealt with this nineteenth-century difficulty at length in our study, "Reform Benedictions for Rabbinic Ordinances," in *Hebrew Union College Annual*, XXXVII [1966], 175–189.)

Wise and those who thought like him thus missed a very good opportunity of grounding their Reform Judaism in the Tradition itself. For what is implied in Rab Iviya's answer is this: the Word of God is not confined to the Five Books of Moses. Each generation has its own unprecedented religious needs, unprovided for by the earlier codes. But God does not remain silent; He is behind the endeavor of the authorized interpreters who take into account the new needs and the unprecedented circumstances. If God's Word were confined to the Five Books of Moses, there could be no Reform Judaism. There could not even have come into existence a Rabbinic Judaism. But if, on the other hand, the Tradition concedes that an innovation of the Hasmonean law court represented a divine "commandment," then, and only then, are we justified in speaking about the "unfolding" Will of God, and about "progressive revelation." (Perhaps, then, Rab Iviya in the fourth century was an even better "Reform Jew" than Rabbi Wise in the nineteenth.)

On reciting the benediction praising God "Who has commanded us to kindle the lights of Hanukkah," it is good to bear in mind the seventeenth chapter of Deuteronomy—and its Pharisaic interpretation which made possible the evolution and development of a Judaism which can be as fresh and as alive "at this season" as it was "in those days."

Indeed, the Talmud raised a question of far-reaching consequences.

The story of Hanukkah, as presented in the Sunday School, is a story of "good guys" (the Maccabees) and "bad guys" (the Greeks, or—with somewhat greater historical accuracy—the Hellenistic Syrians). Of course, the "good guys" won—or there would be no Festival of Hanukkah to celebrate. This makes a good story, and it lends itself beautifully to stage productions. The only trouble is: life is stranger than fiction.

In a little Schocken book, *The Maccabees*, Professor Elias Bickermann takes a second look at the conventional Hanukkah story and contrasts it with what the historical sources themselves have to say on the subject. The results are somewhat

The Magnification of Hanukkah

startling. The glorious Maccabean war turns out to have been first and foremost a Jewish civil war, with the Syrians called in by one of the contending factions. At issue was the question of "Hellenization." There was a powerful section of the Jewish population of Palestine prepared to throw overboard their Jewish heritage and to swallow, hook, line, and sinker, the government-sponsored brand of Hellenism, which had already been willingly accepted in the surrounding territories. Some of the "best families" of Jerusalem were counted in on this. The Maccabees, at first a mere band of guerrillas, became the leaders of those other sections of the population who were determined to remain "loyal to the covenant of their fathers." The Maccabees emerged the victors—but their victory by no means settled the question of Hellenization.

When the victorious Maccabees instituted the Festival of Hanukkah, Bickermann argues, they did something unprecedented in the annals of Judaism. No previous victory in battle had been commemorated by an annual observance in the Jewish calendar. The Greeks, however, were in the habit of fixing this kind of celebration. What is more, in choosing the kindling of lights as the characteristic observance of their victory celebration, the Maccabees imitated a typical Hellenistic custom. The very observance of Hanukkah, then, looks like a Jewish bow in the direction of Hellenism. What, therefore, was the battle all about?

The succeeding history of the Hasmonean dynasty was one of typical Hellenistic princelings—with all the trappings. This is easy to shrug off by reminding ourselves that the later Hasmoneans sided with the Sadducees, and that they are, therefore, not really representative of the "mainstream" of Judaism. But the picture does not change when we look into the documents which form the very basis of Pharisaic-Rabbinic Judaism. Professor Saul Lieberman has written two important books on the subject, *Greek in Jewish Palestine* and *Hellenism in Jewish Palestine*—the titles almost tell the story. And what Professor Lieberman is discussing is not the question of fringe groups in Judaism, of Sadducees and degenerate scions of the Hasmonean house. He is talking about the *Mishnah* and the teachers of the *Mishnah*. He is showing how the Greek language and Greek ideas—and even Hellenistic cultic forms—have entered the main citadel of Judaism and helped shape the very form taken by Jewish legal codes and teachings. Again, we might be tempted to ask, was the Maccabean battle fought in vain?

We find an answer to this question—a negative answer—in Bickermann's work. There were, says Professor Bickermann, two forms of "Hellenization." The one was marked by the willingness to throw away one's Jewish heritage and put the foreign culture in its place; the other tried to find room within the Jewish culture for the good things which Hellenism had to offer. This was the Hellenism of the Maccabees.

What the Festival of Hanukkah commemorates, therefore, is not the struggle of Jewish faith and culture against Hellenism and Greek culture. Rather is it the commemoration of a struggle between those who were ready to assimilate their Judaism to Hellenism, and those who were ready to assimilate valuable aspects of Hellenism to their Judaism.

It is the question of "assimilation" which the celebration of Hanukkah induces us to ask anew each year. "Assimilation"— that much misunderstood word! In some Jewish circles it is given a negative connotation exclusively. If you admit that you are in favor of assimilation, they put you down as opposed to "Jewish survival," as uninterested in Jewish values. But others have read Ahad Ha'am, and know that there is a difference between "assimilation" and mere "imitation." Still others have read Hermann Cohen, and know how to distinguish between "active assimilation" and "passive assimilation."

Assimilation is something that cannot be disposed of by slogan thinking. In its negative aspect, it is pursued as much by the Zionist radical who wants the Jews to be "a nation like unto all the other nations" as it is by the more conventional "assimilationist" who is eager to lose all traces of Judaism and to merge in the crowd. In its positive aspect, it is something that

The Magnification of Hanukkah

has gone on in Judaism since time immemorial, and something that is going on as long as Judaism desires to remain alive. The Maccabees were neither the first nor the last to enrich Judaism with borrowings from Hellas. But it takes study and much thought—and also taste—to know where to draw the line.

And come to think of it, what are we to say about our twentieth-century American Hanukkah?

CHAPTER 5

🖉 *The Hero of the Isaac Story*

What has kept Judaism alive through the ages is not so much the literal meaning of what the non-Jewish world calls the "Old Testament," but rather the scope which that text provided for the ongoing process of interpretation and reinterpretation. Every generation was able to follow the Rabbinic advice of "standing at the foot of Mount Sinai" in its own right, and every generation heard the message of Sinai in words appropriate to its own level of philosophical sophistication.

In Chapter 2 we have attempted to describe the "Bible of the Synagogue" as a whole. In the present chapter, we shall read one particular passage of Scripture as it is reflected through the manifold lenses of that "Bible of the Synagogue." We shall deal with the twenty-second chapter of the Book of Genesis. It is the chapter in which we read about God's commandment to Abraham that he should sacrifice Isaac, about Abraham's

---

Reprinted, with additions, from *The Jewish Frontier*, XXVII, No. 4 (April 1960), 11–14. Copyright © 1960 by The Jewish Frontier Association. The author is grateful for permission to reprint this material.

The Hero of the Isaac Story

willingness to comply with that commandment, about God's stopping the intended act at the very last minute, about the substitution of a ram for the sacrifice of the son, and about the blessing which God bestows upon Abraham as a reward for his absolute obedience. In our Tradition this chapter is called the *Akedah*, which means "the binding."

Of course, the *binding* of Isaac is as far as the intended act of sacrifice was allowed to go. Abraham was stopped by the Angel of the Lord at the very moment when he raised his slaughtering knife. But in some strands of our Tradition the "binding" is treated as if the sacrifice had actually been consummated. Not all those strands go quite as far as the interpretation, mentioned and *rejected* by Ibn Ezra in the twelfth century, that Abraham actually slaughtered Isaac, and that Isaac was later resurrected. But, without visualizing the intermediate steps, there are Rabbinic statements which speak about the "ashes of Isaac" rising upon the altar and making intercession on behalf of Israel. Indeed, the "binding" is often spoken of in terms of an act of atonement, of a *vicarious* atonement, to be precise; it was for the sake of the binding of Isaac that the waters of the Red Sea were divided, and it will be for the sake of the binding of Isaac that, at the end of time, the dead will be resurrected. (The sources have been gathered in Geza Vermes, *Scripture and Tradition in Judaism* [Leiden: E. J. Brill, 1961], pp. 193–227; and in Shalom Spiegel, *The Last Trial* [New York: Pantheon Books, 1967], *passim*.)

All such statements presuppose, of course, that Isaac offered himself willingly for the sacrifice. This view is implied, for example, in the comments of the famous eleventh-century commentator, Rashi, on verse 8 of our chapter. In verse 7 we read Isaac's question: "Behold the fire and the wood; but where is the lamb for a burnt-offering?" And, in verse 8, Abraham answers: "God will provide Himself the lamb for a burnt-offering, my son." And the verse continues: "So they both of them went together." Now, according to Rashi, this verse is to be understood as follows:

"God will provide Himself, and select, a lamb. But if there will be no lamb, then you, my son, will be used for the burnt-offering." And even though Isaac understood that he was about to be slaughtered, they both of them went together, in perfect accord.

There can be no doubt that, in this view, Isaac is the "hero" of the *Akedah* story—at any rate, from the moment that he "understood." Here we get the idea of an Isaac who willingly suffers martyrdom. We get the picture of an Isaac carrying the wood up the mountain—the very wood which was about to be used for his own execution. And the result of all this—an act of atonement and intercession on behalf of Israel!

It was this picture which entered the Jewish liturgy, particularly the liturgy of the High Holy Days, when it is invoked time and again in the Jew's plea for divine pardon and salvation. This becomes all the more appropriate in view of the fact that the *Akedah* is the Scripture lesson for the second day of Rosh Hashanah.

But even on ordinary weekdays, the Jew makes mention of the *Akedah* in his daily morning prayers. "What are we?" he says. "What is our life? What is our goodness? . . . Are not all the mighty men as nought before Thee, the men of renown as though they had never existed? . . . Even the pre-eminence of man above the beast is nought, for all is vanity." But then he immediately continues by saying:

> However, we are Thy people, the sons of Thy covenant, the children of Abraham, Thy friend, to whom Thou didst make the promise at Mount Moriah, the descendants of *Isaac, his only son, who was bound on the altar*, the congregation of Jacob, Thy first-born son . . . [author's italics].

And in this the Jew finds his pre-eminence above the beast, the meaning of life, and the hope for his salvation.

Those ideas are not often voiced when facile attempts are made to contrast Judaism with Christianity, and to show, on a superficial level, where Judaism differs. But those ideas are there, and for centuries they have been of considerable influence

The Hero of the Isaac Story

—even though they may not have been as central in Judaism as the corresponding ideas are in Christianity.

The analogy of the role of Isaac in Judaism to that of Jesus in Christianity once having been established, the question naturally arises: Who was influenced by whom? In some of his recent writings, dealing with early Christianity, Professor Hans-Joachim Schoeps, of the University of Erlangen, has asserted that the Apostle Paul was influenced by Jewish views about the *Akedah* when he formulated his concept of the atoning character of the self-sacrifice of Jesus. Unfortunately, none of the Jewish sources adduced by Schoeps antedates Paul. Paul's dependence upon Jewish ideas can, therefore, be at best considered plausible. But it cannot be proved.

It seems to us, however, that it is just as plausible to assume a Jewish dependence upon Christian ideas. This should not be as startling as it might appear to some readers at first sight. Such doctrines of medieval Judaism as that of the pre-existent soul and of spiritual immortality were taken over from the Hellenistic world of thought. Even the *Jahrzeit* light seems to have been a borrowing from the Church; and many other instances could be listed. It was not only a modern cynic who insisted *wie es sich christelt so jüdelt es sich* (i.e., that Jews are always imitating Christian fads and fashions). Already Rabbi Judah the Pious (d. 1217), in his *Sepher Hasidim* (paragraph 831), made this comment: "As is the custom of the Gentiles so are the customs of the Jews in the majority of places."

When Christianity taught the doctrine of the sacrificial death of its savior, it must have compelled the Synagogue to react to it. And the Synagogue could not reject the doctrine offhand—whatever modern Judaism may have to say on the subject. The feeling of man's insufficiency in the presence of God was well known to the Rabbis of old; and after the destruction of the Temple, the lack of a sacrificial ritual was keenly felt by many, and led to all kinds of substitutions. Among them, the *kapparoth* rite on Atonement Eve—practiced in some circles to this day—is perhaps the most eloquent testimony.

But also the notion that the innocent suffer for the sake of the wicked, and that little children die on account of the sins of others, was a notion not without its protagonists among the ranks of the Rabbis.

Man always does less, and is able to do only less, than what he feels is required of him. Commitment to God, with all one's heart, all one's soul, and all one's might, implies a radical and ultimate commitment. That is why Rabbi Akiba felt that he could live up to it only at the very moment of his martyr's death. Lesser mortals are consciously or unconsciously aware of their shortcomings, of their failure to give their all, to commit their total selves. And how easy it is for this sense of incompleteness to turn into a sense of guilt! And the sense of guilt, in its turn, wants to be assuaged.

Here was the great appeal of the Christian dogma. It pacified the sinner by telling him that God does not expect him to raise himself by his own bootstraps. It has all been done *for* him. The savior has died for him on the cross, and, by his death, has brought atonement for the many.

For obvious reasons, the Synagogue could not accept the Christian claim. The doctrine of the vicarious atonement was only one aspect of the total Christology taught by the Church; and that total Christology had already infringed the boundaries of Jewish monotheism. But divorced from the notion of a God-Man, there was no reason for the Synagogue to deny the idea of a vicarious atonement. There was indeed, as we have tried to indicate, every reason why the Synagogue should accept such a doctrine. And the figure of Isaac, lacking all the traits which made the Christian Christ objectionable to the Synagogue, was the ideal figure around which such a doctrine could center.

The *Akedah*, in other words, was to become the Jewish counterpart to Calvary, and to address itself within the Synagogue to that psychological need which, outside the Synagogue, was met by the Christian dogma. It is in this way that we can account for the many parallels which Rabbinic literature and Jewish liturgy, in dealing with the *Akedah*, offer to the Christian

The Hero of the Isaac Story

picture of the atoning death of Jesus. It is in this way, too, that we can understand why, in several Rabbinic sources, the *Akedah* is spoken of in terms which imply an actual consummation of the intended sacrifice—even though, on a more explicit level, the biblical account speaking of Isaac's being spared could, of course, not be rejected. This, to us, appears to be at least as plausible as the view of Professor Schoeps and of others about the Jewish antecedents of the Christian dogma.

Yet the *Akedah* can only function as the Jewish "Calvary" if Isaac, pure and innocent, willingly accepted the role of the sacrifice. If, then, Isaac is seen in this role, it follows that Isaac must have been the "hero" of the *Akedah* story. Isaac, moreover, was the "hero" in more than one sense. In good literature, the hero must be such that the reader can identify with him. And throughout the centuries of Jewish martyrdom, many a Jew, and many a Jewish community, had occasion to identify themselves with just such a "hero" as Isaac was understood to have been—with the man who willingly chose death "for the sanctification of the Name."

To regard Isaac as the "hero" of the *Akedah* story is, however, only *one* exegetical possibility. An equal, or an even greater, claim might be made for Abraham, the father. Such, at any rate, is the view of Ibn Ezra, in his comments on verse 4 of the *Akedah* chapter. The down-to-earth rationalistic—not to say, prosaic—approach adopted by Ibn Ezra can best be appreciated by reading his comments in full:

> Our Sages, of blessed memory, say that Isaac, at the time of his "binding," was thirty-seven years old. If this were an authentic tradition, we would have to accept it; but, from the point of view of logic, it cannot be right. For then the righteousness of Isaac should have been revealed, and his reward made double that of his father, seeing that, of his own free will, he gave himself over to the slaughter. *But the Scripture does not say the least thing about Isaac!*

Others say that he was five years old. But this, too, cannot be right, since he carried the wood for the burnt-offering.

The most reasonable thing to assume is that he was about thirteen years old, and his father forced him, and bound him *against his will*. The proof of this is the fact that his father kept the secret from him, and said (verse 8): "God will provide Himself the lamb." Had he told him: "*You* are the burnt-offering," *he would surely have fled*.

A greater contrast to Rashi's understanding of the words, "they both of them went together," can hardly be imagined. Far from willingly baring his soul unto death, Isaac had actually to be *tricked* into playing his part!

Who has the correct interpretation of the text—Rashi or Ibn Ezra? Tradition does not decide this question for us. It prints Rashi and Ibn Ezra on either side of the biblical narrative. Perhaps, on a more exalted level of synthesis, both of them may turn out to be right. Certainly, a good case can be made out for regarding Abraham as the "hero," as a reading of Kierkegaard's *Fear and Trembling* will make abundantly clear. So does the Jewish Tradition—in spite of, or in addition to, all its glorification of Isaac's role. The *Akedah* is the last, and the supreme, test of the ten tests which Abraham, this "knight of faith," had to pass.

It did not, however, escape the Masters of the Tradition that the very notion of a "test" given by God to Abraham was not without its theological difficulties. We test something to find out that which we did not know before. Yet God is, by definition, omniscient!

The thirteenth-century Spanish-Jewish commentator, Nachmanides, tries to come to terms with this problem by invoking the Aristotelian notions of "potentiality" and "actuality." He tells us, in his comments on the first verse of the *Akedah*:

The function of this test is, I believe, due to the fact that man has absolute free-will over his actions. If he wants to do something,

The Hero of the Isaac Story

he can do it. And if he does not want to do something, he need not do it. It is called a "test" from the perspective of the testee only. But the Tester (blessed be He) issues a command to him in order to bring the matter from potentiality to actuality, so that he may receive the reward of a good *deed*, and not just the reward of a good intent. . . . And behold, all the "tests" in the Torah are for the benefit of the testee.

The same theme, though with commendable brevity, and with a reference to the ideal of *imitatio Dei*, is taken up by the sixteenth-century Italian-Jewish exegete, Obadiah Sforno:

God tested Abraham so that he should be as loving and as God-fearing in actuality as he already was in potentiality. In this way he would be more like unto his Creator, Who is beneficent to the world in actuality. For indeed the purpose of man's existence is that he should be like unto his Creator as much as possible. Scripture testifies to this by saying: "Let us make man in Our image, after Our likeness."

By linking God's act of "testing" with the ideal of *imitatio Dei*, Sforno has generalized the particular, and thereby he has given us to understand that the "tests" which God imposes on man are those opportunities given to every man of bringing out the best that is within him, of making actual that which has thus far existed in potentiality alone.

Once we have reached this stage of exegesis, it hardly matters any longer who *the* "hero" is. For some, it might mean the readiness for self-sacrifice, as, according to one interpretation, it meant for Isaac. For others, it might mean the readiness to part with what is most precious to them, as, according to the second interpretation, it meant for Abraham. What counts in either case is man's ability to echo Abraham's answer to the divine call: *Hinneni*, "Here am I!"

CHAPTER 6

🕮 *Reflections on a Title*

In our five previous chapters we have had frequent occasion to refer to Rabbinic Judaism, to Rabbinic literature, and to the Rabbis. It is one of the tokens of Jewish continuity that the title, "Rabbi," is still borne by Jewish religious functionaries in this day and age. Yet it is a title which has a checkered career, even as its standing today is not without its problematical aspects. There are some men whose knowledge of Rabbinic literature is, at best, elementary, and whose theology is built on the negation of Rabbinic teachings, who nevertheless insist on being known as "Rabbis." Yet there are others who have fully merited the title of "Rabbi" who will nevertheless insist on being addressed by some other academic title they have acquired. It is all somewhat confusing. In the following pages we shall attempt to bring some clarification to this subject.

Etymologically, of course, the matter is quite simple. "Rabbi" means "my master." The ordained teachers in the period of the

---

Reprinted, with revisions, from *The Jewish Spectator*, May 1961, pp. 9-11. Copyright © 1961 by The Jewish Spectator. The author is grateful for permission to reprint this material.

Mishnah are called "rabbi." In the period of the *Gemara*, the ordained Palestinian teachers continue to bear the title of "rabbi," while the ordained Babylonian teachers acquired the title of "rav." The Palestinian patriarchs went by the name of "rabban" or "rabbenu" ("*our* master," rather than "*my* master").

The ordination by which a man acquired the title of *rabbi* or *rav* was not so much a sacramental ordination, or a handing down of the mantle of charismatic leadership, as it was a legal formality, corresponding to the modern lawyer's being "called to the bar." The formula of ordination, *yoreh yoreh, yadin yadin* ("he may teach, he may judge"), implied permission to render decisions in matters of ritual and of civil law. Not all Rabbis had that permission in both areas. One could be ordained to render decisions in ritual law only, or in civil law only. What is more, some of the greatest teachers quoted in Rabbinic literature never received any kind of ordination. One did not have to be ordained to be listened to with respect—if he had something to say.

Moreover, there was a time when the title "Rabbi" was not yet in existence. Notice that we refer to Hillel and to Shammai —never to Rabbi Hillel or Rabbi Shammai. The title "Rabbi" came into use only *after* Hillel's time. Hillel's grandson, Gamaliel, was the first to bear the title "*rabban*," while "*rabbi*" began to be used only in the following generation.

During the Talmudic period, the title "*rabbi*" or "*rav*" indicated that its holder had received ordination from the Palestinian or the Babylonian authorities. But *after* the Talmudic period, those titles began to be used indiscriminately. According to Simeon Duran (fourteenth/fifteenth century), those titles were used to distinguish the Rabbanite Jews (i.e., the believers in Pharisaic-Rabbinic Judaism) from their Karaite opponents. After a while, however, the Karaites themselves adopted those titles. "*Rabbi*," as used among the non-Karaites, was little more than a courtesy title, corresponding to our use of "Mister," which, going back to the Latin *magister*, has the same basic meaning.

In other words, the title was given to people who had no ordination or authorization at all. (In Yiddish, people still address each other as "Reb," a corruption of *rav* or *rabbi*.)

The original form of rabbinic ordination had come to an end with the closing of the Palestinian academies. There was a futile attempt to revive it in sixteenth-century Palestine by Jacob Berab. The cessation of the original form of ordination is now used by many Orthodox Jews as an argument against the revival of the Sanhedrin in the State of Israel. With no real ordination, what would be the authority of its members?

Although the original term for rabbinic ordination, *semikhah*, is still being used to this day, neither the Orthodox nor the Conservatives nor the Reformers do, in actual fact, bestow the kind of ordination which, in the Talmudic period, conferred the title of "*rabbi*." It is, therefore, not surprising that there are no uniform standards which have to be met by candidates for the rabbinical title.

But standards of sorts there are. In the course of the centuries, congregations looking for men to occupy the position of teacher and judge—which is what the rabbinical office implied until modern times—had to have some kind of guarantee, or recommendation, for the man who was to be chosen. A substitute for the old ordination was devised, probably some time in the fifteenth century. This was the *hattarah hora-ah* ("permission to render decisions"). Though it lacks the full authority of the old *semikhah*, its operative terms, *yoreh yoreh, yadin yadin*, remain the same. In theory, this *hattarah* can be bestowed upon a disciple by anyone who himself holds this authorization. Such, in fact, was the actual procedure for a number of centuries; and it is still being followed by the ultra-Orthodox. However, the granting of the *hattarah* by individual scholars has largely gone out of fashion in Western countries since the Emancipation. It is obvious that this procedure is open to abuse. By and large, modern congregations of all Jewish "denominations" want their rabbis to obtain the *hattarah* from a recognized rabbinical seminary. This, among other things, assures minimum standards of

Reflections on a Title

attainment—at least within each "denomination." A graduate of the Jewish Theological Seminary, or of the Hebrew Union College, or of the Yeshivah, is a "rabbi." In actual practice, however, the American Jewish community is much more liberal in its bestowal of the title.

In our American ecclesiastical vocabulary, a Protestant spiritual leader is a "minister," a Roman Catholic one is a "priest," and a Jewish functionary (with or without ordination) is a "rabbi." First-year rabbinical students, ministering to small congregations during the High Holy Days, thrill to the experience of being called "rabbi" by their (temporary) congregants—before they have so much as opened the first volume of the Talmud. This, as we shall see, is peculiar to the American scene.

If the title "Rabbi" has had a checkered career throughout the centuries, the last one hundred and fifty years of its history have been the most interesting (and confusing!) of them all. When Reform Judaism, as an organized movement, started out in nineteenth-century Germany, the title "Rabbi" had acquired a bad reputation. The rabbi was primarily the supervisor of *kashruth* (i.e., the dietary laws). Or so, at least, he was regarded by the rapidly assimilating members of his flock. He filled none of the pastoral and homiletical functions which are nowadays associated even with the Orthodox rabbinate. Consequently, many of the early Reform rabbis preferred to be known as *Prediger* ("preachers"), and not as rabbis.

This dislike for the rabbinical title was not confined to the Reform camp. It was shared by none other than the man who, in 1821, was appointed as the Orthodox Chief Rabbi of Hamburg (site of the first Reform Temple) with the specific task of leading the "counter-reformation." Isaac Bernays (1792–1849), a man of strictly Orthodox views—and, incidentally, the mentor of Samson Raphael Hirsch—accepted this position on condition that he be called *"hakham,"* and not *"rabbi."* Now, *"hakham"* (lit., "sage") was, and is, the rabbinical title of the Sepharadi

(Spanish and Portuguese) Jews. Bernays was *not* a Sepharadi. His insistence on the Sepharadi title shows, therefore, that he, too, must have realized that the Ashkenazi rabbinical title had lost much of its luster by the beginning of the nineteenth century.

But not all Reform rabbis shared the dislike for the rabbinical title—even as the Orthodox successors of Bernays in Hamburg no longer insisted upon being called *"hakham."* When Abraham Geiger (1810-1874) received the call, in 1838, to become the second rabbi of the Breslau Jewish community, the Orthodox opposition might have been pacified by Geiger's consenting to being a *Prediger*. But Geiger held that a principle was at stake: the liberty of the holder of a rabbinical office to engage in free scientific inquiry. He also claimed to be a leader of authentic Judaism as a whole. At a later date, he refused to become the rabbi of the Reform congregation in Berlin, because, as Geiger saw it, that congregation was only a sectarian offshoot of *the* Jewish community. He, therefore, insisted upon being engaged as a *rabbi* in Breslau, and as a member of the Breslau *beth din*.

Similarly, Samuel Holdheim (1806-1860), the most radical reformer of them all, describes himself as *Rabbiner und Prediger* ("rabbi and preacher") on the title pages of his books. Of course, Holdheim had previously taken steps to clear the rabbinical title of its earlier associations. In his book, *The Autonomy of the Rabbis* (1843), he had argued for the abolition of the juridical functions of the rabbi, and for his recognition as a "spiritual" leader—on a par with the ecclesiastical functionaries of other religious denominations.

With Reform preachers laying claim to the rabbinical title, the Orthodox became restive. The spectacle of questioning the validity of another denomination's ordination has been a familiar one in the Church. It was now to be enacted in Judaism as well. In practice, this meant that the Reform rabbi would be addressed by his Orthodox colleague as "doctor"—whether or not the Reform rabbi had actually obtained an academic doctorate. In the Hebrew and Yiddish press to this day, an Orthodox rabbi will be referred to as "*harav*," while the Conservative and Reform rabbis have to make do with "*rabbi*." If it be argued that this merely means bestowing a Babylonian title on the Orthodox, and a Palestinian one on the "deviationists," the matter can be, and has been, clarified by spelling the word "*rabbi*" (in its English pronunciation) phonetically. (*Resh, aleph, beth, beth, yod, yod.*)

But what happens if a rabbi—of any "denomination"—really does hold a doctor's degree? In Europe this presents no problem. He is "Rabbiner Dr.," and, in England, "Rabbi Dr." In the United States the matter is more complicated. According to Emily Post, a rabbi without a doctor's degree is Rabbi So-and-so, and a rabbi with a doctor's degree becomes The Rev. Dr. So-and-so. The combination "Rabbi Dr." is unknown; and where it is being used in this country, one is not far wrong in suspecting a foreign provenance of the combined-title holder.

This leaves the American rabbi who holds a doctor's degree with the choice of being known either as "Rabbi" or as "Doctor." So far, many of them have opted for the latter. Why? In some instances it was undoubtedly a case of imitating the ways of the Gentiles. If the local Presbyterian minister is a "Rev. Dr.," so is the rabbi! Already in the fifteenth century, Don (*sic*) Isaac Abrabanel criticized the Ashkenazi Jews for aping the Gentiles by calling their rabbis "Doctor."

But not all "Reverend Doctors" are "assimilationists." Some of them are in academic work, where one's doctor's degree may be an essential "status symbol." Others might quite justifiably feel that everybody preaching to a Jewish congregation (with or without ordination) is, in any case, called "Rabbi." But it takes some work and achievement to obtain a doctorate! (The Talmud states that a man should not study Torah in order to be called "Rabbi." But no such Talmudic prohibition seems to hold for the academic doctorate!)

Yet we may expect changes here, too. *Honorary* doctorates have made their appearance. Once they are going to be bestowed in such profusion upon rabbis that it will be hard to find a rabbi who is *not* a doctor, some of those doctors may find it more honorable and meaningful to stress their rabbinical title again. Unless, of course, our rabbinical seminaries take to conferring the honorary *rabbinical* diploma. (One or two cases are already on record.) Then, perhaps, someone is going to follow in the footsteps of Isaac Bernays, and call himself *"hakham."*

It is, however, only in the United States, as we have already remarked, that the rabbinical title is so "loosely" bestowed. Our English brethren are a little more careful. A student who graduates from London's Orthodox Jews' College, or from the Reform Leo Baeck College, receives his "Minister's Certificate." He is known as a "minister," and the correct form of address is "The Rev. Mr. So-and-so." Only after additional years of intensive study of Talmud and Codes does such a minister present himself for an examination which, if successfully passed, leads to the Rabbinical Diploma. Here, then, the rabbinical title still indicates a certain proficiency in Rabbinical literature. Yet there have been outstanding scholars in Anglo-Jewry who never bothered about the rabbinical title. The author of the very useful *Everyman's Talmud,* and editor of the *Soncino Books of the Bible,* was the late *Reverend* Dr. A. Cohen.

Something might be said for adopting the English system in this country. Men whose primary interest in the Jewish ministry is pastoral work, and who have little, if any, interest in higher Jewish studies, might then be Jewish *ministers,* with the title of "Reverend" or "Reverend Doctor," while the rabbinical title would be bestowed only upon those who are scholarly experts in Jewish law and Jewish lore. Something might be said for that, but its adoption seems highly unlikely. For one thing, it is hard, if not impossible, to run counter to popular usage; and in America, the Jewish "minister" *is* the *rabbi.* For another, there have been earlier periods in Jewish history when, as we have already pointed out, "Rabbi" was merely a courtesy title; and ours seems to be another of those periods.

Reflections on a Title

"Rabbi" may be the highest title which Judaism has to confer. But much depends upon *when* and *where* that title is being conferred. In the final analysis, it is the *bearer* of the title who confers honor and dignity upon the rabbinical title, and not vice versa.

CHAPTER 7

The Grip of the Past

The cry of Koheleth that "there is nothing new under the sun" may have voiced his despair, or even his resignation to the inevitable. But to the generations who succeeded him, this conviction about the impossibility of revolutionary innovations was, above all, a reassuring source of comfort. "The thing that hath been, it is that which shall be; and that which is done is that which shall be done; and there is nothing new under the sun. Is there anything whereof it may be said, See, this is new? It hath been already of old time, which was before us" (Ecclesiastes 1:9–10).

It is easy to see how orthodox religion would like to understand itself as being true to this pattern. At a certain point in history, God's Revelation took place. Since the Revelation was that of God, the whole Truth must have been revealed then and there. Granted this premise, there is an undeniable logic in the Talmudic statement that what a scholar is to propound in

---

Reprinted from *Judaism*, VIII, No. 2 (Spring 1959), 132–141. Copyright © 1959 by the American Jewish Congress. The author is grateful for permission to reprint this material.

The Grip of the Past

the distant future was already revealed by God to Moses on Mount Sinai. While future generations might be credited with the ability to elucidate points of law unsuspected by their forebears, on the analogy of the dwarf standing on the shoulders of the giant, there is, at the same time, a pronounced tendency to bow to the authority of those who, in point of time, stood closer to the moment of Revelation. It is more than mere sentiment when the Talmud records the statement: "If the former generations were angels, then we are men. But if they were mere men, then we are but asses." It had its *legal* implications. A teacher of the *Gemara* (i.e., of the generations *after* the *Mishnah*) may argue against another teacher of the *Gemara*. But he may not argue against a teacher of the *Mishnah*, unless he can find support for his views in the statement of another teacher of the *Mishnah*.

And, as in legal dialectics, so it was in philosophical speculation. Saadia Gaon (882–942), the first major systematic Jewish thinker of the Middle Ages, in enumerating the "ways of knowing," lists *Tradition* next to sense perception, reason, and inferential knowledge. It is through Tradition that we are able to benefit from the experience of Revelation vouchsafed to previous generations. And it is Tradition which validates the claim—strongly denied, in Saadia's day, by the Karaites—that the Rabbinic Talmud is indeed identical with the Sinaitic Oral Law.

All this is easily intelligible once we grant the basic Orthodox assumptions; and, in theory, it is still the basis of modern Orthodoxy. Modern spokesmen of this school of thought, fighting for recognition in the marketplace of ideas, may point to the adaptability, and to the potential for development, inherent in Orthodox Judaism—a claim, incidentally, which the objective scientific investigator will not deny. But whereas the latter would account for it in terms of responses conditioned by changing environments, the Orthodox spokesmen would have to seek refuge in their belief in an Oral Law which had already been revealed to Moses on Mount Sinai. There can be no *conscious* change or development in any but minor matters.

It is interesting to see a somewhat similar outlook at what might certainly be called the extreme opposite of the religious spectrum. The Deists of the seventeenth and eighteenth centuries had no use for the ideas of religious development and "progressive revelation." True enough, they vigorously denied the kind of Revelation posited by the Jewish and Christian Scriptures. As far as they knew, the Deity had singled out no one particular people to whom to reveal Himself. The "natural law" was vouchsafed to all men alike, although, admittedly, the "Religion of Nature" had not survived in its pristine purity. Priests had set to work, and by means of introducing creedal and ritual elements, they had brought Religion to the sorry state in which the Deists now found it. Thus, while we are, in part, indebted to the Deists for the science of Comparative Religion, the Deists themselves were completely oblivious of History. The only kind of "progress" or "development" they could see in Religion was the process of corruption and deterioration.

Running through their heterodox writings there is a distant echo of the Christian doctrine of the "Fall," though, as Crane Brinton reminds us, in *The Shaping of the Modern Mind*, the "average enlightened intellectual [in the eighteenth century] was inclined to credit the old Greeks and Romans with having done good spade work, and to believe that what we call the Renaissance and Reformation had begun once more the development of reason." We may also note that the Deists were preceded by Maimonides (1135–1204) in their assumption of the existence of a universal religion of purity which later deteriorated into idolatry.[1]

Thus, while the Orthodox Jew venerates the past, and considers himself its *preserver*, the Deist, precluded by his lack of historical sense from any positive notion of development, sees himself as the past's *restorer*. But this veneration of a—real or imaginary—past is not confined to the two circles we have mentioned. It is, as we well know, the stock-in-trade of every reformer—religious or otherwise.

The Grip of the Past

Take, for example, the Hebrew Prophets—although, because of their place in Orthodox theology, the illustration they offer is somewhat complicated. In the Orthodox scheme of things, the Prophets merely came to reiterate what Moses had already proclaimed. They were neither innovators nor reformers. When Malachi, the last of the Prophets, climaxes his message by saying: "Remember ye the law of Moses My servant, which I commanded unto him in Horeb for all Israel . . . " (Malachi 4:4), his aim and purpose are attributed to all the other Prophets as well.

In the light of critical scholarship, which is inclined to place much of the "Law of Moses" *after* the major Prophets, the latter do stand out as great religious innovators. It is they who are the great pathfinders in Israel's religious quest. It is they who are the real creators of Israel's monotheistic and universalistic faith.

Yet, if we study the writings of the Prophets themselves, without any preconceived notions or prejudices, we shall be hard put to it to find any traces of the Prophets' self-awareness as innovators. They came to *re-call* Israel to the true way—a way known to, and followed by, their more righteous ancestors. Attacking the vices of Israel's recently acquired agricultural and urban civilization, they could point, by way of contrast, to an idyllic picture of the time when "Israel was a child," and when, faithfully and morally, he went after God "in the wilderness, in a land that was not sown."

Again, the Pharisees, next to the Prophets perhaps the most thoroughgoing Reformers of Judaism, as we have tried to show in our first chapter—the Pharisees, too, merely claimed to "interpret" a Law which went back to the Sinaitic Revelation.

Characteristic, too, is the example furnished by Jesus of Nazareth. There is no dearth of literature, both scientific and apologetic, showing that Jesus was a good Jew, that he had no intention of founding a new religion, and demonstrating verse by verse how the Sermon on the Mount can be matched by quotations from the Hebrew Bible and from Rabbinic literature.

HEIRS OF THE PHARISEES

Be that as it may, there can be no doubt that, both in the eyes of his disciples and in those of his opponents, Jesus must have created the impression of being an innovator. It was felt that he had introduced something new into the religious realm of his time. (Whether that which was "new" was good or bad depended upon one's point of view.) And if this is not, strictly speaking, true of the "historical Jesus" (and what, after all, do we really *know* about the "historical Jesus"?), it is certainly true of the portrait of Jesus which emerges from any "harmony of the Gospels." And it is likewise true of the Christ preached by Paul.

Nevertheless, Jesus claimed: "Think not that I am come to destroy the Law and the Prophets. I am not come to destroy, but to fulfil" (Matthew 5:17). Even Paul, whose whole theology is based on the recognition that the rule of the Law had come to an end by reason of the "new dispensation," will, on occasion, argue that "he that loveth another hath fulfilled the Law" (Romans 13:8)—as though there were, after all, still a "Law" which, in one way or another, must be "fulfilled." Indeed, the whole "Old Testament" is annexed, and the very name of "Israel" is pre-empted, by the new Church.

By such means the new religion could profit from the erstwhile prestige of the now rejected "mother religion." And it is often highly amusing to see the very same "Old Testament" institutions, so fiercely attacked by the Church Fathers in their polemics against the Jews, defended by the identical Church Fathers when the attackers were pagan philosophers and Gnostic heretics. The Church stood to gain by claiming Sinai as one of its foundations—in addition to Golgotha.

The pattern is repeated in the history of Christianity itself. The Pope derives his authority from being Peter's successor; and Peter was ordained in his office by Jesus himself. Thus the Roman Catholic Church is the one and only Church founded by Christ. But, when the Reformers came along, they also had no intention of establishing a *new* Church. They merely wanted to restore the pristine purity of the "primitive church."

The Grip of the Past

This latter was, of course, the only "authentic" Church, being so close, in point of time, to Jesus himself, and having been administered by his immediate disciples.

There is no difference in pattern when it comes to the modern attempts at "reforming" Judaism. Reform Judaism, too, was not meant to be a departure from the "authentic" Jewish Tradition. On the contrary, it merely claimed to free Judaism from the doubtful accretions which had accumulated as a result of centuries of Ghetto existence. Reform Judaism wanted to "restore" the "pure" form of "classical" Judaism, and tending to disregard some two thousand years of Jewish history and development, it was, in time, to regard itself as the legitimate heir of "Prophetic Religion."

This kind of approach forced the Orthodox to demonstrate the legitimacy of the Rabbinic succession and the absolute necessity of recognizing the traditional Oral Law in order to make sense of the Written Law. We may compare this with the Roman Catholic claim that it is the Church which gives us the Bible in the first place (and not vice versa), so that the Church which is trusted to have transmitted the authentic Text must also be trusted when it comes to its interpretation.

But there was a logic in the Reform Jewish position which cannot be denied. After all, an Amos or a Jeremiah, being recipients of Revelation in their own right, and living, in point of time, much closer to Moses and Sinai, must have been much nearer to the "source" than, say, Rabbi Judah the Prince in the second century—not to speak of Rabbi Joseph Caro in the sixteenth! If the great Prophets could lead blameless and acceptable lives without benefit of the medieval ritual codes, so could the nineteenth-century German Jew!

It will be recognized that, in the early days of the nineteenth century, both Orthodox and Reformer shared the same basic presupposition: the belief in a divine Revelation which took place at a given time and which alone is the "source of authority" in religion. Consider, for example, the question about the ritual bath (*miqwah*) which was debated by the second conference of Reform rabbis, held in Frankfurt am Main, in 1845. A congregation wanted to know whether, for purposes of fulfilling the commandment of the ritual bath, women could use the municipal bath at which "drawn waters" (*mayim she-ubhim*) were used, which were conducted by a pipeline from the river to the bathhouse, or whether the traditional requirements of immersing in "living waters" were absolute. The Reform rabbis decided, contrary to the accepted norm, that "living waters" were not a *conditio sine qua non*, and that "drawn waters" may be used for this purpose.

What is so remarkable about this decision is that it was reached by men who were quite outspokenly "Reform" in their religious approach. Instead of declaring the whole idea of the ritual bath for women null and void, a radical Reformer like David Einhorn permitted "drawn waters," because, he claimed, the traditional arrangements may have the result of making women forgo the duty of ritual immersion altogether. Though permitting the use of "drawn waters," he still insisted, however, on the Talmudic requirement that the vessel in which the immersion takes place should have a small opening and should be attached to the ground.[2] In this stipulation he was supported by another "radical," Samuel Hirsch.[3] Only Holdheim, though agreeing to this decision *ad hoc*, wanted to see a discussion about the abolition of the whole system of "theocratic-symbolical purification laws."[4] But even Holdheim did not deny the divine origin of the Law as such. He merely argued that its ceremonial and ritual provisions were inapplicable outside a theocratic Jewish state.

Now, those were the same men who advocated the most far-reaching reforms in matters of Sabbath observance, and in the laws of diet, marriage, and divorce. They were also the men who pressed for worship services in the vernacular and for the banishment of Hebrew from the synagogue. (And yet, be it noted, they also insisted on the study of Hebrew in the religious school, and on the retention of Hebrew for the Torah reading,

The Grip of the Past

for Hebrew was, after all, the language in which God had revealed His Law!)

It was all a question of liberalizing the provisions of Talmud and codifiers, or, at most, of declaring a biblical law to be no longer applicable in nineteenth-century Germany—never of making a clean break with what Orthodox and Reformer alike considered to have been the documents of Divine Revelation.

But soon thereafter something happened in the history of thought which was to bring about a radical change in the basic presuppositions. The theory of Evolution, first found to apply in the realm of zoology, was ultimately applied to matters spiritual and religious as well. Once accepted as a plank in Reform Judaism's platform, the theory of Evolution made it impossible to look to the past for authority. One could, of course, still believe in Revelation, although, with the help of the Higher Criticism of the Bible, the particular Revelation at Mount Sinai was more likely to be denied. God reveals Himself in every age. His Revelation is unfolding only very gradually. It never took the form of a communication of the whole and complete Truth—with nothing left to reveal to succeeding generations. The past, at best, shows us, in Breasted's phrase, the "Dawn of Conscience." It cannot possibly be the authority for the present and the future. After all, the Reformers, assembled in Pittsburgh, in 1885, could in all good conscience describe the Bible as "reflecting the primitive ideas of its own age" (second "plank" of the *Pittsburgh Platform*).

Here, then, an obvious break with the past had occurred—a change of perspective which makes the Frankfurt discussion about the *miqwah*, in 1845, appear closer in basic assumptions and motivations to the *pilpul* of the old *yeshibhoth* than to the aspirations of American Reform Judaism. It is for similar reasons that Simeon Bernfeld, in his Hebrew history of the Reform movement, published in 1900, dismisses the whole of American Reform Judaism in the following few lines:

> Various attempts were made afterwards in America, where "rabbis" assembled time and again to "reform Judaism" and to make it

compatible with the requirements of life. But those attempts have no place in a history of *Judaism*. We do not mean to imply that the Jews of America are not a part of the Jewish nation. . . . But we do believe that only that can be called "Reform" which, to a greater or lesser degree, desires a relationship to historical Judaism. American Judaism has no history; and those who come from abroad consciously suppress the memories of the past. And since this is a new settlement, it pays no attention at all to any previous traditions; and its tie to the Judaism of history is very loose indeed.[5]

Curiously enough, the one tie which the historian Bernfeld could still discern, that of Jewish nationhood, was itself most emphatically denied at the time by the American Reformers themselves. That denial is, of course, of greater interest to us in terms of the self-awareness of the American Reformers than as a criterion by which to measure the truth or falsity of Bernfeld's nationalist theory. At any rate, as far as the Reformers were concerned, nationhood was definitely ruled out as a factor of their Judaism (fifth "plank" of the *Pittsburgh Platform*).

If we, then, understand Judaism in terms of what Mordecai Kaplan and his Reconstructionist followers would call the "sancta of the group," the customs and ceremonies of Jewish life, the Pittsburgh Reformers would indeed have had but "a very loose tie indeed to the Judaism of history."

If, finally, Judaism be understood in terms of belief, which was really what the Reformers were getting at, then, in the light of the history of Jewish thought, one may indeed wonder whether a confession of "ethical monotheism" alone (and, basically, that was all that was left to the Pittsburgh Reformers) is what makes Judaism "Jewish." Surely, the authority of the Torah had heretofore constituted no small measure of even the *creedal* content of Judaism.

The stage, therefore, was set for a complete break with the past—a break which, in actual practice, had already occurred. But the remarkable thing is that the break was not consciously admitted in theory. The one or the other Reform Jewish family may have found their true spiritual home in the Unitarian Church, or even in one of the more traditional

Christian denominations. Here and there, a Reform rabbi may have given up his pulpit in favor of more secular and non-denominational endeavors in the area of social betterment. One man, Felix Adler, destined for the Reform rabbinate, actually founded the Ethical Culture movement. But the fact remains that the men assembled in Pittsburgh, in 1885, knew themselves to be Jews, and this in spite of the fact that vast areas of the traditional content of Jewish belief and practice had been summarily rejected, while the theory of modern Jewish nationalism fared no better.

It should be emphasized that we are concerned with the Reformers of 1885. It is true that, *since* that time, American Reform Judaism has undergone quite a different development. It has reacted to the Holocaust in Europe and the emergence of the State of Israel. It has drawn its leadership and its members from Jews of East European antecedents, and it has attempted to find room for their "Jewishness." It has bolstered up a very vague theology with a pronounced Jewish "folk-feeling." It has tried to raise the emotional temperature of its worship services by the large-scale importation of "ceremonies and pageantry" of traditional provenance. It has even, within more recent years, given birth to a group of younger theologians who have "rediscovered" the truth and relevance of such traditional beliefs as those in Revelation, the Covenant, and the Election of Israel. But all of that came at a much later date. It was not foreseen by the men of Pittsburgh.

What matters to us in this context is that, Bernfeld's criticism notwithstanding, the men of the *Pittsburgh Platform* were not aware that their tie to the Judaism of history was "very loose indeed." On the contrary, they were very passionate Jews, and very much concerned about the survival of Judaism on the new soil. What they *called* "Judaism" may have been much closer to Unitarianism or to Ethical Culture than to the Judaism of Tradition. But they did not take the easy way out, although the opportunities were surely not lacking. Instead, they were following the typical pattern of the reformer and the innovator. What they preached and taught was the only "authentic"

Judaism, the Judaism of the early Hebrew Prophets. Theirs was, as Isaac M. Wise had claimed, the *real* "Orthodox" Judaism.

Different, then, as the presuppositions of American Reform Judaism may have been from those of the conferences of European rabbis in Brunswick, Frankfurt, and Breslau, the insistence on the thoroughbred pedigree was common to both. The Bible, as we have noted, may have been regarded as "reflecting the primitive ideas of its own age," but the men who said that about the Bible also said: "We hold that Judaism presents the highest conception of the God idea as taught in our Holy Scriptures and developed and spiritualized by the Jewish teachers, in accordance with the moral and philosophical progress of their respective ages. We maintain that Judaism preserved and defended, midst continual struggles and trials, and under enforced isolation, this God idea as the central religious truth for the human race" (first "plank" of the *Pittsburgh Platform*).

Critics have noted that the Pittsburgh Reformers seem to have been more concerned with the "God idea" than with God Himself, and this criticism may indeed be justified. It may also be true that Kant and Hegel had a good deal more to do with the Pittsburgh "God idea" than did the Holy Scriptures. But all this should not blind us to the remarkable fact that the Pittsburgh Reformers did find it necessary at all to refer to the Scriptures and to the "Jewish teachers." It is here that they most obviously fall into the customary pattern of the reformer.

To speak in terms of an unconscious, quasi-biological, Jewish "will to survive" in order to account for this attempt on the part of the Pittsburgh Reformers to maintain their tie with the Judaism of Tradition would be to take a very narrow and parochial view of the matter. When we spoke of the "customary pattern of the reformer," we had in mind a general, and not a specifically Jewish, phenomenon. Surely, it would be absurd to invoke the Jewish "will to survive" by way of explaining Jesus' and Paul's professed link to the Law of Moses—let alone Luther's claim to have gone back to the state of affairs of the primitive Church!

The Grip of the Past

It would seem to be more plausible to recognize the grip of the past on *all* religious manifestations, whether they appear in the garb of the reformer or in that of the traditionalist. In his essay, "Between the Sacred and the Profane," Ahad Ha'am has described this *universal* phenomenon.[6] The "vessels" of religion are always those associated with an earlier period. Thus, Ahad Ha'am points out, centuries after the invention of the printing press, the hand-written Torah Scroll is still a *sine qua non* of the Synagogue. Similarly, the ancient Egyptians used vessels of stone on certain festivals long after they had graduated to the use of vessels made of more precious materials. The vessels of stone had survived from the Stone Age during which the festivals themselves had originated.

In that same essay (which, incidentally, is directed against the Reform attempt to dispense with traditional "forms") Ahad Ha'am makes a distinction between sacred and profane books— a distinction which may help us to understand why the Pittsburgh Reformers insisted upon their background in the Scriptures, and why Reform Judaism, in general, sees itself as the authentic "Prophetic Religion."

Profane books, Ahad Ha'am points out, tend to be discarded once a knowledge of their subject matter spreads and grows. Not even the trained scientists of our day read the actual works of Copernicus, Kepler, and Newton. But it is quite different with the sacred books. Witness all the different things people, in various ages, have read into, and out of, the Bible. They *had* to "find" their particular views in the Bible; for, had they not found them there, their truth would not have been truth, nor would the Bible have been holy.

Ahad Ha'am was satisfied with the mere recognition of this *fact*. For our own purposes, it will be necessary to delve a little deeper into the reasons and the motivations. Why is it that the reformer or the innovator invariably insists that he is merely a *restorer* of the old? Why is it that the "sacred" is always linked to the "traditional"?

In the case of the individual reformer, who has broken away

from a traditional home background, the reason is not far to seek. He wants to allay the guilt feelings which are inevitably produced by the break with his parental faith. One's attitude toward religion is so inextricably intertwined with his childhood attitudes toward parental authority that a break with one implies a break with the other. It is, therefore, easier on the psyche if the break could be rationalized out of existence. I have not really broken with my parental religion, the reformer says to himself; I have merely developed a deeper understanding of the sources on which that religion is based.

Thus, for example, the sincere Jewish convert to Christianity feels that he has a better understanding of the Hebrew Bible than had been attained by his erstwhile coreligionists. The Reform Jew feels that he understands the Hebrew Prophets better than did the Sages of Sura and Pumbeditha. In German Reform Judaism this process of rationalization went even further. The first generation of German Reformers invoked Talmud and *Shulchan Arukh* to justify their reforms of the worship service. Similar attempts have occasionally even been made on American soil. Perhaps the very retention of the Hebrew language in the American Reform worship service—even if it be confined to but one sentence or two—is evidence of this desire to express continuity, if not actual identity, with the past.

"The psychoanalyses of individuals," says Freud,[7] "have taught us that their earliest impressions, received at a time when they were hardly able to talk, manifest themselves later in an obsessive fashion, although those impressions themselves are not consciously remembered." And Freud significantly adds: "We feel that the same must hold good for the earliest experiences of mankind."

Here, then, we have made the transition from the individual to the group. It can indeed be said for the generality of men that "remote times have a great attraction—sometimes mysteriously so—for the imagination."[8] This attraction of the remote times may, of course, be due to an illusion. As Freud says, "Probably man still stands under the magic spell of his childhood, which a not unbiased memory presents to him as a time of unalloyed bliss." But is it not just possible that there is a substantial basis to those early unconscious memories? The memory of those "childhood experiences" may have been somewhat "biased," but, in view of the universal spread of certain myths, we must assume that they have had at least *some* factual basis, or that they are part of what C. G. Jung calls the "collective unconscious."

Let us consider what Freud calls "the never forgotten dream of a Golden Age." It has become fashionable in the apologetic writings of modern Judaism—inspired as they are by the evolutionary philosophies and by nineteenth-century meliorism—to contrast the pagan myth of a Golden Age in the past with the alleged Hebrew "Prophetic" view of the universal age of peace and brotherhood which is to dawn at the "end of the days." What is usually ignored in such comparisons is the fact that in the Prophets' own understanding of the "messianic era" the latter represents a *return* to the Paradisiacal state of affairs before the "fall."

"The wolf dwelling together with the lamb," in the eleventh chapter of Isaiah, is a projection into the future of the conditions described in the opening chapters of Genesis. And, in Jewish mysticism, Adam, as he was before his "fall," becomes idealized as a cosmic being which contains the whole world in itself, and whose station is superior even to that of Metatron, the first of the angels. The Adam of the Bible corresponds, on the anthropological plane, to *Adam Qadmon*, the ontological primary man.[9]

Myth, fact, or illusion—it all comes to the same. Man's whole orientation in life is, at least partially, determined by the grip of the past. That is why Carl G. Jung[10] finds the really "modern" man to be such a solitary creature. "He is so of necessity and at all times, for every step towards a fuller consciousness of the present removes him further from his original *'participation mystique'* with the mass of men—from submersion in a common unconsciousness. Every step forward means an act of tear-ing himself loose from that all-embracing pristine unconsciousness which claims the bulk of mankind." He thus becomes "unhistorical" in the deepest sense, and has estranged himself "from the mass of men who live entirely within the bounds of tradition."

Now, if there is one thing the reformer does *not* want to be it is to be *solitary*. His temperament is not that of the hermit or the recluse. He wants to influence the world of men; and the world of men, rightly or wrongly, has the tendency to credit the past with a more direct and "authentic" manifestation of the Divine. If the author of the Epistle to the Hebrews wants the recipients of his epistle to grant the fact that God "hath in these last days spoken unto us by His Son," he has to make it quite clear at the outset that it is the same God "who at sundry times and in diverse manners spake in the past unto the fathers by the prophets" (Hebrews 1:1–2).

Thus it may be seen that man's very psychological make-up precludes his ever extricating himself completely from the grip of the past, and perhaps least of all within the realm of his religious development.

Two practical consequences follow from all this for the modern theologian. In the first place, his reforming zeal must be tempered by the recognition that just as, in the words of Leibniz, *natura non facit saltus* ("Nature makes no jump"), so does Revelation (and be it ever so "progressive") make no jumps. But this consequence is hardly more than an advice to act with prudence and circumspection. The second consequence involves a task—the task of taking seriously the universal human testimony that the past has known giants of the spirit whose accomplishments have as yet remained unsurpassed.

NOTES

1. Maimonides, *Yad, Hilkhoth Akkum*, ch. 1.
2. *Protokolle und Aktenstücke der zweiten Rabbiner-Versammlung* (Frankfurt am Main, 1845), p. 186.
3. *Ibid.*, p. 187.
4. *Ibid.*, p. 182.
5. Simeon Bernfeld, *Toledoth Hareformatziyon Hadatith Beyisrael* (Cracow, 1900), p. 234. (My translation from the Hebrew.)
6. *Kol Kithvé Ahad Ha'am*. One-volume edition (Tel-Aviv, 1956), pp. 73f.
7. Sigmund Freud, *Moses and Monotheism* (New York, 1955), p. 167.
8. *Ibid.*, pp. 89f.
9. Cf. Gershom G. Scholem, *Major Trends in Jewish Mysticism* (Jerusalem, 1941), p. 276.
10. Carl G. Jung, *Modern Man in Search of a Soul* (London, 1933), pp. 227f.

CHAPTER 8

🖋 *Not by Bread Alone*

Bread, the "staff of life," the staple of man's sustenance in symbol and in fact, is regarded in the Jewish Tradition as a gift from God. Partaking of it, the pious Jew engages in what is quite consciously seen to be an imitation of a sacrificial act. His hands must have been washed so that he breaks bread in a state of ritual purity similar to that demanded of the priests in the Jerusalem Temple. He says a prayer before breaking bread, and prior to eating it, he dips his slice of bread in salt—even as salt was an absolute prerequisite in the ancient sacrificial cult.[1] A lengthy grace concludes those of his meals during which bread is eaten. And even after the meal, bread continues to be treated with respect. A pious Jew will guard the leftovers and crumbs from willful destruction almost with the same care which a Roman Catholic priest bestows upon the leftovers of the eucharistic wafer.

While the Talmud recognizes the validity of even a simple doxology like "Praised be the Merciful One, the Master of this bread,"[2] the standard form of the Jewish "Grace before Meals" has long been the following: "Praised art Thou, O Lord our

---

Reprinted from *Judaism*, VII, No. 3 (Summer 1958), 229–234. Copyright © 1958 by the American Jewish Congress. The author is grateful for permission to reprint this material.

Not by Bread Alone

God, Ruler of the Universe, who bringest forth bread from the earth." The idea that it is God who brings forth bread from the earth is one at which even liberal religious Jews do not take umbrage. They do not suspect it of primitive anthropomorphism. They do not feel that their knowledge of the natural sciences has taught them better. And why should there be any objection to this simple prayer? Were not the Jews who first uttered it themselves engaged in agricultural pursuits, knowing full well man's own share in the production of bread? God was indeed the Heavenly Provider, but man had to do the plowing, the reaping, the grinding, and the baking. Man may even have to spread manure over his fields before they will yield their produce! And yet, there is the recognition of what moderns might call man's dependence on natural processes, and of what the ancients more readily saw as man's dependence on Nature's God.

When, therefore, it became known, some years ago, that in some of the Israeli settlements they had substituted for the old prayer the phrase, "Praised be the farmer who brings forth bread from the earth," there was a feeling of annoyance by no means confined to Orthodox circles. No, with all his knowledge of the workings of Nature, the modern liberal Jew can still share his ancestors' gratitude to the God "who brings forth bread from the earth."

What the liberal religious Jew finds difficult, if not impossible, to do is to share his ancestors' conviction that the God who brings forth bread from the earth also brings forth His Torah from Heaven. Now, it may seem curious that we should have introduced a discussion of the doctrine of Revelation with a brief disquisition on the Jewish attitude toward bread. But the two subjects happen to be more closely related than might appear at first sight.

Grammatically, the phrase, "bread from the earth" (*lechem min ha-aretz*), has the same structure as the traditional name for Revelation (*torah min hashamayim*, literally: "Torah from Heaven"); and there is a beautiful symmetry in the thought that the God who supplies our material needs from the earth also nourishes our spiritual needs from above. It may, of course, be argued that the word "Heaven" is merely a metonym for God Himself. As such, it does, in fact, frequently occur in Rabbinic literature.[3] There is, then, ample support for David Hoffmann's view[4] that, when the *Mishnah*[5] denies a share in the World-to-Come to him who says that "the Torah is not from Heaven," it is thinking of one who claims that "the Torah is not from God." On the other hand, "Heaven" was surely not understood as a mere metonym for God in that version of the "Blessing over the Torah" which is recorded in the Tractate *Sopherim*,[6] and which reads:

> Praised art Thou, O Lord,
> Who hast given us a Torah from Heaven
> And eternal life on high.
> Praised art Thou, O Lord, Giver of the Torah.

To say to God in a direct address: "Thou hast given us a Torah from God" is not a very likely liturgical phrase; nor, were we to accept such an interpretation, would the poetic parallelism be preserved that matches the "Torah from Heaven" with the "eternal life on high." Besides, the idea that God reveals Himself "from Heaven" is certainly a biblical one![7] Nevertheless, while admitting that the parallel presented by *torah min hashamayim* to *lechem min ha-aretz* first inspired these meditations, we do not want to press the point too far nor wish it to be regarded as the crux of our argument.

We are on firmer ground in drawing attention to the *halakhic* (i.e., legal) relation between the blessing over bread and that over the Torah. The Rabbis were aware of the fact that the only blessing explicitly commanded in the Torah itself is the "Grace after Meals." It is found in Deuteronomy 8:10, "And thou shalt eat, and thou shalt be satisfied, and thou shalt bless the Lord thy God for the good land which He hath given thee." The Torah does not explicitly prescribe a blessing to be recited before or after the reading of the Torah. But in the words,

"He hath given thee," in the law relating to the "Grace after Meals" the *Tosephta*[8] sees a reference to the blessing to be recited over the Torah and the performance of the commandments. This is based on the fact that the same word, "give" occurs in Exodus 24:12, where God says to Moses: "Come up to Me into the mount, and be there; *and I will give thee* the tables of stone, and the law and the commandment, which I have written, that thou mayest teach them." Similar arguments occur in other parts of Rabbinic literature."[9]

Perhaps the most detailed form of the argument deriving the obligation to recite a blessing over the Torah from the biblical commandment to say "Grace after Meals" is to be found in Karaite literature. Rejecting the Rabbinic hermeneutics, the Karaites were forced to employ their own, above all the *kiyyas* (the argument by analogy), in all cases where they wished to retain a Rabbinic observance and had to find their own support for it in the Bible. Thus we find Anan, the founder of the sect, reasoning as follows, in his *Sepher Ha-Mitzwoth*:[10]

Scripture commands the blessing over food in Deuteronomy 8:10. In Ezekiel 3:1 we read about the Prophet's being bidden to "eat this scroll." Now, "this scroll" could only have been the Torah, which is further proved by Ezekiel's report (3:3) that "it was in my mouth as honey for sweetness," seeing that, in Psalm 19:11, the Torah itself is described as "sweeter also than honey." With this analogy between eating and Torah study thus established, it follows, of course, that Torah reading must be accompanied by benedictions just as eating is. No doubt, Anan was more "Rabbinical" here than he would have cared to admit!

The modern mind will find the Rabbinic and the Karaite arguments equally strange, and will wonder whether the venerable institution of thanking God for the Torah really has nothing more solid to rest on than farfetched analogies between Torah reading and eating. Such skepticism is wholesome. We would indeed be doing the ancient Rabbis an injustice were we to imagine them as meditating on the words of Deuteronomy 8:10, and suddenly coming up with the discovery that what is implied here is a blessing over the Torah. It is much more likely that the blessing over the Torah was instituted on its own merits,[11] and that only afterward did the Rabbis look for a "proof-text" in the Bible.

Yet, if the sequence was indeed such as we have tried to indicate, and as the modern reader would naturally be inclined to assume, if, that is to say, we are in a position to look above and beyond the mere formal structure of Rabbinic hermeneutics, there is still a question to which an answer must be attempted. Supposing that the Rabbis were looking for a biblical basis for the blessing over the Torah, why, of all things, did they go to the "Grace after Meals"? Surely, they should not have found it too difficult to come across something more apropos, something more explicitly and intrinsically related to the institution of the Torah blessing which they were trying to promote!

In other words, we suspect that, over and above the merely formal analogy they discovered between the eating of bread and the reading of the Torah, they were aware of a deeper underlying connection. Could it have been the verse in Deuteronomy 8:3, "Man doth not live by bread alone, but by everything that proceedeth out of the mouth of the Lord doth man live"? Or take the beginning of the fifty-fifth chapter of the Book of Isaiah:

> Ho, every one that thirsteth, come ye for water,
> And he that hath no money;
> Come ye, buy and eat;
> Yea, come, buy wine and milk
> Without money and without price.
> Wherefore do ye spend money for that which is not bread?
> And your grain for that which satisfieth not?
> Hearken diligently unto Me, and eat ye that which is good,
> And let your soul delight itself in fatness.

Not only are the traditional Jewish commentators unanimous in regarding this as an invitation to the people to avail itself of *spiritual* sustenance, but, in the light of the context, it is hard

Not by Bread Alone

to assume that the Prophet could have meant anything else. The hunger and the thirst he had in mind was that, as Amos had asserted before him,[12] "of hearing the words of the Lord."

It is, therefore, not simply a matter of an arid legalism if the Rabbis established a relationship between bread and Torah. It was part of Israel's Prophetic tradition. It was also implied in the Festival of *Shavu'oth*, with its twofold aspect of harvest festival and feast of Revelation. As Theodor H. Gaster aptly remarks, "If, in the primitive agricultural rite, man offers God two loaves of the new bread as a symbol of cooperation, in the historical counterpart—by a fine and inspired inversion—God offers to man the two tablets of the Law."[13]

The connection between bread and Torah is of more than historical interest to us. In it may be found the solution of a very modern theological problem. We have already noted that the modern liberal Jew is not deterred by his knowledge of natural processes and agricultural "know-how" from regarding God as the One "who brings forth bread from the earth." But, when it comes to the old doctrine of "Torah from Heaven," the modern liberal Jew balks.

Having been made aware of the human element which went into the composition of the Bible, having learned to prefer the laborious process of *Quellenscheidung* (separation of the various sources and strata) to the "naïve" belief in a Sinaitic Revelation which was *einmalig* (once and for all time), he feels that he can no longer accept the "primitive" dogma of *torah min hashamayim*. Perhaps the responsibility is not altogether his own. He may have been driven to this position by Orthodox intolerance. The Orthodox rabbinate of the nineteenth century was apt to see in the slightest demand for external reforms an evidence of apostasy, a denial of fundamental Jewish dogma. Of course, according to the Rabbinic interpretation of Numbers 15:31, the slightest reservation about the complete divine origin of the entire Torah was sufficient to place one in the category of those who "despise the word of the Lord." And this includes him who believes in the divine origin of the whole Torah, but has reservations about certain laws not explicitly stated there, but merely derived from the text by means of one or another of the Rabbinic hermeneutic rules.[14]

The anti-Sadducean point of such remarks is very obvious, and though such an extremist interpretation of the divine origin of the Torah may have been justified in its time, it is, to say the least, questionable whether it should have been pressed against the Reformers of the nineteenth century. The effect was what in Rabbinic idiom might be described as "a thrusting away with both hands" and as a "closing of the door in front of the potential penitents." The time was to come when the Reformers would accept the Orthodox accusations—and feel proud of them!

That, however, is only one side of the coin. The other has to do with the inner development of the Reform movement itself. Just as in the case of the Rabbinic derivation of the Torah blessing from the law of Deuteronomy 8:10 the practice itself preceded the finding of a basis in Scripture, so, in the case of the Reformers, it will have to be admitted that, by and large, the theological foundations came *after* the practical reforms. In other words, we are not to imagine that an Orthodox Jew studied the Prophets and, on that basis alone, came to the conclusion that the dietary laws were of no religious consequence— whereupon he bit into a ham sandwich. Rather was it the man, already lax in ritual observance, who found support for his deviations from Tradition in what he called "Prophetic Religion."

Seen in this light, the incorporation of the Higher Criticism of the Bible into the theological foundations of Reform Judaism in the twentieth century (though, be it noted, not before, and not by the original apostles of Classical Reform!) becomes intelligible as a kind of "Occam's Razor" for the purpose of dealing with Judaism's adjustment to the practical problems of modern life. Instead of arguing *within* the framework of the traditional *Halakhah* (Jewish Law), which is not always easy, and which, as Conservative Jews well know, always invites the fierce opposition of the Orthodox who can play at the same game, Reform cut the Gordian knot by denying the very premise on which *Halakhah* is predicated, namely the doctrine of "Torah from Heaven."

The Bible became a human, instead of a divine, document. It was read as a record of man's quest for God, rather than as a statement of God's demands on man. In this manner, the detection of the human element became synonymous with disproving the divine authorship.

"For the basis of the old legalism has crumbled away," wrote Claude G. Montefiore.[15] "We no longer believe in the Mosaic and divine origin of the *whole* Pentateuchal law; we no longer believe that all the ordinances date from the same period, and that they are *all* perfect, immutable, and divine. Some of the ceremonial laws may be, in their ultimate origin, much older than Moses, resting as they do upon primordial conceptions, and even upon superstitions or taboos, which have wholly passed away, while others of the ceremonial laws are undoubtedly much later than Moses."

Yet the late Claude G. Montefiore would hardly have approved of the following statement: "For the basis of the old *motzi* [blessing over the bread] has crumbled away. We no longer believe that God is personally concerned with the production of each and every slice of bread, so that the very sandwich we eat could be thought of as a direct gift from God. Some of the ideas behind the *motzi* may be, in their ultimate origin, much older than Judaism, resting as they do upon primordial conceptions, and even upon superstitions and remnants of animism and the worship of fertility gods, which have wholly passed away, while, unlike the ancient Israelite, the modern Jew is fully aware of the processes from gestation through packaging which bring the bread upon his table." Claude G. Montefiore would not have approved of this because, as a deeply religious soul, he was able to perceive the hand of the Creator behind the physical aspects of His creation.

We suggest that a similar view could be taken of the doctrine of "Torah from Heaven"—even by those who feel quite confident that they are able to determine precisely who wrote what, and when, in the post-Mosaic literary history of the so-called Law of Moses. As Franz Rosenzweig wrote to Jakob Rosenheim:

> Even if Wellhausen would turn out to be right in all his theories, ... it would not make the slightest difference to our faith.... We, too, translate the Torah as *one* book. For us, too, it is the work of *one* spirit. We do not know who it was; that it was Moses we cannot believe. Among ourselves we call him by the sign which the Higher Criticism uses to designate the final redactor assumed by it, "R." But we resolve this sign not into "Redactor," but into "*Rabbenu*" [Our Teacher]. For, whoever he was, and whatever sources he might have utilized, he is our Teacher, and his theology is our Teaching.[16]

The time is past when the mere denial of the doctrine of "Torah from Heaven" was deemed capable of solving all the practical problems of Reform Judaism. The assumption of the existence of various strata in the composition of the Pentateuch is no longer such a novelty. Many Conservative Jews share it; and the Protestants, who had originally discovered it, have long since proceeded to listen again for the "Word," and to transcend, though not to ignore, the multifarious stratification of sources in a higher "unity of the Bible."

It is, of course, very likely that a modern interpretation of the doctrine of "Torah from Heaven" is going to make somewhat less sweeping demands than the Rabbinic interpretation of Numbers 15:31, which we discussed above. On the other hand, a doctrine of "progressive revelation"—as preached by Reform Judaism—which does not confine the Word of God to the Written Text might not, after all, be so adverse to finding Revelation in the Oral Torah as well. At any rate, the time may well have come when the doctrine of "Torah from Heaven" should be taken seriously again.

Taking "Torah from Heaven" seriously may not be easy for the modern liberal Jew, but it is not impossible. At least, it is not impossible as long as his rationalism does not prevent him from thanking God for bringing forth bread from the earth. For unless this tribute to Nature's God merely covers up for an apotheosis of Nature herself, the Jew who believes in God's power to produce bread from the soil cannot very well remain deaf to the admonition that "man doth not live by bread alone, but by every thing that proceedeth out of the mouth of the Lord doth man live."

NOTES

1. Cf. Leviticus 2:13.
2. B. Berakhoth 40b.
3. Cf. A. Marmorstein, *The Old Rabbinic Doctrine of God* (London, 1927), I, 105ff.
4. David Hoffmann, ed., *Mischnaiot, Seder Nesikin* (Berlin, 1898), p. 189, Note 9.
5. *Mishnah Sanhedrin* 10:1.
6. *Sopherim* 13:8 (ed. Mueller, p. xxii).
7. Cf., for example, Deuteronomy 4:36.
8. *Tosephta Berakhoth* 7:2 (ed. Zuckermandel, pp. 15f.).
9. Cf. j. *Berakhoth*, ch. VII (11a, b); and *Abudraham*, beginning of ch. III.
10. *Sepher Hamitzvoth*, in *Likkuté Kadmonioth*, ed. Harkavy (St. Petersburg, 1903), II, 17.
11. Cf. the blessing before the reading from the Torah as described in Nehemiah 8:5–8.
12. Amos 8:11.
13. Theodor H. Gaster, *Festivals of the Jewish Year* (New York, 1953), p. 63.
14. B. *Sanhedrin* 99a; and cf. *Sifré* to Numbers 15:31 (ed. Friedmann, p. 33a).
15. Claude G. Montefiore, *Outlines of Liberal Judaism* (London, 1912), pp. 218f.
16. Franz Rosenzweig, *Briefe* (Berlin, 1935), pp. 581f. (My translation from the German.)

CHAPTER 9

ℬ Beyond Fundamentalism and Iconoclasm

Fundamentalism, that is the belief in the literal inerrancy of the Scriptures, coupled with a literalist exegesis, is the distinguishing feature of certain Orthodox sects within modern Protestantism. It is unknown to, indeed it is rejected by, Traditional Judaism. If this sounds startling and strange, the reader should consider the Rabbinic interpretation of the *lex talionis* in Exodus 21:24. "An eye for an eye," according to the ancient Rabbis,[1] must *not* be understood literally. Its "true" meaning is that of *monetary* compensation. Again, the biblical law (Exodus 16:29), "Let no man go out of his place on the seventh day," was understood by the Rabbis to refer not to a man's own house, but to his city. Even so, they permitted a man to walk two thousand cubits *beyond* the city limits, and if food has been deposited there on Friday, yet another two thousand cubits beyond that.[2]

Reprinted, with revisions, from *The Jewish Chronicle* (London, England) of September 25, 1959, p. 23. Copyright © 1959 by The Jewish Chronicle, Ltd. The author is grateful for permission to reprint this material.

Beyond Fundamentalism and Iconoclasm

A literalist interpretation would not have yielded such results. Thus, for example, the ancient Sadducees insisted upon a literal application of "an eye for an eye," while the early Karaites would not allow a man to leave his house on the Sabbath day. Yet both Sadducees and Karaites were bypassed by the course of "normative" Pharisaic-Rabbinic Judaism. The latter, by adhering to the doctrine of a twofold Revelation, encompassing the Oral as well as the Written Torah, was in possession of a built-in mechanism for progress, which made allowance for man's moral advance and the adaptation of the Law to changing circumstances of life.

This applies not only to the legal content of Judaism, but also to its doctrinal and spiritual aspects. Maimonides was neither the first nor the last Jewish thinker to maintain that "those passages in the Bible which, in their literal sense, contain statements that can be refuted by proof must and can be interpreted otherwise."[3] Had proof been forthcoming in his day for the Aristotelian notion of the eternity of matter, he would have been quite prepared, on his own admission, to interpret the Creation story in Genesis accordingly.

Sometimes, indeed, the very non-literalist exegesis of the Rabbis prevented a head-on clash with Science. The eleventh-century commentator Rashi lived a long time before Charles Darwin. It was for reasons unconnected with the modern theory of Evolution that Rashi, in commenting on Genesis 1:1, made the statement: "This passage of Scripture does *not* come to teach the *order* of creation." But, once such a view is taken, it does not become too difficult for the post-Darwinian Orthodox Jew to reconcile his faith with the theory of Evolution. In 1925, in Dayton, Tennessee—in the Protestant American South—a teacher could still be tried in court for teaching the theory of Evolution. In 1929, the Orthodox British Chief Rabbi, Dr. J. H. Hertz, in his Genesis commentary, was able to write: "Thus evolution, far from destroying the *religious* teaching of Genesis 1, is its profound confirmation!"[4]

We today are still in the midst of a process of digestion which involves Traditional Judaism, on the one hand, and certain facts brought to light by nineteenth-century Science, on the other. I am referring specifically to the critical study of the Hebrew Bible, and of the Pentateuch in particular. Applying the same analytical methods to the study of ancient Hebrew literature as had proved useful in the study of other classical literatures, the critics came to the conclusion that not all books in the Bible necessarily came from the pen of the authors to whom they had been traditionally attributed, and that the Pentateuch, in particular, far from being Mosaic, was, in fact, a composite of various legal and narrative strata which reflected the religious evolution of ancient Israel over a period of centuries.

The Orthodox Jewish reaction to those findings took two different forms. In some quarters there was a downright condemnation of this kind of scholarship as sheer blasphemous heresy. Motives were imputed to the Bible critics which were anything but scholarly. Other traditionalist Jewish spokesmen, however, attempted to beat the critics on their own ground. The learned David Hoffmann, principal of the Orthodox Rabbinical Seminary in Berlin, produced a scholarly work marshaling "The Most Important Instances Against the Graf-Wellhausen Hypothesis."[5] Even in circles somewhat more favorably inclined toward the scientific study of the Scriptures there was, and still is, a tendency to date biblical documents as early as possible—or even earlier—as if the value of a biblical passage were somewhat dependent upon its hoary age.

Liberal Jewish circles soon came to terms with the so-called Higher Criticism of the Bible. Not only did the results of the critics seem to substantiate the thesis that Judaism is not, and never has been, static, but evolutionary; but it was also felt that the Law loses its binding force the moment its Mosaic authorship has been disproved.

It appears to us, however, that, understandable as those reactions are in terms of the various schools of modern Jewish thought, the identical fallacy has been committed by Orthodox and Liberal alike. The underlying assumption of both positions

Beyond Fundamentalism and Iconoclasm

is apparently that *literary* history contains the answers to *theological* questions. The problem of Revelation is a theological, not a literary, problem. It has to be faced by the modern Jew on a philosophical and theological level—quite independent of the results of the critical study of ancient Hebrew literature. One man might conceivably maintain the Mosaic authorship of the Pentateuch and yet deny that God reveals Himself to man, while another, with all of his acceptance of the results of criticism, may yet maintain his faith in a God who communicates His will to man.

Naturally, except for the last few verses of Deuteronomy, describing the death and burial of Moses, which were attributed to Joshua, the ancient Rabbis did not suspect that anyone but Moses acted as the human channel for the Divine Revelation contained in the Pentateuch.[6] But neither did they suspect that their successors in the modern world would one day reconcile the Torah with Copernicus and with Darwin! *They* had the task of squaring the teachings of Judaism with the knowledge available in *their* day. The modern Jew must take into account the knowledge available in the twentieth century.

But once the *divine* source of biblical teaching is made the center of our concern, the Orthodox Jew need not fear the assertion of the existence of various layers in the Pentateuch—any more than the Liberal Jew can rationalize his non-observance of traditional provisions by an iconoclastic reference to the "disproved" Mosaic authorship of the Pentateuch.

In its long history, Judaism has come to terms with many an innovation in Philosophy and in Science. Some it accepted sooner than others, but its very survival is in no small measure due to the fact that it ultimately always came to terms with reality. Our approach to biblical criticism will prove to be no exception to this rule.

Two further considerations should be borne in mind: The first is that no scientific discipline must be absolutized. Judaism came to terms with Plato and with Aristotle, but it did not become identical with them. It outlasted them, even as it outlasted its temporary association with early Babylonian scientific notions. Copernicus and Darwin, too, are only stages in man's scientific progress. Judaism has come to terms with them, and it will likewise come to terms with whatever notions may succeed them.

Biblical criticism, too, is a branch of Science—as liable both to progress and to error as any other branch. The biblical criticism of the second half of the twentieth century is not identical with the biblical criticism of the nineteenth. It would, therefore, be wrong to stake one's total religious commitment on the shifting sands of scholarly hypothesis. The views about the history of biblical literature are bound to change. The Jew's commitment to his God must be the one constant element in his life.

The second consideration is this: What the Bible critics study is, in reality, the "Old Testament," the plain, literal text of the Hebrew Bible. Yet, as we have pointed out time and again in these pages, Judaism is *not* based on the literal meaning of the biblical text. The Bible of Judaism is the Bible as interpreted by the Pharisees, by the Midrash and the Talmud, by Rashi and Ibn Ezra, by Maimonides and the Malbim. It is the Bible in which countless generations of Jews have found the Word of God addressed to their particular needs and circumstances. It is the Bible with which they have grown, and which has grown with them. But it is *not* the Bible of Fundamentalism. The Bible of Fundamentalism is indeed endangered by the findings of modern scholarship. *Our* Bible, on the other hand, stands or falls, not in relation to problems of authorship, but by our ability to find in it the Word of God.

NOTES

1. B. *Baba Kamma* 83b–84a.
2. B. *Erubhin* 51a.
3. *Moreh Nebhukhim* II, 25.

4. Joseph H. Hertz, *The Pentateuch and Haftorahs*, Vol. I. Genesis (New York, 1929), p. 55.
5. David Hoffmann, *Die wichtigsten Instanzen gegen die Graf-Wellhausensche Hypothese* (Berlin, 1904).
6. B. *Baba Bathra* 14b–15a.

CHAPTER 10

✍ Revelation and the Modern Jew

When Jews and Christians in the past treasured the books of the Hebrew Bible, it was not on account of their literary beauty or of the light they could shed on ancient history. The Bible occupied the place it did because it was believed to be the Word of God. God had spoken to Israel and, through Israel, to mankind. He had made known His will. He had revealed "the commandments which a man shall do and live thereby." Passages like the nineteenth chapter of the Book of Exodus were taken as a description of the "how" of God's Revelation.

We know the picture of Moses on Mount Sinai. There were the thunders and the lightnings, the sound of the ram's horn, the mountain shaking, the people trembling. And God spoke. And God inscribed the Ten Commandments on the two tablets of stone which Moses was to bring to the people. This is Revelation as the Bible describes it.

Or is it? Doubts must have been felt by many who saw Cecil

Reprinted from *The Journal of Religion*, XLI, No. 1 (January 1961), 28–37. Copyright © 1961 by The University of Chicago Press. The author is grateful for permission to reprint this material.

B. De Mille's magnificent production, *The Ten Commandments*. The film was a sincere effort to do justice to the events narrated in the Book of Exodus. It was faithful to the *literal* meaning of the biblical words. But how many, after seeing the movie, really left the theater with the firm belief that this is the way it *really* happened?

Why should there be occasion for doubt? Why was it that so many film critics, writing for the religious press of this country, felt that the Revelation scene on Mount Sinai involved a cheapening of the biblical text? The reason is not far to seek. It lies in the very fact that the movie took the biblical story literally!

It is obvious that what the Bible *wants* to describe, or to indicate, is the momentous fact that the infinite God had revealed Himself to finite man. Yet this is a concept, a daring thought, which defies adequate description in the language of man. The thunders and the lightnings at Sinai, as they appear in the biblical narrative, are the echo sounding through the ages of what had happened there. They testify to the fact of Revelation, to the impact it had on the people. But it is only the man of prosaic mind, the man lacking in imagination, who would read this biblical account as if it were a news bulletin reporting in every detail what had actually happened. Only the language of *poetry* might dare to capture what had transpired there. And the language of the nineteenth chapter of the Book of Exodus *is* the language of poetry. The trouble with the movie, *The Ten Commandments*, was precisely this: it turned the poetry of the biblical account into the prose of twentieth-century newspaper reporting.

Now, it may well be argued, and with some justification, that the film version of the Ten Commandments has done nothing that is not also done by so-called Fundamentalists. The film, like the Orthodox believers, simply took the biblical words literally. But such an argument is not likely to impress the *Jew*. Judaism, as we have already explained in previous chapters, even in its traditional phases, has never been committed to that kind of literalist exegesis.

Heirs of the Pharisees

Already a fourth-century Rabbi, quoted in the Talmud, maintained that what Israel heard directly from God at Mount Sinai consisted of the first two of the Ten Commandments only. These are, in the Jewish way of counting the Commandments, "I am the Lord thy God" and "Thou shalt have no other gods before Me." The rest of the law was mediated by Moses.[1]

This idea was taken up by the philosopher Maimonides, who offers the following interpretation of the talmudic passage we have quoted:

The first commandment deals with the existence of God, the second with His unity. What the Talmud means by saying that they were directly revealed by God Himself is that those principles *are accessible to unaided human reason!* "For whatever can be established by proof is known by the Prophet in the same way as by any other person." As for the rest of the commandments, they were mediated by Moses, who interpreted for the people a sound which was unintelligible to them.[2]

So far Maimonides. It is true, his explanation may no longer satisfy the twentieth-century religionist. But I consider it an advance over the interpretation given by the movie version of the Ten Commandments. It is also evidence of how little the Jewish Orthodoxy of the past was bound by "Fundamentalist" preconceptions.

But it was an "Orthodoxy" just the same. It posited the supernatural. It affirmed the miraculous. It maintained the authoritative character of a moral and ritual legislation said to have been revealed by God Himself. As such, it was bound to collide with the rationalism of the eighteenth and nineteenth centuries. And out of this collision and conflict, Reform Judaism was born.

Actually, Reform Judaism began without any intention of upsetting the traditional belief in divine Revelation. It began with a simplification of the synagogue service and an abolition of rituals and ceremonies which were no longer felt to be "meaningful." In some of its early manifestations, Reform Judaism

Revelation and the Modern Jew

claimed that only the biblical laws were divinely revealed, but not the laws of the Rabbinic Tradition. Yet soon enough it was realized that any number of ceremonies which had become religiously "meaningless" were *biblical* ceremonies. And so a distinction was made between the moral and ethical laws of the Bible, on the one hand, and the ritual and ceremonial provisions, on the other. The former were held to be eternally valid. The latter were deemed to be time-bound and of human provenance.

Typical of this stage in Reform Jewish thinking are the views of Rabbi Isaac Mayer Wise, the nineteenth-century organizer of American Reform Judaism. He held that the Ten Commandments were revealed by God Himself. The rest of biblical law represents the application made by Moses of the principles contained in the Ten Commandments to the particular conditions with which he was faced.

This, however, was an intermediate step in Reform Jewish thinking. Biblical criticism had come upon the scene in the meantime. And so had Darwinism and Evolution. Scholars not only denied that Moses wrote the five books traditionally ascribed to him, but some of them even doubted the existence of Moses himself. Biblical religion was no longer viewed as something that was handed down from heaven to earth once and for all times. Rather did men begin to speak about the gradual *evolution* of Israel's faith. The Bible, indeed, turned out to be a very human document—a record of man's search for God rather than the transcript of God's commandments for men.

In addition, of course, things were happening in the realm of Philosophy. The Jew who shared the Kantian or the Hegelian concept of God did not find it easy to ascribe the Hebrew Scriptures to an act of Revelation of that kind of God. And all along, the founders of Reform Judaism carried their share of the Deistic heritage, their belief in the "eternal verities" which were universally implanted in the human mind or soul, being in no need of a supernatural Revelation.

HEIRS OF THE PHARISEES

In the eighteenth century it had still been possible for a Jewish philosopher like Moses Mendelssohn, the friend of Lessing, to combine his Deistic philosophy with a faithful observance of the Jewish law. The Revelation of God, in which Mendelssohn believed, was not a Revelation of religious "truths." Those "truths," he claimed in typical Deist fashion, were universally known *before* Sinai. What God revealed to Israel at Mount Sinai was a *legislation* by which Israel, and only Israel, was to be bound—at any rate until such a time as God would revoke it again as publicly and as spectacularly as He had originally revealed it.

But such a view was no longer possible in the nineteenth century—and certainly not in the twentieth. That legislation, cultic and ceremonial provisions, are *man-made* went without saying for the nineteenth-century Reformers. Where Revelation was problematical was in the realm of religious "truths," in the views about God, man, and the world. Did the basic and fundamental Jewish teachings on these subjects originate in a divine Revelation, or did they not?

Peculiarly enough, the word "Revelation" itself never went out of circulation. Modern Jewish thinkers continued to use it—although it no longer had the slightest connection with the thunders and lightnings of Sinai. But they used it in a variety of meanings.

"It is an indisputable fact of history," wrote Kaufmann Kohler, the theologian of American Reform Judaism who died in 1926, "that the Jewish people, on account of its peculiar religious bent, was predestined to be the people of revelation. Its leading spirits, its prophets and psalmists, its lawgivers and inspired writers differ from the seers, singers, and sages of other nations by their unique insight into the moral nature of the Deity."[3]

Similarly, Claude G. Montefiore, famous Hibbert lecturer and founder of a radical brand of Reform Judaism in England who died in 1938, in writing about the Hebrew Prophets stresses "the truths which they uttered, the season when they

Revelation and the Modern Jew

uttered them, the novelty of their utterances, their importance, their influence and their effect"; and he feels that "we may justifiably speak of it as a special sort of inspiration which needs and deserves a heading to itself."[4]

But Kohler and Montefiore are merely re-echoing the sentiments of Abraham Geiger (1810–1874), one of the first German Jewish theoreticians of the Reform Movement, for whom "Revelation" had resolved itself into the fact of the peculiar Jewish *genius* for religion![5]

Now, all three of them—Geiger, Kohler, and Montefiore—were sworn enemies of so-called Jewish nationalism and of Zionism. Nevertheless, their identification of Revelation with some form of Jewish "racial genius" brings them—perhaps quite unknown to themselves—in line with certain trends of Zionist thought.

It is about views of this sort that Professor Emil Fackenheim wrote some years ago: "If we Jews have indeed produced religious genius, we have given it, long ago, to the world; we cannot and dare not keep its insights to ourselves. We try in vain to save Jewish religious particularism on non-supernatural grounds. In the end, we are led to a perversion of classical Jewish doctrine: the substitution, for the worship of God, of the worship of the 'Jewish vision' of God."[6]

But Professor Fackenheim already criticizes the thinkers of the last generation from the perspective of the latest stage in Reform Jewish thinking. We shall come back to that. But first we shall have to look at some other attempts of coming to terms with Revelation in modern times.

It may have been noted in the few quotations we have given so far that there was a tendency among earlier Reform thinkers to identify Revelation with *inspiration*. This is an easier word, and an easier concept to handle. Schleiermacher had prepared the way for this: "Every original and new communication of the universe to man is a revelation. . . . Every intuition and every original feeling proceeds from revelation."[7]

Even a Carl Gustav Jung can use the word "revelation" in

this sense, when he says: "To the patient it is nothing less than a *revelation* when, from the depths of the psyche, something arises to confront him—something strange that is not the 'I' and is therefore beyond the reach of personal caprice."[8]

Again, a contemporary Jewish writer, Professor Jacob Kohn, who is also a Conservative rabbi, gets over the difficulty by using a semantic approach. He rejects Revelation as a "miraculous historical fact," but maintains it as a "rational metaphysical fact." For him, " 'Reveal' and 'discover' are different words for the same fact, viewed in different perspectives. What is 'uncovered' stands 'revealed,' and what is revealed is uncovered. . . . Revelation and discovery are the two poles of the same situation—the divine and the human."[9]

The matter is not, however, a simple question of semantics. As John Baillie reminds us, in his book, *The Idea of Revelation in Recent Thought*, "no true knowledge, no valid act of perceiving or thinking, can be explained by beginning from the human end—whether it be my perception of the number of peas in a particular pod, or my discovery of an argument for the existence of God. In either case my cognition is valid only so far as it is determined by the reality with which I am faced."[10]

"The reality with which I am faced." Ay, there's the rub! The reality which—according to *their* view—faced the nineteenth-century thinkers was an impersonal Absolute. It might even be said that they were hardly aware of being *faced* by a Reality. They themselves were part of that reality, part of that Absolute; they were themselves manifestations of universal spirit.

And it is just in this that they differed so radically from biblical man. Biblical man lived with the constant awareness of the *difference*, of the gulf which separates man from God. And biblical man's God was a *personal* God. That is why biblical man could speak, and think, in terms of God's Revelation, whereas modern man had to equivocate. For, to quote Baillie again, "the object of thought itself undertakes no unveiling. When we thus speak of it, we are personifying it; and

Revelation and the Modern Jew

this fact justifies the statement that, properly speaking, revelation has place only within the relationship from person to person."[11]

It was left to our own time to rediscover the personal God. Kierkegaard, Barth, and Niebuhr have their Jewish counterparts in Buber, Rosenzweig and Abraham J. Heschel. The causes responsible for this rediscovery are beyond the scope of our present topic. But the *consequences* of this rediscovery are directly relevant. One of them is that modern Jews can again speak seriously about Revelation.

Of course, modern Jews are *modern* Jews. They cannot close their eyes to the findings of biblical criticism. They cannot act as if there were no such discipline as the study of comparative religion. They cannot ignore the scientific study of religious origins and evolution. And they cannot—in any *literal* sense—share the traditional belief that God revealed to Israel exactly 248 positive commandments and 365 prohibitions. They cannot even believe that God reveals nice and ready-made theological systems. But they can believe—and some of them *do* believe—that God really reveals Himself.

"My own belief in revelation . . . ," writes Martin Buber, "does not mean that I believe that finished statements about God were handed down from heaven to earth. Rather it means that the human substance is melted by the spiritual fire which visits it, and there now breaks forth from it a word, a statement, which is human in its meaning and form, human conception and human speech, and yet witnesses to Him who stimulated it and to His will."[12]

And Franz Rosenzweig agrees that "Revelation is certainly not Law-giving. It is only this: Revelation. The primary content of revelation is revelation itself."[13]

We today conceive of Revelation—in the words of John Baillie—as "events occurring in the historical experience of mankind, events which are apprehended by faith as the 'mighty acts' of God, and which therefore engender in the mind of man such reflective knowledge of God as it is given him to possess."[14]

123

The "events" themselves are events which take place in the natural order and in history. It is man's God-given ability to place a certain interpretation on them which is evidence of God's Revelation. To quote John Baillie again, "God so chose Israel that He not only led them out of Egypt but also enabled Moses and the prophets to grasp the significance of that exodus. ... The Bible is the written witness to that intercourse of mind and event which is the essence of revelation."[15]

Let us illustrate by a concrete example what we mean: When, in 1940, most of the British and some of the French forces were evacuated from the French mainland at Dunkirk, there were many who felt that a real miracle had happened. The odds against the great rescue work seemed to be so overwhelming. The little steamers and boats from all over England, which were used to augment the resources of the British navy, hardly seemed adequate to the task expected of them. But the evacuation did succeed, and a German victory, which was so close at that time, was averted.

When it was all over, thanksgiving services were held throughout England; and the comparison between Dunkirk and the passing of the Children of Israel through the Red Sea suggested itself to many minds. As a matter of fact, the two events may even be said to have shed light on each other. For just as the event at Dunkirk was a miraculous one, *without* any setting aside of the laws of Nature, so the event at the Red Sea, invested by later generations with all the elements of a supernatural miracle, may have been nothing but a *natural* occurrence, which was felt to have been "miraculous" because it happened at the precise moment when Israel was in need of it.

But here the analogy comes to an end. The event at Dunkirk is already buried in the history books of World War II. There does not seem to be any evidence that, in the thinking of mankind, any great change was wrought on account of what happened at Dunkirk. No new concept of freedom was born there, no added feelings of responsibility of man for his neighbor. That is why we may still refer to Dunkirk as a "miracle." But nobody has yet been able to claim that Dunkirk was a "revelation."

Not so the event at the Red Sea, the climax of the liberation from Egyptian slavery! Here it was God who—in the words of the ancient Rabbinic commentary on the Book of Exodus—"revealed Himself at the sea."[16] Here it was Israel which, there and then, recognized and accepted for themselves the rulership of God, as they exclaimed: "The Lord shall reign for ever and ever" (Exodus 15:18). The liberation from Egyptian bondage—which has once jokingly been called, "The first strike of the bricklayers' union in recorded history"—was here understood as an act of divine *Revelation*. And this necessarily led to the concept of a God who wants man to be free—of God as the Author of Liberty.

And this, in turn, was to lead to a host of provisions in the social legislation of Israel—provisions motivated by the consideration: "And thou shalt remember that thou wast a slave in the land of Egypt, and the Lord thy God brought thee out thence by a mighty hand and an outstretched arm" (Deuteronomy 5:15). Here is the basis for such laws as: "The stranger that sojourneth with you shall be unto you as the home-born among you, and thou shalt love him as thyself; for ye were strangers in the land of Egypt" (Leviticus 19:34).

The event at the Red Sea is but one of many in Israel's history where God is said to have revealed Himself, where God has given man the ability to experience "that intercourse of mind and event which is the essence of revelation."

The question of why does God give this ability to man—why, at certain moments in the course of history, does He raise happenings and events from the level of the routine and the ordinary to that of Revelation—can only be answered by a reference to God's *love*. "With everlasting love hast Thou loved the House of Israel, Thy people," says the Jew in his daily evening service; "Torah and commandments, statutes and judgments hast Thou taught us." Actually, as Franz Rosenzweig would have it, the divine love is the *only* content of Revelation. Man, becoming conscious of the love of God, hears the divine command: "Thou shalt love the Lord thy God with all thy heart, with all thy soul, and with all thy might." Ordinarily, of course,

HEIRS OF THE PHARISEES

love cannot be commanded. Only a lover, in a moment of aroused love, might, and does, demand of his beloved that she return his love, that she reciprocate the love shown to her. But that is precisely what the moment of Revelation does imply. God shows His love, and longs for man's love in return. All the rest is commentary and interpretation.

But as soon as man is able to reciprocate the love, as soon as man is able to hear the commandment, "Thou shalt love the Lord thy God," he cannot stop there. "If I truly love *one* person," writes Erich Fromm in *The Art of Loving*, "I love all persons, I love the world, I love life."[17] Man, aware of the love of God, tries to capture, to make concrete and permanent, this experience of love in terms which will ultimately influence and govern the affairs of all men. And so the experience of God's love for man results in yet *another* commandment: "Thou shalt love thy neighbor as thyself—I am the Lord."

Those two great commandments, in turn, give rise to a host of other commandments—commandments of a ritual nature, in which man shows his love for God and tries to relive the moment of Revelation, and commandments of a moral and ethical nature, which aim at applying in practice and in daily life the commandment about loving one's neighbor. Admittedly, these further commandments are man's *interpretation* of the experience of Revelation. And according to how one values this "interpretation," he either will, or will not, find an inner relation to the legal and ceremonial tradition of the Jewish past.

It is on this point that the two great thinkers of modern Judaism—Martin Buber and Franz Rosenzweig—have failed to agree. "It is only through man in his self-contradiction," Buber writes, "that revelation becomes legislation."[18] Revelation, according to him, is Revelation only when it is directly experienced. One man's *interpretation* of the event can no longer be another man's authentic *Revelation*. Man must hold himself in readiness to be directly addressed by God. Adherence to the mere record of earlier revelations may actually interfere with one's relation to God. Buber, therefore, rejects the traditional law, or

Revelation and the Modern Jew

at least those parts of it through which he has not felt himself personally addressed by God.

Rosenzweig agrees that "Revelation is not Law-giving," and that legislation is but man's *interpretation*. But he nevertheless asks: "But where does this 'interpretation' stop being legitimate? I would never dare to state this in a general sentence; here commences the right of experience to give testimony, positive and negative."[19]

Here, of course, is the problem which the modern Jew has to face: On the one hand, he has to study the Hebrew Bible from a scientific perspective, reading it as the surviving remnants of ancient Hebrew literature. On the other hand, this literature is *also* the record of divine Revelation. On the basis of the older view of Revelation, the mechanical view which conceived of a *divinely* communicated text which is identical with the text now found in the Hebrew Bible, this problem would be insoluble. Or it could be solved by cutting the Gordian knot—by rejecting either the belief in Revelation or the modern scientific approach. In other words, the solution would be found either in an obscurantist Fundamentalism or in a non-religious Humanism. Happily, however, the modern Jew can escape this "either/or" strait jacket.

In a letter which Franz Rosenzweig wrote to a friend who was fearful about the new approach which took Revelation seriously, he said: "If one tells a tale about Hansel and Gretel, it need only be pretty. Neither the witch nor the parents are going to raise an objection about being misrepresented—for they really do not exist at all. But if one wants to tell a tale about God's Revelation, it becomes a far more ticklish business. Here it does not suffice that the story be pretty; it must also be true. Otherwise one runs the risk of having God raise an objection. For, unlike the witch and the parents, God *does* exist. He cannot be indifferent to the kind of tales His children tell about Him—any less than to the name by which they call Him. Yet they remain tales; and you need not worry that the science of literary history will be robbed of a subject matter. All narrative, as such, turns into a tale. That is human. And God wants the human—also in His own Revelation."[20]

John Baillie expressed a similar thought: "It were indeed a strange conception of the divine providential activity which would deny that the biblical writers were divinely assisted in their attempt to communicate to the world the illumination which, for the world's sake, they had themselves received."[21]

This juxtaposition of the quotations from Rosenzweig and from Baillie should indicate that there is a certain similarity between the modern Jewish approach and the modern Christian approach to the problem of Revelation. We are living in the same world, and we share the same culture. Both the Jew and the Christian have to come to terms with what Karl Jaspers once wrote to Rudolf Bultmann: "I do not understand how you can regard something human as the word of God."[22] The solution lies, of course, in distinguishing between the Revelation and its "interpretation." Here there are likely to remain many differences between Judaism and Christianity, even as the problems of "interpretation" will by no means find unanimous solutions among the Jews themselves.

We are still struggling with this problem. Many Jews remain satisfied with the formulations of so-called Classical Reform Judaism, with the views of Geiger, of Kohler, and of Montefiore. Others are Humanists, and denying the existence of a personal God, they have no problem at all with Revelation. But within recent years the views of Buber and of Rosenzweig have found an increasing number of champions among the younger Jewish theologians.

Revelation, however, is not something that only happened in the distant past. The ancient Rabbis already insisted that each Jew, in every generation, must regard himself as though he, too, had been liberated by God from Egyptian slavery. And they stressed the constant reference of the Scriptures to "this day," by demanding that the Jew constantly *re-live* the experience of Sinai. It may, therefore, be suggested in all modesty and humility that, once modern Judaism has finally come to terms with

Revelation and the Modern Jew

the problems posed by Revelation, it, too, will have been blessed by God with that felicitous union of "event" and "interpretation" which is the essence of Revelation.

NOTES

1. B. *Makkoth* 24a.
2. Maimonides, *Guide for the Perplexed*, II, 35.
3. Kaufmann Kohler, *Jewish Theology* (New York, 1918), p. 39.
4. Claude G. Montefiore, *Outlines of Liberal Judaism* (London, 1912), p. 174.
5. Abraham Geiger, *Judaism and Its History*, tr. Maurice Mayer (New York, 1865), pp. 47–64.
6. Emil L. Fackenheim, "Can There Be Judaism Without Revelation?" in *Commentary* (December 1951), p. 567.
7. Friedrich Schleiermacher, *On Religion—Speeches to Its Cultured Despisers*, tr. John Oman (New York, 1958), p. 89.
8. Carl Gustav Jung, *Modern Man in Search of a Soul* (London, 1945), pp. 279f.
9. Jacob Kohn, *The Moral Life of Man* (New York, 1956), pp. 224f.
10. John Baillie, *The Idea of Revelation in Recent Thought* (New York, 1956), p. 22.
11. *Ibid.*, p. 24.
12. Martin Buber, *Eclipse of God* (New York, 1952), pp. 173f.
13. Franz Rosenzweig, *On Jewish Learning*, ed. Nahum N. Glatzer (New York, 1955), p. 118.
14. Baillie, *op. cit.*, p. 62.
15. *Ibid.*, p. 110.
16. *Mekilta, Shirata*, chap. iv, ed. Lauterbach, II, 31; and parallels.
17. Erich Fromm, *The Art of Loving* (New York, 1956), p. 46.
18. Quoted in Franz Rosenzweig, *On Jewish Learning*, pp. 111f.
19. *Ibid.*, p. 118.
20. Franz Rosenzweig, *Briefe* (Berlin, 1935), p. 537 (my translation).
21. Baillie, *op. cit.*, p. 111.
22. Karl Jaspers and Rudolf Bultmann, *Myth and Christianity* (New York, 1958), p. 81.

CHAPTER 11

Reflections on Revelation

It is customary, in presentations of *systematic* theology, to deal with the belief in God before dealing with the belief in Revelation. The possibility (or the fact) of Revelation, in such schematic treatments, is usually "deduced" from the nature of the God whose existence will have been "demonstrated" first. Obviously, it would make no sense at all to speak of Revelation within an atheistic frame of reference.

But, in Judaism at least, the logical approach does not exhaust either the sphere of the Divine or that of Revelation. There is also a historical dimension. Historically speaking, it might even be legitimate to say that the belief in God is not so much a prerequisite for belief in Revelation as that the experience of Revelation is chronologically antecedent to a reasoned belief in God. The *Aggadah* may try to reconstruct the mental processes by which Abraham "found" God. But the Bible itself knows of no such exercises in Natural Theology. It gives Abra-

---

Reprinted, with revisions, from the *CCAR Journal*, XIII, No. 6 (June 1966), 4–11. Copyright © 1966 by the Central Conference of American Rabbis. The author is grateful for permission to reprint this material.

Reflections on Revelation

ham's family history (Genesis 11:27–32); and then, without any further ado, it tells us that God addressed Abram with a command and a blessing, and that Abram obeyed (Genesis 12:1–4).

Long before a Saadiah or a Maimonides set out to "prove" the existence of God, the Prophets, finding God "revealed" in nature and in the historical experience of Israel, saw no need for theological preambles to their "Thus saith the Lord." And when the medieval thinkers constructed their "proofs" for the existence of God, the God whose existence they "proved" had to be the kind of God of whom the earlier biblical revelations could be predicated. Revelation, in other words, or the possibility of Revelation, was not "deduced" from the nature of a God whose existence was "proved" by independent rational means. But Revelation was itself a datum which, through inductive reasoning, led to the definition of the nature of God.

When, therefore, the modern Jewish theologian reopens the question of the existence and nature of God, and the question of Revelation, he cannot really treat the two questions in isolation from each other. It is, of course, quite conceivable that one might arrive at a "God concept" from which no concept of Revelation whatsoever can be "deduced." The Deists of the seventeenth and eighteenth centuries have done so, as have the rationalists of the nineteenth and the naturalists of the twentieth. Such "God concepts" may indeed serve an important function. But they are substitutes for, not restatements of, the biblical God of Israel. From the perspective of those modern "God concepts," therefore, it is not only Revelation, but the God of the Bible Himself who must be regarded as an *überwundener Standpunkt*. Nor, for that matter, does the God of the "religious naturalist" have too much chance of survival in our age. On the one hand, He is in danger of being swallowed up by the proponents of our latter-day "Atheistic Theology" and "Agnosticism." On the other hand, some of His apostles have been known to make claims on His behalf which do not follow at all from their "professed" naturalistic premises. In any event, a definition of God which does not already include the datum

HEIRS OF THE PHARISEES

of Revelation among the evidence on the basis of which it is formulated is not very likely to lead to a serious consideration of Revelation at all. There simply will be no point of transition.

Consider for a moment a Moses, bereft of Revelation, engaged in the task of constructing a rational "God concept." He had sufficient facts at his disposal to help him in such a task. He might even, as Freud has suggested, have learned all about henotheism from Ikhnaton. This god, then, arrived at within the limits of reason alone, was responsible for the order of nature, for the flooding of the Nile, etc. Undoubtedly, too, this god was the guarantor of the stabile order of society: Pharaoh at the top, and the Hebrew slaves at the bottom. That, too, was part of the order of nature. Within that particular setting there was no reason why the "God concept" arrived at by Moses—with or without any help from Ikhnaton—should have inspired him with the thought of leading the Hebrew slaves into freedom. Slavery has been known to limit one's spiritual horizon; and the god of the slave (at any rate, of the slave unfamiliar with the Bible) does not necessarily inspire thoughts of physical liberation. I suspect that some such thought lies behind the *Mekhilta*'s somewhat cryptic remarks about Exodus 24:10. (See *Mekhilta Bachodesh, parashah* V, ed. Horovitz Rabin, pp. 219f.). There, the brick-making in which Israel was engaged prior to the Exodus is said to have blurred their perception of the true nature of God, a nature which became evident to them only after their liberation.

But then, according to the Bible, Moses did not have to construct his "God concept" merely on the basis of the data which his environment furnished him. Moses, according to the Bible (Exodus, chapter 3), experienced a revelation—a revelation which led him from "this great sight" (verse 3) to the "God of the fathers" (verse 6), who cares (verse 7), and who promises liberation (verses 8ff.). Only under the impact of that revelation after the initial encounter does Moses begin to ask questions about the "nature" of God (verse 13). Of course, logically speaking, there would have been no theophany at the Burning

Reflections on Revelation

Bush without a prior existence of God. But it is also—chronologically—true to say that there would have been no awareness on the part of Moses of the *ehyeh asher ehyeh* ("I am the One who will always be present"—Exodus 3:14) without the prior fact of the theophany. This, it would seem, is paradigmatic of what, in Judaism, has been the relation between belief in God and the experience of Revelation.

When Sh. Y. Agnon, in 1959, published his anthology of Rabbinic passages dealing with the Sinaitic Revelation, it was natural for him to entitle his work, *Attem Re-ithem* ("Ye Have Seen"—Exodus 19:19). It was natural because, until fairly recently, Revelation was not a theological abstraction in Judaism, but "happenings," a series of events. "You have seen," "You have heard," "You have been shown," and "You know." Such is the vocabulary of the Bible when it refers to the concrete events which theologians choose to describe as "revelations."

Yet the very concreteness of the events is the root of our modern problem with Revelation. From Judah Halevi (1086–1145) through Moses Mendelssohn (1729–1786) the consideration of Revelation could be shunted from the metaphysical realm to that of history. Six hundred thousand Israelites witnessed the event at Sinai. The Sinaitic Revelation is, therefore, a historical fact. Theorize, if you must; but any theory you evolve will have to accommodate that particular historical fact. We smile today at the naïveté evidenced by such a reliance on merely purported "facts." We claim to know more today than Judah Halevi was able to know about the evolution of ancient Hebrew literature. We also operate with concepts like "later glosses" and "pious forgeries." If the Bible purports to record a "fact," we feel no *prima facie* compulsion to relate to that "fact" with greater credulity than we would relate to "facts" recorded by Homer or in the Quran. If someone would only have had a movie camera with him at the crossing of the Red Sea, if someone could have used a tape recorder at Sinai, and if Moses would only have taken out copyright on the complete Pentateuch—then, indeed, our attitude might be different. But they did not, and our own attitude remains skeptical and negative.

What, in the past, had been the strongest "proof" for Revelation, i.e., its historical concreteness, has, in our day, turned out to be the Achilles' heel of Revelation. If a certain chapter in Leviticus was written by P, rather than by Moses, then—so many of us have argued—there obviously was no Revelation. That is one approach. There also is another—one which I myself have adopted, both in my book, *Ever Since Sinai* (New York, 1961) and in earlier chapters of the present volume. That approach would separate the theological problem of Revelation from the literary problem of the history and the composition of the Bible. God would have made use of J, E, P, D, H, and the rest of the writers and redactors posited by modern biblical scholarship, in much the same way in which it was traditionally (and, as we are now told, mistakenly) supposed that He had made use of Moses. After all, the dogma of Rabbinic Judaism had to do with the *divine* origin of the Torah, not with its assumed Mosaic authorship.

But I must confess that this separation of Revelation from literary history might lend itself (although it does not necessarily have to do so) to the kind of theological abstraction which has only a most tenuous connection with the concrete reality of biblical Revelation. If the concreteness of the event is lost, if I can no longer be told, "You have seen," or "You have heard," then, indeed, the concept of Revelation is robbed of most of its significance as a pointer to the reality of God. It becomes a theological luxury; and the "God concept" of the believer in such a Revelation may not differ very much from the "God concept" of the man who denies Revelation altogether. Yet we cannot ignore modern biblical scholarship, and, in the face of available evidence, we cannot go back to pre-scientific notions of the Bible's literary history.

This problem is solved neither by uncritically "dating" biblical material as "early" as possible nor by siding with Yehezkel Kaufman against Wellhausen. Once the assumption of a Mosaic authorship has been abandoned, and for most of us it remains an irretrievable assumption, then the question of whether D preceded or followed P is a secondary question—without too many implications for modern theology. What really bothers us is something quite different. Granted that the Pentateuch, in the literary form in which we now possess it, is post-Mosaic; granted, too, that some of its legislation could not have been enacted before the period of the monarchy, or even the Babylonian Exile—does the Pentateuch, or does it not, preserve echoes and reminiscences of real happenings and events?

The happenings and the events which I have in mind are not, of course, those which archeology can support or refute. I am not concerned with the precise dimensions of Noah's Ark or with the exact location where the Israelites crossed the Red Sea. What concerns me, rather, is whether, in my people's history, there were events which changed my ancestors' perspective on life and on life's Creator. The Torah says that there were. It speaks of the Exodus from Egypt, of the event at Sinai, and of other occasions to which it ascribes a "revelatory" significance. The Torah says that those events transformed my ancestors' whole way of living and of thinking, transformed it under the impact of God's incursion into history. Nay more, the Torah says specifically that my ancestors came to an awareness of what God is only after they had experienced His presence in His deeds. "You have seen."

Is the Torah speaking the truth, or is it not? Is it all myth, fable, or forgery? Or is there, behind the veil of later embellishments, the living memory of concrete events, the resounding echo of experienced reality? Note, I am not speaking of "the ancient Hebrews." I am speaking about my ancestors, my people. It is at this point of my reflections that Judah Halevi's naïveté no longer appears to be quite so naïve. I may indeed quibble with him about his statistics, and I may be somewhat less certain than he was about what my ancestors actually "saw" and "heard" and "knew." But, at any rate, Halevi seems to be making the implicit assumption that "you cannot fool all of the Jews all of the time." Since this is an assumption made about my very own fathers, I have the natural and filial inclination to accept that assumption. I also have the natural and filial inclination (that is, "natural" *after* one has passed the stage of adolescent rebellion) to accept the testimony of my ancestors—so long as it is not decisively disproved. And the attempt to disprove it would have to do more than establish the post-Mosaic age of the Pentateuch. It would have to do nothing less than prove conclusively (1) that Israel's purported Exodus-Sinai experience did not lead to a radical change in man's view of God and in man's awareness of his responsibilities to his fellow men; and (2) that, if the events did not really take place, later generations of "pious forgers" had something substantial to gain by "inventing" those events—instead of taking the credit for having themselves been immediate recipients of divine revelations.

My reference to "filial inclination" was not facetious. I just do not relate to "ancient Hebrew literature" in the way in which I relate to the remnants of other ancient literatures. I am, of course, aware of the various "strata" and of the work of the successive "redactors." But I do make a distinction between scientific understanding, on the one hand, and iconoclastic "debunking," on the other. The line of demarkation between the two is, alas, not always drawn clearly enough. The exponent of sober scientific understanding has a loyalty to honesty and truth. The "debunker" may also have this loyalty. But he also has something else. He is trying to "prove" something, something that would lend additional justification to a break with his own past which he has already made for other reasons. Whether a modern Jew is an exponent of the sober scientific approach or a "debunker" may perhaps have something to do with his self-acceptance—or otherwise—as a Jew. Perhaps it is at this stage that one either manifests, or fails to manifest, what the late Caesar Seligmann called *der Wille zum Judentum* (the "Will to Judaism"). I know that my fathers have sought the Word of God (addressed to them) in this literature. They have approached it with the desire to learn and to find; and what they have learned and found has sustained them through the generations. And I am trying to follow in their footsteps; and I hope that my children will follow in mine.

The reference to "filial inclination" was also meant to meet another gambit of the anti-revelationists. If you accept the Torah, by what logic can you reject the New Testament, or the Quran, or the Upanishads? Why ancient Hebrew religious literature rather than modern philosophical and psychological literature? The argument is familiar; and it is completely beside the point. For it is not an "either/or" question for me at all. If I live long enough, I shall familiarize myself with as many literatures, religious and secular, as I can. But I have to start with my own. I have to understand myself and my own background before I can attempt the understanding of others. That is the prior claim which the Torah makes on me. Nor does the Torah demand of me that I reject as necessarily false whatever I may find in the literature of others. The Torah claims to be God's Torah for Israel. (And I am part of that Israel.) Yet the Torah does not only not deny that God has had dealings with others, besides Israel; it actually affirms it. Paul asserted that the Gospel had taken the place of the Law; and Mohammed asserted that the Quran had taken the place of both Law and Gospel. But the Torah comes to *re-affirm* the Noahitic Covenant with all mankind, and to place an *additional* inheritance into the hands of the "congregation of Jacob." That is its unique combination of universalism and particularism. Neither one negates the other. And the Torah does something else. It gives me the choice either to affirm or to reject that special inheritance. I have chosen to affirm.

But "filial inclination" alone does not yet establish the nexus between an abstract theological concept of Revelation and the concrete events to which biblical literature testifies. "Filial inclination" accounts for a great deal, but not for everything. I am not only the descendant of my ancestors. I am also myself —a human being placed within his own time and environment.

If the Torah is to be more than an interesting historical document for me, more than a cherished family album, if it is to be evidence of Revelation, then the Torah must do more than impart family history to me. It must speak to me. It must be "verifiable" in terms of my own experiences. Can I, or can I not, "re-live," as Tradition demands, the Exodus from Egypt when I celebrate the annual *seder*? Can I, or can I not, "re-live" as Tradition demands, the "event at Sinai" when I gain new insights through the study of Torah literature? Can I, or can I not, discern, as Tradition urges me to discern, the Torah's pattern of *Heilsgeschichte* in the course of a millennial Jewish history—including our own catastrophic age?

Those are really personal questions; yet Torah, to be meaningful, has to operate also on a personal level. To personal questions there can only be personal answers. In my personal case, they would run like this: Yes, I can "re-live" the Exodus from Egypt. Yes, I can "re-live" the "event at Sinai." I am even able, on occasion, to hear some of the "Thou Shalt's" and "Thou Shalt Not's" addressed to me personally. But, I admit, I still have trouble fitting our age into the pattern of biblical *Heilsgeschichte*, in affirming the dictum, "What happened to the Patriarchs is a portent for their descendants."

I have trouble doing so precisely because, for far too long, we have been defining our "God concepts" all too abstractly, and without reference to all the aspects and facets of God to which Revelation claims to bear testimony. The "God concept" we have defined for ourselves, in the Age of Liberalism, was that of a well-behaved and respectable kind of God. We left it to the professional Bible scholars to write learned treatises about what they called "the demonic aspects" of the biblical Deity. That, of course, was ancient Hebrew myth—which we ourselves had long since outgrown. But they found it—in the documents of Revelation, or, at any rate, in those documents which earlier generations had considered to be the documents of Revelation. The God we worshiped, on the other hand, was altogether rational and kind and loving and "progressive"—and all of that by our human standards of behavior.

Reflections on Revelation

Yet, in our day, God has shown Himself capable of letting things happen which do not comport at all with our notions of what a rational, kind, loving, and "progressive" God should be doing. The God of our a priori definitions just could not have let all those "terrible" things happen. That is why it has now become fashionable to proclaim the "death" of that God, or, at least, to include the element of limitation or of finitude in our definitions of Him.

But a behavior of God which is inexplicable to man does not, after all, seem so remote from the God of whom the Torah speaks, the God of passages like Exodus 4:24 and II Samuel 6:1-7. Still, the mind balks at the full implications. It prefers a God whose behavior is predictable and explicable by human standards. Biblical *Heilsgeschichte* is all well and good as long as it moves in grooves parallel to those of human progress and social meliorism. If it branches out on its own, into unexpected directions, we are at a complete loss. That is what happens when one defines his "God concept" before all the evidence is in, and if one chooses to ignore the evidence furnished by what purports to be Revelation.

To be sure, we are not altogether bereft of an awareness of Revelation even in this, our skeptical age. The experience of slavery in, and liberation from, Egypt serves the Torah as a prime motivation for its social legislation. In our age of genocide and wanton destruction—but also of the end of colonialism—the striving for civil rights and social justice would indicate that the God who reveals Himself in "terrible" events, and who uses them to teach mankind the Law of Life, has not been quite as eclipsed as we sometimes tend to think.

But we do not yet understand it all. We do not understand Auschwitz. And we do not really understand as yet the true significance of the State of Israel. One day, perhaps, we shall have a better understanding of what has happened to us, and of how what has happened to us is related to God and to His ways of making Himself known to us in the events and in the happenings through which we ourselves have lived. If that understanding should ever be vouchsafed unto us, then we, too, may rightfully regard ourselves as direct recipients of Revelation.

A future generation will undoubtedly attempt to rationalize our innermost experiences. A still later generation may even attempt to deny the reality of the events themselves, to demythologize them. But the God who revealed Himself to Moses and the Children of Israel will find His own appropriate means to let man know that, above and beyond man's most sophisticated theological definitions and constructions, there is the God who reveals Himself in concrete situations, the *ehyeh asher ehyeh,* the One who will always be present.

CHAPTER 12

The Christian-Jewish Dialogue

In one way, the Christian-Jewish dialogue has been going on for some nineteen centuries. In another way, it is only just beginning. What has been going on for nineteen centuries can only with difficulty be described as a dialogue, if, by "dialogue," we mean the talk among equals, born of mutual respect and, with full awareness of where the division lies, dedicated to the furtherance of a shared concern. Judaism and Christianity did not talk as equals when Christianity was but a heretical sect on the periphery of Judaism. There was even less equality when Christianity became the state religion of the Roman Empire and when the sword of the state predetermined the outcome of any such exchange of opinions. It was not "dialogue" in which the two faiths engaged then. "Disputation" would be a more appropriate term. Disputations (almost always *forced* on the Jews by the Christians), polemics and apologetics—such were the media of expression.

Reprinted from *Lutheran World* (Geneva, Switzerland), X, No. 4 (October 1963), 373–384. Copyright © 1963 by the Lutheran World Federation. The author is grateful for permission to reprint this material.

Moreover, the past nineteen centuries have usually found the Synagogue in a defensive role, with the Church throwing down the gauntlet. Christianity issued the challenge; Judaism was forced to reply. From its very inception, Christianity felt impelled to convert the Jews, to demonstrate to the Israel "after the flesh" that the very Scriptures of the Sinaitic Covenant find their "fulfillment" at Golgotha. The Synagogue, on the other hand, while defending its own understanding of the Covenant and the promise, felt no need to argue against Christianity as such.

To clarify this last statement, it will be necessary for us to bear in mind the two types of Christian who went into the making of the early Church. The Gentile Christian presented no problem to the Synagogue. On the contrary, we may safely assume that the ancient Rabbis would rather see the Gentile as a Christian than as a pagan. According to old Rabbinic teaching, "there are righteous men among the nations of the world who have a share in the World-to-Come," which is the Rabbinic way of saying that they "will be saved." Indeed, one might almost be tempted to assert that, according to Rabbinic teaching, it was easier for a righteous Gentile to be saved than for a Jew. The former had to abide by seven laws of elementary human morality, which, according to the Rabbis, constituted God's covenant with the sons of Noah, i.e., with the ancestors of the entire human race. These laws included the prohibitions of the overt manifestations of idolatry, of blasphemy, of murder, of theft, of sexual immorality, and of cruelty to animals, and the positive commandment about the establishment of courts of justice. It is noteworthy, moreover, that, according to a later interpretation, the prohibition of overt manifestations of idolatry did *not* extend to what the Rabbis called *shittuph*, the belief that the One God has (divine) associates.

It is easy to see, then, how many a righteous Gentile Christian would qualify, from the Rabbinic point of view, as "a righteous man among the nations of the world," how, in fact, his Christianity would aid him to attain this state—much more so

The Christian-Jewish Dialogue

than did the average form of paganism. When Maimonides, in the twelfth century, spoke of Jesus (and of Mohammed) as being the pioneers of the true Messiah, seeing that they have brought the words of the Torah to the distant ends of the earth (cf. *Hilkhoth Melakhim*, chap. 11, in the—uncensored—Constantinople edition), he was but stating a logical inference derived from this old point of view. Of course, if such a Gentile Christian, in addition to leading a pious and moral life, would deny the Election of the Jews, or their right to the Scriptures, the Rabbis could only retort that such notions were based on a faulty exegesis.

The case of the Jewish Christian, however, was different. He could not attain his "share in the World-to-Come" merely by observing the seven laws of elementary morality. He was heir to the Sinaitic Covenant and bound by all of its provisions. His disobedience of the Law would automatically class him together with all heretics, Gnostic or otherwise, whose antinomism was understood as rebellion against the very foundations of Jewish society. Yet there seem to have been any number of Judeo-Christian sects which strictly abided by the Law of Moses. Whether Paul himself preached non-observance of the Law to the native *Jew* is, at any rate, still a matter of scholarly debate—not to mention the somewhat problematical nature of the utterance of Jesus in Matthew 5:17f. The "Torah-true" Christian did in due course become an impossibility for the Church, though Justin Martyr[1] still, if somewhat grudgingly, admitted his existence. But for the Synagogue he was a distinct, and not only theoretical, possibility.[2]

Again, it was not his belief in Jesus as the Messiah which, in and by itself, placed the Jewish Christian beyond the pale of the Synagogue. None other than the great Rabbi Akiba (early second century), a master-builder of Rabbinic Judaism, had been guilty of wrong messianic identifications. He saw Bar Kokhba, the leader of the Jewish rebellion against Rome, as the promised Messiah. Some of Akiba's colleagues laughed at him, and history itself proved him wrong. But the stature of Akiba has not suffered in the eyes of posterity on account of his "eschatological" mistake.

Yet the very Bar Kokhba rebellion was decisive in bringing about the break between the Synagogue and the Jewish Christians. The latter could not join their fellow countrymen in this fight for freedom—not if the battle was led by a messianic claimant. For the Jewish Christians thought that they *knew* who the Messiah was. It was not Bar Kokhba, but Jesus! What such non-participation means at the time of a nation's life-and-death struggle can easily be imagined. Here we must look for the origin of the identification of "Christian" with "traitor" or "informer," an identification which, alas, was only strengthened in those many centuries of Christian persecution and Jewish martyrdom, when the Jew who saved his life by conversion to the persecuting Church became the incarnate image of disloyalty. It was on the basis of this image, and not as a consequence of Jewish religious law, that the Supreme Court of the State of Israel ruled, some years ago, in the case of the monk, Brother Daniel, that he was *not* a Jew in terms of Israel's Law of the Return.

To the break occasioned by the Bar Kokhba rebellion we must add the developing theology of the Christian Church. To consider Jesus as the Messiah may have been, from the point of view of the Synagogue, a factual mistake. But it was *not* a religious sin. To consider Jesus as part of a divine trinity was another matter altogether. A "Son of Noah" could believe in a divine *shittuph* and still qualify as one of "the righteous men among the nations." A "Son of Israel," however, was bound to such a radical form of monotheism that he was unable to distinguish between a monotheistic trinitarianism and a polytheistic tri-theism. (And how many of the Christians with whom he came into contact did, in fact, make such a distinction?) A Jew who believed in divine "associates" was simply considered an idolater, and could not enjoy, in the eyes of the Synagogue, the status accorded the Gentile Christian. Mariolatry and image-worship only helped to emphasize a break which had oc-

The Christian-Jewish Dialogue

curred even without them. That is why Luther, too, was frustrated in his hopes of winning the Jews over to his Reformation Christianity.

Synagogue and Church went their separate ways and reckoned their years by different calendars. Basic to both of them was the eschatological pattern mapped out by early Rabbinic Judaism. That pattern saw "this world" followed by the "days of the Messiah," and the "days of the Messiah" by the "World-to-Come." The Synagogue saw itself living in "this world." The Church, with its *anno domini*, already thought of itself as existing in the "days of the Messiah." Why did the Synagogue refuse to live by the new calendar? This question can best be answered by a well-known Hasidic story, retold somewhere in the writings of Martin Buber: "A pious rabbi was interrupted in his study of the holy books, when an excited disciple burst into the room, and shouted: 'Master, the Messiah has come!' The rabbi got up and looked out of the window. After a while, he muttered, 'Nothing has changed,' and returned to his studies."

For the Christian, the year 1, or the year 30, is a decisive point in world history. For the Jew, "nothing has changed." The messianic expectations have remained unfulfilled. Note that we speak of "messianic expectations" in the plural. It is futile to argue whether Jesus did, in fact, fit *the* role of the Messiah as envisaged by his contemporaries, or whether he introduced a new messianic concept altogether. There were many different messianic concepts in his days, as there were already in biblical times. Think of the difference between the "horizontal" messianic expectations of the Hebrew Prophets and of the "vertical" messianic intrusion as pictured in the Book of Daniel and later apocalyptic writings. Think of the imagery in such chapters as the second chapter of the Book of Isaiah, where the personal Messiah does not even figure, and of those other passages where the role of a Davidic scion is stressed. Think also of Akiba's messianic claims for Bar Kokhba, who was not a "Son of David," and of the "Messiah, son of Joseph" (who dies in battle) who likewise figures in Rabbinic literature. And now the Dead Sea Scrolls have introduced us to yet another Messiah, one of *priestly* descent.

What all *Jewish* concepts of the Messiah have in common, however, is the view that the Messiah brings about a change in the kind of life being lived on earth and not just in the inner life of the individual. Wars and persecutions must cease. Justice and peace must reign. After all, for the Jew, Jesus is but one in a long chain of men for whom messianic claims have been made. There were others in his own time. There have been many since. The Synagogue had no other resort but to judge such claimants by their own fruits. Says Maimonides, in the passage from which we have already quoted: "If a king of the Davidic dynasty should arise, who meditates on the Torah and busies himself with the commandments as did David, his ancestor, both according to the Written and according to the Oral Torah, and if he compels Israel to walk in the Torah and to repair its breaches, and if he wages the battles of the Lord, then he is under the presumption of being the Messiah. If, furthermore, he should succeed, subdue the nations round about, rebuild the Temple on its place, and gather the outcasts of Israel, then he is certainly the Messiah. But if he does not altogether succeed, or is slain in battle, then it is sure that he is not the one promised by the Torah. Instead, he is like all the other kings of the House of David who were upright and pious, and who then died. God raised him up for the sole purpose of testing the people."

Judged by these criteria, Jesus has not fulfilled the expectations. But if it is claimed that Jesus introduced a *new* messianic concept, then for some two thousand years the Church has been wasting its time, trying to "prove" to the doubting Jews that Jesus has actually "fulfilled" the "Old Testament prophecies." Jewish *Heilsgeschichte* sees in the Exodus from Egypt the pattern of the messianic redemption. Just as the former, in addition to bringing about a spiritual transformation, involved an actual, physical liberation, so the latter cannot be genuine if it does not involve both. Indeed, so important are the actual

The Christian-Jewish Dialogue

conditions of the "days of the Messiah" that modern Reform Judaism can lay its whole stress on the messianic *age*, regarding the "personal Messiah" of prophetic literature as nothing more than a poetic metaphor, i.e., the ideal king, by which imagery the Prophets conveyed their belief in the coming of a just and righteous government. Under the circumstances, the question whether X or Y was the Messiah is a futile question with which to confront the Jew. For him, Jesus can be considered in this role no more and no less than David Reubeni or Sabbatai Zevi. If "nothing has changed," the Messiah, or the Messianic Age, has obviously not come.

This is not to say that the figure of Jesus does not have a certain fascination for many a modern Jew. Not all of them would go as far as did Martin Buber, who said: "From my youth onwards I have found in Jesus my great brother. . . . My own fraternally open relationship to him has grown ever stronger and clearer, and today I see him more strongly and clearly than ever before."[3] But there has been a decided Jewish interest in the subject. Christians would be wrong, however, to see in Buber's "de-Christianized" Jesus, in the historical *Leben Jesu* studies of Claude G. Montefiore, Leo Baeck, and Joseph Klausner, and in the "novelistic" Jesus of Scholem Asch, any indication of a possible Jewish acceptance of the messiahship of Jesus. If anything, all those modern Jewish treatments are predicated on a clear separation between the "Jewish Jesus" and the "Christian Christ." (And they succeed or fail precisely to the extent to which such a separation is, or is not, possible.)

The fact remains that throughout the Middle Ages (which, for the Jew, lasted until the eighteenth century) the Church has been confronting the Synagogue with numerous "Old Testament" texts said to "prove" the messiahship of Jesus. The whole relationship between Church and Synagogue—on the spiritual level, that is; socially and politically it was far uglier—can be described as a never-ending "battle of the proof-texts." The Church made exegetical claims, and the Synagogue denied them. Every self-respecting Church Father had to write at least one *Adversus Judaeos*. Every Jewish convert to Christianity worth his salt had to stage at least one forced disputation, in which he claimed that the Hebrew Bible (and some made the claim for the Talmud as well) "proved" the truths of Christianity. And the Synagogue "replied"—replied, that is, in the only way open to it: in a chain of polemical and apologetical writings, which bear such titles as *The Book of the Shame of the Gentiles, The Refutation of the Dogmas of the Christian Faith,* and *The Strengthening of Faith*—the latter being a verse-by-verse analysis and refutation of christological interpretations of the Hebrew Bible.

Of course, the medieval "battle of the proof-texts" went far beyond Philip's exposition to the Ethiopian eunuch in Acts 8. Not only that Jesus was the Messiah was "proved" now. The doctrine of the Trinity, too, was contained in the Hebrew Bible. The word for "God" in Genesis 1:1 (*Elohim*) is, grammatically speaking, a plural form. (Yes, replied the Jews, but the verb is in the singular!) The threefold "holy" in Isaiah 6:3 refers to Father, Son, and Holy Ghost. (No, said the Jews, it means that God is holy in heaven, holy on earth, and holy unto all eternity.) The "wood" with its life-giving potential, in Exodus 15:25, is a prefiguration of the cross. (No, said the Jews, the Hebrew word in question also means "tree," and it is obviously a reference to the Torah, which is "a tree of life to all that lay hold of it.") And so on, and so forth—not to speak of the word *'almah,* in Isaiah 7:14, which the Christians insisted on translating as "virgin," and which the Jews, with like insistence, refused to render as anything but "young woman."

Were the arguments conclusive? It can hardly be said that either side succeeded very much in convincing the other. A cynical outsider could very well arrive at the kind of conclusion which Heinrich Heine put into the mouth of a spectator at one of the medieval disputations:

> *Wer Recht hat, das weiss ich nicht.*
> *Doch es will mich schier bedünken,*
> *Dass der Rabbi und der Mönch,*
> *Dass sie alle beide stinken.*

(Who is right, I cannot tell.
Yet I am inclined to think
That the rabbi and the monk,
Both of them, do vilely stink.)

Yet underlying all the bitter disputations there was a basic fact which perhaps few of the participants ever consciously realized or adequately evaluated. Maimonides, in the twelfth century, could find room for both Christianity and Islam in the divine scheme of salvation. Joseph Albo, in the fifteenth century, could claim that Judaism, Christianity, and Islam all share the basic dogmas concerning the existence of God, Revelation, and divine Retribution—differing only in their understanding of the details. But, in the heat of combat, how many Christians and Jews realized that there were so many convictions which they shared in common, without which, indeed, all their disputations could not even take place? There may have been discussion as to whether or not God has a son. But there was no argument as to the existence of God Himself. Whether the Law was eternally binding or whether it was merely "a schoolmaster leading unto Christ" could be debated. But both sides took for granted that God had revealed the Law, that there was such a thing as Revelation. Had the Messiah already come, or was he still to come for the first time? That was a matter of discussion—not the faith in a messianic redemption of history as such, which was shared by both sides.

There were other areas of tacitly shared concern. Modern apologetic writing has tended far too much to establish clear-cut dichotomies in order to assert categorically "Where Judaism Differed." It is all too easy to say that Christianity believes in vicarious atonement, while Judaism rejects such a belief; or that Christianity believes in original sin, while Judaism does not. Or again, that Christianity lays its whole emphasis on creed, while Judaism is only concerned with deed. The fact is, as we have already seen in Chapter 4, that, within Rabbinic Judaism, there was a school of thought which understood the twenty-second chapter of the Book of Genesis entirely in terms of vicarious atonement. It is also a fact that there were Rabbis who believed that the serpent (of Genesis, chap. 3) infected Eve with some kind of "filth" which was transmitted from generation to generation—until Israel accepted the Torah at the foot of Mount Sinai.[4] And, furthermore, it is a fact that, while the Church may have been concerned with the formulation of correct belief, it also reckoned with the *nova lex Christi* —just as the Rabbis would never have argued the fine legal points about "the egg laid on a festival-day," if they had not previously taken for granted the *belief* in a God, the *belief* in Revelation, and the *belief* that Scripture contains the Revelation of God.

What is also true, however, is that the interpretation of the Isaac story in terms of vicarious atonement was accepted by some Rabbis and rejected by others. Likewise, the Rabbinic version of the "original sin" story was the opinion of individuals, not of Rabbinic Judaism as a whole. One's eternal salvation did not depend upon his acceptance or rejection of such interpretations. True also is the fact that the Rabbis were more given to discuss and to follow the majority vote on matters like "the egg laid on a festival-day" than on anything remotely resembling the *homoousion-homoiousion* controversy. But what matters in the present context is that, with all the allowance made for differences in emphasis and formulation, Jews and Christians had more in common than they were perhaps willing to admit to themselves.

How much that was only began to become apparent when Judaism and Christianity were both faced by a common opponent: the *weltanschauung* of modernity, the shift from a theocentric to an anthropocentric philosophy, and the substitution of the Religion of Nature for the Religion of Revelation. Both Judaism and Christianity made their peace with modernity along certain fronts, and even ceded some ground along others. Both suffered from the deposition of Theology as the Queen of the Sciences, and both, in the guise of Deism and of "religious" Humanism, had their advocates of total surrender. (In due course, both were to discover that there was a certain irreducible something which could not be rationalized, philosophized, or psychoanalyzed out of existence without thereby destroying the whole. That discovery is a relatively recent achievement. It goes by such names as Neo-Orthodoxy and Religious Existentialism. It is associated, in Christianity, with such names as Søren Kierkegaard, Karl Barth, and Reinhold Niebuhr, and, in Judaism, with Martin Buber, Franz Rosenzweig, and Abraham J. Heschel.)

We must not underestimate the wholesome aspect of this confrontation with secularism, which gained momentum in the eighteenth and nineteenth centuries. For one thing, Jews owe their emancipation to it—something which the Christian Middle Ages would never have considered granting them. For another, it was only now, with the sword of the temporal power withdrawn from the support of the Church, that the true "dialogue" between Judaism and Christianity (as opposed to polemics and apologetics, and forced disputations) could begin. For "dialogue," as we have defined it earlier, is the talk among equals, born of mutual respect and, with full awareness of where the division lies, dedicated to the furtherance of a shared concern.

Political democracy and the secular state guaranteed the equality. The application of scientific methods to the study of the various religious traditions made for the requisite mutual respect. Christian scholars like Hermann L. Strack, R. Travers Herford, and George Foot Moore undertook the study of Rabbinic literature, and published the results of their investigations, not—as some Christian scholars had done before—in order to justify the New Testament condemnation of the Pharisees, or to have a dark foil against which the truth of Christianity would shine all the brighter, but in order to present the Rabbinic religion in its own right and within its own historical setting. The works produced by these Christian scholars are still invaluable aids for Jews in their quest for an understanding of their own religious heritage. Similarly, Jewish scholars like Montefiore, Klausner, Baeck, and Daube, aware of Christianity's origins within Judaism, were attracted to that particular chapter in the history of Jewish thought, and oblivious of traditional prejudices, addressed themselves to an objective evaluation of early Christian sources. Their work has been of value to Christian scholars as well.

The scientific study of religious sources put an end to the old "battle of the proof-texts." Here and there, a zealous Christian of Fundamentalist inclinations will still try to engage a Jew in a discussion of Isaiah 7:14 or of Isaiah 53, even as some Christian missionary societies still try to place in the hands of Jews "Old Testament Prophecy Editions" of the New Testament. But, by and large, where the "battle of the proof-texts" is still being fought at all it is within the ranks of Christianity itself, not between Church and Synagogue. Liberal Christians themselves, led by their own professional Bible scholars, have long since taken over the Synagogue's rejection of the christological interpretation of Hebrew Bible verses—a fact made obvious to all in the more recent Protestant translations of the Bible.

The area of shared concern, the third prerequisite of true "dialogue" according to our definition, is clear to every thinking Jew and Christian. When the choice before twentieth-century man is one between a world with God or a world without God, both Judaism and Christianity know where to cast their votes. And in finding ways and means of bringing the knowledge of God to the people, a fruitful discussion between the two faiths is absolutely in order. Where does God fit into an age of technology and scientific advance? How does the personal God of both the Jewish and the Christian traditions relate to a world-view dominated by the physical sciences? And what about the contemporary stage in the dialectics of Reason and Revelation? All these are questions which Christians and Jews need not ponder in isolation from one another.

Again, it is a truism that we are living in an era of unprecedented social change. But what kind of change is it going to be? Does man have any control over it, or does it operate

The Christian-Jewish Dialogue

according to the iron-clad laws of an inherent materialism? And if man does have control, who or what controls man? Are the diabolical forces unleashed within our own lifetime evidence of man's utter helplessness in shaping his own life, or is there perhaps a way in which man can keep his "evil inclination" in check and work for the establishment of a just and righteous society? Both Judaism and Christianity used to have something to say about this subject in ages past. Are they saying anything today? If so, what are they saying, and how are they saying it? And what practical steps are they taking to translate their talk into action? The problems have become far too complex, the implications far too frightening, for the Church and the Synagogue not to pool their resources in the attempted solutions.

In the past, Synagogue and Church have often differed in their emphases in the formulation of intrinsically related concepts and beliefs. At the risk of making a not altogether warranted generalization, we could say, for example, that the Church used to be more preoccupied than was the Synagogue with the sinful nature of man, while the Synagogue may have been more concerned than was the Church with the psychology (as distinct from the theology) of repentance. Similarly, asceticism has always been more pronounced in Christianity than in Judaism, while Judaism had its own regimen of self-discipline (such as dietary laws, Sabbath rest, etc.) which was often misunderstood and ridiculed by the Church. Has not the time come for us to exchange views on these and other topics, and to do so with a willingness to learn and to understand, rather than to score points in a debate? Is it not just possible that perchance one's own inherited concepts would profit by some widening of horizons? Need the Jew remain in ignorance of the Christian saint's *unio mystica* with his God, or the Christian oblivious of the *amor Dei intellectualis* of the devoted Talmud student? Such are the lines along which we can visualize the "dialogue."

So far we have been concerned with the kind of dialogue

made possible by a "peaceful coexistence" of Judaism and Christianity. But what is the nature of such a coexistence? Have the Middle Ages really been left behind? The "battle of the proof-texts" may be over; but does that mean that the Christian is no longer under an obligation to win Jewish souls for Christ? Must he give up his faith in the ultimate transformation of the "Israel after the flesh" into a believing component of the "Israel of God"? And what of the Jew's view of Christianity? Is Christianity, for the Jew, still only a means for the native pagan to become one of the "righteous men among the nations," living under the "Seven Laws of the Sons of Noah," and preparing the way for the "true" Messiah?

Such questions invariably lurk in the background. It is not considered "polite" to voice them in public. In America, it might spoil the good neighborly relations between Christians and Jews. In Europe, the Christians are—with, alas, only too good reason—embarrassed by what Christian Europe has done to the Jew. How could they preach "Christ crucified" to the pitiful heap of surviving relatives of six million martyred Jews?! How could they bring the "gospel of love" in the name of him who once said, "by their fruits shall ye know them"?! No, it is neither polite nor politic for the Christian, at this time, to be overtly active in the "mission to the Jews." At *this* time. But ultimately? Ultimately, with or without a literal "second coming of Christ," the Jews will be converted. *Teste David cum Sibylla!*

And does not the Jew, too, live in the expectation of an ultimate conversion of the Gentiles to the faith of Israel? The passage from Maimonides, which we have already repeatedly quoted, goes on to say: "But when the true Messiah comes, the nations (missionized by Christianity and Islam) will immediately repent and realize that (together with the laws of the Torah taught to them by Christianity and Islam) their fathers have caused them to inherit falsehood, and their prophets have led them astray." There is no unanimity in Judaism regarding the ultimate conversion of the Gentiles for which the Synagogue daily prays ("Let all the inhabitants of the world perceive and know that unto Thee every knee must bend and every tongue give homage. Before Thee, O Lord our God, let them bow down and worship; and unto Thy glorious Name let them give honor."). Does this "conversion" imply conversion to Israel's cult as well as to Israel's God, or merely, without any specifications as to the particular mode of worship, to Israel's God? There is not even any unanimity among the teachers of the Synagogue as to the binding character, for the *Jew*, of the totality of Torah legislation in the "days of the Messiah." But there can be no doubt that, theologically speaking, Judaism does expect a redeemed mankind to be strict monotheists—in the *Jewish* sense.

Christians often express amazement that the Jews, the people of Deutero-Isaiah, "chosen" to be "a light unto the nations," do not engage in active missionary work. There are Jews, moreover, who emphatically deny that Judaism is a proselytizing faith. Both are wrong. There was a time when Hellenistic Judaism conducted a very active missionary campaign, and when, according to Jesus himself, even the Palestinian Pharisees crossed land and sea to make converts. This active campaign ceased when the Jewish missionary effort became a capital offense soon after Rome had turned Christian. But that is not the whole reason. Jews have always lacked one of the primary motivations of the Christian missionary effort. There is no Jewish counterpart to *salus extra ecclesiam non est*. On the contrary, the very doctrine about the "righteous men among the nations" who will be saved made it unnecessary, from the point of view of the Synagogue, to convert them to Judaism. It was, however, the duty of the Jew to encourage the universal acceptance of the "Seven Laws of the Sons of Noah." The ultimate conversion of the world was understood as one of the "messianic" events. Meanwhile, Israel's "mission" was conceived as a passive one. It is, however, not inconceivable that in the modern world, with its separation of Church and State, there may be a resurgence of Jewish missionary efforts.

In either case, whether the Jew actively engages in missionary work or whether he is merely hoping for the "ultimate" conversion of the world, we have to reckon with the fact that, behind the present "peaceful coexistence" between Synagogue and Church, there is the expectation on the part of each of them to outlive (and to absorb) the other. A recognition of this fact could call into question, not the continuation of "peaceful coexistence" as such, but the possibility of true dialogue. That is why, both from the Christian and from the Jewish side, voices have been raised on behalf of a complete re-evaluation of the roles of Synagogue and Church.

The Rev. Dr. James Parkes, for example, an Anglican clergyman, calls for the recognition of the equal validity of both the Covenant of Sinai and the Covenant of Calvary. In the former, God called to His service a "holy community." In the latter, He addressed Himself to the "saved individual" among the nations. The two covenants in the divine scheme of things are mutually complementary, not mutually exclusive. The "new covenant" does *not* revoke the "old." Christians and Jews, therefore, must not interfere with the divine plan, and must not try to convert each other.

A similar view had already been expressed by the most profound Jewish thinker of the twentieth century, Franz Rosenzweig (1886–1929). Rosenzweig conceded more than any Jew, while remaining a Jew, had conceded before him. He admitted the truth of John 14:6, that "no man comes to the Father" except through Jesus. To which admission, however, Rosenzweig immediately added that the Jew does not have to *come* to the Father. He has been *with* the Father ever since Sinai. The Church, in other words, is the missionary arm of the Synagogue, trying to bring the Gentiles to the destination which Israel had reached when God made the Sinaitic Covenant. This is borne out by the self-definitions of Christians and of Jews. The Christian, according to his own teachings, is born a pagan. He *becomes* a Christian. The Jew, on the other hand, according to his own teachings, is *born* a Jew, born into the

The Christian-Jewish Dialogue

Covenant which was made "with him that standeth here with us this day before the Lord, our God, and also with him that is not here with us this day" (Deuteronomy 29:14). In Rosenzweig's scheme, too, there is no room for the attempts of the one to convert the other.

Whatever may have to be said from the Christian side about the continued validity of "Sinai," there can be no doubt that there is nothing in Judaism to preclude the view that God has made covenants with others, in addition to His Covenant with Israel. The very concept of the "Covenant with the Sons of Noah" shows that Judaism did not limit God's covenanting to the Jews. Yet by the same token Rosenzweig, in affirming the truth of John 14:6, may have taken too narrow a view. It gives Christianity a monopoly which ill accords with the role Islam has played in bringing pagans "to the Father," and which other religions may have played, or may yet be destined to play. But, then, Rosenzweig was writing within a Christian environment, even as the concern of the present chapter is with the Christian-Jewish dialogue, and not with religion in general.

If Judaism and Christianity can, in this sense, grant the validity of each other's Covenants, there need be no reservations about their "peaceful coexistence." Indeed, they could even engage in helpful dialogue. They have, after all, for some two thousand years, uttered the same prayer: "Thy kingdom come!" And when that "kingdom" comes, when the Jew sees the fulfillment of the prophecy, "The Lord shall be king over all the earth; in that day the Lord shall be one, and His name one" (Zechariah 14:9), the Christian, too, will see the fulfillment of prophecy: "Then comes the end, when he delivers the kingdom to God the Father . . . The Son himself will also be subjected to Him who put all things under him, that God may be everything to every one" (I Corinthians 15:24, 28).

So much for the "end." But what of the interim period? Is missionary endeavor altogether ruled out? It seems to us that Parkes and Rosenzweig have both been somewhat unrealistic. We admit that the wholehearted Jew and the wholehearted

Christian have no need to convert each other to their respective faiths; they would, indeed, be untrue to their divine calling were they to do so. But our world is not populated by wholehearted Jews and Christians. It is inhabited by the religiously uprooted, the spiritually destitute. Not every offspring of Jewish parents actualizes his Jewish potential. Not every pagan born into a Christian household does, in fact, become a Christian. The world is full of only nominal Christians and nominal Jews. The Synagogue has a primary obligation to win over the nominal Jew to a full acceptance of the "yoke of the kingdom of Heaven" and the "yoke of the commandments," just as the Church has a primary obligation to lead the nominal Christian to Jesus, and through Jesus, to the Father. But addressing himself to the mass of agnostics, atheists, and religiously uprooted, one cannot always discriminate and distinguish between those of Jewish and those of Gentile origin. Church and Synagogue, in entering the marketplace of ideas, must offer and describe their wares to all comers, must answer the queries of all questioners. And it may well happen that, here and there, the Jewish answer will appeal to the nominal Christian, just as the Christian answer may appeal to the nominal Jew. Of course, Jews consider a wide occurrence of the latter alternative as highly unlikely. Why should the twentieth century be more propitious for the Christian mission to the Jew than the last nineteen centuries have been? But theoretically the possibility of a limited kind of "two-way traffic" must be granted. It must not be interfered with by calling in the arm of the secular state, whether it be the State of Israel in relation to the Christian missions to the Jews, or the states of Christendom in relation to a possible resurgence of Jewish missionary efforts.

But this possibility must never be more than a peripheral concern. It must be granted and openly faced in order to make a true and honest "dialogue" possible. It cannot, however, be the sole content of that "dialogue" itself. That can only be concerned with the tasks and the challenges which confront us in common. And having once begun to "talk with" (rather than to shout at) each other, let us, by all means, keep the conversation going.

Now Trypho paused somewhat, and then said: ... I have been extraordinarily charmed with our intercourse, and I think that these are of like opinion with myself. For we have found more than we expected, or than it was even possible for us to expect. And if we could do this more frequently, we should receive more benefit. ... As regards myself, I replied, I could wish ... that such a discussion should take place every day....

After which they departed, finally praying for my deliverance from the dangers of the sea, and from all ill.

And I prayed also for them.[5]

NOTES

1. Justin Martyr, *Dialogue with Trypho*, ch. XLVII.
2. Cf. A. Marmorstein, *Studies in Jewish Theology* (London, 1950), pp. 179ff.
3. Martin Buber, *Two Types of Faith* (London, 1951), p. 12.
4. B. *Yebamoth* 103b.
5. Justin Martyr, *op. cit.*, ch. CXLII (A. Lukyn Williams' ed).

CHAPTER 13

Prayer in an Unredeemed World

It was at an adult conference of one of the Protestant denominations, held on the campus of an Ohio college. Typical of the era of religious pluralism and mutual understanding was the privilege afforded this writer of serving on the faculty, of sharing his knowledge of, and his approach to, the "Old Testament" with the believers in the New. The biblical book chosen for daily study was Psalms. A question was asked, and an answer was attempted. And the topic of conversation brought us face to face with an aspect of the Christian-Jewish "dialogue."

But first, a few preliminary remarks on the Book of Psalms. While the Christian Church has appropriated the "Old Testament" as a whole, there would hardly seem to be a more "Christian" book in the whole of the Hebrew canon than Psalms—that is, outside of famous chapters like Isaiah 53 and individual verses in other biblical books which have a time-

---

Reprinted from *Commentary* (April 1957), pp. 371-373 (under the title of "A Conference on the Psalms"). Copyright © 1957 by the American Jewish Committee. The author is grateful for permission to reprint this material.

Prayer in an Unredeemed World

honored christological interpretation. It is the Book of Psalms, as a whole, that has won the heart of the Christian, and which is familiar to him from its liturgical use in church services. And it is not only the quaint page headings of the King James Version that make it so essentially a "Christian" book. It is the sentiments themselves, expressed in the Book of Psalms, the pronounced element of "personal religion" which is so often said to be missing in so much else of the "Old Testament." Add to this the fact that the Book of Psalms is the one and only "Old Testament" book that is frequently bound together with pocket editions of the New Testament, and one is no longer taken aback by the amazement so often expressed by pious and sincere Christians when they hear for the first time that Psalms belong to the "Old" Covenant.

And yet even the unprejudiced reader cannot fail to notice, once he engages in a systematic study of Psalms, that there are some very "un-Christian" sentiments expressed in them—sentiments which simply ask for the old stereotypes to be brought out into the open again: the God of Vengeance of the "Old Testament," and the God of Love of the New! The Psalmist is very conscious of his "enemies." He prays for their destruction. In his suffering, he cries out unto the God of Vengeance. There is no "turning of the other cheek" here, no loving of one's enemies. Very clearly, the Psalmist lived by an ethic quite different from the one we read about in the Sermon on the Mount.

And so the question came up. It simply had to be asked. But it was asked without any malice aforethought. It was presented as a sincere request for enlightenment. How can we reconcile the Psalmist's imprecations against his adversaries with what, in our Christian environment, we have been taught to regard as true religious sentiments?

The answer fell into three parts, which might be labeled liturgical, homiletical, and "existential." As far as the liturgical use of Psalms is concerned, we can just omit (in so far as we are not Fundamentalists) whatever verses we find offensive. In prayer we have to be honest. We cannot be expected to mouth phrases, hallowed by ancient usage though they be, which not only do not express what is in our hearts, but give currency to notions opposed to our deepest convictions.

When, for example, Psalm 145 is recited in the American Reform Jewish service, verse 20 is simply omitted. It reads: "The Lord preserveth all them that love Him; but all the wicked will He destroy." (No doubt this omission survives as a legacy from calmer and more optimistic days, when no urgent need was felt to see the wicked destroyed. Alas, in the process, we also had to forgo the comfort of reminding ourselves that "the Lord preserveth all them that love Him.")

Similarly, when modern Jews try to relive liturgically the experience of the Babylonian Exile by meditating on Psalm 137 ("By the rivers of Babylon"), they are liable, at this late stage of the game, to stop with verse 6, without giving vent to their feelings by calling down terrible curses on the "children of Edom" and on the "daughter of Babylon."

Moreover, while our pious ancestors in Rabbinic days may not have shared our cavalier disregard of uncomfortable verses, they tried at least to help themselves by means of "interpretation." Famous is the story, recorded in the Talmud, of Rabbi Meir, who was vexed by the conduct of wicked neighbors and who prayed to God for their destruction. His wife bade him desist, and she quoted by way of proof, of all things, verse 35 of Psalm 104 ("Let the sinners be consumed out of the earth, and let the wicked be no more"). But by changing the vocalization of a single Hebrew word—*chattaim* to *chataim*—she made the verse to mean: "Let sins [sic] be consumed out of the earth, and then the wicked will be no more [because they will have repented]!"

But this first part of our answer is, after all, still on a rather superficial level. It deals with our own use of the Psalms in prayer, with the question of how far a liturgical text can be meaningfully employed some two thousand years after it was written. It leaves unanswered the problem of why the "wicked"

Prayer in an Unredeemed World

should have been dragged into the Psalms in the first place.

In trying to answer this, we are not going to take a short cut which the superficial use of the Higher Criticism might possibly suggest to us. We are not going to dub the verses which offend our susceptibilities as "later interpolations." Rather would we face up to the question of why the original authors "marred" their compositions by the introduction of such hostile sentiments. We can do this best by turning the whole argument around, by saying that it would be impossible to understand the composition of the Psalms *without* the presence of the verses that "mar" them.

For the Psalms—at any rate, the Psalms under discussion in this context—were not written in the quiet of the study. They arose out of actual life situations, out of the kind of crises in which men turn to God. There was neither the leisure nor the inclination to dream up Utopia or Pollyanna. The man who can say, "God's in His heaven, all's right with the world," is in no need of praying for the destruction of the wicked; nor, on the other hand, is he liable to write Psalms which can be meaningful as "personal religion" to a sufferer removed from him in both time and space. And perhaps it is just this which makes the Psalms so meaningful: that there is nothing artificial about them, that we can feel a kinship with those men of flesh and blood and emotions who had experiences not too dissimilar from our own.

The world is not perfect as long as there is evil in it, as long as the wicked are around to harass the godly. But the plan of God is to *make* the world perfect. And this, of necessity, implies the elimination of evil. Yet the evil in this world is not the working out of an abstract principle. Evil is that which evil *men* do. How well, then, can we understand the thirty-fifth verse of Psalm 104 from this point of view, the verse that voices the prayer that "the sinners be consumed out of the earth"! For thirty-four exhilarating verses the poet has been singing the praises of nature and of nature's God. But, after all, he does not live in the "New Jerusalem," but in this not yet perfect world of ours. And so he completes his picture of the glories of nature by giving expression both to his awareness of the experience of wickedness and to his fervent hope that the world will be made perfect by its speedy removal.

Lest it be said that such a hope is too "Jewish," and not "Christian" enough, we are reminded by as authentic a Christian as the late Dean A. P. Stanley that "the duty of keeping alive in the human heart the sense of burning indignation against moral evil—against selfishness, against injustice, against untruth, in ourselves as well as in others—that is as much part of the Christian as of the Jewish dispensation."

This brings us to the third and final part of our answer. In a whole week spent in the studious, devotional, and congenial atmosphere of the adult conference, this writer heard a great deal about Jesus and his love. And many a time he heard him referred to as the Prince of Peace. But he was also given a hymnal (used at the daily vesper services) in which this very Prince of Peace is invoked as "the royal Master" who "leads against the foe." And the followers of this Prince of Peace, laying claim to the title of "Soldiers of the Cross," are bidden to arise, and to gird themselves with their armor bright; for "mighty are your enemies, hard the battle ye must fight."

This, of course, was nothing new. It has long been recognized that the New Testament has its blood-curdling Apocalypse as well as its pacifist Sermon on the Mount; and the picture of the "gentle Jesus, meek and mild," may do less than full justice to the hero of the Gospels. But what the hymns referred to above express so forcefully, even if the purely metaphorical use of the expressions be granted, is the idea of the Church Militant.

The Church Militant! The Church, when all is said and done, is still very much a fighting Church. It sees its challenge and its task in territories still unconquered (again, if you prefer, in a purely metaphorical sense). The Kingdom of God has its "foes" whom the "Soldiers of the Cross" have yet to conquer.

As an outsider who tried to be objective, this writer was not offended by those notions. But he found the terminology certainly most suggestive. Were he engaged in religious polemics, he might perhaps suggest that the Church first follow the advice of Jesus by removing the "log" from its own hymnals before taking offense at the "speck" in the Hebrew Psalter (where the subjugation of the "enemies" is, after all, left in the hands of God Himself). But polemics are not our object here. We seek mutual understanding and enlightenment. And we understand from the hymnology of the Church that the present-day Christian shares with the "Old Testament" Hebrew an awareness of the presence of evil in this world. On this basis we can understand one another, whether the image in which we try to enclose our hopes for the ultimate Redemption be "the Coming of the Messiah," "the Messianic Age," "the Second Coming," or "the Kingdom." Whenever the Jew and the Christian pray: "Thy Kingdom come!" (and the "Lord's Prayer" does share this request with the *Kaddish*), both Jew and Christian give expression to the "existential" awareness that the world in which they live is as yet unredeemed.

In the light of this awareness, the Jew can understand why the Christian calls upon the Incarnate Word to "gird on his mighty sword." The Jew may even be moved to a sympathetic appreciation of the tragic tension involved in Christianity, which, on the one hand, believes that the Redeemer was born 1969 years ago, and which, on the other, *still* has to pray, as did the Apostle Paul (I Corinthians 16:22) in the Aramaic dialect of early Jewish prayer: "*Marana tha!*—Our Lord, come!"

But, by the same token, the Christian need not be repelled, and most certainly need not revert to the Gnostic distinction between the "God of Love" and the "Jewish God" (a distinction which the very Fathers of the Church have been at great pains to refute), when he hears the Psalmist praying:

> O Lord, how manifold are Thy works!
> In wisdom hast Thou made them all;
> the earth is full of Thy creatures. . . .
> I will sing to the Lord as long as I live;
> I will sing praise to my God while I have being.

Heirs of the Pharisees

> May my meditation be pleasing to Him,
> for I rejoice in the Lord.
> Let sinners be consumed from the earth;
> and let the wicked be no more!
> Bless the Lord, O my soul!
> Hallelujah.
>
> (Psalm 104:24, 33–35.)

CHAPTER 14

Criteria for Reform Jewish Observance

Tradition speaks about the "Six Hundred and Thirteen Commandments" of the Torah. But Rabbi Simlai, who first mentioned that number of commandments,[1] did not proceed to enumerate them. Thus it came about that later scholars differed among themselves as to how one could arrive at that number. For if one were to count only the commandments of the Written Torah, the figure would be less than 613. If, however, the commandments of the Oral Torah were to be added to the biblical ones, then the number would far exceed 613. A whole branch of medieval Rabbinic literature is, therefore, devoted to the task of "enumerating the commandments." Various authors argued on behalf of their own counts. However, as time went on, the enumeration of Maimonides, in his *Sepher Hamitzvoth* ("The Book of the Commandments"), achieved the greatest popularity; and it is generally the enumeration of

---

Based on the author's German article, "Beweggründe einer religiös-liberalen Gesetzeserfüllung," which appeared in *Tradition und Erneuerung* (Berne, Switzerland), No. 24 (November 1967), pp. 409–417. Copyright © 1967 by the Swiss Vereinigung für religiös-liberales Judentum. The author is grateful for permission to republish this material in translation.

Maimonides to which reference is made when, in modern writings, there is talk of the "Six Hundred and Thirteen Commandments."

Talk there is indeed of the "Six Hundred and Thirteen Commandments," even though no modern Jew—the most pious included—is observing all of the "Six Hundred and Thirteen Commandments." No Jew today *could* observe them all, even if he so desired. A large number of the "Six Hundred and Thirteen Commandments" has application to the Jerusalem Temple and to the sacrificial cult. Others have reference to the levitical purity of priests and Levites, a subject which, in turn, is again related to the Jerusalem Temple cult. Still others apply only to a Jewish king. In other words, the "Six Hundred and Thirteen Commandments" (whatever they might be, and whatever enumeration of them we might choose to follow) were never meant to be observed by each and every Jew. Nevertheless, the concept of the "Six Hundred and Thirteen Commandments" has become a slogan in modern Jewish life. It is often asserted that Orthodox Jews observe the "Six Hundred and Thirteen Commandments," and that Reform Jews do not.

That this could not possibly be true of any Orthodox Jew we have already seen. But it is also not true that the Reform Jew rejects the "Six Hundred and Thirteen Commandments" as a whole. If the Reform Jew loves his neighbor, then he is observing one of the "Six Hundred and Thirteen Commandments" (by everybody's method of enumerating them). If he refrains from murder, from adultery, and from theft, he is observing a second, a third, and a fourth of the "Six Hundred and Thirteen Commandments." If he pays his employees in time, if he returns a lost article to its owner, and if he honors his father and his mother, then he is observing a fifth, a sixth, and a seventh. There is no need here to keep count of all of the "Six Hundred and Thirteen Commandments" which the Reform Jew does observe. Suffice it to say that, if the Reform Jew leads a reasonably moral and ethical life, his style of life will not be bereft of a goodly number of the "Six Hundred and Thirteen Com-

Criteria for Reform Jewish Observance

mandments." For the traditional count of the "Six Hundred and Thirteen Commandments" does not confine itself to the so-called ritual and ceremonial observances. The love of one's neighbor is no less a part of the "Six Hundred and Thirteen Commandments" than is the practice not to mix meat and milk dishes. Thus neither the Orthodox nor the Reform Jew can be described as either totally observing or totally rejecting the "Six Hundred and Thirteen Commandments." Both are *partial* observers. And it should be added that the ethical commandments are not a monopoly of the Reform Jew. Nor can it be said that even the most radical Reform Jew has completely divested himself of *all* the so-called ceremonial observances.

It is, however, true that, in matters of ritual and ceremonial observance, the Reform Jew maintains less of the traditional heritage than does the Orthodox Jew. In the nineteenth century, Reform Judaism gave up many traditional Jewish observances—because, so it was said then, they were "too Oriental," or because they no longer "spoke to modern man." There was also an attempt to side with the "Prophets" against the "Priests," to regard the Moral Law alone as "divine," and to view the "ceremonial law" as something of purely human origin, which could either be modified or totally abolished.

This was indeed a break with Jewish Tradition—a tradition which knew only of *mitzvoth* (divine commandments), without distinguishing between moral and ritual commandments to the detriment of the latter. "Ritual" and "ceremony" are not authentic Jewish concepts. Besides, more recent Bible scholarship no longer takes it for granted that the Prophets invariably and inevitably took an antagonistic position toward the cult. It is, therefore, rather easy to criticize much of the position of nineteenth-century Reform Judaism from the perspective of the twentieth century.

But, behind the position adopted in the last century, there was nevertheless an important insight to which the twentieth century must not turn a blind eye. In its most radical form, this insight was expressed by Samuel Holdheim (1806-1860). Already the ancient Rabbis had made a distinction between the *mitzvoth* which are obligatory only in the Land of Israel, and those which retain their validity also beyond the borders of the Land of Israel.[2] The Jew of the Diaspora is obligated to fulfill the latter only. Holdheim went one step further. The Torah, he argued, has a twofold content. It contains a strictly religious element, which is eternally valid. But it also contains the legal constitution of the ancient Israelite theocracy; and that constitution is time-conditioned. Since God Himself has abolished the theocracy, by letting Temple and State be destroyed in the year 70 C.E., the constitution of that theocracy has likewise been abolished.[3]

Holdheim drew radical conclusions from this. For example, he asserted that, while the weekly day of rest was an eternally binding religious commandment, the particular day of the week on which it is to be observed has nothing to do with religion, but only with the constitution of the state. In ancient Israel, it happened to be Saturday; but in Prussia it was Sunday. Altogether, Holdheim had the tendency to make life easy for himself by relegating all the commandments he did not particularly care for to the constitution of the ancient Israelite theocracy—depriving them thereby of their binding character.

Of course, Holdheim went too far. Nevertheless, in his view of the Torah and its twofold content, Holdheim was absolutely right. We need not follow him in his critique of Rabbinic Judaism, which he criticized because, in spite of the destruction of the Jewish State, the Rabbis endeavored to maintain its constitution. After all, medieval Judaism could use its own legal constitution very well. Still, it remains true that the Jew who, in the period of the Emancipation, voluntarily accepted his Judaism did so in terms of a commitment to *religion*, and not to the legal constitution of an ancient state. The commandments which he observed were indeed—to use Franz Rosenzweig's terminology—"commandments," and not "legislation."

Criteria for Reform Jewish Observance

Behind the "commandment" there is only God, and not the constitution of a state.

In the final analysis, whether the individual Jew observes many or few "commandments" depends on the seriousness with which he tries to hear the Word of God in the Tradition, and on how many of the old "laws" address him personally as "commandments." This, it should be noted, applies no less to the Western type of Orthodoxy than it does to Reform Judaism. On the one hand, Orthodox Judaism in Western Europe and America has tacitly managed to ignore quite a few paragraphs of the *Shulchan Arukh* (the sixteenth-century code of Jewish practice which, together with its commentaries, is regarded as authoritative by Orthodox Judaism). On the other hand, a man like Franz Rosenzweig was able to accept as "commandments" addressed to him a maximum number of traditional observances —and that on the basis of a liberal approach.

But Reform Judaism did commit two serious errors in the nineteenth century. In the first place, the non-observance of the *mitzvoth* was made to look like one of the demands of Reform Judaism. For example, one of the "planks" of the famous Pittsburgh Platform of 1885 stated, with regard to the Mosaic legislation, that "we accept as binding only its moral laws, and maintain only such ceremonies as elevate and sanctify our lives, but reject all such as are not adapted to the views and habits of modern civilization."[4] This, of course, was quite in Holdheim's spirit. Only the moral commandments were binding! The individual was hardly given an opportunity of hearing —as Franz Rosenzweig heard—"commandments" also among the "ritual" laws.

In such a categorical rejection of a large body of *mitzvoth* there was no less dogmatism than there is in an uncritical acceptance of the totality of the *Shulchan Arukh*. Why should the American Reform rabbis of the nineteenth century have been more entitled to ordain the non-observance of the *mitzvoth* than Orthodoxy was to prescribe the permanent validity of a sixteenth-century code of laws? If Reform Judaism is truly meant to be liberal, then it must be left to the individual to decide which of the commandments he accepts as binding for himself. Indeed, we must even reckon with the possibility of his accepting an ancient piece of legislation as "commandment"—even though it might not be "adapted to the views and habits of modern civilization."

However, in order to be able to make his individual choice, the Reform Jew must have at his disposal a knowledge of the material from which this choice is to be made, a knowledge of the *mitzvoth* handed down by Tradition. This, in turn, necessitates an intensive study of that Tradition. In theory, a Reform Jewish education would have to be much more intensive than an Orthodox one. Only the educated Jew, who is well acquainted with the Tradition, can come to terms with it and can make his own selection from the plethora of traditional observances. Yet, in this respect, a second error was committed in the last century. Once it had been agreed that *only* the moral commandments were binding, it was no longer felt to be necessary to burden religious instruction with the study of the "ritual" *mitzvoth*. Jewish education was reduced to talk about ethical monotheism and to a few chapters of biblical history. While there was a constant stress on the Reform Jew's freedom of choice, he was not made acquainted with the very material from which that choice was to have been made.

The student of Jewish history can understand the reasons which led to this state of affairs. He can, on occasion, even find excuses. Nevertheless, the problems of the twentieth century are of an altogether different kind. We no longer believe that the European Jew becomes a better European, and the American Jew a better American, by shedding his Jewish particularism. Moreover, in view of what we know today about psychology, we have also become somewhat more circumspect in our evalu-

Criteria for Reform Jewish Observance

ation of "ritual" and of the "non-rational." If it was the task of Judaism in the nineteenth century to "adapt" itself to the "views and habits of modern civilization," we, today, are somewhat more critical of that "modern civilization." We rather regard it as the need of the hour to make the nominal Jew into a real Jew. If the nineteenth century felt it to be necessary to tell the Jew what he no longer had to observe, the twentieth century faces the task of leading the Jew back to the sources of Judaism.

Those sources—Bible and Talmud, Midrash and Philosophy, Kabbalah and Codes, poetry and the classics of the scientific study of Judaism—are the property of all Jews. In the obligation to study those sources and to get to know them, there is no difference between the Orthodox and the Liberals, the Conservatives and the Reformers. This is a *mitzvah* which even the most radical of the Reformers cannot afford to ignore—without calling into question his good faith and the seriousness of his convictions. That is why the Tradition said that "the study of the Torah is equal to all the other commandments."[5]

Only if the Reform Jew acts out of a full knowledge can there be talk of Reform Judaism at all. An ignoramus is only—an ignoramus; and, if he acts out of his ignorance, he still remains an ignoramus, and does not automatically become a Reform Jew. Of course, it is quite possible, and even likely, that, under certain circumstances, the Reform orientation *might* lead to the non-observance of a number of traditional laws. It is possible; but it is not inevitable. As we have noted before, Franz Rosenzweig, on the basis of a non-Orthodox theology, was able to make his own a maximum number of traditional observances. But even if the Reform orientation should lead, in a number of cases, to the non-observance of *mitzvoth*, it would be a non-observance based on careful evaluation—and not on mere ignorance. A true Reform Judaism, therefore, and one worthy of that name, would have to cultivate the study of the totality of the Tradition—together with a set of criteria which the individual Reform Jew can apply to that Tradition, in order to make his own selections from it.

What, then, are those criteria? We would suggest the following four.

(1) *What, in a given case, has been the main direction of the millennial Tradition?* In the process of examining the traditional material, one must not remain satisfied with first impressions. Rather should one pursue the meaning of a given observance in the Jewish past. Moreover, since, within a span of four thousand years, the meaning was not always uniformly understood and interpreted, it becomes particularly important to discover the main thrust within the Tradition.

For example, a modern Jew might well be under the impression that the prohibition of work on the Sabbath was simply directed against strenuous physical labor. The weekly day of rest in Judaism, therefore, would be understood in terms of the weekly day of rest, Sunday, in modern Christian and secular society. However, a little more thorough study of Jewish sources will soon lead to the recognition that far more is involved here than the mere abstention from exhausting physical labor. The Jewish Sabbath is the day on which man—who creates and works throughout the week—shows himself to be but a *creature*. God alone is recognized as the Creator. And this recognition finds its expression in the fact that, on the Sabbath, the Jew refrains from acting as a "creator" and from interfering "creatively" in the normal course of nature. Such interference need not even be thought of in terms of physical exertion. The intent of man to impose his will on nature suffices to break the spell of the Sabbath mood.

But if it is the purpose of the Sabbath to express the thought that God, and not man, is the real Creator, then it follows that the abstention from work, commanded in the Torah, is aiming at something over and above man's relaxation and physical recuperation. Consequently, it is not sufficient to argue, as some modern Jews might be tempted to do: "Cooking and baking were hard work in biblical antiquity. But we do not have to exert ourselves to do so. That's why it should be allowed for us on the Sabbath!" An argument of this kind is far too superficial an interpretation of both the biblical and the Rabbinic Sabbath regulations.

Needless to say, the Sabbath law (with all of its commandments and prohibitions) contains and implies far more than we have been able to hint at in connection with the prohibition of work. We merely wanted to furnish an illustration of what we mean by demanding, as *one* of the criteria for a modern Jewish observance, that, in any given case, an investigation be made into the main direction of the millennial Tradition.

(2) The second criterion could be formulated as follows: *In what manner can I best realize the traditional teaching in my life and in the situation in which I find myself?*

If the first criterion was a purely scientific and objective one, then this second criterion already contains a conscious application of the Reform principle. Orthodox Judaism, for example, is, basically and objectively, quite correct in deducing the prohibition of the use of cars and of electricity on the Sabbath from the biblical prohibition of work—with "work" defined according to Rabbinic categories. Tradition may indeed be so construed.

But the Reform Jew must also ask himself: "Do I observe the Sabbath better if, on account of distances involved, I refrain from going to the synagogue on the Sabbath or from visiting friends and the sick? Or is it not just the use of my car which helps me in my observance of the Sabbath, in my particular situation? Does the true observance of the Sabbath compel me to keep my home cold and dark? Or is it not just the use of electricity which helps me to make the Sabbath the 'day of light and joy' it was meant to be?"

In other words, the Reform Jew is far more concerned with the Sabbath itself than he is with the letter of the Sabbath legislation, which testifies to the reality of the Sabbath as experienced by *past* generations. The Reform Jew wants to observe the Sabbath in the "here and now." That is why factors come into play with which the legalists of earlier generations did not have to reckon.

(3) A third criterion is *the voice of my own conscience.* In this criterion, even more than in the second one, we see the liberalism of the Reform Jew and the influence of the Emancipation. The Reform Jew is, for better or worse, characterized—in the words of Leo Baeck—by the "piety of the individual," and not, as was the Jew of the Ghetto, by the "piety of the environment." But, as an individual, he is no longer subject to religious compulsion or to the dictates of any ecclesiastical authority. As an individual, he is free to participate, and free not to participate—even if others believe that they have found the key to the proper observance of the Law in the "here and now"; yes, even if I myself believe that I have found a way in which an old tradition can best be applied to my particular situation. Deducing things from the Law, even bearing in mind the needs of my own particular situation, is not yet the whole story. My conscience still has to assent!

Take, for example, the law which states, in connection with Passover, "And there shall be no leaven seen with thee in all thy borders seven days" (Deuteronomy 16:4). There can be no doubt about the main thrust of the Tradition with regard to this law. Anything remotely subject to the suspicion that it may contain "leaven" ingredients must not only not be "seen" in the Jew's home during Passover. It must not even be in his possession. The application of this law, as interpreted by the Rabbis, could thus lead to the wholesale destruction of food in the Jew's house just before Passover—were it not for the fact that the same Rabbis who elaborated the stringencies of that law also evolved a legal fiction by means of which the full force of the law could be evaded. By "selling" the food to a non-Jew—with a minimum down-payment, and with the understanding that the Jew can buy it all back after the festival—the food need not only not be destroyed, but it can remain on the Jew's premises, provided it be suitably locked up.

There is nothing wrong with legal fictions as such. No legal system can function without them. Indeed, one might even appreciate the inventiveness of the ancient Rabbis which helped them keep their legal system within humane dimensions. But it is one thing to appreciate the phenomenon historically. It is quite another to accept it for oneself, particularly if he does not view his relation to God primarily in terms of a legal system. Thus, while it would be quite possible for the Reform Jew to solve his "leaven" problem along the lines indicated by the Rabbis, possible even within his "here and now," it is quite conceivable that the Reform Jew might say: "Yes, it is possible to do it this way; *but my conscience speaks against it.* I shall refrain from eating leaven during Passover. I shall even keep all leaven out of sight in my home. But I feel no need for the legal fiction of 'selling' my leaven. This would add nothing to my Passover observance. On the contrary, I would not feel quite intellectually honest were I to engage in this legal fiction. My conscience rebels against it."

In terms of the criterion we have outlined here, the Reform Jew would be justified in using such an argument. But he would also have to add the following: "My fellow Jew, however, also has the right to listen to the voice of *his* conscience—even if his conscience makes him 'sell' his leaven for Passover. Seeing that we are both Reform Jews, I cannot resent his 'selling' of the leaven—any more than he is able to regard my non-compliance with this practice as a sin."

(4) While the last-named criterion may well carry within itself the seeds of total religious anarchy, the fourth criterion helps to maintain the balance. It is *the feeling of responsibility toward the Covenant Community.*

After all, we are not speaking about religious liberalism in general. Our concern is with Liberal *Judaism;* and Judaism cannot be abstracted from the faith-community within which Judaism is lived—the faith-community with which God made a covenant at Sinai, and which remained loyal to Him throughout the millennia. This Covenant People, Israel, not only has a historical significance; its significance extends to the realm of redemptive history. Everything, therefore, which contributes to the survival and to the unity of the Covenant Community of Israel must be regarded as a religious commandment. Everything, on the other hand, which hurts the Covenant Community must be avoided.

Bearing this perspective in mind, the Reform Jew will observe many a *mitzvah* toward which he might feel no personal obligation—if, in his religion, it were a matter of the individual only, and not also of the community as a whole. Into this category belong the specific seventh day on which the Jewish Sabbath is to be kept, and all the Jewish festivals, which have to be observed exactly according to the Jewish calendar. After all, it is conceivable that one might be able to celebrate the ideal of Freedom on some evening other than the Eve of the Fifteenth of Nisan. But the *seder,* as a *Jewish* celebration of Freedom, can only be celebrated then. In this connection we must also mention the use of Hebrew in the Jewish worship service. Important as it may be to find room for the vernacular in the synagogue, it is nevertheless true that the worshiping Community of Israel knows itself as such particularly during moments of Hebrew prayer.

The above illustrations are not of a purely theoretical kind. They are all based on questions which, at one time or another, have been raised within Reform Judaism, and on problems to which some very radical solutions have been proposed in the last century. The implementation of some of those proposed solutions did, in fact, lead to a state of affairs where the specifically Jewish elements disappeared more and more, and where many a Reform rabbi felt the need to prove to his congregation that,

Criteria for Reform Jewish Observance

in spite of outward similarities, there still remained a difference between Reform Judaism and (Christian) Unitarianism.

The twentieth century has largely turned away from those radical solutions. And it can be seen, not least from the illustrations which we have adduced, that *the feeling of responsibility toward the Covenant Community* has played a not insignificant role in the change of orientation which has taken place in Reform Judaism. Nevertheless, there still remain important components of the unifying Tradition which Reform Judaism has not yet approached with the necessary sense of responsibility. We shall revert to some of them in the next chapter.

It will not often occur that the four criteria, which we have mentioned, will be in complete accord. They are more liable to be in a constant state of tension. Yet it is just that tension which represents the dynamic element of Reform Judaism, and the guarantee for its remaining a living faith and a living practice. One Jew may rate one criterion higher than does another Jew. But they all will have to reckon with all of the criteria all of the time.

The four criteria, in their aggregate, represent the yardstick which the modern Jew must apply to the inherited Tradition. Yet a yardstick is only—a yardstick. It cannot be the total content of one's religious faith and life. The latter requires more than a yardstick. It needs the material itself, the material of the millennial Tradition. And there are no short cuts to the acquisition of that material. Two thousand years ago, when the Tradition was still relatively young, Hillel stated that "the ignorant man cannot be truly religious."[6] If it was true then, it is all the more true today. Only an intensified Jewish education—of child, youth, and adult—in Reform Jewish circles can make the application of the criteria meaningful. But only an application of the criteria can make the Tradition live.

NOTES

1. B. *Makkoth* 23b.
2. *Mishnah Kiddushin* 1:9; *Sifré Re-eh*, par. 59 (ed. Friedmann, p. 87a).
3. See Samuel Holdheim, *Ueber die Autonomie der Rabbinen* (Schwerin, 1843), pp. 15–57.
4. Cf. David Philipson, *The Reform Movement in Judaism* (New York, 1907), p. 491.
5. *Mishnah Pe-ah* 1:1.
6. *Mishnah Aboth* 2:5.

CHAPTER 15

The Holy Community

We have, in our preceding chapter, discussed the problem of Jewish observance almost as though it were a matter of purely individual choice. In doing so, we have been guided by the awareness that, at least in the West, the machinery of Jewish law, as a fully functioning legal system, has broken down with the coming of the Emancipation. Until the eighteenth century, it was still possible to speak of Jewish "self-government." Even where the punitive power of congregational and rabbinical authorities was severely restricted by the state, the rabbinic use of anathema and excommunication still facilitated a high degree of outward conformity. But all that is now a matter of the past —except for the incorporation of certain aspects of traditional Jewish law within the civil law of the State of Israel. In the West today, even Orthodox Jews bring their disputes in civil law before the secular civil courts, tacitly ignoring the whole fourth part of the *Shulchan Arukh* which codifies the Jewish

---

Parts of this chapter were included in a lecture, "Freedom and Authority," delivered at Congregation Emanuel, Chicago, Illinois, and printed, under the title of "Toward a Modern 'Brotherhood,'" in *The Reconstructionist*, XXVI, No. 16 (December 16, 1960), 11–20. Copyright © 1960 by the Reconstructionist Press. The author is grateful for permission to reprint this material.

civil law. In the few cases where Orthodox Jews settle their disputes before a rabbinical court, they do so voluntarily and as a matter of individual choice. Also in matters of so-called "ritual" observance, the old compulsion has disappeared. Infractions of the dietary laws and of Sabbath regulations, which, in former times, would have called into question the good standing of the "transgressors," no longer prevent those "transgressors" from occupying positions of leadership in Orthodox congregations.

It is thus clear that the old legal system has broken down. Orthodox Judaism may officially continue to act as though this were not the case. Reform Judaism may actually welcome the breakdown of the old legal system, considering the latter to be an outgrown stage in the evolution of Judaism. Conservative Judaism may regard the old legal system as still being in force, while admitting that modern life has created serious difficulties which force a revision of that system. But no thoroughgoing revision has as yet been undertaken by Conservative Judaism. Whatever, therefore, the modern Jew's "denominational" affiliation, the fact remains that all modern Jews, at any rate in the West, act on the basis of individual choice. Some may choose to observe more of the traditional provisions. Others may choose to observe less. But all of them choose. Even the maximum observance of the most observant Jew is an act of free choice.

That is why, in our last chapter, we have been concerned with the criteria to be applied to such a choice. We have spoken of the criteria for "Reform" Jewish observance, because, at this moment, Reform Judaism is the most willing of the various Jewish schools of thought to admit that, in this post-Emancipation age, Jewish observance *is* a matter of individual choice. But in the light of what has just been said about *any* type of Jewish observance, we feel confident that a consideration of the criteria will be helpful also to those modern Jews who are Orthodox or Conservative.

Yet there is something unbalanced about a consideration of Jewish observance which reckons only with the individual Jew. Our fourth criterion, the feeling of responsibility toward the

The Holy Community

Covenant Community, may already have served as an indication that the full dimension of Jewish observance cannot be experienced by the individual merely as an individual. Whatever satisfaction the individual may derive from Jewish observance, the *Jewish* significance of his observance is based on the degree to which this observance is also practiced by fellow Jews. For it is not the least aspect of Jewish observance that it contribute to the cohesion and the survival of the Covenant Community. You cannot love your neighbor, as the Torah commands, if you withdraw from all contact with your neighbor. And there are certain liturgical acts which the Tradition does not allow you to perform in isolation. They require a *minyan*, a quorum, which is representative of the "community."

After a century and a half of increasing anarchy in religious practice, more and more voices are now being raised which call for greater standardization and uniformity. Those voices range all the way from the demand, in some Orthodox circles, that the supreme authority of Rabbinic Judaism, the *sanhedrin*, be reconstituted in the State of Israel, to the reiterated request, by many Reform Jews, for a "guide" to Reform Jewish practice. What all of those suggestions tend to overlook is the absence, at the present time, of any one authority which is recognized at least by all the Jews of its particular way of thinking. Thus the demand for the reconstituted *sanhedrin* has remained unheeded —not least because the thought is repugnant to the more extreme groups within Orthodoxy itself.

As for the more modest Reform request, even that is somewhat unrealistic. In the first place, the Central Conference of American Rabbis, which is the Reform rabbinical body, has never been constituted as a legislative assembly. But, and this is of even greater importance, the leadership of Reform Judaism, at the present time, is divided on even much more serious issues than the matter of a common religious practice. There is disagreement about the nature of God, and even about His very existence. There is disagreement about Revelation. There is disagreement about the Election of Israel and the nature of the

Covenant Community. There is not even unanimity about such a practical question as the legitimacy, or otherwise, of mixed marriages. Indeed, it would not be at all unlikely that, some time in the future, there will be a split in the Reform camp and a realignment of the religious forces in American Judaism —possibly transcending the present "denominational" boundaries which are increasingly becoming irrelevant. But it certainly stands to reason that, right now, the Reform rabbinate is in no position whatever to "lay down the law."

Yet there are two precedents in Jewish history which have a bearing on our problem, and which might contribute insights leading to its solution. One is the "Covenant" (*amanah*) in the days of Ezra, entered into by the exiles returning from Babylon.[1] In the account of that "Covenant" there is a verse which can be helpful to us in our present predicament: "We also lay upon ourselves *mitzvoth*."[2] Those *mitzvoth*, or obligations, are spelled out in some detail. They all have to do with the self-preservation of the small group of returning exiles, who obligated themselves to maintain the sanctuary and its cult, to observe the Sabbath, and to reject mixed marriages.

The precise details do not matter so much in our particular context. What does matter is the fact of the *voluntary* acceptance of Jewish obligations on the part of the people, the "self-imposed" authority behind the standard of observance. This could well serve as a precedent for our own acceptance of certain obligations, of certain *mitzvoth* which are ours to perform, not so much because they represent God's Word to us individually, but because they represent the "constitution" of the "holy community."

But if that precedent, set by the people as a whole, and under circumstances quite different from our own, can no longer be imitated by us in a slavish manner, there yet remains one other precedent in our history which has a very direct relevance to our latter-day problem. We are referring to the *chabhuroth*, the Pharisaic "brotherhoods," organized in the days of the Second Temple. Those "brotherhoods" were formed by Jews who made

The Holy Community

a number of "ritual" laws more stringent for themselves, and who became more particular and meticulous in the laws governing tithing and levitical purity than was the current Jewish practice of their time. The "brotherhoods," as *voluntary* associations, maintained their own superior standards, and they did have very rigorous "entrance requirements."

The exclusivism of the Pharisaic "brotherhoods," their "setting themselves apart" from the rest of the people, may indicate a tendency at variance with the lowest common denominator which, in our own days, is all too often elevated as the "democratic" standard. But it remains to be pointed out that, ultimately, those elite groups set the standards for the people as a whole. Their particular interpretation of the Torah gained virtually universal acceptance, and the very stringency of their "ritual" observance, which they adopted as the badge of their exclusiveness, became, in the course of time, the *norm* of Jewish piety for everyone alike.[3]

We are not suggesting that the Pharisaic "brotherhoods" be imitated in their rigorous observance of the laws of tithing and levitical purity. But we *are* suggesting that the concept of the *chabhurah*, of the "brotherhood," with *self-imposed* obligations, is one deserving of detailed study by those who today are concerned about the "constitution" of the "holy community." We *are* suggesting that it might be possible to solve the problems of present-day religious anarchy on the *local* level—even though the "coast to coast" and the international solutions may as yet lie in the distant future.

Unlike the old-established Jewish communities of Europe, the Jewish congregations in the United States are voluntary associations, established, at least in principle, by like-minded individuals. That is why we have synagogues and temples, established with the avowed purpose of maintaining the Orthodox, the Conservative, the Reform, and the Reconstructionist expressions of Judaism. Now, there would be nothing to stop the founding members of a new congregation (except, perhaps, the temptation to fall for the idolatry of mere numbers) from saying: "We, who are establishing this congregation, bind ourselves to maintain such-and-such observances and such-and-such standards, which are meant to constitute our congregation as an integral part of the Covenant Community of Israel. Whoever wants to join us as a regular member will likewise take upon himself the above-mentioned obligations—over and above such other obligations, as he may already have taken upon himself or as he will yet take upon himself, in an individual capacity."

In the case of congregations already established—and that is the more usual case—it will not be feasible to introduce such a self-imposed authority retroactively. But what will be possible in the case of already established congregations is the formation of *chabhuroth* within the congregation. In itself, this is nothing startlingly new in Jewish life. The traditional synagogue has always known its various brotherhoods and societies devoted to the specific intellectual, spiritual, and philanthropic pursuits of its members. There were permanent societies for the study of the Talmud, for the recitation of Psalms, for the performance of the burial rites, for the dowering of indigent brides, and for many other purposes.[4] The modern *chabhurah* may, in its initial stages, be nothing more and nothing less than a group of people within the congregation who are particularly devoted to the *mitzvah* of the Study of the Torah, and who meet regularly to fulfill it. But, as part of their "constitution," they will also bind themselves to the keeping of certain other *mitzvoth*—not because anybody is forcing them to do so, but because they have discovered the community dimension of Jewish living.

In this manner, the solution of the problem of freedom and authority, of individual rights and community needs, may be approached in our day—with the full awareness of the fact that the old legal system has broken down. Those who constitute the modern *chabhuroth* will be able to relive and to re-enact the "Covenant" made in the days of Ezra, when the people said of themselves: "We also lay upon ourselves *mitzvoth*." And behind that "Covenant" at the beginning of the Second Commonwealth, as behind the self-imposed obligations of the Pharisaic

The Holy Community

"brotherhoods," there is the distinct reminiscence of that other covenant, the Covenant at Sinai, where Israel responded with the words, "We will do, and we will understand" (Exodus 24:7), to the divine mandate that they constitute themselves as "a kingdom of priests and a holy nation" (Exodus 19:6).

Of course, the formation of a *chabhurah* is only a partial solution. It is but one of the things which can be done to restore the dimension of the Covenant Community to the realm of Jewish observance. At least, it is an attempt to deal realistically with the problem of "authority" in Jewish life today. It is an attempt which is predicated on the recognition that, in this day and age, there is neither the machinery nor the theoretical foundation for any authority in religious practice which is imposed from above. If such an authority will become possible again in the distant future (and that, at present, seems highly questionable, nor is it necessarily desirable), then it will grow organically out of the self-imposed authority which individual Jews, coming together in *chabhuroth* or similar groups, have taken upon themselves.

In the meantime, it may be necessary to harmonize the needs of the free individual and the demands of the "holy community" by recognizing that there are three different levels of Jewish observance. In the first place, there are those observances for which we would like to pre-empt the traditional category of "commandments between man and God." They constitute, as it were, the "private domain" of religious observance, the realm in which the individual would have to apply the four criteria which we have discussed in our last chapter. This would be the realm in which the greatest diversity is likely to obtain in modern Jewish life. The specific observance of the Sabbath and of the dietary laws would belong to this realm. So would the habits of private prayer, of family devotions, and the home observance of the festivals. Such are matters "between man and God." They are "private," and not subject to the censorious criticism of outsiders.

A second level, and one which already introduces us to the

dimension of the Covenant Community, is the style of observance of a given congregation or *chabhurah*. By joining a specific congregation, one tacitly assents to the use of the particular prayerbook adopted by that congregation and to the style in which that congregation is accustomed to worship. Here, more than one individual is involved. It becomes a matter of commandments "between Israel and God." And where Israel, as a "holy community," confronts the God of Israel, aspects of Tradition may have to be taken into consideration which are still being ignored by many a modern Jewish congregation.

What we have in mind can perhaps best be illustrated by a trend of thought once developed by the late Leo Baeck. Baeck was a religious liberal who saw the essence of Judaism in ethical monotheism. The totality of biblical and Rabbinic "ceremonial" legislation was, for him, only the "hedge around the Torah." How much of that "hedge" the individual accepted for himself was, according to Baeck, the individual's own affair, something strictly between God and the individual concerned. But, for Baeck, the "hedge around the Torah" was also something else. It was, as he called it, the Constitution of the Jewish People. Whenever, therefore, Jews come together as Jews, and not just as individuals, the "hedge" becomes relevant. The specific example which Baeck used (and it was only one of many possible examples) had to do with the dietary laws. As a liberal, Baeck was not overly concerned with the private dietary habits of the individual Jew. But Baeck insisted that, at a congregational dinner (where Jews come together not only as Jewish individuals, but as members of the Jewish People), the food served would have to be kosher.

Still, on the congregational level, there are bound to remain many differences in practice between one congregation and another. That is why there are so many different congregations, to begin with. We are living in an age of religious pluralism, and the different schools of Jewish religious thought, and the various synagogues influenced by them, will continue to reflect that pluralism. There is, therefore, yet one further level of religious practice—in addition to the individual and the congregational levels—which has to be considered. It is that level on which, in spite of our individual and congregational differences, we all recognize one another as Jews and as members of the same "holy community." We might label this level of observance as the "commandments between Jew and Jew."

The Covenant at Sinai was made "with him who is standing here with us this day before the Lord our God, and also with him who is not here this day" (Deuteronomy 29:14). Tradition knows of two ways in which one becomes a Jew. One is either born into the Covenant Community, and thus acquires his status by virtue of the Covenant (made also "with him who is not here this day"); or one can come into Judaism from the outside by undergoing the accepted rites of conversion. Once one is a Jew, he may turn out to be a good Jew, or a bad Jew, or a sinful Jew; but his "Jewishness" itself cannot be called into question. This sounds liberal and broad-minded enough. Yet it can work only so long as the whole Covenant Community is in agreement on the marriage law in terms of which a "Jewish birth" takes place, and on the details of the conversion procedure by means of which outsiders are accepted into the fold.

It is thus the Jewish law concerning "personal status" which guarantees the underlying unity of the "holy community." But it is precisely the legislation concerning "personal status" (and the requirements for conversion) which Reform Jews, particularly in America, have largely chosen to ignore. They have thereby provoked some Orthodox rabbis (and the government of the State of Israel) into rejecting the validity of Jewish marriages performed under Reform Jewish auspices.

The fault, however, is not all on one side. The traditional Jewish marriage and divorce law is predicated on a status of women in society which no longer corresponds to the actual status of women in the modern world. There are, therefore, changes which will have to be made in Jewish marriage and divorce law, even as changes have always been made before in the millennial development of the Tradition. The Orthodox rabbinate has been remiss in making those changes; and the result has been that a growing number of Jews have ignored the law altogether, if, like many Reform Jews, they have not explicitly rejected it.

In this process, a division is being created in the "holy community," a division which, in succeeding generations, is bound to lead to many cases of hardship and personal tragedy. It is also a growing rift which threatens the underlying unity of all Jews. And once that underlying unity disappears, the present religious pluralism may well turn into complete religious anarchy; and total religious anarchy may spell the end of the Covenant Community, in which alone Judaism as a faith can have its being and significance.

The most urgent requirement, involving the very survival of the Covenant Community, is undoubtedly a meeting of minds of both Orthodox and Reformers on this particular issue. The Orthodox will have to be amenable to an adaptation of the law according to the dynamics which the Tradition itself provides; and the Reformers must be prepared to conform to the law at least in this respect. Ways and means will have to be worked out jointly to prevent the further erosion of the "commandments between Jew and Jew."

For only if the "holy community" remains undivided on the basic level of its existence, only if there can be an unqualified acceptance of one another as fellow Jews, will there be hope for the flourishing growth of individual piety and the productive diversity in religious expression.

NOTES

1. Nehemiah, chap. 8–10.
2. Nehemiah 10:33.
3. See above, Chap. 1, "The Pharisaic Tradition Today," and cf. Jacob Neusner, *Fellowship in Judaism* (London: Vallentine, Mitchell, 1965).
4. Cf. Israel Abrahams, *Jewish Life in the Middle Ages* (London: Goldston, 1932), pp. 331–363.

INDEX OF SCRIPTURAL REFERENCES

(1) HEBREW BIBLE

Genesis 1:1   31, 111, 148
Genesis 11:27–32   130–131
Genesis 12:1–4   131
Genesis 22:1–19   68–75
Genesis 28:18   31, 53
Exodus 3:3–14   132–133
Exodus 4:24   139
Exodus 15:18   125
Exodus 15:25   148
Exodus 16:29   110
Exodus 19:6   187
Exodus 19:19   133
Exodus 20:2–3   40
Exodus 20:25–26   29
Exodus 21:24   27, 110
Exodus 24:7   187
Exodus 24:10   132
Exodus 24:12   103
Leviticus 18:3   41, 50
Leviticus 19:18   126
Leviticus 19:34   125
Leviticus 23:40   25
Leviticus 26:41   48
Numbers 15:31   105, 108
Numbers 23:9   60
Deuteronomy 5:15   125
Deuteronomy 6:5   125–126
Deuteronomy 8:3   103–104
Deuteronomy 8:10   102, 103
Deuteronomy 12:30   45
Deuteronomy 16:4   176
Deuteronomy 16:22   53
Deuteronomy 17:8–11   62
Deuteronomy 18:3   46
Deuteronomy 24:1–4   25
Deuteronomy 21:18–21   9
Deuteronomy 28:19   44
Deuteronomy 29:14   157, 189
II Samuel 6:1–7   139
Isaiah 6:3   148
Isaiah 7:9   21–22
Isaiah 7:14   148, 152
Isaiah 11:6   97
Isaiah 53:1–12   152, 160
Isaiah 55:1–2   104
Isaiah 66:23   57
Jeremiah 23:29   26
Jeremiah 35:6–10   50
Ezekiel 3:1   103
Ezekiel 3:3   103
Ezekiel 5:7   49
Ezekiel 11:12   49–50
Ezekiel 16:3   39–40
Amos 8:11   105
Zechariah 14:9   157
Malachi 2:7   62
Malachi 4:4   87
Psalms 1:1   43
Psalms 19:11   103
Psalms 104:35   162, 165–166
Psalms 106:2   60
Psalms 137:6   162
Psalms 145:20   162
Ecclesiastes 1:9–10   84
Nehemiah, chs. 8–10   184
Nehemiah 10:33   184

(2) NEW TESTAMENT

Matthew 5:17   88, 143
John 14:6   156
Acts 8:26–35   148
Romans 1:26–27   42

Index of Scriptural References

Romans 13:8 88
I Corinthians 15:24, 28 157
I Corinthians 16:22 165
Hebrews 1:1–2 98

INDEX OF RABBINIC PASSAGES

(a) MISHNAH

Pe-ah 1:1   173, 180
Shabbath 6:10   46, 56
Kiddushin 1:9   170, 180
Sanhedrin 10:1   102, 109
Abhodah Zarah 2:1   42, 55
Abhodah Zarah 3:4   51, 56
Aboth 2:5   179, 180
Chullin 4:7   46, 55
Yadayim 3:5   32, 38

(b) TOSEPHTA

Berakhoth 7:2   103, 109
Shabbath chs. 7–8   46, 56
Abhodah Zarah 2:5, 6   43, 55
Abhodah Zarah 2:7   44, 55
Abhodah Zarah 3:2   42, 55

(c) PALESTINIAN TALMUD

Berakhoth, ch. VII   103, 109
Pe-ah II, 6   24, 37
Chagigah I, 7   28, 38

(d) BABYLONIAN TALMUD

Berakhoth 4a   28, 38
Berakhoth 40b   100–101, 109
Shabbath 21b   28, 38
Shabbath 23a   61–62
Shabbath 63a   29, 38
Shabbath 67a, b   46, 56
Erubhin 51a   110, 114
Pesachim 6b   27, 38
Pesachim 49b   11
Yoma 28b   27, 38

Yebamoth 79a   47, 56
Yebamoth 103b   150, 159
Baba Kamma 83b–84a   27, 38, 110, 114
Baba Bathra 14b–15a   113, 115
Sanhedrin 34a   26, 37
Sanhedrin 39b   50, 56
Sanhedrin 96a   12
Sanhedrin 99a   105–106, 109
Makkoth 23b   167, 180
Makkoth 24a   118, 129
Abhodah Zarah 18b   42–43, 55
Menachoth 29b   24, 37

(e) POST-TALMUDIC TRACTATES

Sopherim 13:8   102, 109

(f) MIDRASHIM

Mekilta Pischa, ch. V   47, 56
Mekilta Shirata, ch. IV   125, 129
Mekilta Bachodesh, ch. II   49, 56
Mekilta Bachodesh, ch. V   132
Mekilta Bachodesh, ch. XI   29, 38
Mekilta Kaspa, ch. IV   45–46, 55
Sifra Acharé Moth, par. 9   42, 50, 55, 56
Sifra Acharé Moth, pereq 13   42, 43, 46, 48, 55, 56
Sifra Qedoshim, pereq 9   49, 56
Sifra Qedoshim, pereq 11   42, 49, 55, 56
Sifra Bechuqothai, pereq 8   48, 56
Sifré Shelach, pisqa 112   105–106, 109
Sifré Eqebh, pisqa 40   28, 38

Index of Rabbinic Passages

Sifré Re-eh, pisqa 59   170, 180
Sifré Re-eh, pisqa 81   45, 52, 55, 56
Sifré Shophetim, pisqa 146   53, 56
Midrash Tannaim to Deut. 18:13   46, 56

Genesis Rabbah 1:2   31, 38
Exodus Rabbah 47:1   37, 38
Leviticus Rabbah 22:8   52, 56
Leviticus Rabbah 32:5   47, 56

NAME INDEX

Abaye, 46
Abrabanel, Don Isaac, 81
Abraham, 27, 68–75, 130–131
Abrahams, Israel, 190
Achad Ha'am, 95
Adler, Felix, 93
Agnon, Sh. Y., 133
Agus, Jacob B., 18
Akiba, Rabbi, 11, 24, 32, 72, 143, 145
Albo, Joseph, 149
Amram, David Werner, 37
Anan b. David, 103
Antony, 42
Aristobulus, 42
Aristotle, 40, 59
Asch, Scholem, 147

Baeck, Leo, 147, 151, 176, 188
Baillie, John, 122, 123, 129
Bar Kappara, 47
Bar Kokhba, 143–144, 145
Barth, Karl, 123, 151
Berab, Jacob, 78
Bernays, Isaac, 79–80, 82
Bernfeld, Simeon, 91–92, 99
Bickermann, Elias, 64–65
Breasted, J. H., 91
Brinton, Crane, 86
Buber, Martin, 123, 126–127, 129, 145, 147, 151, 159
Bultmann, Rudolf, 30, 128, 129

Caro, Joseph, 89
Cohen, A., 82
Cohen, Hermann, 34, 66
Copernicus, Nicolas, 95, 114

Da Costa, Uriel, 9–10
Darwin, Charles, 111, 114
Daube, David, 151
David, 28
De Mille, Cecil B., 116–117
Dio Cassius, 42
Duran, Simeon, 77

Einhorn, David, 15–16, 90
Eleazar, Rabbi, 11
Ezekiel, 39–40, 49–50, 53–54, 103
Ezra, 184

Fackenheim, Emil L., 121, 129
Freud, Sigmund, 54, 56, 96–97, 99, 132
Fromm, Erich, 40, 55, 126, 129

Gamaliel, Rabban, 51, 77
Gaster, Theodor H., 105, 111
Geiger, Abraham, 8, 80, 121, 128, 129
Goldman, Solomon, 16

Heine, Heinrich, 148–149
Herford, R. Travers, 8–9, 151
Herod, 42
Hertz, Joseph H., 111, 115
Herzl, Theodor, 60
Heschel, Abraham J., 123, 151
Hillel, 77, 179
Hirsch, Samson Raphael, 79
Hirsch, Samuel, 90
Hoffmann, David, 102, 109, 112, 115
Holdheim, Samuel, 80, 90, 170, 180
Hunna, Rab, 47

195

Name Index

Ibn Ezra, Abraham, 24, 37, 69, 73–74, 114
Ikhnaton, 132
Isaac, 68–75
Iviya, Rab, 62–64

Jacob, 53
Jaspers, Karl, 128, 129
Jeremiah, 26, 50
Jesus, 48, 61, 71, 87–88, 143, 146–147
Joseph, Morris, 10
Josephus, Flavius, 8, 42, 55
Judah, Halevi, 133, 135
Judah Maccabee, 28, 58
Judah the Pious, 71
Judah the Prince, 89
Jung, Carl G., 97–98, 99, 121–122, 129
Justin Martyr, 143, 159
Juvenal, 42

Kaplan, Mordecai M., 92
Kaufman, Yehezkel, 134
Kierkegaard, Søren, 74, 123, 151
Klausner, Joseph, 147, 151
Koheleth, 84
Kohler, Kaufmann, 120, 128
Kohn, Jacob, 122, 129

Lauterbach, Jacob Z., 8
Leibniz, G. W., 98
Levi, Rabbi, 52
Lieberman, Saul, 52, 56, 65
Luther, Martin, 94, 145

Maimonides, Moses, 34, 54, 86, 99, 111, 114, 118, 129, 131, 143, 146, 149, 167–168
Malachi, 87
Marmorstein, Arthur, 109, 159
Meir, Rabbi, 162
Mendelssohn, Moses, 120
Mohammed, 143
Montefiore, Claude G., 107, 109, 120–121, 128, 129, 147, 151

Moore, George Foot, 8, 151
Moses, 24–25, 116, 132–133

Nachmanides, Moses, 74–75
Neusner, Jacob, 190
Niebuhr, Reinhold, 123, 151
Nieto, David, 37

Parkes, James, 156, 157
Paul, 42, 71, 88, 143, 165
Peter, 88
Pfeiffer, Robert H., 13
Philipson, David, 180
Philo, 32

Rashi, 38, 69–70, 74, 111, 114
Rava, 46
Reubeni, David, 147
Riesman, David, 16
Rosenzweig, Franz, 18, 34, 108, 109, 123, 125–128, 129, 151, 156–157, 171, 173

Saadia Gaon, 85, 131
Sabbatai Zezi, 147
Schleiermacher, Friedrich, 121, 129
Schoeps, Hans-Joachim, 71
Scholem, Gershom G., 99
Seligmann, Caesar, 136
Sforno, Obadiah, 75
Shammai, 77
Simlai, Rabbi, 167
Spiegel, Shalom, 69
Stanley, A. P., 164
Strack, Hermann L., 151

Tertullian, 43, 45–46

Vermes, Geza, 69

Weiss, I. H., 55
Wellhausen, Julius, 30, 108, 134
Wise, Isaac M., 15–16, 63, 94, 119

SUBJECT INDEX

Adversus Judaeos, 147
Aggadah, 37, 130
Akedah, 68–75
Am-Ha-aretz, 11–12, 14, 17–18, 173
Amor Dei Intellectualis, 153
Apocalypse, 164
Apocalyptic, 145
Apocrypha, 59
Arena, 44–45
Asceticism, 153
Assimilation, 49, 66–67, 81
Atheistic Theology, 131
Auschwitz, 139

Babylonian Exile, 162
Bar Kokhba Rebellion, 143–144
Bible, 12, 20–24, 26, 29, 30, 33–35, 36, 39, 50, 53, 87, 91, 94, 95, 106–107, 108, 110–111, 112, 114, 116, 124, 127, 133–134, 148, 152, 173; see also Scriptures
Blessing over the Torah, 102, 103, 104
Bread, 100–109
Brother Daniel Case, 144

Caftan, 45
Calendar, 65, 178
Ceremonies, 93, 107, 118–119, 168–169
Chabhurah, 184–187
Chosen People, 155, 183
Christianity, 23, 70–73, 88, 96, 141–159
Christmas, 60
Chukkoth Hagoyim, 40–50; see also "Statutes of the Gentiles"

Church, 43, 54, 71, 72, 80, 88–89, 142, 143, 144, 145, 147, 150, 152, 153, 156, 158, 160, 164
Church Militant, 164
Circus, 44
Collective Unconscious, 97
Conscience, 176–177
Conservative Judaism, 10, 108, 173, 182, 185
Constitutions of the Holy Apostles, 43
Conversion of the Gentiles, 12–13, 48, 154–158
Covenant, 48, 93, 142, 143, 156–157, 177–179, 182–183, 184, 189, 190
Cross, 72, 148

Dead Sea Scrolls, 10–11, 146
Deism, 86, 119, 120, 131, 150
Derash, 30, 31
Dialogue, 141–159, 160
Diaspora, 39, 44, 170
Dietary Laws, 11, 12–13, 79, 90, 153, 169, 182, 187, 188
Disputations, 141, 148–149
Divorce, 25, 90, 189–190
Dunkirk, 124

Education, 17–18, 172, 179
Ehyeh Asher Ehyeh, 133, 140
Emanation, 33
Emancipation, 78, 151, 170, 176, 181
Enemies, 161, 164
Ethical Culture, 93
Ethrog, 25
Evil, 163–164

197

Subject Index

Evolution, 111
Excommunication, 181
Exodus from Egypt, 132–133, 135, 136, 138, 146

Fundamentalism, 17, 110, 114, 127, 152, 161

Gemara, 33, 77, 85
God, 14, 28, 32, 63, 64, 68, 72, 84, 91, 94, 100–102, 116, 118, 121, 122–123, 127, 131–132, 134, 138–139, 148, 149, 150, 152, 157, 161, 174–175, 177, 183
Gospels, 88, 137, 164
Grace after Meals, 100, 102
Grace before Meals, 100–101, 107

Hakham, 79–80, 82
Hanukkah, 28, 57–67
Hasidism, 14, 145
Hasmoneans, 28
Hattarath Hora-ah, 78
Hebrew, 90–91, 96, 178
Hebrew Union College, 79
Heilsgeschichte, 138, 139, 146
Hellenistic-Roman World, 8, 41, 43, 44, 47
Higher Criticism, 21–22, 28, 30, 87, 91, 106, 108, 112, 114, 123, 134, 163
Homoousion-Homoiousion Controversy, 150

Idolatry, 40, 86, 142
"Ignosticism," 131
Imitatio Dei, 75
Immortality, 71
Inspiration, 121
Islam, 149, 154, 157

Jahrzeit, 71
Jewish Theological Seminary of America, 79
Judaeo-Christians, 143

Kaddish, 165
Kapparoth, 71
Karaites, 23, 30, 77, 85, 103, 111
Kiyyas, 103

Law, 24, 42, 62, 77, 88, 94, 105, 106–107, 137, 143, 149

Leaven, 176–177
Legal Fictions, 176–177
Letter of Aristeas, 12–13
Lex Talionis, 9, 31, 110
Liturgy, 58, 70, 161, 162
Lord's Prayer, 165
Love, 125–126

Maccabees, 59–60, 64–65
Magic, 46
Ma'oz Tzur, 59
Maranatha, 165
Mariolatry, 144–145
Marriage, 11, 90, 184, 189–190
Materialism, 152–153
Messiah, 143, 145–146, 149, 154, 165
Messianic Era, 97, 146–147, 165
Midrash, 33, 114, 173
Minhag America, 63
Minyan, 183
Miqwah, 90, 91
Mishnah, 33, 37, 77, 85, 102
Mitzvoth, 169, 172, 173, 178, 184, 186
Mystery Cults, 13
Mysticism, 97

Natural Law, 86
Natural Theology, 130
New Moon, 57–58
New Testament, 8, 10, 137, 151, 160–161, 164
Noahitic Laws, 142, 144, 154, 155
Nova Lex Christi, 150

Oral Law, 9, 23–27, 37, 85, 111, 167
Ordination, 76–77, 78
Original Sin, 149–150
Orthodox Judaism, 41, 78, 85, 105, 111–112, 118, 168–169, 171, 173, 175, 181–182, 183, 185, 189–190

Passover, 58, 176–177, 178
Patria Potestas, 9
Pentateuch, 27, 37, 63, 107, 108, 112, 113, 133, 134–135, 136
Personal Status, 189–190
Peshat, 30–31, 35
Pharisees, 8–19, 62–63, 87, 151, 155

Subject Index

"Pittsburgh Platform," 91–94, 171
Potentiality and Actuality, 74–75
Progressive Revelation, 24, 26, 36, 53, 64, 108
Prophets, 21, 50, 87, 96, 97, 120–121, 145, 147, 169
Protestantism, 13, 14, 15, 23, 33, 108, 152, 160
Psalms, 160–166
Psychoanalysis, 96
Purim, 58

Quellenscheidung, 105; see also Higher Criticism
Quran, 133, 137

Rabban, 77
Rabbi, 76–83
Rabbinic Judaism, 9–10, 13–14, 23, 30, 40, 41, 42, 44, 62, 65, 76, 111, 149
Rav, 77–78
Rechabites, 50
Reconstructionism, 92, 185
Red Sea, 124–125, 133, 135
Reform Judaism, 10, 15–16, 35–36, 41, 59–60, 63, 64, 79, 89–94, 106–107, 108, 112, 118–121, 128, 147, 162, 168–169, 171–174, 175, 178–179, 182, 183, 185, 189, 190
Religion of Nature, 86, 150
Remez, 30, 32
Repentance, 153
Retribution, 149
Revelation, 17, 20, 84–87, 89, 93, 111, 113, 116–129, 130–140, 149, 150
Roman Catholicism, 13, 23–24, 89, 100
Rosh Hashanah, 70

Sabbath, 57, 90, 153, 170, 174–176, 178, 182, 184, 187
Sacrificial Cult, 29, 51–52, 71, 100, 168
Sadducees, 9, 11, 30, 65–66, 111
Sanhedrin, 78, 183
Scriptures, 9, 23, 32, 48, 68, 94, 103, 119, 142; see also Bible
Secularism, 151
Seder, 138, 178

Semikhah (see Ordination)
Separatism, 12–13, 47–49
Sermon on the Mount, 87, 161, 164
Shavu'oth, 105
Shittuph, 142, 144
Shulchan Arukh, 10, 34, 96, 171, 181
"Six Hundred and Thirteen Commandments," 123, 167–169
Slavery, 132
Sod, 30, 32–33
Song of Songs, 32
State of Israel, 93, 101, 139, 144, 158, 181, 189
"Statutes of the Gentiles," 40–55
Streimel, 45
Sukkoth, 25
Systematic Theology, 130

Taboo, 54, 107
Talmud, 8, 11, 12, 24, 25, 28, 33, 34, 35, 37, 47, 50, 61, 62, 64, 82, 85, 91, 100, 114, 118, 148, 162, 173
Ten Commandments, 40, 117, 119
Theater, 44–45
Theocracy, 170
Torah, 22, 26, 27, 31 32, 34, 36, 44, 48, 59, 62–63, 81, 90, 101–109, 113, 135, 137–138, 146, 148, 154
Tradition, 20, 36, 52, 55, 63, 64, 69, 73, 74, 85, 89, 94–95, 100, 119, 138, 167, 169, 172, 174–175, 179, 183, 188
Trinity, 144, 148

Unio Mystica, 153
Union Prayer Book, 35
Unitarianism, 13, 92, 179

Vicarious Atonement, 70–73, 149, 150

"Ways of the Amorite," 46
Written Law, 9, 23, 25, 37, 89, 108, 111, 167

Yeshivah, 35, 79, 91

Zionism, 60, 121
Zohar, 32–33

199

Katherine Spirit of the Dell

Pat Wells

© Copyright 2006 Pat Wells.
All rights reserved. No part of this publication may be reproduced, stored in a retrieval system, or transmitted, in any form or by any means, electronic, mechanical, photocopying, recording, or otherwise, without the written prior permission of the author.

Note for Librarians: A cataloguing record for this book is available from Library and Archives Canada at www.collectionscanada.ca/amicus/index-e.html
ISBN 1-4120-9061-x

Printed in Victoria, BC, Canada. Printed on paper with minimum 30% recycled fibre.
Trafford's print shop runs on "green energy" from solar, wind and other environmentally-friendly power sources.

TRAFFORD
PUBLISHING
Offices in Canada, USA, Ireland and UK

Book sales for North America and international:
Trafford Publishing, 6E–2333 Government St.,
Victoria, BC V8T 4P4 CANADA
phone 250 383 6864 (toll-free 1 888 232 4444)
fax 250 383 6804; email to orders@trafford.com

Book sales in Europe:
Trafford Publishing (UK) Limited, 9 Park End Street, 2nd Floor
Oxford, UK OX1 1HH UNITED KINGDOM
phone +44 (0)1865 722 113 (local rate 0845 230 9601)
facsimile +44 (0)1865 722 868; info.uk@trafford.com

Order online at:
trafford.com/06-0817

10 9 8 7 6 5 4 3 2 1

PREFACE

What I have tried to achieve is to put together the research which I have obtained about what daily life was like in Medieval England, focusing on a village in Suffolk, Barrow (Barewe) near Bury St Edmunds, to help people gain an understanding in a most pleasurable way and to bring to life the structured rules of life under feudalism.

It covers medieval society, with people living their lives under the rules of homage to God, The King and their Lords. Villeins who have become vassals of their Lords, performing services under the Lords' control, the Lords on their part giving
protection and security.

It tells of the wars. What it was like taking part in the Crusade for the hero Sir William Gifford. The many disputes between The King and his Barons.
The clearing of the Jews from Suffolk. The daily functions needed for survival in the 13th century.

The heroine, being Lady Katherine de Passelewe, tells of her background and her childhood living at Clare Castle and her bonding with Sir Richard de Clare's youngest daughter Isabelle. Their education and adolescence spent at Denny Abbey.

Katherine's young love and marriage and raising a family. Her passions, fears and strengths Her responsibility to her vassals.

The main characters are real people who are recorded in the Chronicles.
The fictional contents of the book of Thought, Emotions, Life and Death of which I have a great knowledge with my experience of being a District Nurse for many years

and helping people through these periods of their lives.

The village of Barrow (Barewe) is on a peak of a hill forming a dell at the top. It is less than two miles from the Icknield Way, close to the old Fen Sea. The Church, the Moat site of the Hall which the Giffords built and the site of Denham Castle still remain. The main structure of the Village remains the same as in Medieval Times.

Pat Wells

Chapter 1
CLARE CASTLE

I, Katherine, was born in the year 1227, the only daughter of Hammond de Passelewe, Gentleman of Norman descent and small land owner of the manor of Heigham and Barewe.

We were not a wealthy family, although my ancestors had been in Heigham since they came to England with the great King William. My father was not a warrior so he did not collect the spoils of war. He was indeed a very educated man, skilful in the ways of court and the King's laws and was able to obtain the position of advisor and attorney to 'Sir Richard de Clara', a very rich and powerful Baron who was a successful warrior. Highly respected and admired by both common folk and Barons alike, he held a very important position but often fell foul of the King in his adventures. It was then up to my father to get these problems sorted out with the King, Henry III King of England (1216-1272).

Mother was Maud the daughter of Thomas de Barewe, a gentleman of good house. She first met my father at Clare Castle whilst she was working as a governess to the Clare children. Her father was not a big land owner but held the village of Barewe for the great William Marshal who was Rector Regni for England. On his death bed - apparently to appease God for his sins - he gave the village of Barewe to the very powerful Abbey of St. Edmunds.

My uncle, Alexander de Barewe who was a monk at the Abbey, acquired Barewe from the Abbots and gave it to my mother and her sister Alice. Alice was married to William of St. Albans and Islington, a very wealthy gentleman. They lived in a grand manor of St. Albans in Hertfordshire.

Father was a very good catch for Mother as she

was of an Anglo-Saxon line. The Saxons, having been conquered by the Normans in 1066, were considered second-class by society who were mostly made up of Norman descent. Not being from a wealthy family, she was unable to take much land or monies with her for her marriage dowry. In appearance, Mother was very slim and tall with chestnut coloured hair - very handsome rather than being beautiful. Her deportment and grace were excellent and she had an air of being very proud about her. She was well educated, quick and bright and most worldly for a young woman in her position.

    Sir Richard de Clare's wife, the Baroness Eleanor, a handsome, elegant woman who commanded as much power as her husband, held from the Ladies of the realm. She was a very good friend to Mother over the years; it was she who had encouraged the match between my mother and father.

    Mother grew to adore her husband but this didn't last very long as he died when I was just six months old. It seemed that he got some sort of infection whilst at the King's palace in London. He was seen by the Royal Physician and bled to get rid of the infection .The next day, as he felt improved, he decided to go back to Heigham, a great distance of some eighty miles, where there would be no one better than his beloved Maud to take care of him. Whilst riding home, the weather changed and there was an extremely fierce thunder storm with such rapid rain that there was flash flooding everywhere. Father had decided to ride his favourite horse, which obviously was a lot quicker than taking the carriage. He did make it to Heigham but in a very poor condition. Mother was sent for as she was away at Clare Castle at the time. By the time she got there, he was very ill and within two days he had died. Mother said that it was because he got so wet and cold.

Chapter 1

Suitors came from near and far following Father's demise, wanting to marry Mother so they could obtain the Manors and lands which she held. She refused them all. Being a strong and capable woman, she did not wish to lose control of the Manor or that of my upbringing by re-marrying. This was frowned on by society as women were not meant to manage their own affairs. What society thought of Mother did not bother her as she was used to hearing whispers about how she was not of pure blood as she was from Anglo-Saxon lineage.

She was given a great deal of support by her friend the Baroness who relied on her to help to run her own family. It was the Baroness who talked Sir Richard into giving Mother part of Father's old job. Of course, she would not be able to go to London to talk with the King like Father did, but she would be able to keep the accounts and, with the help of the Bailiffs, run the Castle and Manor when the Clares were away, as often they were.

I spent most of my early years growing up in the beautiful Clare Castle which was so very large it was like a kingdom within a kingdom. I was treated the same as the five Clare children as a member of their family. I was of a similar age to Isabelle, the youngest of the children. We were brought up together, sharing sleeping arrangements, food, clothes and everything else, including my mother, as the Baroness was away a great deal in London at Court and other society functions.

From my earliest years, I can remember Isabelle's round rosy face with great big brown sparkling eyes and beautiful dark curls which she wore on the top of her head. We both felt secure when we were together and uneasy when we were apart.   Emma, Richard, Gilbert and Thomas were the rest of the Clare children. Mother had some import into their early upbringing when she was governess to them before her marriage to Father.

Emma, the eldest, was the beauty of the family, being tall and very fair with the Clare's large brown eyes. When she moved, she seemed to float and when I was very young I would stare at her waiting for her to fly away. She was so very vain and was sure that when she grew older she would become a princess. I even heard Sir Richard say "So you shall my beauty."

Young Richard, the eldest son, was a miniature of his Father: bold, brave and demanded respect, especially from his younger brothers.

Gilbert, the next in line, was very much like young Richard in appearance, being tall and strong for his years. He would not give in to Richard or let his brother have his own way. "I am just as fine a man as you and will always be so," he would say.

Thomas, the youngest son, I liked the best out of the boys. He was always so friendly, had a very good sense of humour and always saw the funny side of things. He was loved by most people and was indeed the Baroness's favourite son.

Emma was over ten years older than Isabelle so it was decided that she should go to London and stay with the Beaumont family, where she would have company of the Beaumont girls who were of a similar age and she would finish her education with these young ladies. The Baroness often stayed with the Beaumonts when in London and would then see Emma.

All the boys also went away to be educated and to train as Squires and would progress into becoming Knights under the care of Barons who were allies of Sir Richard.

This left Mother, Isabelle and myself at the Castle with the Baroness and the Baron coming and going, which made for great happiness.

There was a resident priest at the castle called Father Joe and Mother spent a great deal of effort keeping out of his way, as it seems he had desires on her and the Manors. He said he would give up his priesthood if Mother would marry him, which was the last thing on her mind. Father Joe would follow her everywhere; she would turn round and he would be there. "How charming you look today my dear," was his favourite saying. The Baroness would giggle and visiting guests would grin. They all knew of his intentions and ambitions

When not trying to get Mother's attentions, he could be found in the kitchen cutting pieces of meat off the spit, whilst the spit boys were still turning the spit. Following the meat, he would drink a whole jug of ale whilst warming his buttocks at the fire, often scorching the back of his gown, much to the delight of the spit boys. It quite cheered the boys up making their hard day a little lighter. We children used to have a good laugh when we saw him walking about with smoke coming from between his legs.

"Why, he looked more like Satan than a man of God," said Thomas as he would walk behind the priest, copying the odd gesture the priest was making, much to our approval.

Life was fun and good at Clare and I enjoyed the time I spent there. The years passed and when Isabelle and myself were eleven years old, our lives were to change. We were sent for by the Baroness with Mother in attendance. The Baroness announced to both of us "You will both be going to Denny Abbey."

"Oh no," exclaimed Isabelle, " I am not going to become a nun."

Chapter 1

The Baroness and Mother both laughed.

"God would not have you, Isabelle, why you are far too wild. You are going there to make you into a gentle godly young lady so you will be able to go to London to the Court to finish your education. Then you will be able to become a Lady-in-Waiting to the Princess and find yourself a husband like your sister Emma, who was born both feminine and gentle and didn't compete with every male. It did not matter to her that she could not ride a horse at a great speed or throw a stick a greater distance than anyone else," said the Baroness, who did not approve of Isabelle's boyish ways.

"Katherine will not be going to Court! Why is she going to Denny Abbey?" asked Isabelle.

"She calms you and she may become a nun - who knows?" replied the Baroness.

Isabelle and myself were not happy following this news. We were both so free here, we could do most of the things we wanted to. We both had ponies and rode most days, winter and summer. In the vast enclosures of the Manor, it was quite safe for us. For Sir Richard had many enemies who might take us as hostages, which had happened to some other baron's daughters. Riding and the ponies was Isabelle's main love for she had a wonderful seat and could out-ride her brothers. Sir Richard was an unusual man and thought his daughter should have every opportunity. He would laugh and say that Isabelle "was the best son he had."

It was a cold January afternoon when the Clare's carriage returned, along with the escorts of guard from Denny Abbey with the Abbess Berta. She was greeted by the Baroness and escorted to her chamber where she refreshed herself and was then taken to the Ladies' Chamber where the Baroness and Mother were waiting for her.

Chapter 1

Isabelle and I were in the library when we heard the noise of the servants hurrying to take their places in the court yard to welcome the Abbess. We peered out of the window but could not get a good view of her, as the servants were in the way.

"Let's go, quickly, to the storage chamber and hide," said Isabelle, running towards the door.

"No, Isabelle! It will only make everything worse. You are being so silly." We both then sat down and waited, not saying a word. Then Jane the housekeeper came into the library to escort us to the Ladies' Chamber.

On entering the chamber, we both stared at the Abbess Berta, a small round nun with much authority about her person but who had a lovely naughty sparkle in her eyes and I could feel a great sense of fun. She was sitting between Mother and the Baroness.

Isabelle and I both curtsied to her for she held a very high position as Abbess and she was a Lady in her own right before she had become a nun. She was a distant kin to the Baroness, belonging to the Gifford family who had intertwined in marriage with the Clares many times over the years.

Berta beckoned to Isabelle. "Come here child. You are quite pretty with those beautiful eyes, but you lack grace," she said, passing Isabelle a prayer book. "Read pages 15 to16, please." Isabelle did as she was asked. "You read the words good and clear but you do not understand what you are reading about! Isabelle, you are like a young duck but, with hard work and commitment from you and myself, you will grow into a beautiful swan. I understand that you have a very strong character and are full of courage like your father. I shall be pleased to work with you. You may go, child." Isabelle left slamming the door.

The Baroness glared at Berta who was giving orders in her domain. Berta looked at me. "Come closer my child. Well, what have we here? Most unusual hair colouring - strands of gold and red on the same head; bright green eyes, skin the colour of lilies, while being tall and slim." I dropped my head and felt my face turn red.

"Hold your head up, child; we never look at our feet. Look me in the eyes."

I did as she ordered, feeling a little nervous. Passing me the prayer book, she said "Read pages 20 to 22 please." I finished reading. "Well, how well your spirit has matured. You may go now."

"Thank you, Your Highness. Oh! I mean 'Your Grace'. I am so sorry," I said, making a curtsey to her as I took my leave, noticing that she was smiling.

Isabelle was waiting outside the door. "Who does that woman think she is? That is, if she is a woman under that gown. Oh! I wish my father was here, he would not have me going to any Convent if I did not want to go. Father, please come home," she said sadly as she stamped her foot crossly and turned her back towards me, not allowing me to see the tears in her eyes.

"I am sure it won't be that bad, we will have to look on it as a kind of adventure," I said, trying to cheer myself and Isabelle up.

"I do not want to go and live with that woman and a bunch of nuns," was her reply.

Isabelle and myself were very quiet for the next few days. Mother noticed this and knew how unhappy we felt about the Convent.

After dinner that night, we went to Mother's bedroom. Mother placed the pillows on her bed in a comfortable position, then the three of us descended on to the bed. She sat in the middle of us both with her arms around us, as she often had before whenever we had a problem.

"Why you are both going to Denny Abbey is to learn about your inner selves and learn how to understand other people, their emotions and needs and what would be expected from you for God, your King and your Lords. How to grow strong and powerful in your heart and mind. You will both develop this and lead a simple and productive life with the help of the Abbess and her nuns.

There will also be lighter times and you will have some fun. There will be other young ladies there. I know that the Willoughby girls will be there, as will Marie, cousin of the Queen, who will be studying with you.

You know how much myself and the Baron and Baroness love you both and we would not send you if we thought you would be unhappy."

Whilst I was listening to Mother, I was staring at the painting on the wall of the chamber of Christ on the cross with little drops of blood dripping from his hands and thinking that it cannot be as bad as having nails banged into one's body. I then felt much calmer and started to look forward to going to Denny, but it was not the same for Isabelle.

Chapter 2
THE JOURNEY

Two weeks had passed since the Abbess was at the Castle and the time had come for us to depart to Denny, which was quite close to Ely.

It was a beautiful sunny day but very frosty. The coach for our journey was being made ready in the court yard. Maggy, who was personal maid to myself and Isabelle, was busy putting large stones that had been heated in the kitchen fire on to the floor of the carriage. These were also used to heat our beds in the winter. Warm sheepskins had been placed on the seats in the carriage. The servants and driver were putting the luggage on the roof.

Inside the Castle, the servants had gathered in the hall to say their goodbyes to us. The housekeeper Jane had made me a posy of dried herbs. "We are all going to miss you very much, Katherine," she said, giving me the posy of dried herbs for the journey.

"I will miss you, Jane, and everyone else," I said, giving her a little kiss on the cheek. Jane wiped a little tear from her eye.

Mother and the Baroness made their entrance. "Where is Isabelle?" asked the Baroness.

"She is sick," replied Maggy. "Far too ill to get out of bed today."

"Poor child!" exclaimed the Baroness with a very stern look on her face. "We must see what I can do." She quickly ascended the stairs followed closely by Jane, Mother and myself. She opened the door of our room. There were loud groans coming from Isabelle.

"What's the problem?" asked the Baroness sternly.

"It is my stomach, it is full of pain, I feel so ill," answered Isabelle.

Chapter 2

"Well, it is fortunate that are you are going to the Convent today; who is there better than the Sisters to nurse one back to health." The Baroness turned and went to make her exit.

"Wait," shouted Isabelle, "Why, I do believe I am feeling improved." With this statement, she jumped out of bed. "Send Maggy up, please, to help me get ready." Isabelle was full of pride and would not wish to make her entrance to the Convent any way other than being near to perfect.

We went back down the stairs to wait for Isabelle. When she came down, she was wearing a red gown with a fur cloak which Sir Richard had brought back from France on his last visit there. I could see that the Baroness did not approve of what she had chosen to wear but did not say anything to Isabelle. For we could all see how unhappy she was feeling. I had chosen a grey gown and cloak of the same colour. I had a problem with bright colours because of the red in my hair.

"Are you ready now?" asked the Baroness. She gave us both a big hug. "It is not going to be that bad, Isabelle. We shall be getting regular reports and we shall know how you are getting on." We were helped into the carriage, accompanied by Mother and her maid Lucy.

The escort of the Household Troop was made up of the Captain and three mounted cavalry and two archers who were seated on the outside of the carriage, one next to the driver and the other at the rear of the carriage. Sir Richard always left about twenty household troops, mostly archers, at the Castle to protect it when he was away. Nearby, he had a training ground where some boys as young as ten were trained in the Swedish drill and the Prussian discipline. These boys were mostly the sons of his vassals. They were trained for over a year.

A large army was kept by Sir Richard, half of which was made up of Mercenary soldiers and a few Flemish Knights, men from Flanders and some Danes. The rest were from his own manors and, as he had some 98 manors in England, he was not short of sworn vassals. Like most Barons, Sir Richard was always in the saddle looking for the spoils of war in this country and in France, as all the men had to be fed and some paid.

It was such a lovely day and really delightful driving through the woods, watching the wild life and the beauty of the frost on the trees and shrubs.

"Look at that stag. My, what a fine head he has, the size of his antlers is just like a small tree on his head," I said with amazement.

"He is indeed a fine old gentleman," Mother answered.

"I am sure my father would like his head on the wall of our hall," Isabelle giggled.

When we got to the manor of Denston, there were a few people and children who were picking up wood for the fires and they stopped to wave to us. Isabelle and I waved back.

"May I have some coins to throw to them?" asked Isabelle. Mother gave her some small coins, smiling and thinking how sweet Isabelle was being.

"I like to see them scrambling and fighting as they all descend upon the coins. I find it quite exciting," said Isabelle, throwing more coins.

"Really, Isabelle, you are being really nasty today," said Mother, getting very vexed with Isabelle.

Our next stop was to be at our home in Heigham. Mother had arranged previously for all of us to stop there

Chapter 2

for food and to rest the horses and water them. I was looking forward to this stop for it had been some time since I had last been home and Isabelle had never been to my home. Mother and I usually went to Heigham when the Clares were at their Manor in the West Country.

When we went through the gates to the Manor, Betsy our housekeeper and her daughter Poppy and the Bailiff were waiting in the court yard for us. We were helped out of the carriage and Betsy and Poppy curtsied to us.

"How are you, Poppy? It is good to see you, it has been some time," I said giving her hand a squeeze. "I am alright. I have missed you, Katherine," said Poppy.

"This is Isabelle; you have heard me speak about her many times, haven't you?" I asked. "Pleased to meet you, My Lady," Poppy answered with a curtsey.

"Katherine speaks about you also, Poppy," was Isabelle's reply. We quickly went into the hall because it was very cold.

"Food is ready, come to the fire," said Betsy, helping us off with our cloaks. "We have rabbit stew with some of cook's delicious oat bread, followed by goat's cheese and it is accompanied with some very fine ale into which I have put a hot poker from the fire, to make a warm drink for you."

Meanwhile, the rest of the escort had been taken into the kitchen to have food there. I was thinking about the young kitchen maids, how they would be giggling behind their hands and whispering to each other about who was the most handsome of the troops. How the cook would be keeping a sharp eye and listening to what was going on and perhaps put the men in their place if they should speak wrongly, for cook would feel that the maids were her charges while in her kitchen.

Chapter 2

When we had finished eating, Mother expressed that there was something that she wanted to show her visitors before we all left. We all climbed up to the turrets of the Hall; as the Hall was on a hill one could see for miles. "Look towards the west and you can see the Fen Sea. From the reflection of the sun it looks that some of it is iced over today. Look at the hill yonder that is Ely or the Isle of Eels." Mother turned to the other side of the turrets. "You can see the town of Bury St Edmunds, which lays in a valley. It is such beautiful countryside and you can see the River Lark winding its way around it and one can see the roof of the Abbey."

It was time to continue on our journey. New hot stones had been placed into the carriage. We all felt very comfortable, full and warm as the carriage moved off. Before we had finished waving our goobyes, Mother and Lucy had dropped off to sleep. Isabelle and myself were looking out of the carriage, talking about the different scenery we were seeing.

Making sure that Mother was asleep before she spoke, Isabelle said "That young Captain is so very handsome! Do not you think so, Katherine?"

"I have not noticed, Isabelle," I answered.

"Katherine, you are telling little white lies. You know that you are. I saw you looking at him and turning your head away so that you did not get naughty thoughts. You think that you are so good, Katherine."

"Be quiet, Isabelle, you are now being rather silly," I answered.

The carriage came to a stop and Mother quickly woke up. The Captain opened the carriage door.

"I thought that the young ladies would like to see this, My Lady." We got out of the carriage and walked down a little path. There in front of us was part of the Fen Sea which had frozen over; we were at a place called Islam and the whole of the residents of the Manor must have been skating on the sea. There were races going on, children chasing each other. There was a man who had made a fire on the beach and he was roasting turnips in it.

"Captain, why are the people not about their business?" Mother asked.

"Well, My Lady, most people here in Islam work with the boats and ferries and maintain them and supply them with goods which they may need and they cannot do so with the sea frozen."

There was an elderly woman quite close to us.

"Bring her over here," directed Mother. She was brought over, accompanied by two young children. "Nothing to worry about. I would just like to know where they all get their skates from."

"They make them, My Lady. They get strong branches from the oak tree in the spring, then they soak them through the summer in goose fat, turning them often, then they dry them and shape them and soak and dry them again." Mother was pleased and gave the old woman a coin.

"May you be blessed, My Lady," said the old woman, who was so pleased she kept looking at the coin as she moved away.

We returned to the carriage. Isabelle took the opportunity on the way back to chat to the Captain which I could see was not to Mother's liking, causing her to speak to Isabelle.

"Child, what is the matter with you today? You know that you are not behaving in the way a Lady should."

"I was just making conversation to be polite," she answered, turning her head away from Mother because she knew she had done wrong.

Chapter 2

"You were not being polite, you were flirting. Let's have no more of this now," Mother said sharply. We proceeded in the carriage at a much faster speed.

"I would like to have a go at skating," stated Isabelle, feeling very sorry for herself. Mother just ignored this. We crossed through several fords in the rivers which was quite exciting and Lucy had to put covers at the windows so that we did not get muddy. It was not long before we had stopped for the gates to be opened at the Convent.

We proceeded into the courtyard where we were greeted by four nuns. Three of them dealt with the escort and our possessions. The third one said her name was Clover and that we should follow her.

She took us to our chamber which was very bare. There was a large bed with enough room for two and a table with a wash bowl and jug on it. On the wall there was a picture of the Virgin Mary and Child.

"Will you come with me please, Your Ladyship?" asked Clover, "I will take you to the guest room." Mother was to stay just one night.

Isabelle and myself just stood and looked at the chamber. Then Isabelle threw her arms around me.

"We have not been wicked, why should we be punished like this? It is so cold," she moaned.

"We will tell Mother in the morning, she would not want us to be unhappy and cold," I said, trying to cheer Isabelle and myself up.

The door opened and there stood a young novice nun about the same age as us. She had a very spotty face and her nose was blue from the cold. I looked at Isabelle whose mouth had fallen open. I knew what she was thinking about, that we would look the same in a few weeks.

"Welcome, my name is Ruth. Will you follow me

Chapter 2

please?"

We did as she asked and we were taken to the study of the Abbess. We entered the chamber and our eyes lit up at the sight of the fire which was burning a log and we both moved toward it to warm ourselves.

Mother and Clover were already there. The door opened and Berta the Abbess appeared. We curtsied to her.

"Please sit down," she said, pointing to a well-spread table. We each had broth followed by cheese and bread. There was plenty of wine.

"This is a very fine wine," stated Mother.

"It is our own, it has been put down for five years," Berta said with great pride.

Mother took a small pouch off her belt which contained gold coins which was the payment for us staying there. This was quickly taken by Clover.

"Well, young ladies, you will see around the Convent tomorrow. You will arise when you hear the gong in the morning. Then there will be refreshments served in the refectory. I will assign Ruth to you both to help you settle in. Please remember that she is not your servant and must not be spoken to as such." Berta took a breath then continued to speak "You will receive tuition in the Holy Book. You will learn also how to serve God, the King and your Lords. I will teach you myself about life at the Palace and etiquette there."

"You will also be expected to contribute to life at the Convent. It might be that you will help Sister Opel, who is the healing Sister in the infirmary, to give Holy Water and pray for the souls of the sick or help to teach the children in the school."

"Are there any questions you wish to ask me?"

There was no reply. So Berta stopped speaking and had a sip of wine.

Chapter 2

"We have finished the meal and the wine. I suggest that I take you back to your chamber now. You must be tired," said Clover.

Chapter 3
BERTA

We returned to our chamber. Lucy was already there. She had lit the candles and got one of the stones from the carriage and had it heated and then had been working on the bed to make it warm for us. Then she had wrapped our nightgowns around the stone to get them warm and placed our nightcaps on top of it.

"Come my ladies, I will help you prepare for the night," directed Lucy. "Lady Isabelle, shall I take your brightly coloured gowns back to Clare and have you sent some darker coloured ones?"

"Yes please," stated Isabelle who had realized that her gowns were rather too fancy for a Convent.

We climbed into bed and Lucy passed each of us a comb for our hair. We had never had to care for our hair ourselves; Maggy always took care of it. Lucy helped Isabelle with hers. "You will have to help Isabelle with her hair, Katherine," directed Lucy, battling with the tight curls. "Otherwise her hair will get into a terrible muddle."

"The bed is lovely and comfortable, thank you Lucy," I said and she smiled.

At that moment, Mother came into the room. "Thank you, Lucy," she said. Lucy left the room. Mother put our caps on our heads and gave us each a gentle kiss. "Well," she said, looking questionably at us and sitting herself down on the bed.

"How will it come about that Berta will be able to have us taught about the life and etiquette at the Palace and how to behave in the company of men and all the worldly subjects that she said that we would learn when she has led such a sheltered life in the Convent?" I asked curiously.

"Berta has not always lived at the Convent and if

you promise that you will not repeat what I am going to tell you, I will let you into some facts that are not generally known," Mother said softly.

"We promise," we both replied together.

"Following the death of King John, William Marshal took over the responsibility for the care and upbringing of King Henry, who was just nine years old at the time. This was a difficult job at the time for William, as he was so often away at war.

William would not leave the young King at Court as he had many enemies among them, some of them Barons and Churchmen. William left Henry in the safety of the Giffords at their castle in Herefordshire, which was the home of Berta's father and family.

While there, the young King grew up with the Gifford children, becoming especially close to Berta, like you two have become close.

William Marshal died in 1219 and Hubert de Burgh took over the responsibility for Henry. The King then spent most of his time at the Palace; he became very lonely following William's death, as William was very kind to the young King and it was said that William showed more love to him than he did to his own son.

King Henry's mother was Isabel of Angouleme, she was granddaughter of King Louis of France. She was not very maternal and in 1220 she re-married Hugh X of Lusigman and went to live in France. The King remained at the Palace. He was just thirteen years old at this time and was very sensitive and had an air of innocence about him. He was not interested in Barons and Archbishops and their politics.

So, when Berta was thirteen she came to live at the Palace. Henry was overjoyed; their friendship blossomed again and they spent a great deal of time together. Berta would hunt with the King for she was a

Chapter 3

very good horsewoman. The King had been introduced to tournaments by William and really enjoyed the sport. He did not have a champion but did the jousting himself and it was always Berta's kerchief that he attached to his lances. The crunch came when the King had two small crowns made for himself and Berta.

There was a very important Banquet with foreign dignitaries. This Banquet was meant to put the King on display for those very rich Counts and Princes of Europe who would like their daughters to become Queen of England by paying a large dowry to help England out of her financial troubles caused by all the wars and also become her allies. The King and Berta, wearing their crowns, made their entry by skipping down the main hall holding hands, much to the shock of the Barons and dignitaries. Berta and the King could not stop laughing at the look of shock on everybody's faces.

A council meeting was called with the Archbishops and Barons who were so embarrassed over the King's behaviour. It was decided that Berta had too much influence over the King and that she would have to go.

Some of the churchmen said that she must be a witch and must have put a spell on the King and that she should be executed.

Richard Earl of Cornwall, the King's brother, was sent for to give evidence against her but Richard spoke up for her saying that they were only over-friendly because Henry and Berta had grown up together. When they were children, the King liked to have fun and play jokes on people, because Berta and Henry were the same build and had the same coloured hair. They would exchange clothes with each other and the King would make out that he was Berta and she would be the King. They even tricked William Marshal once when he came

Chapter 3

looking for the King and saw the back view of Berta thinking that she was Henry. She ran off with William chasing her. When he caught her and saw who it was, everyone had a laugh and there was much jollity.

Berta never missed her prayers and Henry and Berta spent a great deal of time reading the Holy Book. There were Bishops and Barons in the Gifford family and they quickly suggested that Berta should be married to the Church and God and become a nun.

The Archbishop Langston suggested that Berta should be taken to the monastery at St. Albans, which has now become a joint monastery, with an order that the King should not know where she was till he came to his senses and understood that the needs of England must come first.

So it came about the King shut himself in his rooms for weeks and would only take his meals there.

It was said that Berta did not shed a tear but refused to talk to anyone, even close family.

There was a monk at the monastery called Matthew Paris who had great sympathy for the King and Berta and he managed to get a letter from Berta to the King.

The King then visited the monastery and Berta in secret. These visits went on for a while. Then Berta was brought here where, in time, she became an Abbess. Now you both have an understanding and admiration of Berta, we will leave it at that and you must both go to sleep." Mother put out the candle and left, closing the door quietly.

The room was so dark. Isabelle and I held each other's hands. We didn't speak a word to each other for quite a while. I had such strong feelings, I felt so sad for Berta - how lonely she must be. God must have been very cross with her, he must have thought that she loved

Chapter 3

the King more than she loved Him. I know that I have read in the Holy Book that says He is a jealous God. Berta must have asked forgiveness from God to have become a nun. These were the thoughts that were going through my head; I know that Isabelle was having similar thoughts.

Isabelle then spoke, "Berta must have really missed riding and her horses. I know that I am going to miss the ponies. Do you think that Berta and the King made love with each other and have a secret child somewhere? I now feel a lot more comfortable about Berta, at least it shows that she is human after all."

"We must go to sleep now. Berta and the King would not have made love if they were not married." I said sternly.

Chapter 4
THE CONVENT

The gong went so very loud. I was sure that I had only just closed my eyes. I sprang out of bed and then shook Isabelle to wake her up.

"Go away, I want to sleep," said Isabelle, turning over to face the other direction.

"Oh! It is so cold," I said, shivering. Lucy had laid our clothes out on the stools. I quickly got my clothes on. "Come Isabelle you must get up."

She made a little effort. "It is far too cold to get up." I then helped Isabelle with her clothes as she was still half asleep and getting in a muddle.

The door opened and Ruth came in. "I have come to take you to chapel, come quickly please," she said moving quickly out the door. We followed. We had not combed our hair and both felt a mess. "We must relieve ourselves," I stated. Ruth pointed to a door.

We went to the refectory. There we were given a piece of bread and some warm goat's milk. We sat at a large table, there were six nuns also sitting at the table eating their bread. They each nodded to us. We nodded back.

"This is really exciting," said Isabelle as she soaked her hard, stale bread in the goat's milk.

"Mother is not here," I exclaimed.

"She is a guest and she will have her food in her room. I am to show you both around the Convent and then take you to the library where you will say your farewells to her," said Ruth.

Ruth took us first to the church. It was quite small but very beautiful; it had been decorated with lots of green plants and twigs.

There was a beautiful painted fresco of Etheldreda. The church had been dedicated to Etheldreda by the nuns who had fled Ely in 870 when

Chapter 4

the Danes had burnt their Convent down and chased the nuns away. The nuns had hidden in the fens till the Danes had gone and then made their way to Waterbeach, where they were helped by local people to build a Convent on the little island of Denny. There they settled.

We then went to the south end of the church where we walked through the cloisters which was quite draughty. Isabelle and I were shivering.

"Is it always this cold, Ruth?" I asked.

"You will get used to it in time, it is warmer in the summer," said Ruth.

"I don't think that we will survive till the summer," said Isabelle with her teeth chattering.

"I will take you to the calefactory, the warming chamber, you will be able to warm yourselves by the fire," said Ruth, feeling sorry for us.

There were no other people in the chamber, so Isabelle lifted the back of her gown and warmed her buttocks and thighs at the fire.

"You remind me of Father Joe!" I laughed. Isabelle dropped the back of her gown and joined me in laughter.

"Who is Father Joe?" said Ruth, looking puzzled.

"It doesn't matter," I replied.

"I sleep in the dormitory above here, it is much warmer than your room," said Ruth with a grin.

We left the calefactory and walked past meeting rooms and studies to the other side of the church to the infirmary. There were four nuns on duty there, nursing the sick. Neither Isabelle nor myself had seen an ill person before. They were not very wholesome, so very thin and some of them had their bones showing through their skin.

"It smells," said Isabelle.

Chapter 4

"You will soon get used to the smell and you will not notice after a while and Sister Opal says that it is good for the soul," informed Ruth.

"I think that my soul is happy as it is," said Isabelle, retreating quickly out of the door.

We next went into the cellar which was full of wine and food. "We grow all our own vegetables and keep our own livestock," informed Ruth.

There were four cockerels hanging up by their feet to drain the blood.

"What is in those large vats?" I asked.

"In the spring we kill some lambs and put them into salt brine. That is what is in the vats. The other vats contain pulses, and some have cider in them," explained Ruth. "Come now, we must make our way to the library, your mother will be waiting for us," she said.

"Well, you can see that you two are not used to getting up so early, make sure that you comb your hair in future," said Mother, giving us both a big hug. "I must get back to Clare."

I felt quite sick with the thought of her going. I loved her so much. Isabelle looked sad. "Must you go now?" she said. Mother didn't answer but just left. We quickly followed her out to the waiting carriage. The Captain of the escort nodded to us both. Mother was helped into the carriage and we waved goodbye. Just as the carriage went through the gates, another carriage entered.

"That will be the Willoughby Sisters. They will be studying with you. The taller one is called Margaret, the other one is Jane," explained Ruth.

Margaret was tall and slim, with brown hair fixed tidily off her face. She had heavy features. Her age was about fourteen years. Her sister Jane was plumper, with smaller features and a smiling face; she was about a

Chapter 4

year younger.

Ruth introduced us. As we went back into the Convent, the two girls seemed excited at learning who Isabelle was. They each caught hold of one of Isabelle's arms. "We have been desperate to meet you, we have heard so much about your family. Our father is a colleague of Earl Clare and has fought by his side many times."

The Willoughby girls did not speak to me and I walked behind them with Ruth. Isabelle was quite shocked. At the Castle, nobody gave her that sort of attention and she was quite flattered.

"You have free time for the rest of the day to settle in," said Ruth.

"Come to our chamber and talk with us while we get unpacked," said Jane, pulling Isabelle.

I went back to the library on my own and selected some of the many wonderful books to look at. I sat myself down at the table, when the door opened.

"You must either be Isabelle or Katherine."

"I am Katherine," I replied. I could not but notice how dark her eyes were; they were so dark that they looked black; they were fringed by thick black lashes. Her skin was the colour of dark olives, she looked more Spanish than French.

"I am Marie. We are here, Katherine, to learn from each other. From you I will learn English language as spoken by the villeins which I hear that you are fluent in. I, in exchange, will teach you the skills and charms of succeeding at Court or in the journey of life". With this she swirled around, swishing out her gown and the most beautiful petticoats which she wore underneath her gown. Her gown was plain grey. She wore her dark hair tied neatly back. She was dressed quite proper for life in the Convent.

Chapter 4

I wondered how someone so young could teach me about life. I knew from our very first meeting that Marie and I would become very good friends.

"Where is Isabelle? Clover sent me to fetch you both, she wants to give us the rota for the next few weeks," said Marie.

"I must ask: why is it so important for you to learn Middle English from me?" I said.

"I have come to England to give support to my cousin, Queen Eleanor of the Province. I will learn about the ordinary people of England, their ways and their lives and the Queen will understand about them from me and win their affections and will not be thought of as a foreigner and maybe, in time, the people of England will learn to love their Queen. Come, we must go now," said Marie, beckoning to me.

The weeks went by and Isabelle and I settled into the life of the Convent better than we thought we would. Isabelle had found her strengths and grew in character. She found that she was very good at teaching the local children who came into the school. She had developed a sense of humour and made up and told the most wonderful stories about horses and animals and told the stories that her father had told to us about his times in foreign lands and the battles which he had taken part in.

Isabelle also taught the children how to behave when in the company of their masters. They also learnt a little French. For their part, they taught her the games which they played. The children grew very fond of her and she was the favourite out of us girls with the children.

I was good at working in the infirmary and became a very good nurse under the tuition of Sister Opal. I learnt how to mix medicine from herbs; some we cultivated ourselves and some I would go to the spinney

Chapter 4

and pick.

The Convent for many years has been used by the Knights Templar who are the Convent's benefactors and used the Convent on returning to England from the Holy Land when they needed peace to revitalize themselves. Some of them would have the most terrible fevers. We would try to nurse them back to health by praying and using the Holy Water on them and treating their ailments. While nursing them, the men would often ask me if they were in Heaven for they thought that I was an angel. I think it was because of the colour of my titian hair.

The Knights did have their own physicians and surgeons, who sometimes visited when they knew there was a very sick Knight who needed their help.

When a Knight died, as sadly it did happen, it was our duty to cut their hair but not their beards for it was forbidden for them to cut their beards as they were required to wear them long. They were then dressed in a white habit as fitting for a Knight of Christ.

We also nursed local people; we only took the very sick into the Convent. For the rest of the people who had a health problem we ran a clinic. We tried our best to treat all the aliments of those who were sick and hurt who attended the clinics. We used syrups for coughs (given mostly to children during the long winter), hot and cold compresses for injuries, poultices for boils (of which we saw many), ointments and creams for other wounds. We made all the remedies which we used for treatments ourselves from herbs and plants. Of course we treated our own nuns.

From working in the infirmary, I learnt good composure: how to direct and speak to people and give orders in an emergency.

Chapter 5

SPRING

As well as working in the infirmary, I also worked in the library with Marie, copying the scrolls that were written by Bede some four hundred years ago and other writings by other scholars.

Marie and myself had become very close; she had such a good brain and was very worldly for her years and taught me so much. Her speaking of English had become very good so when we were together in the library we spoke no French, just English. Berta had suggested to Mother that Marie should spend two days with us at Heigham for Marie to get an understanding of the rural life of people. This was agreed.

On arriving, we were greeted by Mother. Betsy had prepared a special meal for us. "Betsy, are you sure that you are not French for I have not tasted such good food since I left France?" said Marie, wearing a great big smile.

Betsy went quite red in the face and curtsied to Marie for making the compliment, for Betsy was speechless with pride.

The next day, Marie could not wait to see the manors. We took Poppy with us as we were walking and she knew which paths were not so muddy. We visited our two churches, one at Barewe and the one at Heigham, calling in to visit my cousin the Reverend Thomas Passlewe, who Mother had given the living of the two churches and taking refreshments with him and his wife Mary, who was so pleased to see us and had prepared a very good spread which she had laid out with all her best vessels. Mary was quite taken with Marie and would not stop curtseying to her and saying over and over again "I am so honoured to have the cousin of our most gracious Queen take refreshments with us in

Chapter 5

our most modest dwelling," much to the embarrassment of Marie.

The next visit was to the mill. Marie was quite interested in seeing the grain ground but did not care for the dust which made us all cough. She was quite surprised at seeing children as young as five feeding the thresher with sheaves of grain.

"Should children so young be doing such dangerous work?" she asked me.

"Children have to work for their families as soon as they can. It makes a better life for all," I informed her.

We next made a short visit to the farm of William Say who was a Freeman. He paid rent to Mother, not in money but in kind - perhaps a pig or lamb or whatever was agreed. Being a Freeman, his stock and crops belonged to him and he could sell them where he wanted to.

Poppy then led the way to her father's smallholding to meet the rest of her family. She had five older brothers of working age, her grandmother Martha looked after their needs while their mother Betsy was away working at the hall for us. On meeting Marie, all the boys' mouths dropped open and they could do nothing but stare at Marie. They had never seen anyone with such dark beauty and grace. Marie did try to speak with them while we were drinking our Alder Flower wine and nibbling on a wheat biscuit.

"Do you all work together on the land or look after stock?" She directed her question to the young men who were clustered together in the small chamber. She only received a stutter back.

"They all do different work, My Lady," said Poppy, trying to make the best of a poor situation.

"Thank you so much, Grandmother Martha, for the hospitality," Marie said as we were about to take our leave.

"The pleasure is mine, Your Ladyship." Grandmother Martha gave Poppy a kiss goodbye.

Poppy's eldest brother Joe opened the door for us, following a discreet kick on his ankle from his sister, to remind him to do so.

When we were outside, Marie said with a laugh, "The cat has got their tongue - I think is what you say? They are not like French young men who are never without words." As we returned to Heigham, Marie could see that Poppy was upset.

"I am so sorry, Poppy, I should not make fun of your family, they really are quite delightful."

Poppy was still feeling very hurt and I felt a little sad for her. The next day, we returned to the Convent. Marie said that she had enjoyed her visit and had learnt a lot. I do not know why, but I felt a little ashamed and wished that Marie had seen me in my setting at Clare. We were greeted by the rest of the girls who asked how we got on.

"It was very good," said Marie. "The countryside was so beautiful. Katherine's mother is a delight and so knowledgeable. Betsy is a wonderful cook. I have not tasted such good food since I left Normandy."

Then she laughed and told them about Betsy's sons and made fun of them. The girls all giggled.

I was really cross and embarrassed. "I am tired and I am going to bed now," I said sharply.

The next day I went to the infirmary and was greeted by Sister Opal. "We are short of herbs and also need some willow bark. Will you gather some please, Katherine?" she said kindly.

It was such a beautiful May morning. I loved going to the spinney. I felt free for a short while. I could sing and talk to the birds while I picked the herbs and be

Chapter 5

quite silly, which was a change from having to be so serious at the Convent.

I had filled my baskets with herbs and had left the spinney and went to the clearing where I sat down on the grass. I removed my shoes and stockings for I had got little bits of bramble in them. I also removed my head covering to pick the bits out of my hair.

The sun felt so lovely on my skin that I lifted my skirt a little higher and pushed my toes into the grass; it was such a lovely feeling.

I don't know why but I got up and started to dance some of the steps that Marie had taught us. I was twisting around when I looked up and saw four men at the top of the hill watching me.

I panicked and ran as fast as I could back into the spinney to a hollow oak tree amongst the bushes, which I climbed into.

One of the men had dismounted from his horse and had entered the spinney on foot and he had stopped right in front of the tree. He was so close to me. My heart was beating so fast. I was so afraid. I quickly prayed to God to keep me safe.

There was a little peephole in the tree which I had been looking out of. He was so close that I could see the colour of his eyes which were a beautiful violet blue. His skin was tanned and he had a scar on his cheek, his hair was fair. He was tall and very handsome but looked so sad. I could not stop staring at him. I noticed that he wore a Coat of Arms upon his chest but could not quite see it. As I stared, I became quite weak at the knees but felt very excited. I had stopped praying and could not bring myself to continue to do so. I felt that it was not me standing there but someone I didn't recognize.

He looked around and then left the spinney. I waited quite a while to make sure that he had gone and

Chapter 5

then I left the tree. I felt the pain in my feet. I looked down and saw how torn they were with many thorns embedded in them. I had no time to stop to remove the thorns. I had to return to the clearing for my shoes. When I got there, my stockings and shoes had gone. The baskets were still there. I picked the baskets up and started to make my way back to the Convent, worrying about what I was going to do without any shoes and my gown was muddy and had blood on it. I must make sure that no one sees me.

I got back to my room and flung myself on the bed and cried. I could not understand what had happened to me. I was so confused and could not think of anything except the man.

Isabelle came into the room "Oh! What on earth have you been doing? Your poor feet!" she exclaimed, coming over to the bed and lifting my feet up.

I burst into more tears. "What am I going to do?" I blurted out. "I have lost my shoes and stockings." I tried to explain what had happened.

"How exciting!" said Isabelle, wide-eyed. "I wonder who the man is? He must be a Knight if he bears a Coat of Arms. I might know him."

Isabelle sat down on the bed with me and wiped my eyes on the bottom of her gown. "Don't cry any more, you have made your face all puffy and hot and I know what to do. I will go and fetch Marie. Her feet are about the same size as yours and she will have some spare shoes and you have clean stockings," she said brightly.

I sat there, staring at the picture of the Virgin Mary. I just could not stop thinking about that fair man. He must have bewitched me.

Isabelle and Marie came back with the shoes. "We must clean her up and do something with her feet. You go to the infirmary and get some comfrey cream

Chapter 5

and a binder," directed Marie. While Isabelle was gone, Marie pulled the thorns from my feet and bathed them.

"I have been bewitched. I cannot clear my head of the thoughts of the man I saw and my stomach is turning over and over and my heart is beating fast, just feel," I said, taking her hand and putting it on my heart.

"You have not been bewitched, you have changed from a girl into a woman. You have fallen in love," she said, smiling.

"Marie, how could I fall in love with someone I don't know and know nothing about?

"It does happen - and quite often I believe," she answered.

Isabelle came back with the cream and binder. Marie put the cream on my feet and the sting in them started to go. "I will not need the binder," I said, putting the stockings and shoes on myself.

"We will not tell anyone about what happened to you, it will be a secret between ourselves," said Marie.

The days went by as usual and no one else except we three knew about that day, although the girls and nuns said that I had changed. This was because the man was always in my thoughts. Sister Opal would raise her voice and tell me to stop day-dreaming.

It was now summer and we had been at the Convent for nearly two years. Berta said that we had now all grown into mature and capable young women and it was time for us to leave.

Marie was to be the first to leave. She came into our room to say her goodbyes. She looked so beautiful. She wore a bright red velvet gown edged with cream-coloured lace at the neck and wrists, her dark hair was worn high on her head and was covered with the cream lace which framed her face, emphasising her dark skin and beautiful eyes.

Chapter 5

"You must both come and visit me at the Palace as soon as I am settled and have got things under my control," she laughed. You must meet my cousin Eleanor and the King. I shall miss you both so much but will always have the fondest memories of you."

"I hope, Marie, that the Queen will allow you to come and stay with us at Clare Castle. We will be able to have such fun together," suggested Isabelle.

We both felt so sad as we hugged Marie. Clover came into the room. "Your carriage is here," said Clover. We went out into the court yard to wave goodbye.

My mother came to take us home the following week. We said our goodbyes to everyone. Berta said that she will be coming to visit us when we have settled in again at Clare Castle.

Chapter 6
HEIGHAM

Mother had brought Maggie with her to fetch us. Isabelle and myself thought that we would both be returning to Clare Castle but this was not to be so.

Mother explained that it was her idea for Isabelle's brother Thomas to take over the running of Clare Castle and his father's affairs.

"It will be good for Thomas. Since he was wounded in battle, he has been at a loss; it will give him some interest. I have spent some time working with him so he knows how to go about it and seems quite good at managing the affairs. I have become very tired," she said "and would like to spend more time at Heigham. The Baroness did agree and we thought that it will be good for you two, now you are mature young ladies, to finish your development apart. You will not always be able to be together, will you?"

"No," I replied but I had never thought about life without Isabelle.

"It will be so boring without Katherine and who is going to look after me when Mother is away? I certainly will not have Thomas telling me what to do," Isabelle said, directing her question to Mother.

"Isabelle, you are now a grown woman and are quite capable of looking after yourself. You will not be on your own at the Castle. Maggie and all the other servants will be there."

"The Baroness is planning a grand Banquet to introduce you both into society," said Mother, smiling.

"Oh! When?" squealed Isabelle.

"We haven't a date as yet," explained Mother.

The carriage arrived at Heigham and we all took refreshments.

Mother and I then said our goodbyes to Isabelle

Chapter 6

and Maggie as the Captain helped them into the carriage. I quickly ran to give Isabelle a kiss on the cheek.

"I shall be so miserable, I know that I will," said Isabelle, looking quite sad.

Then there was a sparkle in her eyes. "Don't you think that the Captain should ride in the carriage with us?" said Isabelle, as she made eye contact with me.

"No, Isabelle," I said sharply. I wondered how she would ever manage without my guidance, as I watched the carriage leave.

I felt both sad and happy: happy that Mother and I would be spending more time together and in our own home as I am sure that I would be very capable of helping her run the manors and the Hall and would be able to bring new ideas to the manors.

Mother had already spent some time at Heigham, making a few changes.

"I am afraid that the Manor and the Hall have been neglected, the Bailiff has done his best while I have been away but it needs a woman's touch. I have brought extra help in from the Manor to turn the Hall into our permanent home. We will make our plans together, Katherine. I have saved quite a bit of money while living at Clare. I will release Poppy from her duties and she will be able to help you get your room as you want it. We will inspect the manors together to see what needs to be improved upon. For we must now make sure that we can get an income from our manors. There will also be other changes; we will not be taking any more meals in the kitchen. It is important that we get Heigham back into society, otherwise we will end up being a couple of hermits," she said laughing.

The next few weeks were such fun .With the help of Poppy, we sorted out the store rooms and found objects that we had not seen before. They had been put there many years ago by the Paselewes and had been forgotten. I asked Mother if I might have two rooms of my own - one for sleeping in and one for a study where I could be private and, when Isabelle came, I would be able to take her there for a chat. I would also like there to be a guest room close by my rooms. Mother agreed and got the carpenter to make an adjoining door between the two rooms. This was done quite quickly as most of the structure of the Hall was wooden.

Poppy and I spent the mornings getting the chambers how I wanted them. We had come across two beautiful tapestries in the store chambers which we cleaned. Then we put the one of the angels telling Mary that she was going to have the child of God into my bed chamber. The other, of two unicorns in the forest, was put into my study. They did brighten up the plaster walls. Poppy also cleaned the large candle bowls and their chains.

We found an old box of beautiful dresses which had been put away several years ago and made herbal cushions out of some of them, but the better ones we could still wear.

"This is such a beautiful dress," said Poppy, holding a dress up next to her body.

"You may have that dress, it just the right colour for you, Poppy."

"Oh, no, that is much too grand for me. I have never had a silk dress before," said an excited Poppy, accepting it gratefully.

After the midday meal, the groom had the horses ready. Mother, the Bailiff and myself would visit different parts of the Manor to see what was needed to be done. There were quite a lot of repairs to be done at the watermill, the outhouses and the dairy. We also visited the smithy as Mother wanted some new cooking vessels made.

I spoke to Mother about Poppy moving out of the servants' chamber and having a chamber of her own and that Poppy should become a lady's maid to me. Of course, Mother agreed. Over the years, both Mother and myself had taught Poppy how to speak and understand French and since I had been home from the Convent I had also been trying to teach her etiquette so that when I would visit Clare, Poppy would be able to come with me.

Over the weeks, the Hall had become very pretty and comfortable and I could not wait to have visitors to stay.

The next day, a messenger came from the Convent. Berta had sent a note to say that she would like to visit us with some urgency. Mother gave the messenger a reply to say that the middle of next week would be convenient and we will all be looking forward to her visit and will prepare a chamber for her stay.

"I wonder what the urgency is?" exclaimed Mother.

"We will be entertaining sooner than we thought," I said, quite excited.

"I must get the Bailiff to send a man over to the Hall of the Convent at Risby to fetch some wine for there is no finer wine. I do not think that Berta would enjoy our Alder Flower wine very much," she said.

Poppy and I made the chamber ready for Berta. We placed lavender and rose water on a small table for her to refresh her skin and some sage and nettle water for her to clean her mouth and teeth. Fresh spring water from Barewe to drink, they say that there is none better. We made little parcels of herbs to go under her head cushion to make sure that she gets a good night's sleep and, of course, there was the Holy Book in case Berta should need it. I felt that we should prepare the chamber ourselves and not leave the job to the servants.

Chapter 6

Our carriage was also returned the same day. It had been with the smithy who had been doing a lot of work on it as it had rusted as Mother had not used it for many years. She had always used one of the Clare's carriages when she needed one. Ours was now so smart and the wheels now went round and no longer were just dragged along by the horses. It was now just as fine as the Clare's carriages.

We decided that on Sunday we would go to the church at Barewe and then we would be able to use the carriage. When Sunday came, Poppy had put on the silk dress that I had given her. She looked so different because the dress was so grand it had also made her improve her deportment and she wore her hair piled high on her head.

"Why, Poppy, you look so grown up and elegant," said Mother. Poppy was so pleased with this remark that she could not stop smiling.

When we reached the church, the villeins were already inside the church. When they saw Poppy they all stared at her and nudged each other. I wondered if we had made things difficult for Poppy in her own community. We sat in our own pew which was at the side of the altar. I could not but notice that Poppy kept turning her head to look at a young man and he did nothing but stare at Poppy. When we left the church and walked past him he just said quite loudly "Poppy." Poppy turned her head the other way.

I did not mention the young man to Poppy in the carriage as we were taking my cousin the Reverend Passelewe and his wife Mary back to the Hall for a meal, as I did not want to embarrass Poppy.

I could see that they disapproved of the way in which Poppy was dressed. I smiled to myself when I saw the look of disapproval when Poppy sat at the table with us for a meal.

That evening Mother was tired and retired to bed early, leaving Poppy and myself alone. "Well, what about the young man who could not take his eyes off you?" I asked.

"What young man?" said Poppy, turning her head away.

I just said "Poppy."

"It is Will Sommers's son, Richard," she said quietly. Will Sommers was a Freeman and owned a wood on the outskirts of Barewe. The whole family worked as woodsmen, they were quite well off. Mother had recently bought all the wood she needed for work on the Manor from them.

"How well do you know him, Poppy?" I asked.

"I do not know him, I just know of him," she said, with her face turning red.

I did not speak any more that evening about him.

"How did you feel about all the chatter at the church about you and the way that people stared at you?" I asked.

"I felt very awkward at first and wished that I was not there, then I thought 'What is the problem?' As long as I don't let it become one, it can do me no harm," was her reply.

"That's right," I said. "It is now time that you helped me get ready for bed, Poppy."

When in bed, I thought about Poppy and Richard Sommers, and my thoughts turned to my fair young man. I was wondering if I should ever see him again. This time, my breast went hard and my limbs became weak. My heart beat so fast and I felt so hot. I could feel his face close to mine. I quickly jumped out of bed and I fell to my knees.

"Dear God, please forgive my sins." I then got back

into bed and closed my eyes so tight hoping that I would clear my head of him. He just refused to move out of my head; when he did start to fade away, he would hold my hand and pull me close to him. I found it so difficult to sleep because I wanted to be with him.

Chapter 7
BERTA'S VISIT

Berta arrived on Wednesday. Poppy was told that she would serve at the table and act as ladies' maid to Berta.

Betsy had excelled herself with the meal which made an impression on Berta. "What a wonderful meal and the wine must be from Risby for there is no finer. Its taste and aroma is that of heather and can only come from that area," she stated with a great big grin.

"The hall looks so pretty and so comfortable," she said so kindly.

"Well, what is the urgency?" asked Mother.

"To the study," directed Berta.

Mother led the way, followed by Berta and myself. We made ourselves comfortable and fixed our eyes on Berta.

"Well, it is the future. I am getting very tired and the years are passing with great speed and I would like to spend more time in my beloved Herefordshire where I spent my childhood. I will need someone to take charge of the Convent when I am not there. We have all missed you every day, Katherine. Sister Opal talks every day about you, how much she misses you in the infirmary. You have the right skills and with a little more training you would be able to manage the Convent very well. So we would like you to take Holy Orders. Of course, you must make your own decision," she stated.

Mother and I just stared at each other, then Mother looked away. "What a great honour," she said, just looking into space.

As a child, I thought that I would give my life to the Lord but now that I am a woman, although I will serve the Lord it will not be in that way.

So I said "No, you have really honoured me and I

Chapter 7

am most proud. I am no longer pure in mind or soul. So I could never become a nun."

Mother and Berta both stared at me in much surprise. "What do you mean?" asked Berta and Mother together.

I had to tell them about that May day in the spinney and the fair young man. How the young man was always in my thoughts both day and night. How I prayed for forgiveness but was still bewitched.

"What does this young man look like?" asked Berta.

I described him to her and she looked quite surprised; she did not seem disappointed as I thought she would.

"I must send a message to the Convent to let them know that I will be delayed in my return, for I must now travel to Clare and this must also be arranged," she said, looking very thoughtful.

"I will send some messengers," said Mother.

"Tell me, Katherine, does this being bewitched frighten you?" asked Berta.

"No, not really! In fact, I feel quite excited. I feel a little frightened when I close my eyes and I see his face and his mouth opens as if he is going to speak to me and another face comes out of his mouth and again the mouth opens and another face of him comes out of the mouth and it keeps repeating on and on and I just cannot clear my head of him. I am so sorry Berta," I said.

"You have done nothing wrong, my dear," she said kindly.

Mother came back into the room. "All arranged, the messengers are on their way," she said.

The next morning Berta and Mother spent all the morning in the study. I knew they were discussing me. I spent the whole morning walking about, I just could not relax. Even Poppy and Betsey were looking puzzled for they knew that something was going on.

Late in the morning Berta left for Clare. Mother hardly spoke to me and her face looked very strained.

"Mother, are you vexed with me?" I asked.

"No, Katherine, I am not cross with you. I just feel a little unsettled. I just have been living in such harmony since you have been home and I see that change must come," she said softly giving me a hug.

"I don't understand, Mother," I said.

"Let that be enough of this silliness," she said.

Berta visited us on her way back to the Convent. Mother and Berta quickly went to the study and shut the door behind them excluding me. They were not there very long before Berta said her farewells. But before she left she said to me, getting into her carriage, "Katherine, the Ball will be the in the second week of February and the Baroness wishes you to go to Clare three weeks before to prepare yourself."

It was now December and for the last few weeks we had been preparing gifts for the poor of the Manor. Betsy had been cooking dripping cakes made from the fat in the bottom of the spit tray and Mother had four pigs slaughtered. These were cut up into portions and then put into brine. We also looked out the things that we no longer needed and these will also be given as gifts.

On Christmas Eve there was a queue outside the Manor. The villeins were let in between midday and dusk. On their arrival, they were given hot Alder Flower wine which had spices added. Some would bring a container and take the wine away. I would give the gifts out and Mother would put her hand on their shoulder and say "May God bless you." It was a good feeling to be able to do this for our people.

The next two weeks seemed to go very slowly. I

Chapter 7

saw less of Poppy; she was always asking for time to either go to her home or to do something. When Richard Sommers brought wood she would hurry him into the kitchen.

"Poppy, we will be going to Clare the second week in January. It will be the first chance you will have to be my lady in waiting," I said. She did not look happy about this news and just said "Oh!"

"I thought that you would be very happy." I said.

"I am looking forward to it but it is a long way from here and it will be a long time away from home."

"Well, Poppy, if you are so fond of Barewe you can stay there. I am quite sure that the Baroness can provide me with a lady in waiting," I said crossly. "Stay here," I said, quickly hurrying to the kitchen.

"Betsy, I want to speak with you," I said sharply. She followed me back to the hall. "What is going on with Poppy?" I asked

"Well, My Lady. Will Sommers has asked my husband Tom, Poppy and myself to go and share a meal with his family on Sunday," she said quietly.

"Why should that make Poppy behave oddly?" I asked crossly.

"Well, I think that Richard wants to marry Poppy and I expect that Will Sommers wants to know what Poppy will be able to take to the marriage," she said quite brightly.

"We will not allow Poppy to marry," I said, raising my voice.

"Why, Katherine?" Betsey questioned.

"How dare you question me? Address me correctly please," I said crossly.

"I am sorry, My Lady," she said and gave me a little curtsey.

I do not think that Betsey had seen me so cross

before, and I did not even know this part of myself. "Go now and do your work," I said sadly. I then hurried off to find Mother. I told her what had happened.

"How can Poppy be so selfish after all the time we have spent on her and the opportunity which we have given her. She knew nothing till we taught her and now I cannot bear to look at her," I said

"Do not let this become a problem, Katherine, you are not thinking. You must always be in control," she replied. "What I shall do is to inform Poppy and Betsy that she must wait one year before she marries and then we will give our blessings, if you are pleased with the service which she gives. Poppy and her husband will get a worthwhile wedding present," said Mother calmly.

Mother went and spoke to both Betsey and Poppy and told them what would happen. Betsy seemed pleased; afterwards she spoke to Poppy in private.

During the next week, Betsey came and spoke to Mother and said that Richard had asked Poppy to marry him and she had said 'yes'. Will Somers was pleased with the arrangement and delighted that Poppy would bring a gift from us to the marriage.

Poppy was now in a very happy mood about her coming marriage, even though she would have to wait a year. She really enjoyed getting her clothes ready for Clare and helping me sort out what I wanted to take with me.

Mother was to come to stay at Clare a week before the Ball to help the Baroness with the preparations.

Chapter 8
THE BANQUET

The day had come and Poppy and I were off to Clare. Mother gave me a big hug and said "See you soon."

Poppy was very excited. We were leaving the Manor and were at Barewe Hill when Richard appeared. The carriage stopped. Richard opened the door and whispered in Poppy's ear and gave her a bunch of snowdrops. The carriage moved off. "I am so happy," said Poppy, smelling the flowers and smiling to herself. It was Poppy's first time as ladies' maid outside our home.

"I hope that you will not be too lonely, Poppy? I will not have much time to spend with you. I am sure that Maggie, Isabelle's maid, will take care of you, you must learn from her."

It would be my first time staying at the Castle as a mature woman. I would have to make sure that everything I did must be correct for all eyes would be on me as I was new to society. With this thought, I took a deep breath and sat upright in the coach. For the rest of the journey, Poppy and I were very quiet for we were both deep in our thoughts.

We arrived at the Castle and there in the court yard were Isabelle waiting for us along with Jane, the keeper of the keys and, of course, Maggie.

"Katherine! Katherine!" Isabelle shouted, "I have missed you so much," she said, giving me a kiss on the cheek.

"And I you, so much," I replied.

"The Baroness will receive you later, she is so very busy. Come now, I will take you to your chamber," said Jane.

We were followed by the rest of the party, for they

would have to unpack the trunks.

While ascending the stairs I took the opportunity to introduce Poppy to Maggie.

"If you shadow me, Poppy, you will soon learn the layout of the Castle," said Maggie kindly.

"Come to my study later so that we might chat," said Isabelle, taking hold of my hand and giving me a tug as soon as I arrived at my chamber.

"Well, what have you been up to, Katherine?" she asked. I told her about Berta's visit and all the other things that had happened.

"What about your fair young man?" she asked.

"Oh! He is still with me every minute of the day and night," I said with a sigh.

"Well, he might be at the Banquet as he wears a Coat of Arms. That is, if he is still in England," she said, deep in thought. "We had better freshen up before the evening meal and I will collect you and we will go together to meet Mother," directed Isabelle.

Isabelle took me to the dining hall. The Baroness was seated at the table.
"Why, Katherine, last time you were here you were a child. Now stands a beautiful young woman."

Isabelle giggled; both myself and the Baroness stared at her. "Sit down and take your places," said the Baroness.

"I am so pleased to be here for it is so full of happy memories," I stated.

"How lovely to see you Katherine, it has been quite a while," said Thomas, Isabelle's brother.

"I think that it must be some three years since I last saw you, Thomas. I have missed you all so much," I explained.

"Father is still away and the rest of the family has not arrived as yet, they should be here tomorrow," replied Thomas.

"Well, Katherine, are you looking forward to the Banquet?" asked the Baroness.

"Very much, but I am a little nervous," I said.

"You will be with Sir Richard and myself and Isabelle at the main entrance of the Great Hall. When we welcome the most important guests, Sir Richard will introduce Isabelle and then you as Lady Katherine de Passelewe, his ward."

"I am most honoured, Baroness, as I am sure that Mother would be also," I said, thanking her.

"You are held with affections as if you were one of our daughters," she said.

"Come, now we have finished our meal we will go to the drawing chamber, there is something which I want to show you both," she said, hurrying off with Isabelle and myself following her.

On the table in the drawing chamber was a large box. "This is from the Province," she said, taking two notes from the box. She gave us each a note. "Read yours, Isabelle," she directed.

"Sorry that I am unable to be with you for your debut, as is the King and my cousin Eleanor. I have sent you a gift of this beautiful Spanish silk. For you Isabelle I have chosen the colour scarlet for it will show off your beautiful dark eyes and hair. It is also the colour for someone as bold and strong as you. I miss you and will always hold you in my highest regards. Love Marie."

"Oh! Look at the silk, it is wonderful, enough to make a gown," she said twirling around.

"Read yours, Katherine," said the Baroness.

"Katherine. Oh! How, I have missed you. My poor brain has been vegetating listening to the silly chit-chat that goes on amongst the Ladies of the Court. None of them seems to be able to match your intellect. For you I have selected the colour silvery green silk to match your eyes and show off your beautiful hair. I wish so much that I could be with you at Clare, just to see the envy on the other ladies' faces when you make your entrance and they cast their eyes on your grace and beauty. I do hope that you find your fair young man. Your friend for always. Love Marie."

As I looked at my silk, I noticed that there was a sketch of two gowns with Isabelle and my names under each gown, which Marie must have thought most suitable for us. Isabelle and the Baroness both looked at the sketch.

"Why, they are just lovely, so different. They don't just hang from the shoulder, they come into the waist and the sleeves are so full, just like wings," exclaimed Isabelle.

"The sleeves are gathered in at the wrists as well," I said.

"I must send a message to the gown maker at Bury St. Edmunds to come at once and get started on making these gowns," stated the Baroness.

The next days went so quickly, there was so much to do. Sir Richard was now home. He had given orders to some of his men to help with jobs in the Castle. They helped unload the carts. There was so much food arriving. There were bullocks, pigs, sheep, swans, rabbits, pulses and much ale and wine. There were the entertainers camping outside the Castle gates: jugglers, musicians and fools.

Mother had also arrived now. "You must both go into the tub before the kitchen gets too busy," she said.

The tub was a great big barrel which was as tall as my shoulder and wide enough to get three people in. We didn't go into the tub very often, as it was a lot of trouble to fill and empty it. It would be stood in the

Chapter 8

kitchen near to the fire, but not too near for we would not want to become smoky.

Maggie, Lucy and Poppy prepared the tub for us. They put the leaves of the horse chestnut tree in the water. These leaves would make the water silky and clean us. They had put boxes for us to climb on; they would now hold our hands and lower us into the water.

We had our bathing gowns on for it would not be right for anyone to see our bodies. Isabelle and I were lowered into the water. It was so deep that our gowns floated up on to our faces. We all laughed so much. Isabelle caught hold of my hands and we jumped up and down, splashing the maids. We went right under the water and rubbed our heads to clean our hair. We were helped out when the water cooled. We dried our private body ourselves under the wet gown and then were handed our under- garments which we put on under the gown and then the maids could remove the wet gowns.

Mother was to share my chamber with me so I hurried there and she helped me with my hair which was very tangled.

The next day the guests started to arrive. They were asked to stay in their chambers and refreshment would be brought to them, for the following day would be the Banquet and the main hall needed to be prepared.

It was the morning of the Banquet and I woke at dawn. Mother was up already and was finishing off the details for the Baroness. The castle was so noisy with laughter and shouting. Many of the guests had not been to bed and were retiring to their chambers for some sleep. I went to Isabelle's chamber to wake her up.

"Oh! Isabelle! The smell of wine along the passage from people's breath is disgusting," I said.

"Katherine, get into bed. I am so tired I didn't get to bed till the early hours. Emma and my brothers arrived and I had not seen them for such a long time. We needed to catch up with the news," she said, turning over in the bed.

"No. I shall go out into the herb garden and pick some herbs which I need," I said, but Isabelle had already returned to her sleep.

I picked the herbs which I needed, then sat down on the bench; it was such a beautiful, bright morning and quite warm for the time of the year. Thomas came into the garden and sat down next to me.

"Well, Katherine, what do you think about poor old Thomas who can only walk dragging his leg?" he said, looking me in the eyes.

"Thomas I just think how brave you have been. It is not how you move but the person you are, Thomas," I said.

"Well, Katherine, when I saw you yesterday I just could not understand how I did not notice in the past how beautiful you were. It may be that I looked upon you as a sister and now I see you as a woman." He paused. "Katherine I am very attracted to you and I would like it if we could spend more time together. Perhaps after the Banquet you could stay on at Clare for a while and we could do things together. Ride and just spend time getting to know each other again," he said.

I was quite shocked and did not really know what to say. "Thomas, you have taken me by surprise. I do love you but just as you would love a dear brother. When I was a child you brought fun into my life, you used to make us all laugh. Do you remember Father Joe's smoky gown?" I said, smiling.

"Yes," he said "I do remember," looking at me for an answer.

"Thomas, I do not know what to say. I have known no other males but you and your brothers and dearly love you all as family," I said, getting to my feet ready to retreat.

I curtsied to him and said very formally "I must go now, My Lord", hurrying back to my chamber. Thomas just sat and watched me retreat.

I had a very heavy feeling in my stomach. I thought about Thomas who was now wounded and how he limps and felt very sad. I just hope that I spoke correctly. I must speak to Mother with some urgency about what has happened. This should be a very happy day, now I feel very unhappy; I do not wish to hurt Thomas's feelings. I got back to my chamber and sat on the bed.

"My Lady," said Poppy carrying in some food, "I have some bread with apple and bramble jelly on it and some milk to drink."

"Have you seen Mother?" I asked.

"Yes, I have, she is between the hall and the kitchen overseeing thing. It is best to keep out of her way, everyone is so sharp today, especially the cooks," she replied.

Isabelle came into the chamber and said that Emma wanted to see me and is waiting in her study. "Emma wants to go through the dances which we will be doing to make sure that we are up to date with them and using the correct steps," she said. Emma was married to a French Baron; he had not travelled with her but had stayed in Normandy. Emma had travelled with her retinue, made up of three young men and three women.

"My dear Katherine! Why, you are not a little girl any more," she greeted me with a hug.

"How lovely to see you, Emma," I replied.

"Your flute," said Emma to one of the young men. "We have not got much time to practise. We will start off with the Estampie."

Two of the men took Isabelle's and my hands and led us to the centre of the room. The flute accompanied us and we started to dance. We finished this dance. "Now the Rotta, followed by the Branles Galor, and then I will dance the Manfredina - you two can watch. For it is new and must be danced seductively. You must make your partner desire you, Queen Eleanor dances it this way all the time," said Emma.

We finished dancing and Emma commenced. She certainly danced it very seductively, tossing her head and getting her body very close to her partner and lifting her gown above her ankle and then stamping her foot. There was no doubt that Emma had a gift of movement.

Mother came into the chamber. "Katherine, Isabelle what are you doing? You should be getting ready for the Banquet," she said.

Mother and myself went off to our chamber. "Mother I need to speak to you in private, it is very important," I said.

"We haven't any time now, Katherine," she said.

Poppy was already there, waiting to help me get changed. I first bathed my face in Camomile water to bring out the fairness of my skin. Then Poppy applied some Red Poppy cream we had made during the summer to my lips and cheeks to give me a glow. I was then helped to get into my dress. The silk was so very fine it sort of floated. I had pumps for my feet made in the same cloth. Poppy helped me with my hair. I had it drawn off my face and the hair was braided from the top of my head with dried Lady's Mantle, Artemisia {silver Queen) to reflect the silver in my gown and fresh Geranium leaves to match the green of my gown.

Mother held a mirror for me to look into. I could

Chapter 8

not believe that it was me I was looking at.

"Well!" said Mother, "Marie has chosen so well for you, Katherine. She is indeed a good friend."

Poppy helped Mother into her dress. Mother still wore black in society to show that she was still in mourning for Father. She did have a little white frill at the neck and wrists.

Isabelle burst in "Mother and Father are ready to make their entrance; are you ready?" she said.

"Isabelle, you look so striking in scarlet, you could not wear a better colour," I said.

We hurried to where Sir Richard and his party were waiting for us. We took our places, Emma was being escorted by her brother Richard, Isabelle was with Gilbert and I was with Thomas.

"You girls look wonderful," said Sir Richard very proudly. "They certainly do," replied the Baroness.

We made our entrance into the hall led by the accompaniment of the bagpipes.
The guests stopped their chattering as we entered and then started to whisper about us - who we were and what we looked like. We made our way to where the important guests would be presented to us.

The first was Richard Earl of Cornwall, being the King's brother, followed by the Knights and their Ladies; Simon de Montford Beaumont, John de Warne, William Walpole, Peter Gifford from Wickenhambrook, Thomas Gifford of Stoke by Nayland. There were Knights whose names I cannot remember or where they were from. They each kissed my hand and said "My Lady, My Honour."

We were getting close to the end of the queue and a little bored when I noticed the Knight being presented to Isabelle had a scar on his face. I knew that I had seen him before; it was my fair young man.

Chapter 8

He took my hand. I felt weak at the knees. I remembered Sister Opel's voice saying "Keep control of the situation."

I heard a voice saying "Sir William Gifford of Weston." He did not kiss my hand, we both just looked each other in the eyes. It must have been for some time, then I heard Sir Richard's voice, saying very loudly "Will." Will quickly kissed my hand and moved off. I dared not follow him with my eyes, much as I wanted to.

We went through to the banquet hall and took our places. Sir Richard picked up a tumbler of wine. "For God, King and Country." The guests picked their tumblers up and repeated the same, then commenced to eat.

The family had been split up and were seated amongst the nobility. Mother and I were seated between Lord and Lady De Vere and Lord and Lady De Say. At the other side of the table there were two empty seats. I looked about me to see if I could see where Isabelle was seated, also looking to see if I could see where William Gifford was seated. Then, across the table just about to take their seats, were Sir Thomas and William Gifford.

"Lady Passelewe and Lady Katherine," they both said, bowing their heads as they took their places at the table.

"What a fine spread," said Sir Thomas.

William and I had made eye contact again, I tried to look away with great difficulty.

"You are Sir Thomas Gifford from Stoke on Nayland, are you not?" Mother questioned Thomas and then continued to ask him about his parents and their health.

"My cousin Sir William Gifford of Weston," Thomas announced.

"I am honoured, Ladies," said William.

Chapter 8

"You are the ward of Sir Richard, Katherine. Do you live here at the Castle?" asked William.

"No, my Lord, I live at Heigham with my Mother. I did spend many years at Clare while I was growing up," I said. We continued to eat while Mother made most of the conversation.

"Lady De Passelewe, may I take Lady Katherine to the other hall to watch the dancing, if she would honour me?"

"You may," said Mother.

Sir William took hold of my hand and led me through the jugglers and fools who were entertaining the guests while they were eating. I could not but gaze at how tall and broad Sir William was and how his fair hair curled at his shoulders.

We entered the hall where Emma and Isabelle were already dancing the Trotto, accompanied by the bagpipes, shawn, framed drums and tambourines. This was a very fast, merry dance.

As I watched, I could feel William's eyes upon me. I turned towards him and he smiled so beautifully at me. "Have I seen you before, Katherine?" he asked.

"Yes, My Lord, at Denny. You were there with other Knights. I was picking herbs and took fright as I did not know who you were and ran into the spinney," I explained.

"I am so sorry, Katherine, I would not have wished to alarm you. I am so sorry. We all thought that you were a beautiful Imp. Come now, Katherine, we must dance," he said, smiling again.

We had finished dancing and there was Isabelle with her brother Gilbert.
Gilbert took my hand and led me back to dance the next dance. I could tell by the sparkle in Isabelle's eyes that she was up to something. I knew that because of

William's scar she was aware that he was my fair young man. I turned my head as much as I could to see what she was doing. I could see that she was chatting away to William at great speed.

Following the dance, Gilbert escorted me back to where Isabelle and William were, saying how beautiful I looked and how every man there would be thinking the same. "You must have confidence in yourself, Katherine and follow your desires."

I thought that was a very odd thing to say. I would have asked him to explain but we were already back with William and Isabelle. "Come Gilbert, we must dance again." she said, hurrying away.

William quickly took hold of my hand and led me into a chamber where music was being played by a harp, accompanied by some lutes. There were not many people there listening to the music. We sat in the corner so that we might talk.

"I want you to tell me about that day when I first saw you at Denny and about the rest of your life. I have to return to the west of England within the next two days. For I am overseeing the building of a castle on the Welsh border and the King wants it to be finished at great haste," he explained.

I told him about that day back in May and how I had lost my shoes. I did not say how I cried or how upset I was.

"Your shoes are with Berta, she is my Aunt, we were on our way to the Convent when we saw you," he said.

"I did not know that Berta was your Aunt," I said.

"You have become very important to me, Katherine, in such a short while for I am very attracted to you. In fact, more than attracted - and I believe that you feel the same?" he said taking hold of both of my hands.

Chapter 8

It was so embarrassing and how could Isabelle betray my confidence? The beats of my heart were racing. What shall I say? "Be truthful" I had been taught.

"Yes, My Lord, I am. But I know nothing about you," I said, looking him straight in the eyes.

"Be patient, you will learn about me. Tomorrow I will have to meet with Sir Richard as you are his ward and also with your Mother. I think that it may be difficult as they will still be busy with the guests, but it must be done," he said, very determined.

"Come now, I must return you to your Mother, she will be worrying for we have been quite a while," he said, taking hold of my hand and leading me back to the banquet hall.

Mother was still talking with Lady De Vere. William waited for his moment and then asked Mother if he may speak to her and Sir Richard both together tomorrow about a very important matter.

Then he asked Mother to come and watch the dancing with us in the other hall. We all returned to the hall and Isabelle came over to speak to us with the young Earl of Essex who she had been dancing with. We all chatted together till it was time to retire.

Chapter 9
WILL'S STORY

The next day I woke early and although I was still tired, I just lay in bed and let the events of the day before filter through my head.

What did William really mean? Did I really hear correctly? What was he saying or was my mind playing tricks on me? Was he going to speak to Sir Richard and Mother to ask if he could spend time with me to get to know me, like Thomas said?

Oh, Thomas! I have not spoken to Mother about Thomas as yet. What is happening? I seem to be getting into such a muddle! How could Isabelle betray me like she did? How will I feel when I see William again, will my face turn bright red? Did he really mean what he said? Or was it the atmosphere of the Banquet and perhaps the wine talking?

I jumped out of bed. What shall I wear this morning? I felt so tired and heavy. I certainly was not attractive today. I washed my face in camomile and cleaned my teeth and tongue in sage, as my mouth felt so horrible. Poppy came in with the breakfast.

"I will not take breakfast this morning."

"Do you not feel well? "You look terrible, My Lady, did you not get much sleep?" saying it with a twinkle in her eye.

"Thank you for that, Poppy. Still I must brighten up, I am just so tired. I will wear my blue gown today, that will make me look more alive," I said, seeing my reflection in the mirror as I walked by, not liking what I saw. Isabelle came into the chamber.

"You may go, Poppy," I said.

"How could you, Isabelle? How could you embarrass me so?" I said crossly.

"I was helping you. William is the man you want.

Chapter 9

You would have never told him so I did it for you, all you would have done was to go on dreaming about him. I have made things happen. You should be very pleased with me and not cross," she said, annoyed, pouting her lips as only Isabelle could when she was annoyed.

"I am sure you are right, but what happens now? I am afraid to leave this chamber for I do not know what to do or what comes next. I shall have to hide from everyone," I said.

I told Isabelle about her brother Thomas and what he had said to me.

"I will explain to Thomas how you feel about William. I will stay with you throughout the day and help you in every situation. Come now, let's go and say goodbye to all the guests," she said with a smile.

Mother greeted us at the bottom of the stairs. "Sir Richard will have a meeting with William and myself following the evening meal, most of the guests will have left by then," she said.

I still didn't get the chance to tell her about Thomas as she hurried off so quickly.

"Come now, let us take a walk in the garden," said Isabelle. We had not been in the garden very long when William appeared.

"Ladies," said William, greeting us with a bow.

"Would you like to walk with us, we are on our way to the stables?" said Isabelle, very confident for she knew that she could speak about horses for hours.

"Very honoured to do so," replied William.

Isabelle did most of the talking, with William making a comment very infrequently. For William only had eyes for me and I for him. He did ask us what we thought about his Aunt Berta and if we were on the receiving end of her sharp tongue. Both Isabelle and I laughed. For we knew what he meant and I replied

Chapter 9

that she also has a heart of gold.

"Well, at first I always tried to avoid her, I was sure that she had the power to look into one's brain and read its thoughts. In time, when I got to know her better, I knew that she just wanted what was best for us." Isabelle looked at me to see my reactions, in case she should not have spoken so. I just smiled at her.

The evening came and Sir Richard, accompanied by the Baroness, Mother and William, went into the study. They had not been in there very long when they sent for me. I took my place between Mother and the Baroness.

"Well, William?" said Sir Richard.

"I felt that you should learn about my background of the last four years and the events that took place before I ask you, Sir Richard and Lady de Passelewe, a very important question."

"Four years ago, I left to fight in the Holy War along with my men. I sailed to Dieppe. There I met up with several Knights and their men and we rode together to Marseille where five ships were waiting for us to take us to the garrison at Acre. There we collected our supplies and more horses and were allocated some mercenaries who would be paid by results when we returned. The Knights Templar had left money for their pay. We were also given our orders and territories.

I was to join up with Sir John Beaumont; it was our job to recapture the castles and territories. As you know, the war had not been going too well for the Christians. We were to ride to join up with Hugh the Fourth Duke of Burgundy; Henry, Count of Bar; Amaury de Monford. There were already many French Knights getting restless for action. Peter of Dreux led 200 French Knights in successful ambush of a non-military Muslim convoy en route to Damascus. Of course I did not

Chapter 9

approve about such actions but it was too late for me to do anything about it. You know what French knights are like," Will said, looking at Sir Richard who just nodded.

"I then joined Henry of Bar and about 500 Knights and some infantry in many raids, which took place on Muslim camps near Gaza. Myself and Sir John Beaumont fought for about nine months in this area before we departed in different directions.   At Gaza we demobilized. The men were paid off and fresh Knights and men returned to the captured territories to hold these areas. I took my own men and proceeded towards Jerusalem along the shores of the Sea of Galilee.

We were all looking forward to getting to Jerusalem and got careless. For we rode straight into an ambush. The horses took fright, for a few minutes we were without defence. I gave orders for the infantry to form their triangle with the supply wagons in the centre of them while I and the cavalry rode off at great speed with the Saracens light cavalry in pursuit of us. At my orders we reformed and, turning on the Saracens cavalry, we fought with great bravery and much experience although we were out-numbered. It was during this battle that a sabre, which was meant to behead me, caught my face. I could see that we were so out-numbered and was thinking the worst.

I then noticed a cloud of dust moving fast towards us, I was still fighting and trying to watch what was causing the dust, when I saw many horsemen shouting and swinging their sabres. I thought that our end was in sight. To my surprise, the Saracens started to flee with the men in pursuit of them, driving them into the hills.

We paused breathlessly. I was about to instruct my men to also pursue the Saracens when their leader returned, holding his hand above his head to signal to us to stay where we were.

He was dressed in goat skins and had so much unkempt hair and his beard in fact was so thick that you could not see the colour of his skin but all that could be seen were two dark blue sparkling eyes. I knew by the colour of his eyes that he was white.

"Why, a Gifford, which one are you?" he said, looking at my Coat of Arms.

I was shocked. "Why, you must be Walter's son. You are so much like your mother," he said.

"I am William, you are correct. Who must I thank for the courageous help we were given? I am in debt of a most knowledgeable gentleman."

"Why, you do not know this monster of the desert? I am your uncle Osbert, your father's brother, Osbert the wicked one," he said, bursting into laughter. "Come now, we will go back for your men. I have sent some of my men to help them," he said.

We rode back to my men, there were a few wounded but no dead. I had my face treated and made sure that the men also had their wounds bound.

"We will ride back to the camp with your cavalry and I will leave mine to bring your infantry back," he said.

I felt quite nervous about doing this but had little choice. My men did not like the arrangements either. On the way back to the camp, my uncle explained to me how he came to be in Levant.

"Well, it was an affair of the heart. I fell deeply in love with a nun from the Convent of Wilton who said that she returned my feelings. I did not have a licence to marry her so I took her away to Normandy, with her consent of course. When we got to Normandy, she wanted to return to the Convent. So I accompanied her back to the Convent where I paid the Mother Superior

Chapter 9

much gold to take her back, not knowing that the Mother had already complained about me to the King saying that I had taken the nun against her wishes.

The King sent for me. He said that for penance he would take my land and holdings and have the sheriffs of Salisbury, Wilton and Amesbury have their men beat me with sticks around their markets and through their churches. I was to give the King my gilt spurs, horse trappings and not wear the girdle of a Knight and should serve for three years in the Holy Land. Of course I have been here a lot longer and have quite enjoyed it living in the community that I do. Still, that was all in the past.

We arrived at the camp which was like a small town. People of all different colours and cultures, men, women, children, tradesmen, craftsmen and priests all going about their business.

At a large tent we dismounted. I followed Osbert into the tent where he was greeted by two women who helped him off with his goatskin cloak and his boots. One poured some wine for us while the other went off to get some food.

"Take your armour off, William, I will put it into safe keeping. You will not need it if you wish to fight by my side. I can stand on high ground and see the sun reflecting off Knight's armour for miles so, if I can see it, so can the Saracens. You shall be taught along with your men a different way to fight and be fitted out with goatskins to wear. You will also find it much better to use an Arabic scimitar, their metal is much lighter than we can make it but just as strong as our sabre. You may also ride one of my Arabic horses, you will find it much swifter and it might even save your life," he said with a smile.

I was having problems with the wound on my cheek, it was still bleeding and covered with flies.

Chapter 9

"Get Bea, Rebecca," said Osbert to one of the women.

A youth came back with Rebecca. He was very young for he had not yet got a growth on his face and his body was still that of a child. He carried a box from which he took a dagger. He pointed to a couch.

"Bea is mute. Lay on the couch and have your wound treated. I am going for a walk," said Osbert.

I did as I was told. Bea poured hot water into a container and cleaned the wound, he was so gentle. He then took the dagger and gently put it into the wound. It was very hot and the pain was very great but I could not shout out in front of this boy and the women. He then put a mixture of honey and some sort of herb into the wound then covered it with a sticky tree bark which stayed put. I thanked him. Bea held up five fingers. "It stays on for five days."

I watched Bea leave the tent; I was quite puzzled by this boy. I knew that something was not quite right but could not think what it was.

The next day my men arrived. They were pleased to see me and I them. We had a look around the camp together and found a place to pitch our tents. I moved out of Osbert's tent and had my tent rigged amongst my men.

The following day, my men and myself were given goatskins to wear which were better than our clothes to protect us from the late afternoon blow which came most days. It was a great wind, which caused a sandstorm, and the sand stung your skin as it hit you. Although the goat's skin was quite light, it protected against the sand and did not show up in the desert as our armour and clothes did. We also had days of training learning how Osbert and his men fought.

We were ready for our first task which was to

Chapter 9

attack a camp of Turks who were causing problems in the area. They were situated east of the river Euphrates. We rode several days to get there. Always at my side was Bea who rode and controlled a horse with great skill. In fact, Bea was a wonderful warrior: brave, fearless with wonderful desert skills. I had great admiration for him and I learned to communicate quite well and we became good friends. I found myself watching Bea quite often; his mannerisms I had not seen before in a youth for he moved as would a maid. I had not fought before with such a young warrior and it was quite a puzzle to me.

Bea's four older brothers were also riding with us. They were all sons of the Sultan Selim from one of the territories in Persia who, from a child, had to live in the desert with his people after they had become Christians. The price they paid was the loss of their lands and being driven out into the desert.

We were very successful and got rid of the Turks. We returned to the camp where there was much merriment with lots of wine flowing and a great feast. I sat with Osbert and Rebecca, who was one of his ladies.

"Rebecca wants to find you a maiden, she says that you must be lonely," said Osbert.

"Thank Rebecca. If I should need company I can find my own maiden."

We were enjoying the feast when Selim and his family joined us. Selim beckoned to Osbert who left the feast to speak with Selim. After some time, Osbert returned to the feast.

"Selim wishes that you and his daughter Princess Bea should become betrothed, for it is Bea's wish. Her mother was French, Will, she died many years ago and I think myself, Will, that it would be a good match for you. For you are not betrothed in England, are you?" asked

Osbert.

I was quite shocked and was quiet and thoughtful for a while. "Do you mean Bea, the boy I ride with?" I asked, looking at Osbert.

"I do indeed, Will," Osbert started to laugh in his deep throat laugh which caused people to look at him. "Fancy thinking that Bea was a boy!" He laughed even louder, holding his stomach and turning red in the face.

I was quite embarrassed. "The joke is on me, Osbert," I said quite sharply.

"I must see Bea and communicate with her, Osbert. I have grown quite fond of Bea mostly because of his, I mean 'her'great bravery," I said, which caused Osbert to start laughing again.

Between Osbert splattering and laughing, he directed one of Selim's sons to go and fetch Bea. Then Osbert sent Rebecca away so that Selim could sit next to him and we waited.

Bea appeared. She was dressed in women's apparel. All eyes were upon her, I do not think that anyone had ever seen her like this before. I had not. For most of the time, her face had been grubby and she was dressed as a man. I had not really looked closely at her face. Her beauty and grace stunned me. Her eyes had been painted in the style of the Egyptian ladies. Bea wore a beautiful gown with lots of gold and precious gems.

"Why, Bea, the Queen of Sheba could not match your beauty."

I took her hand and we walked away together to a place which was quiet and private. We sat down and our eyes were locked together.

"Bea you are most beautiful and I hold you in the greatest esteem and I am most fond of you. If you marry me and I should be fortunate and live through the battles

Chapter 9

which I must take part in, I will then be returning to England, my home, which you, if you become my wife, would come with me, away from your home and family and would find life in my country quite different."

Bea put both of her hands on her heart and then put them on to my heart; she then took a ring and put it on to my betrothal finger and then took my face with both her hands and kissed my lips very hard.

"If that is your wish then it shall be so," I said gladly. I did not know if I would ever be able to return to England. I did pledge my life to fight for God and free Jerusalem for the Christians.

"Come now, we must inform your father and Osbert," I said, taking hold of Bea's hand. They were all full of joy that we had become betrothed.

"No time to waste. Bea is in all her finery and has never looked more beautiful or more happy,"said Osbert.

He called to the Priest who was also at the feast. We were married. I did not imagine that when I woke that morning I would be returning to my tent at night with a wife."

"You have a wife then," said the Baroness, quite shocked as were the rest of those who sat around the table.

"No, My Lady I have not," said Will, dropping his head sadly. "If you will bear with me a little longer, I will conclude my story as quickly as I can," stated Will. Turning his head to make contact with everyone at the table, he stopped at me and we stared at each other.

My heart had sunk. Where was my dream? I was meant to be his first love. How could he love another woman? Will seemed to know what I was feeling. He let his head drop again as he continued his story.

"Bea continued to fight at my side, even when she was carrying my child. She would not have it any other

Chapter 9

way. We were both happy as we were allowed to be taking the conditions of war. A son was born to us. We named him 'Walter, Selim, Longueville San Peur, Gifford in honour of our Fathers and Forefathers.

It was not many weeks after the birth of my son that a message came from the French Knight Theobald saying that in Jerusalem the Tower of David had been stormed by As-Salih of Damascus and that we needed to give help to Theobald to recapture the Tower.

I had to say goodbye to Bea and my dearest little son. My men and myself had to ride with much haste to Jerusalem, where it took us several weeks fighting alongside several Knights and their armies to recapture The Tower of David. We returned with great speed back to the camp. I could not wait to see Bea and my beautiful son. I had made up my mind to return to England with my family.

Before we got to the camp we could see smoke coming from between the surrounding hills. I have never galloped my horse so fast before. Arriving at the camp entrance, I could see at the top of the flagpole which usually flew the flag of The Crusade the body of an infant. I knew that it was the body of my son Walter. A young Arab who we used as a scout swiftly climbed the pole and brought the body down and placed it in my arms. I looked at Walter's sweet little face framed by a mass of thick dark hair shining with threads of gold and red. I focused my eyes upon his deep blue eyes, gently closing them with my fingers as the tears flowed down my face landing on his little nose. I kissed his little cherry lips.

"Bea, mother of my son, where are you, are you alive or dead? God why have you punished me like this? Have I not been a good servant to you, fighting your war, how could you let this happen to me? What of my wife?"

Chapter 9

I shouted with much hate and passion.

I should have been off on my horse, galloping to find Bea but could not do so. My legs had turned to jelly and would no longer support me. I crumbled to the ground where I sat for two days just holding Walter in my arms, neither hearing nor talking. Seemingly Osbert had been away those two days looking for our women and children that may have survived the sacking of the camp.

"Get up," he shouted on his return. "What are you doing? Firstly you are a Knight and then a Gifford, do you dare to put me and my kin to shame?"

I heard him but took no notice and I did not want to get up.
Osbert then took a large container of water and tipped it over me and my son. Full of rage, I got to my feet. How could he insult my son? I reached for my dagger but it was gone so was my sword. I could not punish God but I could do so to Osbert. With all my strength, I plunged towards Osbert. He quickly kicked my legs from beneath me and I fell to the ground, he then kicked me on the thigh. He took Walter from my arms and gave his body to the women.

"You have held him in your arms long enough, he needs to be made ready for his journey to Heaven, do not deny your son that, Will," he said gently. "Make your peace with God then you may come to my tent," said Osbert, walking off.

I sat down again and let Osbert's words flow through my mind. I am a Knight. I should wear a sheaf of valour around my heart, I had let it crack, I have lost honour. It was my pride; I wanted to take my son home to my grandfather Elias and the rest of the family for he was their new heir. With much effort, I quickly made my peace with God and asked forgiveness.

Chapter 9

I went to Osbert's tent. As I arrived, Bea's father and brothers had returned with her body; she had been tortured and raped. They carefully laid her body on the bed, then they threw the body of the leader of those who had sacked the camp at my feet. I did not ask what revenge they had taken, I did not want to know. Rebecca came into the tent carrying Walter in her arms. I took him from her and taking the vest which was bearing my Coat of Arms, I then lay Walter in Bea's arms, covered them with the vest and kissed them both goodbye. The Priest was called who blessed them and said a few words, which I did not hear as I could only watch my beloveds being covered with sand, knowing that I would not see them again until I go to God's Kingdom, if I should be fortunate.

I said to all those that were there that I and my men would be returning to England. Bea's father clasped my hand and said "Will, you have made my daughter Bea so happy in her short life and I thank you for that, also for giving me a grandson of whom I am so proud and for that I and my family will always hold you affectionately in our hearts."

I turned my head and looked at Bea's brothers who were nodding in agreement.

"I have nothing here any more but sadness and guilt. I will remember you all," I directed to everyone as I shook their hands in good-bye.

Osbert gave me a letter for the King and said that he would be following me in a few months to England.

That is my story. I hope that you will consider me a fit Knight for Katherine's hand in marriage, that is if Katherine is agreeable," said Will, getting to his feet.

I was in torment, filled with so much emotion. So sad for Will and his family and so sad for myself. This was not my dream. It should not be like this. I felt that I

Chapter 9

should rush out of the chamber for my head was spinning. I was having a problem to clear my head and I knew that I must be in control. I looked at Will and I knew how much I loved him.

"Sit down Will," said Sir Richard. "You are a fine Knight, there are not many better. As for Katherine's hand in marriage, I was hoping that she would marry my son Thomas who also loves her dearly and such a marriage would bring much joy to me and my family. To be fair to you, I think that Lady de Passelewe must make the decision," said Sir Richard, looking at Mother.

"I am so honoured, My Lord, that you should want Katherine as your daughter and as you know how fond of Thomas I am, I wish to hear what Katherine has to say," said Mother, looking at me.

"I also love Thomas but as a dear brother who I have grown up with and there is no other family that I would like to be part of and I will always remember how fortunate I have been to live amongst people who I love and honour and owe so much to. I hope that in your hearts in time you will forgive me and learn to love me again. I feel in my heart that there can be no other man in the world that I can love as I love William. So I will marry Will," I said, moving towards him.

The Baroness just got up and left the chamber without speaking another word.

"It will be so then, if you agree," said Sir Richard, looking towards Mother for her reply.

"The decision is Katherine's," said Mother, leaving the chamber with Sir Richard.

"Katherine, thank you so much, I will always love you and we will be so happy together," said Will, taking me in his arms and kissing me so gently.

"I must retire now Will. I feel it will be better tomorrow when everyone has had some time to think about us. For it has been such a shock for everyone, learning about your marriage to Bea and having a son Walter and the terrible things that happened to them," I said

"Well, that was then and this is now, we must look forward to the future. I know that we have not known each other for very long. My dearest Katherine, the moment I saw you I just knew that we were meant for each other. I love you so much, my whole body and mind are full of love for you. I did love Bea and always will but that does not mean that I love you less for I could not love you more."

He put his arms around me and we kissed. I just melted and felt the same as that day when I first saw him in the spinney.

"Please, William, I do not have a chaperone. We must not," I said, pulling away and feeling very hot.

"I just cannot wait for the time when I make you my wife and we will be as one."

"Do not speak about such matters, Will. It is not allowed," I said quite firmly.

"I must make an early start in the morning. I must return to the West Country where I have commitment to the King to keep the security on the borders of Hereford safe from the Welsh and of course I must let my father, grandfather and brother Walter know our good news. Would you like to get married in Worcester or Hereford Cathedral, Katherine?" asked William, quite excited.

"Will, I was thinking about getting married in one of our churches and having quite a small wedding," I said quietly.

"Well, we will have two weddings - one at your home and one in a Cathedral in the Gifford's holdings. I am sure that my brother, being a Bishop, will be able to work something out," he said thoughtfully. "I will also

Chapter 9

have to find a home for us in the west of the country as I will have to be close to my work and commitments," he said, looking me in the eyes. I feel that he must have realized that I would feel quite shocked about leaving the area where I had always lived. The truth being that I had not really thought about life outside my own cocoon and I would also have to leave Mother for she would never leave her Manor.

"It will take me some weeks to sort everything out, Katherine, for I will also have to have an appointment with the King and that will mean that I may have to travel to Normandy or France as the King seems to spend a great deal of time abroad now. I will get messages to you, Katherine, to let you know how things are progressing," he said, once more pulling me close to him and saying "Goodbye my love."

It was very difficult but I said "Good-bye Will," with a smile which I had to force on my face.

I quickly run up the stairs full of emotions. Happy about the coming marriage and sad about all the problems it seemed to be bring with it. Isabelle was waiting for me at the top of the stairs.

"Well what has happened? Are you going to marry William?" she said.

"Yes," I stated with a smile.

"Why have you got tears in your eyes then, what is wrong?" she said, very puzzled. I informed her about all the problems.

"Katherine, you will be marrying a Knight, you will belong to him. I can't see any problems. Just stop worrying and let Will and your Mother work it all out. They will know what is best for you and Will. You are being very silly, Katherine."   Laughing, she gave me a hug. "Why, it is me who is supposed to be the silly one and you the level headed one!" We were both

Chapter 9

laughing together.

Chapter 10
THE DAYS BEFORE THE WEDDING

The next day Mother and I started our journey home; Poppy had left the evening before to return to Heigham. So much had happened, I felt like a different person from the one who had started the journey to Clare for the Banquet. Mother was very quiet for the start of the journey.

"Are you not happy with my decision to marry William? You are so quiet," I said.

"Yes, Katherine, I like William very much. We of course have not known him very long but he comes from a very good old family. Above all my other feelings, I want you, Katherine, to have a happy life, to be loved and cared for and I will do everything within my control to see that is what you achieve. I know how happy I was with your father in the few years we had together and how I value those years. It was not easy for me when you said 'yes' to William. For I always thought of you being married to Thomas, which would have been in line with the plans I had made in my head during the recent years. You have given your heart to William so William it will be," she said with a smile.

"Mother, I love William so much and so want to be with him but I did not think there would be so many difficulties and my head is in a spin."

"There will be problems but we will be able to work it out and get control of each situation. Sir Richard, William and myself did have some discussions. William did state that you should live with his father Walter till he can get one of their castles or manors made ready to live in." She looked at me, waiting for my reaction.

"I will find it very hard leaving you and my home and I am sure that I will be so sad and lonely when William is away from home, as he will be from time to time," I said.

"Barewe, as you know, was left to me and my sister Alice by my dear brother and I have been holding and running Alice's half of the Manor for her. For a wedding present I have decided to give to William my half of Barewe. Then you will be able to reconstruct the hall at Barewe for it needs a lot of work done on it to make another home for you and William," she said, taking my hand and squeezing it.

"How wonderful, Mother, then I will not be leaving you and my home," I said happily.

"Well, it's up to William if he wants to make it one of your homes," she expressed.

"We are at the gates of the Hall and Betsy and Poppy are in the yard waiting for us," I said, waving to them. We got out of the coach and they curtsied to us.

"I am to be married," I said with a spring in my steps as we entered the Hall.

"When?" asked Poppy.

"As soon as arrangements can be made," I said, full of pride.

"Before me, then?" asked Poppy.

"May I ask who it is you are marrying?" asked Betsy, quite surprised.

"Sir William Gifford of Weston," I answered.

"Betsy and Poppy, you are our great friends and we are most fond of you both but in future you must address both Katherine and myself as your 'Lady' and of course Sir William as your 'Lordship'. It has not mattered in the past but now there will be lots of nobility coming to the Hall, so it must be so," stated Mother.

"Will there be many changes, My Lady?" asked Betsy, a little crossly.

"There will be a few," said Mother quite sharply.

Poppy took my boxes to my chamber; while she

Chapter 10

unpacked I asked her about Richard Sommers and her relationship with him and his family.

"Both families are getting on well together and we are very happy and are looking forward to the day when we can marry, My Lady," said Poppy, making her point.

Two weeks had gone and there had been no message from William and I was feeling quite sad. We had not yet made any plans for The Wedding, although Mother had got extra women into the Hall to give it a very good clean. I had been making drawings of how I would like my wedding dress to look.

Then came a message from Berta saying that she was going to Weston on horseback escorted by Sir Thomas Gifford of Stoke by Nayland, Will's cousin . She would really enjoy riding all that way on a horse and I know that she will be full of praises about us and the coming marriage when she speaks with William's family at Weston. She said that she would not be spending much time there and would call at Heigham on her way back and bring news for us.

I had written to Marie to tell her my good news and ask her if possible could she wait on me at my wedding, along with Isabelle. Mother had also been writing and had told her sister Alice about my coming marriage and how she was going to give her part of Barewe to William. She had a reply from Alice who said that her husband, Sir William of St Albans, was not too happy about the arrangements.

Within a week, I got a reply from Marie saying how happy she was for me about my news. She said that if the Wedding was the right date then she would love to wait on me if it did not clash with her duties to her cousin the Queen and, of course, the King. She explained about her duties at the Palace. How the Queen was away so much in France and how the Queen had taken Emma, Isabelle's sister, under her wing and was not really a very good influence on Emma who did not need much encouragement to raise eyebrows. "We shall say no more," wrote Marie. "My cousin says that my duties are to escort the King while the Queen is out of the country and do all the boring jobs that the miserable old Barons say she should be doing. The Queen says that the King no longer has any fun in his soul and that England is a miserable place with weather that cries tears all the time, whereas in France the weather laughs sun most of the time and makes her feel good. She says that all I have to do is to keep the King happy so he does not keep moaning at her.

    I have grown fond of the King, our minds are in tune with each other. We play chess together and I am helping the King with his plans for a great Cathedral which will be a great Minster for London.

    The King says that it is a way that he can express the love he has for his very first love, which he has never lost but which he had to forfeit. He will not give any details about the Lady, just that his heart bleeds for her every day.

    I knew who that Lady was, who he loved so much and thought how romantic it was that he should still love her. I also knew that it was not the right way for him to feel but I do know how difficult it is sometimes for one to control one's feelings." Marie's note continued: "I know what you are thinking, Katherine, but the King and I are just good friends. He says that I am such a rare woman that he would not spoil me and that there are plenty of harlots surrounding him, when he needs that sort of company. He says that he hopes in time that I should fall in love with a good strong man. Then he says 'not too soon' for he would miss my company and beauty. I trust, Katherine, that you will burn this note straight away and not tell anyone about what I have written, not even Isabelle or your mother. I hope that one day you will meet Henry, I have told him so much about you. Then you will understand what a lovely man he is. He is not weak as the Barons and Bishops say. If I can't make the wedding, my best wishes will be with you both. Great love from Marie."

    I did as Marie asked and burned the note. I felt from reading her words that she had already given her heart to King Henry and I felt so sad for her.

    Ten days had passed when Berta returned, so tired and quite dirty from her traveling. She said that she had much news but must wash and rest before she was able to give it to us. Mother quickly got Poppy to take her to her chamber and help her wash and make herself comfortable before she took her rest.

    I have never known time go so slowly, I just could not settle. Mother was helping Besty make the table ready for the evening meal. Berta returned from her rest after about two and a half hours. Mother, Berta and myself sat at the table for our evening meal; I could not eat or take my eyes off Berta as she started to drink her wine.

    "I had better speak," said Berta, looking at Mother "or Katherine will waste away," she said, laughing. I quickly started to eat as Berta started to speak.

    "I just managed to miss Will by a day for he had ridden off with his uncle Osbert to France to see the King. William suggested that Osbert should take over his duty for the King in the West Country and that the King may be able to suggest work for William here in the East. Of course this can only happen if Osbert is reinstated and forgiven by the King. So we must all pray that this will happen.

    My brother Walter and my nephew Walter are

Chapter 10

very happy about the Wedding. They said that the Wedding may be here. Nephew Walter will preside over the ceremony and my brother would like you, Katherine, to wear Will's mother's wedding dress," she said, giving me a parcel.

"Oh, thank you, Holy Mother," I answered, wondering what the dress would be like and whether it would fit me.

"They said that they will make arrangements to stay at St. Edmunds Abbey before the Wedding and that they will make the arrangements also for Will's men-at-arms to camp somewhere close. Will sent you this note, Katherine," said Berta, taking a large mouthful of wine.

"Will you both excuse me please? I have eaten enough and wish to retire," I stated. Mother nodded and I said 'Goodnight'. I got to my chamber, sat on my bed and, with trembling fingers, opened the letter from Will.

"To the Lady of my heart, Katherine.

You are in my thoughts both day and night and I cannot wait till we are as one. We do not know much about each other. It is our strong love we have for each other that has brought us together. I must let you see into my soul, my dearest Katherine. For, as you know now, I had a love before - Bea - and although she and my dearest son are not with me in body, I have not stopped loving them for they have taken part of my heart. This doesn't mean that I love you any less for I could not love you more. I do hope that you will not feel jealous of these feelings which I have. I hope that you will also be able to love this part of me and let their spirit into our family which you and I are about to make. You will understand if I have dark days and restless nights caused by the guilt which I feel and will always be with me as I did not give them enough protection when they needed it.

Chapter 10

I feel that God has given you to me and this has helped me heal and get rid of some of the anger which I felt towards Him.

Berta must now be with you and given you the news on how happy my family is for me. We will get the work in the Hall at Barewe done, then we will be able to make the Hall one of our homes.

Take care my love, we will be together soon. All my Love, Will."

I just sat and thought. I remembered how shocked and sad I felt when Will told us at Clare that he had been married and had a child. I had thought about Bea and wondered if I would become second best to Bea. Now I understand Will and trust him and this will strengthen our love for each other.

In the morning I showed the letter to Mother. She just gave me hug and she said that she would straight away send some men to start the renovation and get a team of women in to clean the Hall at Barewe.

Berta had already left, making an early start to return to Denny. She had said before she left that Isabelle would be visiting within the next few days to spend some time with me before the Wedding. Isabelle will be going to live at Court and so we will not be able to see much of each other because of all the changes. I was so pleased about her coming visit.

I tried on my wedding gown with the help of Mother and Poppy. It was so beautiful - quite plain and simple, just what I wanted and it fitted so well.

Isabelle arrived the next day and will be staying until after the wedding. She had brought the dress she would be wearing as my attendant; it was blue, edged with gold at the neck and at the bottom of the skirt with golden sleeves. For the next few days, both manors were so busy with nearly everyone getting things ready for the Wedding. There were many carts coming and going. Mother hardly went to bed making plans and directing people. Barewe Hall was finished very quickly and Isabelle and myself put the finishing touches to it. Mother said that Betsy would get the servants that would work at the Hall into shape so that they knew what they were about.

"I think that it will be a good idea if Will's family stay at Barewe Hall before the Wedding instead of staying at the Abbey. For I am sure that the Hall would be more comfortable for them and it is quite a long way for them to travel on such an important day.

"That is a wonderful idea, Mother."

"Also I wonder what you thought, Katherine, if Poppy got married to Richard the week after your wedding, for the church would still be looking lovely and Poppy is so keen to get married."

" Yes, and Poppy and Richard would be able to live in a cottage close to Barewe Hall so that Poppy could still work for me. Also it would be useful if Richard could also work for us."

"Well it would be up to Richard - remember that he is a Freeman and may not want to work for William. It will also make Poppy free following her wedding," Mother stated.

This made me think "What on earth would I do without Poppy's help?"

"You will manage and I am sure we could find some other maid," Mother answered.

We had all been working so hard and were getting tired; nearly everything was in place so Mother said we must all take time off to relax before the Big Day.

Chapter 11
THE WEDDING

Although we had been so busy, it was lovely to have Isabelle staying, there was so much laughter all the time. I would joke with Isabelle about all the suitors she will have once she has settled into life in the Palace society.

"That's why I am there," said Isabelle." I hope that all the handsome men have not gone and that I am not left with all the fat ugly ones," she said with a frown.

"Well, I am sure that Marie will help you to find the kind of men you like," I said.

"Well, she has not found one for herself yet, according to Emma," expressed Isabelle. "Still, it will be lovely to see Marie again. I think that we should go riding, I need to see more of the countryside, I need some fresh air," she said, moving towards the door.

When we got to the stables, Isabelle laughed, "Why, the horses are so old. I hope that we will not kill them by taking them out!" she giggled.

"We haven't had time to think about the horses. We did not need them when we lived with you at Clare," I said, a little vexed.

We did enjoy our ride around the countryside. When we returned to the Hall there was a message from Will to say that he would be here in two days time. I felt so excited and nervous. Mother said that we must send some messages off, to Sir Richard and the Countess, to Berta and the other guests to say that the Wedding will be in five days time. Sir Richard and his party, William's father and Berta will be staying here, William and his friends will stay at Barewe Hall. I will have to find accommodation for the other guests, perhaps with the De-Says at Denham Hall and Saxham Hall will accommodate some of them.

"My Lady," said Poppy. "I thought that I should say that people in Barewe are worried about Sir William taking over the Manor. They don't know him and think that there will be many changes."

"There will be changes but I am sure that Sir William will be fair. I have not got time now to speak to them, I will get the Bailiff to have a word with them," Mother answered. "Poppy, Katherine and I have decided that you may marry Richard in the week following Katherine's wedding if you wish as the church will still be looking beautiful," said Mother with a smile.

Poppy gave a jump of delight. "Oh! Thank you so much, My Ladies," Poppy said, pulling her shoulders up to her neck and giving a big grin.

"I will give you a gown, Poppy, for your wedding, I will be having all new gowns to go to Court with," said Isabelle, wanting to contribute to the situation.

"Now, back to your work, Poppy, we still have so much to do," said Mother.

The two days had gone and a messenger came and said that William's cortège had just left Grantchester and should be at Barewe about noon. I felt so happy but very nervous and squeezed Isabelle's hand. Isabelle has been a great support and we have been so close for so many years and now we will be going in different directions as we start the next part of our lives.

"I will always love you, Isabelle," I said.

"Me too, I will always love you," said Isabelle.

"We will go to All Saints Barewe to meet William on horse back, I feel that it will be more dignified to greet them that way," Mother said to Isabelle and me.

"We must get ready and leave soon," I said.

The streets of Barewe were lined with people who had left the fields and their work to greet their new Lord. The first sighting of the cortège was when the sun reflected light from the armour as they came over the hill at Needles Eye. Then I saw William and his cousin Thomas in front with their colour bearers. Behind them were men of arms on horse back, then a carriage, followed by more horsemen, then came many carts which carried supplies and possessions. There were about forty men at arms on foot. William's army will be camped at Denham castle, an old fort, which was last used by William Marshal's men. The people of Barewe all cheered when William greeted me. We then followed William to the carriage which carried his father and brother, where we welcomed them. They then followed us to Heigham, while the men were taken to Denham.

On arriving and following the courtesies, the guests were taken to their chambers were they could refresh themselves following their long journey.

Will took my hand and we went into the garden and when we were a short distance from the Hall we embraced. Then we exchanged news. William told me that his audience with the King had been most successful. The King was quite surprised to see Osbert. William told me word for word about the audience which he and Osbert had with the King.

"Why, you old rogue. Are you able to control your lust now?" he said with a smile.

"I ask your forgiveness, Your Majesty," said Osbert, kneeling to pay homage to the King.

"You have my forgiveness, you may get up. I have heard about your great success in the Crusade. You fought much longer than you needed to regain your honour. I will give you back your spurs of a Knight; also I will give you back two thirds of your lands for I must keep a third for payment for having your manors looked after."

"Thank you," said Osbert looking at the ground.

"Well, William, I have also had news about your exploits in the Crusade. Your grandfather Elias must be very proud of you. I have also heard about your coming marriage to Lady Katherine De Passelewe and hear that she is quite a beauty and has been a good friend to the Queen's cousin Marie," said the King, waiting for my reply.

"I am indeed most fortunate, My King. It is my coming marriage that caused me to request an audience with you, Your Majesty, for I would now like to reside in Suffolk. Osbert would be willing to take over my duties on the Welsh Borders. If this will suit you, King Henry, I would be most grateful," I said.

The King thought. "Yes, I do need more strength in Suffolk and along the East coast there. Osbert is quite capable of keeping the Welsh out of my country. I will get you to liaise with Sir Richard De Clare. I give you my blessing for your coming marriage and give my regards to the beautiful Katherine and you, Osbert, be on your best behaviour!" He laughed as he said goodbye.

"Before we left, Marie asked for me to visit her, which I did. She said how she had been longing to meet me and she said that she feels that she knows me well from the feelings which Katherine held for me and is very sad that she will not be able to be at the Wedding. Then she gave me a parcel for you saying that you must open it before the Wedding Day and when you are on your own. She said 'Sir William, you are so fortunate to be marrying Katherine for I know no other who would make a better wife and I wish you both great happiness.'"

"Did you admire her beauty?" I asked.

"Yes I did, also her grace and charm and I thought that she was very sincere," he said.

Then Sir Thomas came and found us and said that there

was a meal ready and we must now go and eat. Following the meal, Will and his brother left for Barewe Hall where they would be staying; their servants would already be there.

Over the next few days, the guests started to arrive; everything started to fall into place thanks to Mother's good planning.

The next day William thought that it would be a good idea to have the folk of the Manor celebrate the Wedding too, and the coming of their new Lord to the Manor. So he said that he would get some of his men to construct a large spit on the green. He would then take some of the young men of the wedding party to hunt boar in Barewe forest and that he would also have the men build a spit at the camp at Denham. He thought it better to keep his men separate from the manor folk. He will also have some men take a cart and get some more ale from the monks at Risby to go with the roasted boars.

The Countess played hostess to all the Ladies in the Hall. They spent most of the time catching up with the gossip; this left Mother free to put the finishing touches to the Wedding the next day.

The next morning I woke early. I needed to pick the flowers for my hair. While I was preparing the flowers in my chamber, Mother came in for a chat for she was sure that later she would not have much time to speak with me. She told me once again how much she loved me and how happy she was for me.

"My dearest daughter, I have come to tell you that you were the most precious gift that your dear father gave to me. I loved your father so much just as you love William. On my wedding night I felt nervous and a little frightened, as I expect it is the way you are feeling." I nodded in reply.

"I am sure that William will be very gentle with you. The union between a man and a woman who are in love is wonderful and you must think how much I love William and trust him. I will pray tonight that your union will bring forth children."

Isabelle came into the chamber full of excitement, followed closely by poor Poppy, who Isabelle had running around in circles fetching and carrying things for her. Isabelle, like Mother and myself, wanted everything to be perfect. The weather had done its best - it was such a beautiful day.

Our dresses were laid out while Isabelle and I put the finishing touches to our posies. These were to complement the decorations in the church which was in the same style of the church of St. Etheldreda at Denny. I had decided to wear my hair loose, intertwined with flowers.

"I am not too sure about you wearing your hair loose in church. I think that it may be frowned upon," said Mother. But Isabelle used her charms on Mother. "Lady de Passelewe, the Ladies at Court are not covering their heads, even when they attend church, it is very modern not to."

We got our wedding clothes on, then Poppy helped us with our hair. The guests were now leaving for All Saint's Church. Then it was time for Mother and Isabelle to leave for the church. The time had come for Sir Richard and myself to leave.

In the carriage, Sir Richard said, "I wish you much happiness. I had hoped that you would have become my daughter by marrying Thomas." He paused then he said "I like William very much, he is fine man and I am sure that he will take great care of you and that you will be very happy."

We had arrived at the church and the people of

Chapter 11

the Manor had picked flowers and made a path of them up to the church. There was a large crowd standing each side of the path, all clapping.

At the porch of the church where Isabelle was waiting, there also stood Berta, Sister Opal and Ruth. I was so surprised, I was not expecting the nuns at the Wedding. Berta and Opal and Ruth walked in front of Sir Richard and myself, carrying a cross, while Isabelle walked behind. William and Thomas were waiting at the altar and they both turned and smiled at me. Walter, Will's brother the Archbishop of Gloucester started the wedding service. He turned to Sir Richard and said, "What have you got to say?"

Sir Richard said, "I give my ward, the Lady Katherine de Passlewe, to Sir William Gifford of Weston lineage of Osbern de Bolbec, Sire de Lonquerville for his wife to love and care for. I relinquish my responsibility for the Lady Katherine."

The Archbishop said, "Lady Katherine, will you hold Sir William above all others, save God and the King, to love and obey him till death?"

"I will, Your Grace," I said.

"You, Sir William, will you take this woman Lady Katherine into your family to love and to cherish and protect?"

"I will," said William, looking at me.

The Archbishop then put a jewelled tiara which carried the Gifford's Coat of Arms on my head and said, "You are now man and wife."

Chapter 12
THE NEW LIFE

As we left the church, the fanfare sounded and the crowed cheered as William and I got into the carriage. Will embraced me and said how happy he was and how beautiful I looked.

I replied, "Will I can't believe that I am your wife. I keep thinking that I am dreaming and that I will wake up and you will not be there."

"I will always be there for you, my Lady Katherine Gifford," he said with a laugh and once more kissed me and embraced me till we were back at Heigham.
The Banquet was held in the garden and there was music everywhere. Some of the guests ate in the hall for the sun was so hot. There was much entertainment with Jugglers, Tumblers and Fools.

Late in the evening, some of the younger guests said that they would make their way to Barewe Green to see the folk of the Manor celebrating.

William and I said our farewells as we made for Barewe Hall in the carriage. Mother made arrangements for the guests that had been staying at Barewe Hall to stay at Heigham, so William and I could be on our own for the night.

We were greeted by the servants. William told them that they may have the night off to join the celebrations, but to be back in the morning.

When they had gone, William picked me up and carried me up the stairs to the bedchamber. It was made to look pretty and smelt lovely and Poppy had brought all the personal things which I needed, including the night robe which was in the parcel from Marie. It was so beautiful and delicate, the colour of ivory. William said "Make yourself comfortable, Katherine, there is something that I need to do downstairs."

Chapter 12

I just smiled at him. My stomach was turning over and over, again and again. I kept thinking how much I loved William and I knew that the union between William and me was God's wish.

I refreshed my body with lavender water; the day had been so hot and it was still very warm. I quickly put the night robe on, it looked and felt so comfortable. William came back before I had time to braid my hair and put my night cap on.

"Well, it is my beautiful wood nymph again!" he said, taking me by the hand and leading me downstairs and out into the grounds. He led me to where the moonbeam was reflecting on the ground. "Please dance for me the dance you were doing when I first saw you at Denny."

I was quite surprised. I skipped and twirled in the moonlight with my hair and robe billowing out and, as I danced, he joined me pulling me close to him. He then led me to a bed of straw which he had laid earlier. I lay down on the straw while William started to take his clothes off. I did not know where to look. "Katherine, my dearest, do not turn your head away, we are now as one," he said, laying next to me and pulling me close to his body. My heart was beating so fast and loud that I was sure he would hear it. He gently stroked the hair off my face and kissed me gently. His hands stroked my body which he caressed. I felt quite calm now and my body seemed to melt as his hands gently stroked my thighs, brushing my robe upwards. I felt his muscular body next to mine as he kissed me once again while he gently pulled my legs apart, touching that part of my body which is not spoken about. He then entered me with that part of his body which makes him a man. I felt so tight and thought that I may tear, I just thought about how much I loved him and it made me more comfortable.

He was holding me so close, I responded by putting my arms around his strong body.

"How wonderful you are, I am such a fortunate husband," he said. The warmth from William's body entered mine as we laid on our sides in a tight embrace, dropping off to sleep. We woke at dawn.

"The servants will be back soon. Come, my beautiful wife," he said as he led me up the stairs to our bed chamber, where we once more embraced.

When it was time for us to rise, William brought the jug of hot water which had been left outside the chamber door for us to wash. We then made our way downstairs to where breakfast had been laid. On the table was bread, oatcakes and jam. Eggs were brought to the table once we sat down, there were also a jug of ale and apple juice

"This day, Katherine, we will saddle the horses and ride around the Manor and surrounds. Then you can introduce me to my villeins and tenants and I will be able to see just what works need to be done. I must get most of the rebuilding done before winter sets in and while I still have my men here to do most of the work. I need to make Barewe more productive if it is to support us and our family. My men at arms will also need feeding. I have quite a bit of bounty from the Crusade but do not wish to live from it, for it will not last very long. Most of my men wish to go back to the west of England where they have families, so I need to replace them. This means I will have to take at least one young man from each family to join my men at arms and of course they will need training," William said as he looked at me.

"Oh, William, the people of Barewe will not like that. For they need their sons to work the land," I said, very anxiously.

"They don't get any choice, Katherine," he

Chapter 12

answered.

"I think that we should get Mother to speak to them and explain," I said.

"Katherine, please do not worry over this. It is not your worry or that of your Mother and nobody will talk to them. It will be announced in church and they will be told when to go to Denham for recruitment," he said quite sharply.

There was a pause. "Sadly, my dearest, during the next week or so I will have to be away from you. For I must visit the Barons here in the East to let them know the King's plans for the East of England. I have to see the Duke of Norfolk and The Earls of Buckingham of which most are kin of ours. Of course I will have to see Sir Richard first. He must have had a draft through from the King by now. We need to make the East more secure for the King feels that it is very vulnerable from the French at the moment," he said, giving me a kiss as I was looking very sad and thoughtful.

"I think that we should go to Heigham to say goodbye to your family and the remaining guests," I said, getting up quickly.

"Yes, we must make haste," he said.

After we had said our goodbyes to the guests at Heigham, William questioned Mother about the other half of the Manor of Barewe for Mother was only able to give her half of the Manor called Alderfield to William, for her sister was left the other half. William asked Mother if she thought that her sister Alice's husband, William, would be willing to sell the rest of the Manor to us, if William went to see him. Mother said that she, with the help of Sir Richard, had levied fines for the Freewarren of Barrewe and Advowson of All Saints Barewe which both were granted in 1241 but had only just come through this year 1242. "So in time you will own all of the

Manor, William."

William said, "That is really very good; for now we will be able to get the Manor working very well."

We then went about doing what we had planned for the rest of the day. When we got home following our evening meal, William started to make out his plans on parchment. There would be many changes.

"I have had Will Sommers deliver some timbers and will get the men on to enlarging the stables here straight away. The forge will need to be much larger as I will need more than one smithy working there. There will be a need for lots of equipment for my army and we will need to have a carriage built. I take it that there is a wheelwright in the Manor?" Will asked.

"There is an old man at Heigham who used to be a wheelwright but he has not made wheels for some time," I said.

"Well, he must teach his trade to a younger man. Opposite the forge I will have a rabbit warren built. It will be a large warren. We will be able to sell the rabbits in the towns on market days and supply the great halls, for eating rabbit has become very fashionable. I will spend money on having more livestock so that we will be able to trade and sell all the surplus to our needs. In time we will have a new Hall built for us. It will be built of stone, not wood like this one and it will be on the site where there is the remains of that old fort that is close to the church. There is much to be done so you, Katherine, will have to take charge when I am away from the Manor. I will see that we have some very good bailiffs to see that our orders are carried out. I would like you, Katherine, to take charge of our accounts. I know that you are very capable of doing that," he said with a smile.

"Yes, I really want to be useful," I said.

"Come now my love, it is time for bed," he said.

Chapter 12

I was so pleased for I was very tired and I just loved to lay in Will's arms.

I woke early in the morning; Will was still asleep I sat up and just studied him. His golden eyelashes were so thick and curled upwards, his skin was still tanned. The scar on his face started level with his eyes and curled towards his chin, it was quite deep and was covered in fair down. His nose was quite straight but not too large. His fair hair curled on his broad shoulders. I gently stroked the hair on his chest, so as not to wake him. I could not help myself. I then lay down next to him putting my arm across his chest.

Within days the village had become so busy. Will's recruitment plans had gone well; many of the young men of the Manor seemed pleased to join the army. Will gave each man who was selected a coin. Many men came from towns and some had already been in other armies.

The time had come for Will to go on his visits to the Barons. He had guards at the Hall at all times. I did not really like it but he said that, as he was a Knight, over his life he had made many enemies who could cause him problems and he must see that I am safe and protected at all times. Also that I would be in more danger when he was away.

I really missed William when he went on his travels to visit the Barons and I felt quite lonely. I had thought it important that I stayed at Barewe Hall rather than go to stay with Mother as was suggested. I was Will's wife and I must stay at home and make sure that the daily routines run smoothly. The first job was to ride around the Manor with the Bailiff to see if there were any problems with the repairs and building that was in progress. The first place I looked at was the dwelling which was being built quite close to the Hall for Poppy and Richard to live in, now that they are married. It would be easy for Poppy still to work at the Hall and she would be available at all times if I should need her. The men were getting on well with the building at the forge. There was so much work going on all over the Manor.

I stopped at the church and told the Bailiff to wait outside for me. I covered my head and went inside to pray. I asked God to forgive my sins. I did not want Him to think that I might love William more than I loved Him. I then thanked him for my happiness and for everything I had. I asked God for strength and guidance to do His wishes. For sometimes in this new life I did get a little confused. Of course, then I asked God to look after William and keep him safe and to return him to me soon.

When I returned, Poppy was at the Hall waiting for me. She had seen all the maids and the cook to make sure that they were doing their jobs correctly. I had made Poppy 'keeper of the keys'. She would be in charge of the inside of the Hall when I was away, as the Bailiff is to the Manor. I asked Poppy if she was happy being married to Richard; she said that she was. I wanted to tell her how happy I was but of course I could not as I was her mistress. When Poppy left, I quickly wrote to Isabelle for I could tell her about my marriage and how happy I was; I really needed to tell someone. Isabelle was now in Normandy with the Royal Court so I had to send a messenger with the letter to the De Clares. I knew that they would make sure that it reached Isabelle.

It was three weeks before William got home. We were so pleased to see each other. "The Barons were all in good spirits, Katherine, and everything was most successful and they agreed with the plans which Sir Richard and I had made for the East of England." He also said "I called into Stoke by Nayland to see Sir

Thomas before he went off to do his duties in the Crusades. I was able to give him some advice and some contacts who would be of great help to him."

I told him, "I have had a few problems while you have been away."

He replied, "I will hold court in two days time and get the problems put right."

"Where will you hold court? It is known in the old Celtic Law that if court is held under a great old Oak Tree, people will always speak the truth. For they fear the old Oak's strength and powers. This is where my grandfather held court under the great Oak which stands in the grounds of the Hall. It is a very large tree, about two or three hundred years old."

"Yes, Katherine," William laughed, "I will hold court there if it pleases my little Wood Nymph."

During our evening meal, Will said that he needed to have an audience with Reverend Thomas de Passelewe. "Your cousin needs to contribute a little more to life in the Manor than he does now. He can clerk and scribe for me. I will need him at the courts to do so. He will also teach some of the villains; it will improve their work to learn to read and also he will see that all the villeins improve their French speech so I can understand them better when they speak," he said.

"That will be quite difficult, Will," I said.

"This is very good rabbit," he said, not answering my reply.

"It is from our own warren and I know how much you like roast rabbit," I said quite pleased.

"In two weeks time we will go to the West of England to visit my grandfather Elias, and you will also be able meet my brother John. There is so much I want you to see, Katherine. I am sure that you will love to ride up the hills which divide Wales from England and see the wonderful views."

"How marvellous! Will we use the coach or will we be riding?" I asked.

"We will ride, it will be quicker. We will only need to take a small escort with us," Will replied.

As we retired for the night, I asked "Will, may I go and watch the court for I have not seen one in progress before? Mother always discussed the problems in the Manor with the Bailiff and then he would sort it in the way Mother wanted it dealt with."

"You may and you shall take your seat next to mine, my Lady Wife," he said.

The day of the court had arrived. There was quite a gathering under the old Oak tree. The Bailiff and several of Will's officers were there.

"Case 1. A fight between five men. Three villeins, being John Newman, Adam Calwe and Simon Black of this Manor and Joe Norman and John West from the army at Denham," the Bailiff stated.

"What have you two to say?" said William, facing the two men from the army.

"Guilty to fighting but it was to protect our honour, My Lord," said John West, the spokesman.

"In what way was your honour threatened?" Will asked.

"We were called 'Norman Scum'" John West answered.

Then Will looked at the other three men and asked, "You do not like Normans?"

It was Adam Calwe who replied to Will. "My Lord, it was only myself that spoke those words and I hope that you will forgive me, My Lord. These men insulted my sister who was with us at the time which made me wild and the words that I used were not meant as they sounded. I have nothing against Normans, My Lord, it was a word that I had always known as a curse, since I was young."

"I am so glad, Adam, that you like Normans and I hope that I never hear of you using that curse again. Next Sunday at Church you will be given time to speak in church and tell all the Manor how much you like people of Norman descent. John and Simon will stand next to you and support you as they did in the fight. As for you two," he said, looking at Norman and West, "you will do extra guard duty without a break," informed Will.

"Case Two. Copulation between Thomas Warner, a married Freeman and a maiden Agnes Turner aged twelve years," the Bailiff announced.

"Is this true, Agnes?" Will asked.

"Yes, I am with child My Lord," Agnes replied.

"When did this take place, and where?" Will asked Agnes.

"Four months ago in June in the woods, My Lord."

"Have you copulated with any other men or boys? Be truthful for if you are not truthful you will be punished very severely," Will said.

"Thomas Warner is the only man I have been with," Agnes said with tears.

"Thomas Warner, did you cover this maiden?" asked Will.

"Yes, she is a temptress. Agnes came to help at the farm and she followed me everywhere. I told my wife to keep her out of my way as she seemed to be everywhere, she did not cover her body as a maiden should and would smile wickedly at me and knock against my body. I would swear at her and say, 'Get out of my way.' The day it happened, I was confused and emotional as my wife was in labour with our fourth child and the house was full of women. I went for a walk in the woods to get out of their way. I sat under a tree to think. When Agnes came running she was hot and had the front of her top garment undone, showing her womanly parts. She said that she was hot and she laid next to me, lifting her skirt. I asked what was she doing and she said that she was so hot and wanted to cool down. Agnes then took my hand and put it on her thigh and said, "Feel how hot I am." She then pushed her body against mine. I am really sorry but I could not help myself and gave myself to the Devil and sinned. I love my family and wife so very much and did not wish to bring this shame upon them, My Lord," he said very quietly for he saw me sitting there and knew that this was something that should not be spoken about in front of a Lady.

Will called Joe Turner, Agnes's father and asked him if he would allow Agnes to remain in his home with her child to provide for it.

"I cannot do so, My Lord, for I have five children and cannot feed another mouth," he said.

"Thomas Warner and wife, will you take the child born to Agnes into your family and give it your name Warner and bring it up as your own child?" Will asked them both.

"No!" screamed Thomas Warner's wife.

"Joe Turner, will you take Agnes and her child back in your family and keep them if I rule that Thomas gives you a field and a goat, three hens and money of two shillings each year to keep them?"

"Yes," said Joe, looking very pleased for this was very generous.

"My Lord," said Thomas, "I will take the child into my family and it shall be treated no different from my other children. I will love it, so will my wife and the other children."

"You, Thomas, before this sin with Agnes, you

were a good, hard-working and truthful man. You will give Agnes sixpence while she is nursing the child and when it is weaned you will take it and see that your wife treats it kindly. You will allow Agnes to see it on Easter Day and Christmas Day if she so wishes. Both you and Agnes will stand in church on the Sabbath as sinners."

I was quite pleased at the wise way William had ruled. For if it had been that Agnes had been with more than one man she would have had to leave the Manor and beg in town for food. She may have been taken into the home of a woman who had been in the same situation and would be made to sell her favours to men or she may have gone with the other women who follow the army and give favours in exchange for food.

Case Three was a family whose father had died without leaving a Will and as he was a Freeman with land and with a grown up family, Will had to divide the land, cattle and chattels amongst the family. Will only heard the three cases as it had taken quite a while.

When we got back to the Hall, I was very sick and quite weak and faint and I had to go to my chamber and could not eat. Will thought that it must have been the rabbit which we had eaten the day before which upset me.

Chapter 13

WINTER MONTHS

The next day I was still feeling ill, very weak and still being sick. I tried to get up and go downstairs but I came over faint and had to return to bed. William sent Poppy up to help make me comfortable. When she saw me she suggested to Will that he should send for Mother.

The coach came bringing Mother and Betsy. They both came into the bed chamber, Mother felt my brow. "Tepid sponging please, Betsy," she said. Betsy sent Poppy to get the water. Mother then felt my breast. "Your breasts are hard which tells us that you are pregnant, Katherine," she said, smiling.

I vomited again. "I am so pleased, Mother, but my stomach is so sore," I said, vomiting again.

"Katherine cannot go on like this, My Lady," Betsy said.

"Betsy, go and make a drink of camomile, lemon and honey. Poppy go and fetch a rosemary cushion. We will make you comfortable then we will send Will up to you for you to give him the good news," Mother said, taking charge.

I had the drink which settled my stomach and made me more comfortable then Mother went downstairs and sent Will up. He sat on the bed and took hold of my hand then, smiling, I told him our good news.

"Katherine! How can I ever thank you enough? My own dearest wife, you have made me so happy. I am so sorry that it is making you feel so ill."

"I am feeling much better now," I said, as he kissed me.

The next day when I woke up I drank the camomile drink which had been left for me the night before to drink before I got up, waiting in bed to give it time to work. Poppy had made a bracelet of cloves on Mother's suggestion which I put on while Poppy helped get me dressed. Then, feeling much improved, I was able to go downstairs. I was to have a baked apple and just one small oatcake for breakfast and to 'eat lightly' Mother had said. For dinner I was to have chicken and lovage leaf soup and to make sure that they also used the stem of the plant when cooking it. For supper I was to have vegetable broth containing plenty of ginger. If I ate like this, I would no longer feel sick or be sick anymore.

  Mother had also said to William that I should not travel to the West of England. For riding a horse or in a bumpy carriage might make me lose the baby. Both Will and I were so disappointed about us not being able to go together, he wanted so much to show me his old home.

  The next few weeks the days got dark, cold and wet and most of the time I stayed indoors. William was away from home quite a bit and just when he thought that he had several days to spend with me, a messenger came from Osbert asking Will if he would go into Wales with him. For the King wanted the Welsh to understand that the King would not stand for the rebels coming into England and trying to plunder the people on the borders. The King's message was for the Welsh Princes to get control of the situation or else he would have to do so himself. William had met most of the Princes in the past and had got on quite well with them and they trusted him, so he had to go.

  I was quite worried about Will going. It would be the first time that he might have to use his newly-trained army. People in the Manor were also worrying for most families had one of their men going with Will. It had been many years since any men from Barewe had had to do any fighting. Then Will decided that he would not take the foot army with him for, if he did, it would take two to three weeks just to get there and he did not want it to be such a great period of time. He wanted to get the troubles sorted and get back home to me, so he said he would just take the cavalry and be able to travel at great speed. Prayers were said each Sunday in church for Will and the men that went with him, asking God for their safe return.

    I had a chamber made ready for Mother so that she could stay quite often with me because I got quite lonely but Mother was right and I no longer had a problem with being sick and now felt quite well.

    Christmas would be upon us soon; both Mother and I wondered what we would do for the Manor folks. We no longer had a surplus of livestock to use as gifts as many of the animals were killed for the Wedding and to feed Will's army. William had mentioned before he knew that he would be away in the West Country that he would hold a hunt and shoot some stags. We would have them butchered into small pieces and use these for Christmas gifts for the villeins which would also make food for the army. Now it would be unlikely that Will and his men would be home for Christmas which made me very sad. Mother stated that "even the King cannot do as he wishes if events happen beyond his control. He even has to go to war, just as Will must if the situation arises and if you should have sons, Katherine, they will have to do the same; that is the way of things."

    The only gift that Mother could think of was that she had all the meat left over from the Wedding put down in brine and with that we will be able to have lots of Rinstead Soup. Rinstead Soup is made from the salted meat, fresh vegetables and, of course, lots of herbs. We will have it cooked for gifts for the villeins which they will be able to use for a base for their winter

Chapter 13

stockpots.

We had a lovely crisp day and Mother suggested that we should take a party into the woods to collect holly, mistletoe and ferns to decorate the Hall and Churches.

"It will do us all good. We will take the Bailiff, Poppy and two of the maids and the horse and cart to put our harvest into. I think that it will quite fun and to get out into the fresh air is what we all need."

"Yes, Mother, you are so right and we can pick crab apples with which we would be able to have jellies made."

I really enjoyed decorating the Hall and making it look pretty. Mother said that it looked so lovely that she thought I should do some entertaining - only Ladies of course as my husband was away. It would not be expected by society to entertain men.

"I think that we should invite the Ladies from Gifford Hall, Wickhambrook. That will be Lady Gifford and her handicapped daughter, The De-Says from Denham Hall and the four Fitzlucus ladies and their mother from Saxham Hall. We will invite them for dinner (which is taken before midday in society)."

"Of course we must have a little gift for each of them," I said, quite excited.

"I have many fans at Heigham which Sir Richard had given me as gifts on his return from his many travels in France. We will be able to give each of the Ladies one for a present."

"Yes, Mother, that will do fine," I agreed.

The day arrived for us to entertain the Ladies. Tables had been prepared with salt pork with crab apple jelly, cold chicken and pease pudding. There were also plenty of sweet jellies and spiced custards and stewed apples. To drink there was wine and hot Alder wine. The grooms were waiting outside the Hall to take the horses from the Ladies as they arrived.

The first to arrive was Lady Gifford and her daughter Stella who had suffered from birth with an affliction known as 'moon sickness'; Stella's face was round and flat with very round eyes. Her mother was quite old when she was born, it is said that often older women have children with the affliction. I found Stella a delight - very bright and happy. Some people say that her problem makes fools but there was nothing silly about Stella. Lady Gifford was a small, round, jolly woman with fun- loving eyes.

"Welcome to the Gifford Clan, Katherine. I see, Katherine, that the Gifford family will soon be increasing in size," she said with her eyes focused on my stomach as I greeted her.

Lady De Say arrived next with her two daughters. Lady Anne was quite tall of medium build with mid brown hair and hazel eyes; her sister was shorter and quite plump with dark curls and a fresh complexion, who hurried to survey the food table. Following closely behind them was Lady Fitzlucas and her four daughters: May, Mary, Maud and Maize, so much alike in appearance, like four peas from the same pod. Smart and very well groomed, all with their heads covered in sweet little bonnets
but without beauty. They stood or sat all in line and spoke in sequence. The end one on the right would start a conversation and, after a few words, the sister next to her would continue for about six words and would look at her sister on the left who would continue. After the fourth sister, the first sister would continue till they came to the end of the conversation. I was quite amazed. Lady Gifford, like myself and Mother, had not met them before and Lady Gifford allowed her mouth to drop open and

Chapter 13

Stella could not stop giggling. Lady Fitzlucas said crossly to Stella, looking her straight in the eyes, "You poor child."

"I think we should eat now," Mother said, quickly directing everyone to the food table to stop an incident arising.

The Fitzlucas young ladies sat next to each other in the same order and all at the same time did they each reach for the same choices of food. Lady Emma ate at great speed.

"The food is so good, really tasty food. So good indeed," she said, eating a large amount, preferring the sweet jellies and custards. When everyone had finished eating we left the table and the Fitzlucas's sat in the same order in their line. Lady Fitzlucas produced a tapestry for each of them to sew.

"Idle hands make for sinful hands. Do you agree, Lady De Say?" she asked.

We all admired the tapestries as the four young women held them out in sequence for us to see.

Lady De Say announced that "Anne and Emma would play the Lute together for many a tune."

"Katherine, would you dance with me please?" Stella asked. "I will," I replied. The dance was of Stella's making which was mostly made up of skipping. "It is such fun, Stella, but I must stop now," I said for I thought that we would be dancing for the rest of the day.

Mother got the gifts which we had for them and all the Ladies were most pleased, for the fans were of the very best quality. Then they all left saying their farewells. Mother and I both sighed in relief, looked at each other and laughed.

"I think that is enough entertainment for a good few months," Mother said and I agreed.

Christmas Day was now upon us and Will had not

got home. We went to church to celebrate the birth of our Lord Jesus. The service was just about to conclude when the church door burst opened and there stood Will. I was so happy and surprised. I hurried to where he was standing and we greeted each other.

"Why, you are so dirty, Will and your stallion is caked in mud," I said.

"We have ridden non stop both night and day. I wanted to get back to you, Katherine, for Christmas. I want us to spend our first Christmas together and here I stand with you on Christmas Day. Let's get back to the Hall."

Will had only travelled back with two of the Captains of his cavalry; he said that they would spend Christmas Day with us. I told Will that we had asked my cousin and his wife to spend the day with us also.

"Where is the rest of your cavalry?" I asked, thinking that something dreadful must have happened to them.

Will laughed "Why, they are playing at being Yeomen."

"Yeomen, Will?" I said, surprised.

"Yes, they are bringing back livestock and carts of my chattel from Hereford. We need these to help Barewe thrive in the future. They should be back about the time of the start of the New Year if everything goes to plan," he stated.

We enjoyed our meal and wines and we all felt quite happy but Will and his men were so tired that we decided to retire to bed earlier than we would have usually done.

I was so pleased for I loved to lay in Will's arms and cuddle up, feeling so warm and snug. It was the best part of my Christmas.

The next day was the day when we gave presents

Chapter 13

to each other. Will covered my eyes with a kerchief and, holding me close, gently led me outside. When he took the kerchief from my eyes, we were outside the stables. There stood the groom holding a beautiful bay mare which had a silver mane.

"I know that you will not be able to get much pleasure from her as yet but the time will come. She is very gentle. I have tried her out and she is very swift and easy to handle," Will said, looking for my reaction.

"Oh, she is so beautiful. Thank you so much, Will. I will call her Crystal for her pelt and mane sparkle in the sunlight. I just love her." I said.

Then Will lifted me up and sat me on her back and led me around the field. When we got back to the stables, there were dogs barking which I thought strange for we do not keep dogs in the stables. Will opened the door and very large dogs came running out. Will shouted at them and they all sat at his feet.

"I have never seen such large dogs before, Will." I said.

"They are called Wolf Hounds, they are my hunting dogs, I brought them all the way back from Hereford. They ran all the way back at the side of the horses," he said with pride.

"What are they called?" I asked.

"The largest of the dogs is called Madog in the honour of a Welsh Prince. The black dog is Saracen and the two bitches are Meg and Mag. I will have a place built for them for I will need all the stables," he said, stroking them.

When we went back into the Hall, I gave Will my gift to him, which I felt was very small. I had made him some sugar fudge for I knew that he loved sweet food. I had flavoured the fudge with sweet herbs: geranium, rosemary, lemon balm and ginger. It was wrapped in a large kerchief which I had made and embroidered with our Coat of Arms on it and gathered up the edges and tied it with a stem of lavender. Will was delighted with the gift and kept looking at the kerchief which I had sewn for him.

It was several days after the beginning of the New Year when Will's cavalry arrived with the livestock; there was a small herd of ponies, ten of them in number. Will had said that they have a special coat which can weather the winter and that they can stay out and do not need to be put into stables and that we would be able to breed from them and sell the foals. There were rams that were from a strong stock and will help to strengthen our herds of sheep, also a few calves.

"I have another present for you, Katherine, and it is not from me. One of the Welsh Princes had learnt that I had married and sent the gift for my wife," said Will, taking me to a cart where he took out a basket. Inside the basket were two very small puppies. I took one of the puppies from the basket, it was red in colour with a fox-type face with pointed ears and funny little legs and it didn't have a tail.

"In Wales these little dogs are used to turn the spits instead of young boys, several are fixed into a wooden wheel. They walk round and round inside the wheel, they are also good at herding the cattle," Will informed me. The other little dog was red with a white chest.

"I will not have them turn the spit, Will," I said quickly.

"You would not have enough dogs for that, they are just dogs for the Hall to keep rats out," he replied.

Will spent the next few weeks mostly at home getting the Manor started in the way in which he wanted it to develop. When he was in the Hall he was very busy

Chapter 13

writing letters and drawing up more plans for the Manor while I was busy preparing for our coming child. Mother had returned to Heigham and had sent to us the crib which had been in our family for many years, along with babies' clothes and other items for the child. I found some soft cloth and renewed the inside of the crib, making it very pretty and comfortable. Will ordered some new sheep fleeces from the shepherd for the crib for there is nothing finer to lay the baby on.

Following supper, we would sit by the fire. Will would be roasting chestnuts, while I played and nursed the two puppies. They would fall asleep in their basket which we had by the fire while Will and I would have a tumbler of mead and eat the nuts. I was at the stage in my pregnancy when the baby was moving about in my stomach and Will would put his hand on my stomach and feel it move and he would smile and speak loving words about his son.   I would say, "Will, it might be a daughter."

"No, Katherine, it is not a daughter; our baby is a son and a very fine one at that," he would say. Then he would hold me close and often we would both fall asleep in each other's arms. I felt so happy and secure until a messenger came from the King.

He said that the King had left with a small army to try to regain Normandy. He would join up with a rebel Count 'Count de la Marche' at Taillebourg on the River Charente. The King of France, Louis IX, had the same problems as King Henry had with rebel Barons, for Louis had several rebel Counts in Normandy and the South of France. King Henry wanted Will to ride with haste with his cavalry to strengthen the defence of the Suffolk coast line. The Duke of Norfolk would be doing the same along the Norfolk coast and the same would be happening in Lincolnshire and Essex.

Chapter 13

"William, why does the King have to make War on Normandy?" I said, very alarmed.

William explained that really Normandy did belong to England and that it was the King's father, King John, who lost Normandy to the French. Following King John's death, Louis, with some rebel English Barons, tried to take Lincolnshire. The rebel Barons of England had promised the English crown to Louis. It was The Great William Marshal who fought at Lincoln and retained the Crown for Henry who was just a young boy at the time.

"My grandfather fought with William Marshal," said Will with pride. "King Louis was defeated and thrown into the Tower. The loyal Barons released Louis on the understanding that Louis should restore Normandy back to England but King Louis went back on his word and it did not happen. So you see, my dearest, it is a question of pride," Will said, holding me close.

"Will, I wonder if Isabelle will be in danger for she is in France?" I asked.

"I would have thought that the English Court are on their way back to the Palace. Sir Richard de Clare will be fighting at the King's side for he has much experience fighting in wars in France," Will said, deep in thought.

I could tell by the expression on Will's face that he was not happy with the King's decision to keep him in England. I know that Will would rather be fighting with the King in France. It was a question of honour. In my thoughts I was thanking Marie for I knew of the influence she had with the King and she would have used this. For she would have known that I would not want Will fighting in France at this time in our life.

"I think, Katherine, that perhaps you should go and stay with Berta at the Convent while I am away. You will be much safer. For the rebel Barons who support

Chapter 13

King Louis will take advantage on those who are loyal to King Henry and do mischief and plunder where they can. They will not do anything against the Brides of Christ," he said, looking very worried.

"No, Will, this is our home, this is where I should be. I could not leave the folk of Barewe in times of trouble," I said quite strongly.

"Yes, I do understand. I will ring both Manors with the foot soldiers and put extra guards at the Hall," he said, pulling me close to him.

"I must leave now, Katherine. I must go to the fort at Denham and prepare the men and give them my orders. Then I must leave with my squire and the cavalry. I do not know how long I will be away but I do know that I shall miss you so much every day that I am away." He kissed me then stooped and kissed my large stomach. "Goodbye my little one. Take care of yourself, my beautiful wife," he said, then left.

I picked one of the puppies up, which was playing at my feet and sat myself down by the fire and watched the flames dance, while my tears slowly flowed down my cheeks. I must be brave for Will and for my child's sake.

Chapter 14
BRIGHTER DAYS

It was now April, the month in which I should give birth to my child. I had not seen William since he had left for the Suffolk Coast. I had a letter from him saying that he was fine. He was busy having forts built along the coast. He also had to travel to London several times to get money from the King's Purse Holder to pay the mercenaries and some of the army.

In his letter, Will wrote that the war in Normandy had gone very wrong for King Henry. The King had to retreat from Taillebourg to Saintes where a short bloody battle had taken place and King Henry's army was defeated and had to flee to Bordeaux where he still is.

King Louis had sickness in the French camp and Louis caught the fever and had to return to Paris. The fever had carried off many of his army and King Louis became very ill indeed. William went to London to see Simon de Montfort, Earl of Leicester, who was brother-in-law to King Henry, to see if he was to raise another army to try once more to take Normandy back from the French. Most of the other Barons did not agree, saying that the war had already cost too much money. I am sure that if the Barons had agreed to go to war again, William would have gone with them which made it quite a relief to me that he would not be going to war.

The days had now become much warmer and longer, the flowers and shrubs had started to bloom and there were leaves upon the trees. Each day I went to visit Crystal, taking her an apple. I used to like brushing her mane and then I would ask the groom to exercise her around the field. She was very frisky as she did not get as much exercise as she would have liked. I would feel much closer to Will while I watched her gallop. The groom had asked me if she could be put out in the

Chapter 14

meadow now during the day time. I told him 'No' for I had learnt from Isabelle that, in the spring, horses can eat too many of the new green shoots of the grass and get colic and sometimes die. I walked parts of the Manor each day accompanied either by Mother or Poppy. I had to keep control and make sure that everything was going to William's plans.

Poppy was now also pregnant and her baby was due about three months after mine. Poppy had become a Freewoman on marrying Richard and she could leave the Manor and did not have to work for me if she didn't want to. We had a very good home built for her and Richard. The hut had two large chambers instead of the usual one. They got it rent free while Poppy worked at the Hall and Richard, if he did work for Will, was often given a coin for payment. I did have other maids but they had not grown up in the Hall and did not have Poppy's manners or learning.

We had a cousin of Poppy's called Sarah who was just eleven; she would help with the baby when it was born. Sarah was the oldest child of six and was very experienced in looking after babies. I had made sure that Poppy had time to train Sarah in good manners and to conduct herself to please my wishes. Sarah had been interviewed by Mother and the Rector to make sure that she was fit in both health and spiritual attitude. She was asked questions about Our Lord, what she thought about and was she pure in heart and mind and could she tell of anything bad which she had done. When she had answered these questions, she was told to remove her gown. Mother and my cousin would look carefully at her body to make sure that there were no marks of the Devil on her, like a third nipple where the Devil could come at night and suckle from it. They would look to see if there was any skin blemish that was not normal to a young woman of her age. Sarah's body was found to be normal.

A small chamber was made ready for me to give birth to the child. The floor was covered with dried nettles, Alder flowers and lemon balm strewed thickly across the floor to keep fleas away. There were vessels of rose and lavender water to be used to cool, sooth and relax. Madonna Lilies had been boiled in wine to drink to calm the pain. Sister Opal had sent from the Convent some poppy seeds which had been brought back from the East by the Knights Templar to be chewed when in pain. There was also an infusion of Milkweed to take to increase the milk flow. I had already been drinking rosemary water each day which will help make for an easier birth.

It was the twenty third of April when I first got pains. I told Mother and she said that it would be better for me to keep walking around the chamber and sit down now and again than to lay down. The pains became more frequent and much stronger. Mother asked me as she escorted me to the birthing chamber if I would like a cart to go to Risby to fetch the Herb Woman. I said "No, I have asked Our Lord for help for a safe delivery."

Poppy and Betsy were already in the chamber, Poppy helped me take my gowns off and put a birth gown on, it was much shorter and opened down the front and it had been blessed in the Church. I was then made comfortable on the bed. Mother sat and held my hand while Betsy and Poppy sat on the floor. Betsy was a large woman, very round from eating her wonderful meals, and she made us all laugh by saying she did not know if she would ever be able to get off the floor again.

It had been less than an hour and I could feel the baby pushing down and a terrible stretching. "You must help the child now, Katherine, you must push," said

Chapter 14

Betsy.

Mother and Poppy held a willow branch above my head which had been made smooth. I gripped it with both hands; I would squeeze the branch, this would give me great strength to push and will ease the pain. I breathed large breaths and pushed with all my strength. It was not too long when Betsy said joyfully that she could see the head.

"Push hard, Katherine," Mother said. "You are nearly there."

Betsy with just two fingers helped the baby out gently, tilting the baby's shoulders and as I was pushing, I could feel the rest of the baby slip out.

"Well done, Lady Katherine, you have a little Will," said Betsy as she laid my son on my stomach.

"Just a little more pushing, Katherine, to dispel the afterbirth," said Mother, placing my hand on little Will's head which I fondled as I pushed the afterbirth out. Poppy then took the baby and bathed him and then wrapped him in a swaddle and then she gave him back to me to cradle. I smiled as the tears of happiness ran down my cheeks. I was thinking about my dear husband and how proud he would be of us both. Mother then took Will to a wooden cross which we had in the room and, taking the Holy Water from the table, she put a little of it on to her finger and made the Sign of the Cross on Will's brow.

"We thank you so much dear God," she said and we all said "A-men."

Betsy said that I must rest now. Mother put little Will in the crib which Poppy had heated with large hot stones. Mother said that she would spend the night in the chamber with me. Betsy cleaned me and made me comfortable and then I fell asleep feeling very pleased with myself.

Chapter 14

At dawn I woke and Mother gave Will to me and I put him to my breast. This was a wonderful feeling, so warm and serene it made me feel so important. When he had finished feeding, both Mother and I studied him. He had very long, thick white hair for a baby, his eyes were violet blue, the same as Will's. His skin was very fair with silky down covering his little face.

"He has Will's nose," Mother expressed. "He is so beautiful, Mother," I said.

I spoke very quietly to little Will, telling him how proud his father would be of him. It seemed that he had his eyes fixed upon me and was understanding what I said.

The days went by and although most of the time I felt happy there were times when I felt very sad. William didn't yet know that he had a son. There had not been any message from him and I could not quite understand why, for he would have known that the baby was due. I had said to Mother that I must get a message to Will to let him know that he had a son and how much we wanted to see him.

"How can you, Katherine? You don't know where he is. He might have gone to Bordeaux to see the King. Sir Richard is still in France so he will not know where William is. William, I am sure, will be here as soon he can. You must be patient," she said.

The next day was a lovely sunny day. Sarah had got very confident looking after little Will and was very good with him and he seemed to like her. I thought that I would take a walk to the stables to see Crystal and take her an apple. When I got there and saw her, I asked the groom to put her bridle on. I was now feeling very fit and wanted so much to ride her. I mounted her and walked her around the meadow, then we had a little trot and I decided to take her for a trot around the Manor.

Chapter 14

It felt very good to be out and to have some time to myself. I decided to ride towards Heigham. I had not gone far when I saw three horsemen approaching in the distance. I just knew that one of them was William. I started to gallop towards him and he was doing the same; it was just a matter of minutes and we were together. William jumped off his horse and lifted me down and we embraced.

"Katherine, my love, we are together at last." He kissed me once more and then his eyes looked down to my stomach as he put his hand on it. "Why, you have lost your lump!" he said with a laugh. "How is my son?"

"How do you know that we have a son? It might be a daughter," I replied.

"I have always known that we would have a son, for you are so clever my love," he said, helping me back on to Crystal.

"Now I cannot wait to see him," he said as we galloped back to the Hall.

We dismounted and Will grabbed my hand as we burst into the Hall and our feet hardly touched the ground as Will pulled me up the stairs to the chamber where little Will laid in his crib. William lifted his son from the crib and held him, looking at Will's little face. Little Will opened his eyes and seemed to gaze at William.

"Why, he is so handsome," said Will as took the baby downstairs, followed by me and Sarah who was carrying the crib down.

"You may go and have a break now, Sarah. His Lordship wants to spend some time with his son," I said.

William was sitting cradling his son. I told him how worried I had been as I had not got a message from for such a long time.

"With much haste I had to go to London to seek out Richard Earl of Cornwall, the King's brother. For I had heard that many of the powerful Barons were very vexed with King Henry's defeat and very grieved that he had not returned to England but had gone on to Gascony, where he was joined by Queen Eleanor and much of the Court. The Barons had heard that much jollity was going on and were very aggrieved about the King's irresponsibility. I have always found the King to be most fair. He has been supportive to me and he forgave Osbert. I knew that Richard of Cornwall had always been loyal to his brother, whether the King was in the right or wrong. I had an audience with the Earl and told him about the way the Barons were feeling and that there were so many Barons who were thinking that the King had no interest in England. Richard said that it would be best if I would take a message to the King in Gascony. He would write to advise the King to come back to England with haste. In the meantime, Earl Richard would meet with most of the Barons and try to pacify them. As you know, Katherine, Gasscony is in the far south of France and I had to travel many miles." Will said all this without taking his eyes off little Will. He was also fondling the baby's hands and stroking his face.

"Were Isabelle and Marie with the Court still?" I asked.

"I saw Isabelle, she was in good health but wants to return to England as soon as possible, she said that she has had enough of the French Court. She told me that her father, Sir Richard, had been wounded and was on his way back to Clare. Isabelle asked about you and was so pleased that we would be having a child and that she would visit us as soon as she can get back to Clare. She could not leave the Court for she had to wait for Emma as they had arranged to travel together. I asked Isabelle about Marie and she told me that Marie had problems at home and had to return to her family.

Chapter 14

Isabelle did not know what sort of problems." Will looked at me to see my response.

"I am so pleased that you saw Isabelle and that she is quite safe. Is King Henry returning to England, William?" I asked.

"I really do not know. He read the message and tore it up and wrote a reply for me to take back to his brother without saying anything about it. He asked me how the castles were coming on and asked about you. I told the King that I wished to leave as soon as possible for I wanted to know if I was a father yet. He said that I should take my leave as soon as I wish which I did, Katherine." As Will said this, Little Will started to cry.

"I must go and feed him now, Will," I said.

During the next few weeks, Will settled down to a much calmer life. He was very pleased with the way the Manor had progressed and how industrious the villeins had been. William said that for a reward we will all celebrate on Mid-summers Day.

It was wonderful to have Will home again; we would go riding together, taking the hunting dogs into the woods with us. Will said that he would have a sheep skin holster made to put Little Will into for he was big enough to come with us and Will would wear the holster on his chest. This way Little Will would learn about horses from an early age like they do in the East. The best part of William being home was to share our bed together at night.

Chapter 15
THE GOOD LIFE

Life was good with William home. William was earning the reputation of being a good Lord. We did have some problems. The De Says did not like having the army camp at Denham Castle so close to their Hall. It was not so much the camp or the men there but the women and children who followed the armies and offer favours in exchange for money or food and formed their own community outside the army camp.

William went and visited Lord and Lady De Say, to get the problem sorted out.

"Welcome Sir Gifford," said Lord De Say in a very formal way. In appearance, Lord De Say was very round with a very large belly which must have made it very difficult for him to get out of bed in the morning. He had very little hair on his head and his face was always bright red. He was not a warrior but it is said that he is not short of money. He had difficulty with his breathing when he talked because of all the fat which he had to carry on his person. Lady De Say was quite a handsome, tall woman, as thin as her husband was fat.

"It is becoming what hell must be like here. Our daughters cannot go for a walk or ride their horses without getting jeers. The women steal eggs and sometimes they even take the fowls from our farm. They milk the cows before our maids get to the meadow in the morning to milk them. I have even had to take my whip to some of them because of the unsavoury words coming out of their mouths as I was riding past them. I am sorry to have to speak to you about this matter, My Lord," said Lord De Says.

"He is sorry, Sir Gifford, but if things do not improve we will have to take the problem to the King,"

Chapter 15

said Lady De Say who was very vexed about the situation.

"Well, let us calm down and see how we can improve this situation. Denham Castle belongs to the King and it is here to protect the East of England," they were told by Will. "What I will have done is have some men patrol and protect your territories. I will also have a stock erected to punish those who steal and cause problems and make your lands out of bounds to those who live outside the Castle. I am sure that these measures will work and, because of your inconvenience, I will ask the King to let you off payment for half a Knight's fees. I hope that this meets to both your satisfactions," William said, as he directed his gaze at Lady De Say. She nodded and curtsied to Will as he held his hand out to Lord De Say to seal the agreement. Then he took his leave.

Mother went to Clare Castle to help the Countess nurse Sir Richard, whose health was very poor since he got wounded. Isabelle still had not returned to Clare.

William had taken me and Little Will to the West of England to visit his family and his Grandfather Elias. We were accompanied by Berta and, as you know, Elias was her father and he was getting very old and Berta wanted to spend some time with him. We had named our son William Elias Hammond Gifford. The Elias was to honour the great-grandfather and Hammond was my father's name. We had asked Elias to bless Little Will for Elias had become a monk to appease God for those he had killed and plundered while being a warrior. I just loved Herefordshire, the large hills and beautiful rivers were so different to Suffolk where the water just lays and turns into mud because there are not many hills to make the water flow. William and I went riding on the mountains accompanied by Uncle Osbert who I got on with so very well. He was so amusing and kept us in much laughter. William's whole family were so lovely to me and William was so proud of me and Little Will.

Poppy was looking after Barewe Hall for us. Poppy now had a little daughter called Rosie. Richard had taken time off from his work as a woodsman to help Poppy and William rewarded him.

We returned to Barewe in the autumn. William had to be away on his duties to check the Suffolk coast to see how the Castles were progressing and whether they were being erected correctly to the plans. William said that he would be away for two or three weeks and if he needed to go and see the King it would be more like five. He thought and then said he really should report to the King who was now home in London. William had left a list of all the work that needed to be done on the Manor to prepare us for the winter and I was to see that the bailiffs made sure that everything was done. It had been a very good harvest and the rabbit warrens were really doing very well and we were able to sell rabbits to the Halls. We also supplied the Abbey in Bury St. Edmunds with them. The ponies which Will had brought from Wales had settled in well and Will had brought one back to the stables and it was to be trained and made ready for when Little Will was able to sit on it safely.

I now understood that a large portion of my life would be spent on my own as William would be away from the Manor very often. I had now grown much in character and was strong like Mother and able to run the Manor very well when Will was away.

It was just weeks away from Christmas when William got home. One of the first questions I asked Will was would he still be at home for Christmas?

Chapter 15

"Yes, unless something should happen. Matters at the Palace are in a state of turmoil with the Barons at each others' throats - some of them supporting the King, others against him. The King's brother-in-law Simon de Montford is now back in England from the Crusade and he is not helping the King's situation by agreeing with those Barons who are against the King. The King's brother is trying to calm the situation and is speaking to the rival Barons putting the King's point of view to them. He is well respected and they do take notice of him. That might change when they find out that he is to marry the Queen Eleanor's sister Sanchia. 'Another foreigner close to the Crown' they will say."

"What are your views, William?" I asked.

"Of course, I support the King. You must remember that the King lived with my father and grandfather as a child, when he was the charge of William Marshal. I am afraid that sometimes the King is his own worst enemy, he is rather like his father, King John and when the Barons do not agree with him, he still has his own way and wishes and will not listen to what they have to say," answered William.

"Well, the King is right, he was chosen by God to rule," I replied.

"We all have to listen and take advice at times. I have had enough of London now, I need to see my son and I also wish to clear my mind of such things for a time," he said.

Little Will could sit up on his own now and was mobile, crawling about the floor which was spread with reeds and herbs which Little Will tried to eat with his two teeth which he had now grown. William picked him up gave him a kiss, held him out to take a look at him then threw him up into the air and caught him. Little Will laughed and really enjoyed it. I was quite alarmed.

Life was calm for a while. For William's Christmas present I was able to tell him that he was to be a father again. Baby John Godfrey Osbert was born in August. In appearance, he was just like Little Will. John's hair was more golden than that of Will for his was quite white.

William was just away a few days at a time which was much better.

Sir Richard de Clare had died and Richard, his eldest son, had taken over Clare Castle and was now the Earl of Gloucester. Mother had returned home to Heigham. She told me that Richard was a great friend of Simon de Montford which the Countess did not approve of, for her husband was always very loyal to the King. Simon was into the Barons and the Churchmen governing and tried to make the King obey the rules of the Magna Carta.

Isabelle was at Clare when her father died. She did come and visit us for a few days. I noticed that she was not her usual bubbly self. She was in a hurry to get back to Gascony for she was going to get married to a Count.

"I am not full of love for the Count but he is very kind to me and allows me to have a free spirit and spoils me and is so much like my father who always understood me. The Count is twice my age but that does not matter, he has a wonderful stable with very fine horses. The country and weather is very beautiful and I will be able to spend most of the time out of doors. Anything is better than life at Court, it is not for me. I am not like my sister Emma who loves the life at Court and would not want to be anywhere else."

"Isabelle, are you sure you should be getting married, when you are not full of love for the Count?" I asked.

"I am very fond of the Count. He loves horses and rides so very well and he does not bore me. That is enough for me and he is so very rich."

"Have you seen Marie, Isabelle?" I asked.

"No, I have not seen Marie since she left Court to go home. The gossip at the Court was that pressure was put on her to leave the Court for some of the Barons thought that Marie had too much influence over the King. I know what Marie had told me that Richard Earl of Cornwall had asked Marie to become his wife. Marie had said that, as much as she liked him, she didn't want to become his wife. I believe that is the reason why she went home. Of course now the Earl is to be married to the Queen's sister, Sanchia. Foolish fellow! Still, since the King's son Edward was born, Prince Edward has brought the King and Queen closer together, they both adore Edward and all three of them are mostly always together nowadays. The Queen is very mature now. The King is so many years older than her and I think that things were very difficult for her in the early years of her marriage because she had to always be with many young people, dancing the night away," stated Isabelle.

"Isabelle are you not going to do the same and marry someone who is a lot older than you?"

"Enough, Katherine, I am nothing like the Queen."

Isabelle was always saying how much she loved my sons. "You will soon have your own family," I said.

"That is my main reason for marrying and, of course, I would not be able to manage on an allowance that my brother Richard would allow me. He would not be so generous as my father was."

As we said our farewells and hugged each other, Isabelle said that her best years were when we were both children together at Clare and at the Convent. There were tears in both of our eyes. I was wondering if we would ever see each other again. For Gascony was so unsettled; the King had sent Simon de Montford to try to sort it out.

William had started having the much needed repair work done on All Saints Church. I believe that no repairs had been done on the church since one of my ancestors, Sir Ralph de Passelewe, had re-built the old Anglo-Saxon wooden church in stone in the early part of 1100. The work on the church was costing a great deal of money. William also wanted to build us a new Hall, he wanted for it to be built of stone. William had chosen the site; it would be just south of the church where there was the site of an old wooden fort. He had already got men digging a moat when they were not busy with other jobs. The site was surrounded by many springs and we would be able to have a good deep moat there.

William said that it will be many years before we will be able to afford to start the structure of the Hall. We did now get money from trading goods from the Manor. William also got payment from the Royal Purse for helping to defend Suffolk and for other jobs he did for the King, but it was often quite difficult to get payment and he had to keep asking for it, which made William very vexed. He had leased his castle and land in Hereford and had some money from that. It cost quite a lot of money to maintain the army so William decided to make his army much smaller. He loaned half the men to Osbert who was having problems with the Welsh. Osbert would then feed them and pay the ones which were on payment.

"We will have to be careful with our money, Katherine, for a while if we want our plans to take shape."

Chapter 16
OUR SON WILLIAM

It was now the year 1253 and I had been married for ten years. The Manor of Barewe was peaceful, it was also flourishing and its people were happy and well fed. Most of the children had some basic education at the church. William had made it a rule that they should spend two hours a week in the time when they were not working to learn how to count and learn about coinage and how to speak and understand simple French. The Reverend and his wife Mary taught the children and sometimes Mother helped. William thought that for the Manor to flourish they would need these skills to encourage the children to want to learn. When William was out inspecting the Manor, he would often halt his horse and speak to a child in French. If the child replied correctly in French, William would give them a small coin. So the children managed to learn French quite quickly.

I now had a beautiful three year old daughter called Alice Maud Isabelle. Her hair was a little lighter than mine with more golden hair than red in it. She had large deep green eyes and pale skin with little freckles across the bridge of her nose. She followed her brothers everywhere and loved to ride her little Welsh pony.

Mother and I educated the children ourselves. The boys learned Latin, reading and writing. Alice did drawing and was read stories from the Holy Book and then she would be asked questions on what she had read.

Little Will was known as 'Ham' now. It was quite difficult with two Williams in the family. When Ham was a baby, Mother use to pick him up and call him her 'little Hammond' after his grandfather. The name over the years got shortened to 'Ham'. Ham's character was forming well; he was brave, fearless, very confident and sometimes full of himself. He had a wonderful seat on a horse and liked to spend much of his time with his father. William would ride and hunt with both the boys.

Sir Thomas Gifford the Younger was back from the Crusades now and visited us quite often and the boys both liked him very much. William had made arrangements for Ham to train as a Knight under the care of Thomas, at Stoke by Nayland. This is where William had become a Knight under the care of Sir Thomas the Senior.

Thomas had been staying with us. William and Thomas had decided to go hunting for a boar. William said that he would take Ham with them. John was quite upset that he was not going with them. They were to hunt on foot. Will had a special smaller pike made for Ham to use, it would be the first time that Ham would be in on the kill. The boys did not usually go hunting boar with Will for it was quite dangerous. Usually Ham and John took their bows and hunted roe deer and small animals when Will took them hunting.

In the woods, some villeins were waiting for William and his party. The villeins had already found where there was a boar and William gave a signal. The villeins then commenced to drive the boar out of the thicket. They had the use of Will's hunting dogs which they had tethered. The villeins had to run fast to keep up with the boar and dogs. All the dogs would be barking which frightened the boar. They chased it into the clearing were William was standing with Thomas, with Ham in between them. The villeins then halted with the dogs. The boar stopped a short distance from William, Ham and Thomas. It knew that there were men and dogs behind it; it had not much choice, it would have to fight for its life. It looked at the three of them, started to paw the ground, expelling vapour out of its nostrils which looked as if it was on fire within its body It put its head down and charged at the three of them. As it approached, William and Thomas put their pikes into each side of the boar's neck to hold it still. Ham quickly ran forward and, with much force, plunged his spike into the boar's brain. Then William and Thomas pushed their pikes hard into the boar until it dropped. Ham picked up the sword which had been placed on the ground ready to use and plunged it into the boar's heart. The boar was dead and the pikes were removed. The villeins then dealt with the body; they knew what parts their Lord would want and the rest would be shared between them and, of course, the dogs would get some bones.

That evening we had a special meal and Ham was allowed to eat with us, our guest Thomas and Mother for he was being welcomed into manhood. We all stood and raised our glasses to Ham for the bravery he had shown that day. William wished him Honour, Bravery, Courage and much Charm. William said that he was sure that he would make a great Knight one day. "To make sure that happens, tomorrow you will go with Sir Thomas to Stoke by Nayland and commence your training. You will become a Page to the Ladies there."

William said this and looked straight at me. I was quite vexed. I knew that Ham would be going to Nayland but not so soon and William had not left any time for preparation or for us to get used to the idea. I looked at Ham; he was surprised but he was smiling. Sir Thomas then made a promise that with all his ability he would see that Ham grew into an honoured Knight.

Tomorrow Ham will ride off with Thomas and Ham will no longer be our little boy. That night as I lay next to Will my pillow was wet with tears. William turned me towards him then, sitting up, he gently wiped my tears away.

"Why, Katherine? You should be feeling proud," he said.

"I am so proud, William, but Ham is so young. It does not feel right in my mind or heart that he should leave us who love him so much. Other people will nurture and develop Ham's character. Just think of ladies like Isabelle's sister, Emma, leading by example of a shallow adult," I said, turning my head away with tears running down my cheeks again.

"The Ladies of Stoke by Nayland are nothing like Emma. Lady Margaret is still Head Lady of the Manor. She was my Lady when I went there as a young boy to be a Page and she was always kind to me. Why, she is Thomas's mother. Thomas is like my brother, I am closer to him than I am to my brothers. Thomas loves us all and will treat Ham as his own son. You must trust me Katherine with our most precious gift. Would you want our son not to be able to function without his mother at his side?"

"Oh William, I am so sorry but this is how I feel. I love Ham so much. I will pray to God each day to give me strength. I know that things must be this way for Ham to succeed in life, but in my heart it does not feel right," I said.

I could not sleep that night. My head would not clear of thoughts. I remembered the first night when Mother left Isabelle and myself at the Convent. I did have Isabelle and we were able to support each other. Ham will be all on his own wondering what was happing at home. Everyone except Thomas would be strange to him; I knew that he would miss us so much. I saw Ham in my mind, sitting on a stool; he was smart and well groomed, playing a lute to the Ladies, while the Ladies were sewing their tapestries and chatting.

As a Page he would fetch and carry for them. He would learn to obey and to be graceful, also charming and learn the courtly manners. Ham will continue his education studying Latin, learning about the Coat of Arms, their meaning and recognizing at a glance which family are bearing those Arms. I could see him in later years as a Squire, waiting on his Lord at the table, keeping the Lord's clothes and armour in order. The Lord would teach him to use the sword and lance while riding. I can see him now with Sir Thomas at a tournament carrying Thomas's shield with the Coat of Arms on it, showing it to the crowds. I see him fighting in battle with Thomas at his side. I must have been dreaming for I jumped out of bed in fright.

William was still asleep. I took the candle and went to the chamber where the boys sleep. John and Ham share a bed together. I held the candle above their heads, looking at their fair hair and beautiful soft skin, noticing the length of their eye lashes. I closed my eyes and sighed; these were my two babies, pure and innocent. Next year John will be leaving to go to be a Page at the Manor of William's younger brother, Sir Godfrey of Boyton. These enjoyable years which I have had with my family will never be the same. William had woken up. He came and took my hand, leading me back to our chamber. We did not speak a word; William just gave me a hug. I felt quite guilty thinking how lucky I was having Will to love me and to take care of all of us.

The next day Ham was ready to leave with Thomas. Ham would revert back to his name 'William' while living at Nayland. He had said his goodbyes to his brother and sister and the servants. William and Ham had their 'Father and Son' chat. The grooms had brought the horses from the stables.

"Are you ready, William?" asked Thomas.

Chapter 16

"Yes ... but," he said and, turning to me and taking my hand, led me into the inner chamber. There he threw his arms around me and we kissed and hugged each other.

"I thought that it would not be manly to say in front of Sir Thomas and Father how much I love you and how much I will miss you all but please do not be sad about me, Mother, I will be brave and make you all proud of me," my brave son said.

"I am already so proud of you and our love which we have for each other will keep us close and of course I will write to you often. Now you must leave," I said as we returned to the others.

He mounted his horse and he looked so small as he rode off with Sir Thomas. I took my other two children by the hand and we went inside. Everyone was so quiet. William suggested that we should all go out for a ride; it would get our minds off other subjects.

The following day William was summoned by the new Sir Richard de Clare The Earl of Gloucester to visit Clare. He was to hold a meeting with other Earls and Barons. The meeting was about a problem between the King and Sir Simon de Montfort.

In 1248 the King was having problems in Gascony with some of the French Barons and Simon de Montford was sent to try and sort it out. There Simon inevitably made enemies and the King recalled him. On his return, the King and Simon had done nothing but quarrel. The King said that Simon had betrayed him. Simon had called the King a liar. Now the King has put Simon on trial as a traitor. Sir Richard is very close to Simon and trying to get support for him from the other Lords.

When William returned from Clare some three days later, he looked very worried. I asked him what was wrong. He said that so many of the Barons were disillusioned with the King for having so many foreign favourites who seemed to have so much influence over him. The Barons blamed these 'French foreigners' for giving advice to the King which caused the war with the Welsh.

"There is so much bad feeling at Court that, in the future, I can see there being another 'Baron's War', Katherine. The Barons were full of admiration for my brother John. They spoke of how distinguished in fighting the Welsh he was and of his bravery," said Will, smiling.

I was quite shocked for that would be one of the worst wars we could have. It would mean brother against brother and friend against friend as each fights on the side in which their loyalties lie. I was thinking about whose side Sir Thomas would be on and about my son if there should be a war.

Two months have gone by now and William said that he must travel to London to get his payment from the King - money that had been owing to him for some time. He said that he would go by way of Stoke by Nayland and spend the night there, then he would be able to see Ham. Following London, he said that he would go straight to the West Country to see his family to ascertain where their loyalties will lie if there should be a war with Simon de Montfort against the Royalists. He said that he would also bring his men back as the Welsh Marches seem to be calm now and that he most likely would need the men himself.

It was about ten days after Will had left when a messenger came with a letter from Ham. I eagerly opened it and read.

'My Dearest Mother and Family. I was so pleased to see Father and Sir Thomas gave me leave as Father

Chapter 16

decided to spend an extra day at Stoke to be with me. I was able to show him around some of the Manor which Father said had changed a great deal since he had grown up there. I introduced him to my friend Henry who is also a Page, he is a son of Sir Robert D'Olley of Oxford Castle. Father told Henry that he knew his Father and must send his regards when he next writes home. We shared a chamber together and there is just one large bed in the chamber which we shared, I did not mind sharing a bed for I had learnt from my experience of sharing a bed with John that you can keep each other warm in the winter when there are often many draughts. We have a large wooden box which is divided in the centre; we each have a side of the box to keep our personal things in. I felt a little sad when Father left; as I watched him ride away I wished that I could be riding at his side. I did tell Father that I am finding it quite difficult being a Page. I have never had to sit for such long periods of time and to be quiet and to speak when I am spoken to. I found it much easier to kill the boar than to spend so much time with the Ladies. Father said that he found it quite hard as well but it is a question of discipline and if I listen to what the Ladies are saying I will learn what I will need to know. He said once I am a Squire it will be much more exciting and that I will enjoy it.

    Lady Margaret is so kind to me, she said that it was just like having my father with her again and reminds her of the years that have gone but which she remembers with such fondness.

    The Manor is so very large. The Gifford Family here must be very rich. They own many hamlets as well as the Manor. They own Belstead, Shelly, Polstead, Higham and Layham, to mention a few. Most days there are visitors who come to the Hall and I have to wait on them. I am having music lessons and I like learning the Lute but am not very fond of the singing lessons. Our Music Master is a very short man with a very pointed beard with small eyes just like little brown pebbles. I think that it is because he is so short that he always seems to be standing on his toes. The boys here call him 'Goat Face'. We will be having a Dance Master soon. Some of the squires say that we have to take the ladies' part some times when we are learning the dances; we are not looking forward to that! In my free time I go riding, sometimes Henry rides with me. He does not ride as well as myself and he has never been hunting. He said that his father does not get time to hunt as he is very busy with the University. Sir Thomas said that we will go hunting and we will teach Henry how to hunt. I am really looking forward to going hunting and of course I am looking forward to when I get some leave and can come home for a while for I do miss you all so much.

How are John and Alice? I have told everyone about them. How funny John can be sometimes and how hard Alice tries to keep up with us on her little pony and our little dogs with little short legs running their hearts out to be part of our fun and are always with us. Henry says that he would be most pleased to meet our family and would like to visit Barewe. I have told Father that now I am a man I do not want to be known as 'Ham' any more but William the Younger like I am known here. Love to you all. Your loving son William.'

I was so pleased with his letter. I put it carefully in my box in which I keep my treasures. I felt so lonely and sad. I went and found John and Alice and told them that I had received a letter from Ham and what it contained and how in future we must call him William and not Ham any more.

Chapter 16

"That is really odd, Mother, for Ham is his name and William is Father's name. Are we to call Father 'Ham'?" Alice asked. I explained to her how William was his real name and why we called him Ham in the first place. Then I hugged them both, counting my blessings that I have still got them for this period in time.

Chapter 17
THE MAKING OF A KNIGHT

It is dawn and it is going to be a beautiful day. I am so happy and excited for today, the 12th day of March 1264, William and I are travelling to Stoke by Nayland for on Sunday my eldest son William will become a Knight.

I just stood and looked at my dearest husband asleep in our bed. He is still very handsome but his forehead now carries a lot of lines of wear and tear of life and there is now white in his beard and hair. It is not often these days that we share a bed together; most of the time he is seated on his horse travelling away from home on the King's business. Times are still quite troublesome but no way was I going to let the affairs of government spoil my weekend. I have, over the past few years, had some very dark, lonely days. Today I have the feel of Spring in my steps and on my lips I cannot help but to wear a smile. I leant over William and gave him a kiss on his lips to wake him up. It did not seem to wake him so I had to kiss him with more force, while pulling his beard. So quickly he took me by surprise with his arms clutching around me as he rolled me on to the bed.

"Why, who is this bold lady of such beauty and passion, could she be my virtuous wife?" I could not speak for Will kissed me so hard, taking my breath away as he caressed the curves of my body.

"William, you said that we must make an early start today," I said as Poppy was banging on the door informing us that it was time to rise.

"William, let me go!" I said.

"Do my duties call me every minute of every day?" he said with a sigh.

"William, today is not duties, the next few days

will be days of pride and joy," I said, taking his hand and pulling him out of the bed.

We had already packed. I had had two new gowns made with matching bonnets. These gowns were made by a cloth merchant from Burwell called Calwe who buys his silks from Spain and France. I chose lavender colour to wear at Young William's ceremony and a darker blue colour for a new riding skirt and cloak. To bring money in for my personal use, I now have a very flourishing herb garden which contains most known herbs. Folk come from many miles to buy or trade the herbs which they need from us; this money William allows me to keep. I did not very often have new gowns made, I saved most of the money towards our new Manor Hall which we still had not had built.

Mother had also been invited to Nayland but now she is much older and for the last few years she has been getting very painful joints and to ride a horse quite a distance would be very difficult for her. She still remains beautiful and doesn't look her age. Her hair is still mostly red but with silver streaks in it.

We now have an addition to the family. This is Hugh, our nine year old son, who has bright red hair and large brown eyes and a plump face to match his quite round body. Poor Hugh has been a very sickly child and quite difficult to raise. Each winter he gets a cough which causes him difficulty in breathing and his face and limbs turn blue. I treat him with a mixture of Har Hume; in the East this is called the Seed of Horus. We boil this with the stems and leaves of comfrey which is made into a drink which stops the coughing and helps him to breathe as normal. Then he is fed tripe cooked in goat's milk, which makes a poultice inside his chest. He does not care much for eating the tripe but this seems to work well for Hugh. This advice was given to me by the herb woman from Risby. This year we will be sending Hugh to finish his education at the Abbey of Bury St. Edmunds, we do not think that he would be fit enough to be a Knight like his brothers. Mother and Sarah will look after Hugh while we are away. They both know how to treat him if he should be ill

William and I left for Stoke by Nayland. Poppy travelled with us as my ladies' maid, two Captains from the army and two grooms with four horses carrying our clothes and the present for our host. We were greeted by Sir Thomas Senior and Lady Margaret and Sir Thomas the Younger and his betrothed, Lady Joanna de Vere. William the Younger was not there to greet us; he had already commenced his 'Vigil' in the Church. William would put his armour on the Altar and then pray and keep guard over his armour till dawn. In the morning, he would put on a robe of white linen as a sign of purity. Over this, he would place a crimson mantle to show the blood he must shed and on his legs he will wear black hose to remind him of his death. Then, kneeling before the Lord, he will promise to defend The Faith of Christ to protect the Ladies and to be faithful to his brother Knights.

We were shown to our chambers; the wall of one chamber was decorated in the style of the chase. There was one large bed with French screens around it to keep the draught out. William was most pleased for there was a table with crystallised fruits and petite sweetmeats upon it and he quickly helped himself to them. In the next chamber there was a large bed and a table on which there were herbed waters, nosegays and small perfumed cushions to encourage a good night's sleep.

"Poppy may have that chamber, we will use the other chamber," said William.

We got refreshed and changed quickly; I did not

wear my new dress, I shall wear that tomorrow. I wore an ivory coloured dress on which Mother and I had sewn patterns of birds and flowers; I covered my head with ivory lace to match my gown. "Come now, Katherine, we will go and find the small refectory where we will be eating," said William, quite eager.

We entered the refectory and our hosts all stood and welcomed us in. There was a wonderful spread upon the table. All different sorts of meats; there was swan, hare, hog and many small birds. We commenced with fowl broth followed by eel blanc-mange and then ate the meats served with barley and oat breads followed with stewed apples served with almond milk and saffron and of course there were many good wines.

Lady Margaret was most charming. We talked about when my William was a young boy staying with her and about each others' families. Then the subject got on to the King and the council of Barons.

"I gather that the Pope has ruled that King Henry was forced under duress to sign the Provision of Oxford in 1258 which the Pope says has no substance and this is supported by King Louis IX. King Henry, who is now most pleased with the decision, has now gone back to ruling on his own and not listening to the Barons' wishes which has vexed most of the Barons. I gather that Simon de Montfort has started to raise rebels against the King. He is already supported by the Franciscans and the Oxford students and, of course, Simon's four sons," said Sir Thomas.

"Of course Gilbert de Clare, the new Earl of Gloucester, is following in his brother Richard's footsteps and will join forces with Simon following Richard's demise," said William.

"Oh, Katherine, what will you do about your daughter Alice, is she not living with Isabelle in the

Clare's castle at Gloucester?" asked Lady Margaret.

"You won't be able to leave Alice there, William," said Thomas the Younger.

"The De Clares will never harm Alice, they are as my brothers, we were brought up together. Isabelle is my best friend, she has always been so," I said, quite vexed.

"My dearest Lady Katherine, they may be as your brothers but your husband will be their foe and, as Alice is William's daughter, she must be moved soon," said Sir Thomas.

"War has not been declared as yet, we still have time," said William, very calmly.

Conversation continued but I do not know of what the speech was saying. I could only think about the safety of my children. My son William will be a Knight tomorrow, he will take part in battles fighting for his King against my family the De Clares. Did not my mother raise them all? How can we ever fight on opposite sides?

"My Lady Katherine. You look very tired. Would you like me to escort you to your chamber? I am about to retire myself," said Lady de Vere, getting up.

We bid Goodnight. William stayed with the men; I could see that they still had much to talk about.

"Do not fret, Katherine, I am sure that our Lords will work out what is best to do," said Lady de Vere gently.

I entered my chamber. Poppy was there to help me off with my gown. She could see how upset I was. I explained that within the next few weeks there would be a war between the Royalists and Simon de Montfort and many of the Barons supported by the people of London, the Franciscans and the students of Oxford, to name just a few of the groups. How Isabelle and her brothers would become our enemies.

There was a large cross in the corner of the chamber. Poppy and I knelt down and prayed to have our families kept safe, together with our people in Barewe. I also had to pray for Isabelle and her family, although they would be on the opposite side and, of course, I prayed for peace. I felt much better after I had prayed and a little bit ashamed that I may have let William down amongst our hosts for being so emotional. I would not think about the coming war again, then it will not spoil my special day tomorrow.

The next morning William took me for a walk in the grounds, pointing out places where he used to have fun with the other squires. While walking in the grounds, William said that he would send our son William to Gloucester to fetch Alice from Isabelle's and take her to a Convent in Gloucester were she would be safe. I asked William if Alice might not come and live at home.

"It is bad enough that I must leave you and Hugh and your mother on your own as I will be away fighting and Alice is a young, beautiful woman and very vulnerable. We could not risk having her spoilt, could we Katherine?" William said, holding me close.

The guests had started to arrive with many of Knights that were coming for the Tournament which would follow the Church Ceremony. William will be competing in the Tournament.

"Why, there is Sir William de Valence and Sir John de Warnne, a neighbour of ours from Wolf Hall, Hardgrave," said William.

"We should go and get ready for the ceremony now Will," I said. I was putting on my new gown and William was looking out of the window watching the guests arrive.

"There is a large party arriving, carrying the De

Clare's banner, just coming through the gates," said Will.

I ran to the window, "Why, it is Alice, Isabelle and Gilbert!" I said, very surprised.

William went down to greet them. Poppy helped me quickly finish getting ready. Before I was ready, Alice and Isabelle burst through the doors. I embraced Alice and pushed her away and looked at her. How fine she looked, she was now fourteen years old and a beautiful young woman.

"Katherine, I thought that Alice should see her brother become a Knight and I wanted to see you and of course the ceremony," said Isabelle, throwing her arms around me and kissing my cheek.

"I was so surprised to see you both and of course so delighted," I said, smiling.

"Doesn't Alice look beautiful? You wait till you see her in the new gown I have had made for her; I had to buy the cloth, the colour was just made for Alice." Isabelle and Alice went to get ready for the ceremony.

They will join William and me to enter the church. Gilbert will not be attending the ceremony, he will be practising on the tournament field as will most of the Knights.

"That beautiful woman is never my little girl, surely Katherine - is she?" Will said, unable to move from shock for it had been some time since he had last seen Alice.

Alice greeted him as he put his arms around her. "Father, my gown! Do not crush my gown!" exclaimed Alice, smoothing her gown. She was fourteen years old now and in the last few months had transformed from a boyish young girl to this indeed very attractive young woman who stood beside us.

We entered the church which was already full. Our son William was still at the Altar praying in his white linen robe and crimson mantle. Sir Thomas the Younger was sitting on a throne-type chair close to the Altar. Sir Roger le Chaumberleyn - who was a good friend of Sir Thomas and had educated young William at his time at Stoke - read the proclamation on how brave, fearless and honourable William had been in his training as a Knight. This was read to the brother Knights who could question anything if they so wished. Then William was called to his Lord, Sir Thomas.   Kneeling before his Lord, he promised to defend The Faith of Christ, to protect ladies, and to be faithful to his brother Knights. Then rising, Sir Thomas girded him with a sword belt 'The Belt of Knighthood'. Piece by piece, his armour was fastened on. Lastly gilded spurs were fixed to his heels and a new Sir Knight had been made. The Knights raised their swords and said loudly together "Welcome brother Knight, Sir William Gifford."

    I could see how proud my husband was. Next year it will be John who is made a Knight if everything is well by then. John could not be at his brother's ceremony as he was away with his Lord Godfrey of Boyton, John's uncle.

Chapter 18
THE TOURNAMENT

After the ceremony we went to a small chamber where we able to have some food. Young Will was very thirsty and hungry as he had not eaten since early the day before and it also enabled us to be together as a family, including Isabelle of course. Young Will and Alice were so pleased to see each other; it had been some time since they last had been together.

"Why, this pretty young maiden could not be that boyish young sister of mine!" he said embracing her.

"This extremely handsome Sir Knight cannot be that spindly long-legged youth known as Will can it?" said Isabelle, laughing and joining in the fun. Then she gave to William a beautiful golden crucifix on a chain saying "For you, most honoured Sir Knight."

Then Alice curtsied to Will and took hold of his right hand, putting on a ring which had been made for him embossed with the Gifford Arms. "Most honoured, dearest brother I am so proud of you," she said.

"So many thanks to you all for all the love and kindness you have always shown me," he said

"Come now, young Will, we must make ready for the tournament," said his father, leaving Isabelle, Alice and myself alone.

"Isabelle, you have been so kind to us all, thank you so much," I said.

"Well, I am a very rich widow, the Count left me so rich. You know that I use the title of The Countess of Gloucester while I am in England and my French title when at my chateau in France. My brother is the Earl of Gloucester so I can use 'Gloucester' in my title. If I used my French title while in England, there may be many who might think that I was one of those 'Court foreigners' and you know that would not go down well

Chapter 18

with me. I will be going to Gascony along with my daughters and my brother's wives and families. If you, Katherine, Alice and Hugh would like to live at one of my chateaux in France you would be very welcome and you would all be safe there and I will not be thinking about your safety all the time," she said, pleading with me.

"Thank you so much, Isabelle, I am so pleased that you are going to Gascony for we will not have to worry about you. I thank you for the care you have given to Alice over the last years and how you have helped her grow into this beauty. I must stay at our Manor at Barewe, that is where I want to be. Alice will be going to Denny Abbey for safety and Hugh will be going to the Abbey of St. Edmunds. He was going there next year anyway to finish his education. So it will just be Mother and myself and my people that I shall have to take care of," I said, taking hold of Isabelle's hand.

"Gilbert said that he would not be able to guarantee Alice's safety and it would not be fair if anything should happen to her father or brother while she was under our care. That's why I brought her back to you for there seems to very little doubt that the Giffords and the De Clares will be opposing each other. You know that I will always love you all, whatever the outcome," said Isabelle, crying.

"Come now, let us enjoy the rest of the time we have together," I said.

"Let's go outside and see what is going on before we take our seats," said Alice. So that is what we did.

As we approached the tournament field, we could hear the trumpets and the music. Round the enclosure there were all different coloured pavilions. The first which we passed was the pavilion for the five challenging Knights. The outside of the pavilion was adorned with each of the Knight's colours, Coats of

Arms and pennons of those who were taking part in the tournament. Inside there were carpets and tapestries and brightly coloured cushions. Isabelle's sister-in-law, also Lady Warnne, together with other supporters of the De Clares were there. We greeted them and had a word. There was a joke about Isabelle supporting the foe and we all laughed, even if we did not think it amusing. Next to this pavilion there was accommodation for the horses, grooms and smithies. Then came a pavilion for the Yeoman, Nobility and the rich Jews. This was followed by groups of local people seated on the grass. Behind them were many stalls containing foods, beverages and all sorts of things to sell. On the opposite side of the field to the challengers was the accommodation for the Home Knight's horses, grooms and smithies. Next to this was the main pavilion where we would sit along with Sir Thomas and Lady Margaret and their guests. Then came the seating for the Manor servants.

We took our seats as the fanfare sounded. The Knights came riding in from opposite ends of the field. The spectators all cheered and made much noise, some making sounds that were not too friendly as the Knights lined up in their groups of five each side of the main pavilion, each one with his squire standing next to him holding his colours. My husband's squire of many years, called Zac, was unable to be with him for William had allowed him to leave to go to Hereford where his father was very ill. Zac had never wanted to become a Knight, although he had all the training as one. This sometimes happened. So William had loaned a squire from Sir Thomas Senior. Young William had a young squire who had only been a year in training at Stoke. He was Geoffrey and from now on will be riding with Will as his squire and will have to support him and finish his training.

Chapter 18

Sir Roger le Chaumberleyn proclaimed the laws of the tournament. The five challengers were to undertake the five Home Knights, secondly any of the Home Knights proposing to combat may, if he please, select a special antagonist from among the challengers by touching his shield. If he did it with the reverse of his lance, the trail of skill will be the arms of courtesy under the new law of our gracious King Henry III. This means that at the extremity of the lance, a piece of round flat board has been fixed over the point so that no danger will be encountered, except the shock of horse and rider. Thirdly, reward will be given of ten points for dismounting one's opponent, ten points is given to the opponent of a Knight who has to retire because of injury, five points for breaking a lance.

The five Knights as Challengers points gained will be added together, along with the points gained in the second tournament, following a break, of foot combat with round-edged heavy swords, points scored in the usual way. The same scoring will count for the Home Knights. The reward will be given to the five who have scored best.

The prize being of an Arab Stallion bred for speed and courage in the East and a pouch of gold given by Sir William Gifford of Weston and Barewe, lineage from Osbern de Bolbec Sire de Longueville San Peur Duke of Normandy.

Sir Roger announced the titles of all the Knights taking part. Then he asked for the first Home Knight to come forward to approach the challengers. Sir William de Valence came forward and touched the shield of Sir Gilbert de Clare. Then both Knights rode up to the main pavilion and paid their courtesy to Sir Thomas and to the Lady of their choice to whom they wish to show their valour. Sir William de Valence tilted his lance to his lady wife and she placed her kerchief on it, which then he placed in his gauntlet with a little edge of it showing. Sir Gilbert had done the same and was displaying his wife's kerchief. The two Knights took their places on opposite ends of the field each side of the centre barrier. The spectators all cheered and shouted. The Knights pulled their visors down and focused their eyes upon Sir Thomas who held his hand up high. He dropped his hand which was the signal for both Knights to race with great speed to the middle space, where their lances clashed so hard that the stallions both rebounded backwards. They rode on to the end of the field where they both turned to face each other again, to recommence the encounter. There were to be three jousts between the two competing Knights. Both Valence and Gilbert competed without any score; as they retired, some of the spectators hissed at them as they had come to see blood.

    The next two Knights were Sir Thomas the Younger and the Earl of Leicester. Sir Thomas was bearing the kerchief of his betrothed Lady Joanna. After the third encounter there were still no points, which was accompanied by more hissing from the crowd. Next to compete was my beloved husband; he was against the Earl of Essex. My stomach was turning over as I put my trembling hand out to give William my kerchief. Will faced Essex. When Sir Thomas's hand dropped, William's stallion galloped off with great acceleration, approaching Essex with such force before he was midfield. The clash was so strong that it caused Essex's stallion to rear up but Essex managed to keep his seat. The crowd cheered.

    William had spent a great deal of time breeding Arab heavy horses that were trained for speed for tournaments. They faced each other again and as Sir

Chapter 18

Thomas's hand dropped, Will looked as if he was flying following spurring his horse. Essex swerved to catch Will's shield at an angle to bring him down but William came with such force that Essex caught his shield awkwardly, which caused his lance to split. William had gained five points. The crowd cheered as the Knights retired. Sir Vere and Sir Warnner were next, they were gentlemen of a similar age with lots of experience but their encounter was without any points. As they left the field, some spectators shouted "Bring on some young blood."

It was young Will's turn next, he was going last against Sir Thomas de Clare. Will presented his lance to Lady Margaret for her kerchief and she was most honoured. I was feeling quite sick in case Will was dehorsed; my hands were quite glowing, a thing that a Lady's hands should not do. Isabelle said that she could not look as he was her brother and my son. I could not say a word; I could not but think at how handsome William looked. He had a very good stallion which his father had bred for him. Sir Thomas's hand dropped and the encounters began but were not fruitful.

Sir Rodger announced that the Home Knights had been awarded five points which would be carried forward to the 'Heavy Sword Tournament'. He said that there would be a break before that to watch the falcons display.

We watched the falcons. Then it was time for the second part of the tournament to commence. This was with the blunted broad sword on foot melée of all the ten Knights taking part together. They would start with their opposition who they fought in the jousting tournament. They had to fight until a sand timer had run through, then that combat would be finished. They would then go to fight the next challenger till they had fought all five

Knights. There would be a sand marshal who watched the time and signalled to a herald who sounded the trumpet, which signalled time to stop. Then there were another five marshals, one being attached to each pair of Knights to see that they obeyed the rules and they also awarded the points. These were as ten points for submitting or retiring because of injury, five points for hitting the main body area. The Knights were not allowed to put blows to the head area or below the waist. They were allowed to use body and leg force against their opponent.

    The Knights were lined up and the trumpet marked the start of the first combat. It was quite difficult to watch all the Knights fighting at once. I really only had eyes for my husband and son. I was mostly worried about young Will for he had not had as much experience as the other Knights and did not have the body weight of most of them for this kind of combat.

    In the first bout there had not been any Knight knocked to the floor, there was a lot of noise of the swords hitting the armour. I did not know what the points were. In the second bout my son was against The Earl of Leicester and my husband against Gilbert. All of a sudden, some of the crowd started to shout while others groaned as our Sir de Vere was knocked to the ground by the Earl of Essex. The next bout was uneventful. William was against the Earl of Leicester and William the Younger was against Gilbert.

    In the fourth bout my son was against Essex, I was really worried about this bout as Essex had already knocked Vere to the ground but my son was young, fit and agile so this gave me hope. William was against Thomas de Clare. By the end of this bout both my men were safe.

    Before the last bout there was a longer break

while the marshals added up the points which had been awarded. A marshal announced that the challengers were five points ahead. Then the trumpet sounded to start the bout. Young Will was against Sir John de Warnne, William was against The Earl of Leicester. It must have been getting close to the end of the bout when Sir John gave such a heavy strong swing of his sword. He was the heaviest Knight in this tournament. The blow would surely knock Will to the ground but somehow Will managed to jump backwards out of the way of the sword and Sir John over-balanced as he followed through on his swing and there was nothing to stop it. So Sir John hit the ground. The crowd went mad and the rich among the crowd showered the field with coins for young Will and his squire gathered them up.

As the points of both tournaments were counted together it gave the overall reward to the Home Knights. The Home group rode to the centre pavilion to Sir Thomas who declared young William 'Victor and Champion'. The prize was shared between the Home Knights.

Sir Roger le Chaumberleyn suggested that everyone should enjoy the rest of the day. To the left of the field there could be found bull-baiting and feats of archery for the men. To the right of the field the ladies would find music, dancing, jugglers and fools. Sir Thomas, the Home Knights and their Ladies went into the Hall to celebrate.

Chapter 19
THE WAR

When we arrived home, there was a large crowd at the Hall gates waiting to greet Will on becoming a Knight.

"Welcome your new Lord," announced William. Will rode forward.

The crowd all cheered "Long life to our Lord," they shouted.

"There will be some hogs killed to be roasted on the green and plenty of mead for you all to celebrate your new Lord," said William smiling.

Some man in the crowd shouted out, "Are we at war yet?"

"No, I will let you all know as soon as I hear. Enjoy the celebrations for now, for there will difficult times ahead of us," said William.

Inside the Hall we were greeted by Mother, Hugh and Poppy. They were so pleased to see Will and Alice for it had been some time since they had last seen them.

"You're a Knight now Will, are you going to war?" asked Hugh.

"Not yet, Hugh," answered Will.

We had a family celebration, we talked and laughed a lot. William told us of his plans. "As soon as the troubles with the government have been put down we will start building our new Hall with great speed. We will have pages and squires to train, our own tournaments and there will be a great banquet as grand as the ones the De Clares hold. My beautiful Ladies will each have new gowns and bonnets, including you, Mother Maud. We will all have some fun for we have not had much during the last few years. I wish that our John could have been with us at this time. I am so proud of you all," said William, I do believe with a tear in his eyes.

Chapter 19

The next few days we did have fun, we all went riding in the woods together as a family and hunting there with the bow. Then William had to spend some of the time at Denham Castle giving orders to the Captains on how they wanted the army got ready for war.

Then came a message for William from King Henry. William read it and told us that the King had been campaigning in the south east of England to put some trouble down and he is making his way south, he has heard that Simon de Montfort, along with Gilbert de Clare, has a large army made up with Londoners and students who are marching towards the King and Prince Edward. "The King wants me and Will to take my army and ride to Scotland to get the help of the King's son-in-law King Alexander II to bring his army to help fight Simon and the Clares. This will take time and I hope that the King and Edward will be able to hold their lines till we can get back with help," said William.

"I will leave some archers at out-lying areas around Barewe, Heigham and Denham and a Captain to keep charge of security. The men of the Manor will have to do guard duties as well. I will get the bailiffs to work with the Captain to give the men some training and know what jobs they will have to do to keep the Manor safe."

My husband and Young Will rode off early the next day with their squires and the army. William had already taken Alice to the Convent at Denny along with a large box containing our treasures and great deal of gold, which we had put away for building the new Hall. It would be safe with Berta who would hide it away and keep it safe for us. Although Berta is getting quite old now, she is still very much in control at the Convent. The armies of both sides of the war would leave the Convent alone for they would not want The Wrath of God upon them when they were at war. That just left me, Hugh and Mother at the Hall.

That day I made the effort to hide my emotions. I made sure that I wore a smile on my face most of the time in and outside the Hall. When I went to bed that night, I cried into my cushion for this was my husband and sons who I may never see again and we had not heard from William's brother Godfrey. We do not know if he and our son John will be fighting on the same side as the rest of the family.

Every day I went to the church to pray for my family and that there will soon be peace. I also asked for strength to help to keep control in all situations that might arise. The next two weeks were uneventful. I was working very hard keeping control of the Manor, making sure that it was functioning the same as usual. Being short of labour, because the men had to do guard duties and defence training now and did not have so much time to do their usual work, I had to make sure that the grooms were looking after the young foals correctly. William had taken extra horses with him for he would be going north with his squire and four of the cavalry to Scotland. They needed the spare horses so they could rest their horses by changing them as they would be galloping at great speed. The main army with Will in command went south.

Then just before dawn one morning there was such a large crash. I jumped out of bed, putting on my cloak quickly and hurried downstairs. There stood men with a large battering ram. They had a white cross on their chests and backs. I knew that they were not Royalist but Simon's men. My heart was in my mouth; I must keep control and keep my wits about me. Mother and Hugh were coming down the stairs as some of the men were running up them, there were men going in all directions all over the Hall. They rounded up all the

Chapter 19

servants that were in the Hall to where we were. My little dogs that lived in the Hall attacked some of the men's ankles, the dogs knew that the men should not be there. The men kicked out at them, one of the men picked up one of the dogs who bit his hand, the man threw the dog at the wall.

"I will have that dog roasted on the fire for my meal today," he said.

While all eyes were on the man and the dog, no one noticed that Hugh had picked up the fire iron and quickly, with all his strength, swung the iron into the back of the man's legs, causing the man to fall backwards on to the floor. The rest of the men laughed to see a boy doing that to him.

"You're a dead now boy," the man shouted.

"That he is not," shouted a very large black man who had just come into the chamber. The way the rest of the men looked at the coloured man, I took it he was a higher rank than the others.

"The man bowed his head to me. "Lady Katherine, it is many years since we last met," he said with a smile.

I thought quickly; there were not many coloured people in this country, some had been brought from the East. The only one I knew of was when I was a girl at Clare. There was a black boy who helped in the grounds of the Castle. He had a sunny personality and was always smiling, he would watch Isabelle and myself with his eyes as we walked in the grounds and we often gave him an apple.

"How are you? It has been many years indeed since we last met," I said with great relief.

Then through the door entered a Knight and his squire; it was Gilbert de Clare.

"You may all leave the Hall," directed Gilbert to

the soldiers.

Mother and I curtsied to Gilbert who acknowledged us.

"Refreshments for Sir Gilbert and his squire," I directed the servants.

"Take the male servants out of the Hall and put them under guard. The women may go about their work," said Gilbert, giving orders to his squire. The food and wine were brought in and sat upon the table. Gilbert sat down at the table. "Join me please, Katherine. Lady De Passelewe, you and the boy may take your leave, best if you go to your chambers."

He waited until Mother and Hugh had left. "Have you heard, Katherine, that the King and Edward are now our prisoners? The King was defeated at Lewis and fled to Cluniac Priory. We waited outside the Priory, not letting any food in, for the King to give himself up, which he did. We had already taken Edward prisoner. They are now on their **way to a castle in Hereford where they will be held as prisoners.**"

"My Lord, what of my husband and sons?" I said, making a sign of Our Lord on my chest, closing my eyes and quietly praying to hear of their safety.

"There were many Barons and Nobility killed in battle but I did not see your husband's colours amongst the blood and mud on the battlefield. I do not know if your family is dead or alive. I could not see Will being taken prisoner, it is not his style.
Katherine, I have not seen your hair loose and flowing around your shoulder since you were a child. You are even more beautiful than I thought with your head not covered," he said, taking hold of my hand.

I quickly snatched my hand away. "My Lord, I do not approve of what you are saying," I said in a strong tone.

Chapter 19

"I will not be quiet, Katherine, you will sit and listen to what I have to say. I have wanted you as a woman since I saw you all grown up at the Ball you shared with my sister, so did my brother Thomas, as you know. I learnt from Isabelle how you were besotted with Will for a long time and I knew that I did not stand a chance with you as you had already said that you did not want my brother. I even, if you remember, encouraged you and Will to be together because I wanted you to be happy as I would wish my sister to be." He paused as he ran his hand through my hair, turning my face towards him.

"My Lord, may I remind you that you are a Knight," I said, removing my seat away from him but remaining seated.

"Now, Katherine, if your beloved William is alive or dead you will have nothing. Think about that, Katherine! I will be the second most powerful man in England. Your sons who live, I will be able to give them Manors, Lands and Positions. All you have to do is to be my lady to live as such. I will honour you above all other women, including my wife and daughters."

"Your wife, Gilbert. She is the women you married, you promised to love and protect her. She is the mother of your children. How can you think so shallow of me? You have known me so many years. I would never cause another human so much pain," I said, scolding him.

"I have never loved my wife, it was a marriage of convenience. The time we spend together is a pain to each of us, we have nothing in common, she is a most silly woman. Thank goodness that I have Isabelle at my castle to set an example for my daughters, I could not bear them to grow up like their mother with nothing in their heads. I needed a wife to share love and

Chapter 19

companionship with, Katherine. I have never had time to find one who could give me that. I knew that I could not love or desire a woman as I do you. I did not put thought into who I should marry, I just did not care. I needed an heir and that is all it meant to me." Gilbert did speak as if he meant every word.

"I do feel sorry that you have an unhappy marriage. I do love you very much Gilbert but as I love Thomas and Isabelle. We have all grown up together, you are all as my family and I will have no other man in my bed than my husband, whether he is alive or dead. You say that I and my sons will now have nothing. We will still have our honour and each other, even if we have very little bread in our mouths," I said, holding my head high.

He now stood up. "My army are now killing some of your livestock to feed themselves. We need fresh horses so I shall be taking the best of William's stable and then we shall leave. If you should change your mind then contact me, Katherine."

"Gilbert, for some of that love you said you have for me, would you leave the silver bay mare in the stable who belongs to me?"

He did not speak and left the Hall. I just sat with my head between my hands, my whole body trembling as I relaxed for it had taken so much of my energy to hold myself together and keep control while Gilbert was here. What has happened to my husband and sons? What will life now hold for us?

Mother came hurrying in and poured us both a large glass of wine, while I told her the news. I didn't tell her about the feelings Gilbert had for me.

Chapter 20
THE WAR CONTINUES

The next day I rode around the Manor with the Bailiff to see how much damage had been done. Two bullocks and two hogs had been slaughtered. The main loss was in the stables where the Arab stallions that Will had bred had been taken. We were left with some old mares and the young foals; Gilbert had left my beloved Crystal. I fed her an apple while I stroked her and kissed her muzzle. While in my thoughts, I was thinking how heartbroken Will would be, following how interested he had been in his breeding programme.

"We will just have to start breeding again once the foals are old enough," I told the groom.

The Bailiff informed me that some young maidens had been spoilt by some of the soldiers. I thought, and then I said that he must send a cart to Risby to fetch the Herb Woman to the Hall. "You may tell her what has happened so that she can bring with her what is needed," I directed.

When she arrived at the Hall she was carrying a large basket full of herbs and potions. She said that she would make a potion for the girls to drink so that they would not have any child that belongs to the Devil. "It will make them sick but will clean them out and save their soul."

I went with her into the kitchen to watch what she was doing. She took just a little amount of some ground root of Belladonna, it is very poisonous, then a good measure of Goldenseal followed with a handful of juniper berries, all heated up together and mixed with water. "That will do the job," she said. Then she took some Hyssopus and made a solution from it. "They must sit in the solution for as long as they can for three days. It does sting but that is what makes it work," she said,

Chapter 20

holding her hand out for some coins which I gave her, thanking her as she left.

I sent for my cousin the Reverend De Passelewe and told him what had happened to the girls and what must be done. The potion must be blessed before it is given to the girls, a quarter of the potion to each of the four girls to drink from the challis which you bless it in. He said that he would pray with them to God first, to ask the Lord to take away their sins. I gave each of the girls the solution which they would mix with water to sit in for each of the three days. I told each of the girls that if they could find a man to marry them at a later date, I would give their husband a coin of quite great value. I thought that would solve the problem because it was not really the girls who caused the problems.

The weeks went by and we were left alone at Barewe without any enemy armies visiting the Manor. I heard news by way of the Abbey in Bury that Simon de Montfort and the Earl of Gloucester (Gilbert) and The Bishop of Chichester had administration of the government of England. But peace was far from the minds of many of the Royalists and there were bursts of unrest all over England from rebels. More than likely led by my William, for I had heard from the Abbey that a Friar had brought a message from William, that he had joined up with his elderly uncle Osbert and they were fighting in the same manner as they did against the Saracens, not dressed as Knights but in disguise to obtain advantage. In the message it stated that both our sons were safe in France waiting for when the time was right so that they could come back with a Royalist Army. I was so relieved to get this news, although I still went on worrying about their safety and welfare.

It was some months later that I heard again that Gilbert and his brother had turned against Montfort,

Chapter 20

mainly that Gilbert could not get on with Montfort's sons and resented the dominance of the now elderly Simon. It seems that Gilbert had joined up with Sir Roger de Mortimer VI, a Royalist at Ludlow. In the meantime, William and Osbert had got entrance of Hereford Castle and helped Prince Edward to make his escape from captivity. They rode together to join up with Mortimer. William and Osbert's armies were already there, so was the Royalist army from France.

Faced with adversaries, Simon de Montfort eventually went to join one of his sons, Simon the Younger, at Kenilworth. On the second of August 1265 he crossed the River Severn, on the third he arrived at Evesham that night with a tired, hungry army - in all he had 6,000 men. **Simon was joined there by the Welsh army who, over the years, had grown to hate King Henry and Edward. They were mostly spearmen.**

Evesham was not a very good place to be, it was surrounded by the River Avon which loops around Evesham in the shape of a U. In the morning of the fourth of August, **Prince Edward trapped Montfort at Evesham after marching all night from Worcester.** The Prince had about 10,000 men, the bulk of his men being on Greenhill to the north of Evesham with The Avon to the east and west, the remainder being stationed to the south on the east bank of the river which stopped Simon being able to escape by the bridge across the Avon. While this was going on, William and Osbert rode to Hereford, remembering that they both knew Hereford so well as the county belonged to the family. They made entry once again at the castle and released the King.

Meanwhile, back at Evesham Simon moved his army towards the Prince's position. He formed his army in lines with cavalry in the front, the English infantry in

Chapter 20

the centre and the Welsh spearmen at the rear. Montfort intended to smash his way through the centre of the Prince's Army. Gloucester came in to the rear of the army, attacking the Welsh who broke lines and fled. It took just two hours to defeat the Montfort army. **Montfort was killed along with eighteen Barons, 160 Knights and 4,000 men.** This was indeed a very sad day. There were family members in each of the opposing armies, father against sons, brother against brother. I prayed to God that my family were all on the same side. There were people whom I had known that had been in the losing army.

Chapter 21

COMING HOME

"The bells at the Abbey in Bury St. Edmunds are ringing, the war is over," shouted the Bailiff, banging at the door at dawn. We all hurried down the stairs. The servants already had the door open. "Go with the groom and ride as fast as you can to the Abbey and find out which side had victory. See that you return here straight away; we will all be waiting to know who now rules. It is very important that we know so that we can make plans, which will be very different in the way we will act," I said, giving him a note for the Abbot.

The time the Bailiff was away seemed so long. It was past noon when he returned. We met him in the court yard; the servants from the Hall were all in the yard waiting for the news for most of them had some kin or a friend who were in William's army.

"It is the King. The King has won."

Everyone cheered, "God save the King," they all shouted. I could not speak a word, the words would not come out of my mouth. I just hugged Mother and Hugh with tears running slowly down my cheeks. The servants were hugging each other and dancing and skipping together. We went into the Hall and had a bottle of our best wine, to raise our tumblers to the Royalist army. Then we all knelt and prayed to God, that our men may be safe.

"We must have the church bells rung. The whole Manor must go to church to give thanks for how the war has ended," said Mother.

It was several days before we heard the bells ring again. Once again the Bailiff was at the hall. "Our army has been seen on the Icknield Way. It will just be a short time before they are all home," he said.

I instructed the cook to get the food ready, she

had been preparing for days a great feast for the family. I had the Bailiff see that four hogs were killed and made ready to roast on the green for the army and for the Manor to celebrate their home coming.

The army marched in, all very dirty and dusty. The crowd all cheered and waved branches and threw petals over the troops to give them a heroes' welcome. I could see all of my three men at the head of the troops. This time I had trouble standing on my legs which went as if they were jelly.

William dismounted. He just took my hand and knelt at my feet, looking up into my eyes. How could my good, brave Lord pay me this homage? I felt so humble as the people once again cheered as William stood up and escorted me into the Hall followed by my sons. We kissed and hugged and kissed again, even Poppy got a kiss from Will because she was always where the family was.

"Alice is not here," said John.

"She is still at Denny," I said.

"I will fetch her then, she must be here," said John.

"I will come with you," said Will.

"My box is at the Abbey. So you can bring that back as well," said William.

"I have had the small chamber prepared for you with three large tubs containing herbs and hot water for you to bathe in to get rid of that dirt and your pains. When you have finished bathing, you can then go and fetch Alice," I said

They did this then rode off at speed.

William, when he was clean, just had some bread and cheese with some ale. He said that he was tired and would take some rest in the chamber while the boys are away. He took my hand and led me to our chamber.

Chapter 21

When the children arrived home, we were able to start our celebrations. There was much chatter and laughter and, of course, we all had to re-live the battle. I then asked them all to be quiet and I told them how brave young Hugh had been when the horrible soldier was going to kill one of the dogs and was threatening us. How Hugh had picked up the fire iron and hit the soldier behind his legs so that he had to fall to the ground. Hugh then stood in front of myself and Mother to protect us. Then, led by William, they all stood and raised their tumblers to Hugh, each of them speaking praise about his bravery. I think that this day was one of the happiest of my life.

William then spoke about his plans for the Manor. "We will start again on building the new Hall. I will get a very good stone mason from East Scotland who was in charge of constructing the castles which were built on the Welsh Marches. I had finished the plans for the Hall a while ago. This Scottish mason works well and we understand each other. Because we have educated our people well to make sure that they are well trained in their many skills and that now we have flourished as a Manor and are now the size of a small town, I shall apply to the King for a charter to be able to hold a market. I am sure that we will be able to make it as successful as the one in Bury St. Edmunds. I will also ask if we may hold a fair, then we will be able to hold some tournaments."

"I am afraid that we will only be having John here to stay for the next three weeks before he has to go away again," said William, very serious, then he smiled and said "Uncle Godfrey is making arrangements for next month, for John to take his oath for 'The Making of a Knight'. It had to be delayed because of the troubles." We all stood and raised our tumblers to John

"As for that most beautiful young lady, who has

had the good fortune to inherit her mother's and grandmother's beauty, I was somewhat astounded during the campaign at the amount of young Knights who asked my consent to present their virtues to you. So must we start thinking about a husband for you Alice?"

"Everywhere I went Knights were asking questions about Alice," said John.

"And me," joined in Will.

Alice was now blushing.

"That's enough now," I said, thinking to myself "Oh, not yet, I do not want to see Alice leave home so soon."

"What plans for you Hugh? Now that you are a lot stronger and your health is now quite good. Your mother and I have decided that you should finish your education at the Abbey in Bury. St. Edmunds following in your Uncle Walter's footsteps; you will then be able to enter the Church."

"That will be a terrible bore. I would rather train as a Knight," said Hugh, looking at his brothers for support, but none was available.

"Your plans, Will?" asked his Father.

"I have some business which I need to clear up at Stoke by Nayland," answered Will.

"Lady Business," said John with a laugh.

We all looked at Will who was glaring at John. "It is just business," he said not intending to give us further information.

We all went to Boyton as a family to see John become a Knight which we all enjoyed. Then we returned to Barewe where there was a message for Will and John from Prince Edward. It was to ask if Will and John would ride with Edward and some other young Knights to Kenilworth where there was an uprising from the supporters of Montfort. He preferred to ride with

Chapter 21

Knights of a similar age or younger than himself and liked to be known as 'Lord Edward' by them. He was a fine looking, tall young man, known to many as 'Long Shanks' because of his very long limbs. He was a fine swordsman with a very good, sharp brain and was excellent at planning military operations and was known for enjoying the combat in battles.

The uprising was soon put down. Will and John did not return home straight after the battle. They had been asked, along with other Knights, to return with Edward to his seat at Guildford. For while fighting, Lord Edward had a message that his wife, Eleanor of Castile, had given birth to their first child, a boy who was to be called John. Eleanor was less than ten years old when Edward married her in 1254; he was only fifteen years himself. During the time that Edward and his father were in prison, Eleanor fled to France. Guildford was Eleanor's favourite castle, she liked to be able to get away from Edward's mother who was very domineering towards her as the Queen was to most people. Lord Edward wanted to celebrate the birth of his son with the Knights who he now considered his friends.

When they did return home, which was after some time, they were full of the life at Guildford. Will told us what it was like.
"When we first saw Guildford Castle, the sun was shining on it. We were on top of a hill about a league away from the castle which was also on top of a hill but it looked as if it was just floating in a purple sea. This was caused because the castle was surrounded by the thickest heather that we have ever seen. It was in full bloom and a gentle breeze was moving the heather as if it were waves on the sea. It was built with stone which I know would interest you, Father, because you have been involved with the building of so many castles. It

had a shell keep and a very small strong tower. King Henry had recently had the Palace moved to the bailey and it had been built most luxuriously. The Royal chambers have beautiful painted frescos of musicians and beautiful dancing maidens on the walls and there are Persian rugs everywhere and many treasures that had been brought back from the Crusades. Six of us shared one chamber and we had a very large tub which was decorated very fine and four servants brought the hot water; three of us could get into the tub together. The servants said that the Princess bathes every day, even when the weather is very cold and she never catches a chill. Most days were spent in the fields, out on the heath or on the chase. There was Archery, Jousting, and Sword-play. Lord Edward won the Sword-play of course but both John and I beat him at Jousting. The next day we chased the deer and the boar. Edward does not like ladies to take part in the chase. He states 'Gentlemen only.' King Henry has had a special cut made where we race our stallions. John won two of the races and I got a second and third. It was the way you have bred the stallions. Edward said that he must buy some stock from you. On quieter days we played stone-hurling and club-ball; after dusk there were minstrels, fools to entertain us and chess and back-gammon to play.

    Most of the Knights had left and John and I were about to say our farewells. Lord Edward asked us to stay longer as his wife has been watching us and would like to get to know us better."

    "We felt quite uncomfortable and could not understand the request," said John who continued to tell their story. "This is where Eleanor won our hearts. She asked us both to escort her in the gardens and asked us to help her pick some flowers; neither of us has ever picked flowers before and we told her so."

"Shame on you," she said. "You must pick the flowers and then study each one. This will teach you about beauty for if you can understand the beauty of each flower, you will understand the different kinds of beauty that each woman carries."   Eleanor is so gentle and very kind and thoughtful to everyone, whether they are nobility or the servants. She is not a beauty but was so well educated, clever and worldly. Eleanor took great interest in Barewe and in you all; she asked a lot of questions about Alice."

"Then when we were about to leave for home, Lord Edward said that his wife would like Alice to come and be a companion to her."

"My wife wishes to have a lady-in-waiting who has not been influenced by my mother or the Court at the Palace - a young woman who has not been spoilt and could learn my wife's ways," said Lord Edward.

"He has written a letter for you, Father," said John. I asked the boys not to say anything to Alice till William and I had had time to discuss the letter.

I was not too happy. I thought about Emma and her shallow life at Court. Above all I wanted Alice to be happy, as happy as I have been. William thought that we should speak to Alice and see what type of life she would like to lead. He did say that she knows what life was like at the De Clares, with nobility coming and going all the time. "If she does want to go, we must spend a good deal of our money on new gowns and bonnets for her. It also looks that Will and John will be coming and going to Edward's castles so there will be plenty of news from home," said William, seeming quite happy with the thought of Alice going to Guildford.

When we did tell Alice, she did not jump with joy but gave it a great deal of thought, asking lots of questions of her brothers about Lord Edward and Eleanor and who were the other ladies there. She asked William if she did not like it there could she return home. William said that he would fetch her himself. Alice then came to me and put her arms around me, kissing me on the cheek and said that she would like to go as companion to Eleanor. So she got her new gowns (four of them with pumps and bonnets to match), six new under-gowns and bodices and three night and bathing garments. We all had to sit and view as she put on each gown and paraded in front of us. She had pale green and blue gowns and a silver one with a touch of pink in it, a fawn with cream, a white one edged with gold and a black gown with lots of white lace on it. John even asked Will to play the lute so he could dance with his sister in her silver gown which John said he liked the best. Will's favourite was the pale green and her father preferred the white one. Alice just loved them all and I am sure she would have slept in them if she could because it was such a job to get her to take them off. The day had come for Alice to leave. Her two brothers were escorting her. She was taking so much with her that they had to take a cart as well. For her lady's maid she was taking one of Poppy's daughters, Jane who, at some three years older than Alice, was a most sensible, bright girl. William had given Alice three gold coins. She will get an allowance from Eleanor. We said our goodbyes with lots of hugs and a few tears from me and Alice.

  In 1267 the King granted the Charter jointly to Lady Maude Passelewe and Sir William Gifford to hold a Saturday Market. He also granted for a fair to be held prior to the feast of John the Baptist. William wanted where possible for work on the Manor to be completed by Saturday

  The villeins will be able to make their crafts and

Chapter 21

wares and sell their goods themselves. Each villein who wants to sell his goods must give his name to the Bailiff and tell him what goods they would be selling. The Bailiff would give the list to William who would see that supplies and materials are available for their very first trading; then they must buy the materials themselves out of the profits. From their profits they would be able to take the cost of the raw supplies, then from what is left they would be allowed to keep half and the other half going to the Hall. This caused great excitement in the Manor and gave a purpose to the villeins' lives.

Chapter 22
LIFE CHANGES

Will spent much time with Lady Margaret at Stoke, the attraction being a certain young Lady whose mother was a good friend of Lady Margaret and visited her quite often. The young Lady was Lady Amicia Wimpole from Arrington, Grantchester. Often Will would escort Lady Margaret to Wimpole Hall for gatherings, to hunt, ride and socialise. Will and Amicia would spend a great deal of time together just walking and talking.

Then came the time when William and I were invited to spend time at Wimpole Hall; we were looking forward to going. Will was very private about his feelings for Amicia and we had not yet met her. She was a little bit of a mystery. I had managed to get small amounts of information out of Will about her. I knew that her hair was the brown colour of chestnuts and that her eyes were also brown and that she was not quite as tall as Alice.

"Will, I do need to know a little bit more about Amicia. We are going to meet her parents and as we know nothing about this young Lady you put us at a disadvantage. It will be bad etiquette to treat Amicia as a stranger; we do know a little about Lord and Lady Wimpole."

"Well, Mother, Amicia is very pretty and most charming with a very quick brain and wit. She is not shy but quite bold and takes a great interest in the world around her. Amicia can draw and paint with much talent; she has painted a picture of me seated on my stallion. I have never heard music so sweet as when Amicia plays the harp and she carries much grace when she dances and I love her very much. Do you know enough now or do you require any other information?" said Will with a grin on his face.

Chapter 22

"Thank you William I can see that she is quite a delight."

I understood from my husband that Lord Wimpole was not a warrior, more of an academic. William did not know too much about the Wimpoles but he knew that they had been friends with Lady Margaret for some time. Margaret's husband Lord Thomas was like my William and did not really enjoy socializing so he was not as close to them as was his wife.

We did enjoy our stay there. William was interested in the Manor and the countryside and of course we went to church; their church at Wimpole was very handsome indeed.

While we were there, Young Will asked Lord Wimpole for his daughter's hand in marriage.

"I have seen how fond of you my daughter is and have watched you closely when the two of you are together. I am very proud that Amicia will become a member of such a distinguished family. So I give my blessings to you, William, you may ask Amicia to be your wife," said Lord Wimpole.

"Thank you so much, My Lord. I will love and protect Amicia and I am sure that I will make her very happy," promised Will, feeling very pleased with himself.

While we had been staying at Wimpole Manor, the summer weather had been so hot, quite uncomfortable and we had difficulty sleeping at night. Arrangements had been made for us all to ride out to a far part of the Manor where the Rivers Granta and Cam meet; it is very pretty there with lots of willow trees which make for shade. Lady Wimpole thought that we may all cool down a little.

In our party were Sir Thomas and Lady Margaret, Sir Thomas the Younger and Lady Joanna, our hosts and their other two younger daughters with their governess. Then there were Will and Amicia, William and I. There must have been about thirty servants who brought a feast of food along with tables and seats. The spit boys came; their job was to fan us with fans made out of tree-bark, hoping to keep us cooler. The men fished in the river, while the ladies took their boots off and bathed their feet in the river. There were musicians who played to us, while we all chatted. Will and Amicia went for a walk along the river bank. When they came back, Amicia announced that Will had asked her to marry him and that she had accepted. Amicia showed everyone the ring that Will had given to her which was a very large ruby set among opals. The musicians played and there was much rejoicing; Will and Amicia had not as yet made a date for their marriage.

    The next day, William and I returned to Barewe; Will said that he would stay at Wimpole for a while to be with Amicia. We gave Will's news to Mother when we got back; she was most pleased and asked what Amicia was like. I told her that she was a very pretty sweet girl, quite petite and you could see that she was very much in love with our Will. Mother said that John had gone off to Boyton to see his Uncle Godfrey and from there he was going on to visit his Grandfather Walter.

    William and I had some time on our own, Mother had returned to her Hall at Heigham. We enjoyed this time but William did get very tired these days. Besides running the Manor he still spent time about the King's work. We were now most prosperous. The Hall was still being built but very slowly, it was quite difficult to get the craftsmen which were needed as most were employed in the Royal Service as both the King and Lord Edward were building many castles.

    It was now 1270. Will and John had been summoned to go to Guildford Castle as Lord Edward

Chapter 22

wanted to see them both. When they returned home, which was a week later, I wondered what had happened for Alice was with them.

"Why have you come home, Alice, are you not happy?" I asked.

"I was very happy with Princess Eleanor, she was very good and kind to me. Lord Edward is going on the Crusade. Eleanor says that she cannot bear to be parted from Lord Edward again as she loves him so much and when she is apart from him each breath of air she takes pains her so much. Edward returns her love and just adores her. I pleaded to her that I may go on the Crusade with her. She stated that it would not be right for me, because I was too young and far too beautiful, that all the Knights would be falling in love with me. This would take my brothers' minds off the fighting as they would be worrying about me. Also Lord Edward would not wish to have women riding with him. Eleanor took my hands and said 'I will miss you Alice. I have really enjoyed your company. To leave my young sons fills me with guilt and I shall never be able to replace those years which I shall miss so much, but we must all make sacrifices in life. Prince John is five now and Prince Henry is three, they no longer need their mother as when they were younger. They will be going to stay at Windsor Castle with their grandfather King Henry, much to he King's delight for he loves the boys' company and I think that they are both sure that he is there just to play with them.' Eleanor thought it best for me to come home for she felt that I would not fit in with the ladies of Windsor. She said that she is not happy with them, when she stays there. So here I am," explained Alice.

"So you are both going on the Crusade with Lord Edward?" I directed my question to my sons.

"Yes we are, Mother. Tomorrow I will ride to

Granchester to let Amicia know that I am going on the Crusade and that we will not be able to marry till I return. John will join me the next day at Wimpole Hall and we will be riding on to London together where we will meet up with Lord Edward and the other Knights."

William just said to his sons that he thought that they will enjoy the Crusade and is so proud that they have both taken up the Cross. I did know in my heart that one day they would both take some part in God's War but I still feel quite unhappy about it.

It is now 1272. Will and John are still away on the Crusade in the Holy Land. Hugh has settled into life at the Abbey. William does quite an amount of trade with the Abbey so sees Hugh quite often and Hugh comes home on leave and sometimes brings a friend with him to stay. He takes great interest in the Manor and its people and is the most popular out of my three sons with the local folk. When at home, he often spends time in Poppy's family where he is treated as one of them. They just call him 'Hugh' and not 'Your Lordship' which his Father does not approve of. William seems closer to Will and John than he is to Hugh and I often have to remind William that a boy of Hugh's age needs his father to take an interest in him.

Alice had the attention of a Lord Warnne, a kin to our neighbour from Wolf Hall. I believe he would have liked to ask William for Alice's hand in marriage but Alice had made up her mind that it should not be so. Then Alice announced that she would like to take Holy Orders and become a 'Bride of Christ' and wished to go to Denny Convent. Although it would be a great honour, both William and myself felt sad about her decision. We told her that if she should change her mind after becoming a novice she must not feel ashamed and should ask to come home. Alice loved pretty gowns and

Chapter 22

spent a great deal of time on her appearance and I could not really see her as a nun.

William got a message from King Henry that he wished for William to visit him at his London Palace. On arriving at the Palace, William was shocked at how ill the King looked

"Come here, my dear friend," the King said while William was paying homage to him.

"My Majesty, my best of greetings to you, I hope that your health is good," said William.

"No, my health is not good, my spirits are low. Since the sudden death of my little grandson Prince John, I have this hollow within me; I cannot feed, the food gets stuck in my throat. I am surrounded by silly people who spend hours speaking about nothing. My people do not like me. I have to watch that I do not get a dagger in my back from some of the Barons. They feel that they should rule this country. Am I not their King? Was I not appointed by God to be so? The Pope says so and that I do not have to pay attention to the Churchmen and the Barons. They took the Love of my Life away from me when I was a young man but they could not take that love from my heart which I have always carried there for her. With that love I have built the great Minster which is now finished. The Minster will always be filled with our love and everyone who visits there will be the richer for it.

William, you have always been a good servant to me and the whole of the Giffords have been loyal to me. For this, William, I have made you the Sheriff of the Shire of Suffolk answering to no-one but myself. You will have to keep a strong arm on the De Clares and the Earl of Norfolk who just live to obtain power. I know that you will be able to do so with the help of your two strong sons. You can see that I am at the end of my life, there is no more that I can now do for this country," said the King as he put his trembling arm out to William to give him a sealed letter.

"How is your Aunt Berta, William? The letter is for her. Goodbye my friend," said the King, not giving William any time to answer, as the King made his exit from the chamber.

William felt really sad returning from the Palace. He took the letter straight to Berta who thanked him for it and asked how the King was. He told her. William was able to spend some time with Alice. He said that she seemed quite happy and enjoyed teaching the children.

The King died in November and was the first to be buried in his beautiful Minster. Lord Edward and Eleanor were in the kingdom of Sicily when Edward heard of his father's death.

On returning to England, Eleanor gave birth to a daughter, Princess Joan, who was born in Acre in the year 1272. This was the second baby born to Eleanor whilst on the Crusade. The first was Princess Katherine who died at birth on September the 5th 1271. It is said that it was at the time when she first received the news of the death of her son John who had died on August 3rd 1271 which caused Princess Katherine to be born too early. Things became more difficult when an attempt was made to assassinate King Edward with a poisoned dagger. Eleanor saved the King's life by sucking the poison out of the wound and then had the flesh cut away. The journey home was very slow because of the delays; also Edward went to Paris where he paid homage to his cousin, King Philippe III for his French lands. Eleanor gave birth again to a son Prince Alphonso, named after her brother; he was born on November 24th 1273.

It was not until the 2nd of August 1274 that they

were able to step on English land at Dover, following a very rough crossing, leaving everyone filling quite ill. Edward was crowned in the new Minster on August the 19th 1274.

Edward had learnt a lot from the civil war in which he had fought with his father and he knew that things had to change. He embarked on the restoration of royal authority with inquiries into on whose authority the landowners held their lands. He summoned representatives of the shires and boroughs to parliaments to improve relations with the communities and to get their support for his policies, taking away some of the power which the Barons held. This made him more popular with his subjects than his father had been.

This made life even busier for my William for he had to travel and take part in parliaments, being the Sheriff of Suffolk.

Chapter 23
EDWARD'S NEW ENGLAND

Will and John were now back from the Crusade. Will had gone straight to Wimpole Hall to make arrangements for his wedding. John was going to work with his father, for William had so much to do. The Sheriff's position was always very full and time consuming but since Edward had been King there had been many changes made and Edward wanted them enforced, which made for much more work.

Edward was having the law brought up to date. He wanted to check the power of the Barons and Bishops. He had advice from great judges like Hengham and great help from his Chancellor Robert Burnell, who advised him to use the Italian financiers rather than the Jews to whom his father, King Henry, owed a great deal of money. In his first Parliament, he covered the whole field of law and an Act called the 'Statute of Westminster' was brought about. He wanted to know on what authority the Barons and the Church held their lands.

William as Sheriff would have to visit all the land owners in Suffolk and record their rights in holding their lands and Manors. Lords may pass their lands on to their kin as long as it was going to be used for profit. It must not be given to the Church, monasteries or other corporations as a gift for favours. If the lands should be given, the Lords would lose the right to it and it would be returned to the Crown. Edward was aware of how rich and powerful the Church was growing from taxes they put on their tenants and trades men in the towns, causing many of them to be unable to make a living.

William was told by Edward to put pressure on the Jews. He wanted a list of all the Jews in Suffolk. They were to pay extra taxes and any who could not pay were to be arrested. William did not like doing this but did not have any choice. He also had to collect all of the Crown's money owed from their rents as well as holding courts in the towns of the Shire. Because of collecting the Crown's money and his position of being Sheriff, William had to ride with a small army to protect himself and the large amount of money which he collected. John shared the collecting of rents with William and had to have his own small army. William and John spent a great deal of time away from home.

    I was also very busy with the Manor and organising the Saturday Market. We had a market every Saturday in the Summer but less often in the Winter. It was a very large market taking place around the church and there were also stalls all the way down Paynethorpe Street. It was not just the residents of Barewe who were selling their wares but trades people from surrounding Manors and towns. Those who were not residents had to pay a groat (four pennies) to the Barewe Manor for being allowed to sell their goods. The market was very important to us and to our people.

    Mr Calwe, the Jewish gentleman from Burwell who made our gowns, had a cloth stall and his wife and daughters had a stall with ready-made gowns and bonnets. There was Mrs Goodfellow from Wickhambrook whose stall displayed gloves and mittens made from leather and cloth. The Herb Women from Risby had a stall and gave health advice for a farthing; and of course there were Tinklers.

    One of Poppy's sons, Joe, had a stall with carvings which he had whittled which were always very popular. John Holme's wife Margery had made all different cheeses from her goats and sheep and Ann Aleyn made brawn, pork cheeses and faggots for her stall. Ann Newman, with the help of her family, made brushes and brooms from the broom plant that grows wild between Barewe and Heigham. There were not many folk from the Manor who did not have a stall. There were also pits where cock fighting took place, hand wrestling and dice playing. They had to pay two groats for their pits or rings which were not allowed to be too close to the Church because men gambled on these events and, as I said to William, I did not feel that God would approve. William said that it would not be a market without these events.

The people who came to the market were from most of the Manors in the area and surrounding towns. There were Knights and their Ladies, Monks, Friars, Yeoman and all different classes of people. The Bailiff had to make sure that the stall holders cleaned up when the market was finished; we took much pride at the Manor keeping it clean and tidy.

When William was at home he still had much of the King's accounts and scribing to do. He had employed a clerk known as Charles Barnwell who lived at the Hall and also travelled with William when he was away. William was very upset about the pressure he had to put on the Jews. He had two of them arrested and they had to be taken to the prison at Norwich Castle where King Edward wanted the Jews from this area kept.

When William was at home he got many visits from Friars and Abbots who were upset about the King's Law of Mortmain under which they would lose their lands to the Crown. The corporate body of the churches and monasteries were the most worried and William was worried that his brother Walter would be affected by this law. For in 1266 William's grandfather Elias gave the shire of Hereford to the Church so that Walter could become Archbishop of York - Walter was already Bishop of Wells and Bath. William was very cross that the shire would be handed over to the Crown for if Elias had not given the shire to the Church, it would still belong to the family, whose heir is our Will. Often William would be working in his chamber well into the night and when I woke up I would go into his chamber and often he would have fallen asleep with his quill still in his hand.

It was now the time of Will and Amicia's marriage. John had travelled to Denny to bring Alice back to Barewe as she had been given leave to attend Will's marriage. So she was able to travel with John, William and I to Wimpole Hall where we were to spend three nights together. Hugh, who was ordained as a priest and is now twenty years old, was not going to the marriage as he would be taking the services in All Saints Church as my cousin the Reverend Passelewe was sick and had taken to his bed.

It was a beautiful wedding. Amicia's gown was made of white silk, the silk cloth came from Sudbury. The proprietor of the silk mill had obtained the worms from the East and had been able to breed them successfully to make the silk. Amicia's maids in waiting were her two sisters in gowns of gold and Alice who wore her habit. She carried a most beautiful large lily and looked so beautiful. The young Knights at the wedding could not take their eyes off Alice and were queuing up to speak to John so that they could be in the company of Alice. There were many Lords and Ladies there; Will had asked King Edward to attend the wedding but he was unable to do so. Lord and Lady Wimpole had made sure that the day would be perfect. The banquet was wonderful - there were musicians and fools and other entertainers who were excellent. It was so wonderful to have most of my family together for a short time.

Will is having a Hall built at Waldingfield, which is

still in Suffolk and it is to be called 'Gifford and Hollymead Hall.' Lord Wimpole had given Will the land as a dowry to build the Hall. Will had obtained gold as spoils of war while in Crusade and William had also given him money as a wedding present. William has also sent all the masons and builders that were working on our Manor to Waldingfield to build Will's Hall for he needed it more than we needed our new Hall.

When we reached Saxham on the way back from the wedding, we were met by the Bailiff who wanted to speak to William.

"I wanted to warn you, My Lord, before you enter the Manor. It was Saturday after the market that something horrible happened. Mr Calwe, the Jew was the last leaving the market as it takes him a while to put his wares away. He and his wife and daughters had just reached the cross road between Barewe and Heigham on their way back to Exning when he was attacked by a highwayman who was armed with a cutlass. He asked Mr Calwe to hand over his money but Mr Calwe refused. Then the highwayman grabbed hold of one of the young women. Mr Calwe jumped off the cart clutching a large stick and went for the highwayman who swung his cutlass, catching Mr Calwe's neck and cut his throat.

Richard Sommers was returning from Kentford following delivering wood. With him he had Big Bill Liddle who, seeing what had happened, stood up in the cart and, picking up a large log and swinging it around, he threw the log at the highwayman, hitting him on the head and making him fall off his horse. Richard and Bill pounced on him, overpowering him and removing his cutlass. They put the highwayman in the cart and Big Bill sat on him as they went with speed back to Barewe where we put him in the stocks. Mrs Calwe and her daughters tried to help Mr Calwe but he died quite

Chapter 23

quickly. Jane Brown took Mrs Calwe and her daughters into her home to comfort them. I went and told Lord Hugh what had happened. By this time the news had spread and there was a large crowd at the stocks throwing eggs and stones at the highwayman. They were shouting "An eye for an eye. Send him to Hell."

The crowd went quiet when Lord Hugh arrived. Lord Hugh went over to the highwayman, caught hold of the man's hair, pulled his head up and looked into his face. He recognized the highwayman as the man in De Clare's army who had entered the Hall and threatened Lord Hugh and Lady Katherine. By this time the crowd was chanting "Death, death, death."

Lord Hugh asked the highwayman what he had to say. "Go to hell," he said and he spat at Lord Hugh. "Have a gallows built and hang him," said Lord Hugh sharply.

I asked if it would be best to wait till his father returned because there must be a trial. "He is guilty; we have enough witnesses, hang him. I will take his confession if he wishes to make one," said Lord Hugh.

"I beg you, My Lord, wait for Lord William," I said but Lord Hugh did not take any notice of me. I did my best, My Lord," said the Bailiff.

"The highwayman would not give his name and did not want to confess. He was hanged in the early hours of Sunday morning and there he still swings in the wind," said the Bailiff with his eyes looking at the ground.

William did not say a word, he just kicked at his horses and rode off with great speed towards our Hall. The rest off us rode up to the cross roads of Paynethorpe Street and Denham Lane, where the gallows had been built. I could see that the man who was hanging there was the same soldier who had threatened us and had hurt the dog.

Chapter 23

Arriving back at the Hall, I could hear William and Hugh in William's chamber. I knocked at the door and entered.

"Hugh, what were you thinking about? How could you allow a gallows to be built and a hanging to take place? On whose authority did you give your consent to a hanging?" asked William.

"On yours - are you not the Sheriff of Suffolk? The highwayman was guilty; there were enough witnesses who saw Mr Calwe get murdered," said Hugh, raising his voice.

"You can't just go round using my power. Under King Edward's new laws I cannot now put anyone to death. I have to get permission from the King's Court. I will now be hearing from the King. He will ask if I have not got control over Suffolk, my Manor, and even my sons. I could lose all my lands and property, Hugh," said William, holding his head.

There was a pause, we just all stood and looked at each other.

"As a Man of the Cloth you should at least have thought about giving compassion. Get out of my sight, Hugh. Go back to the Abbey," said William, leaving the chamber and slamming the door.

I put my arm around Hugh saying "Your father is in shock, when he calms down he will realise that you made a mistake and will forgive you, Hugh. It will be best if you go to Heigham and stay with your grandmother. You will still be able to take the services at the Church. I think that it will be embarrassing for you to return to the Abbey at the moment and your grandmother will enjoy your company."

Just a few days had gone when William got a summons from the King to go before him. John went to London with his father. At the Palace they had an

Chapter 23

audience with the King; William and John paid homage to him.

"Well, Gifford! I thought that you were in Suffolk to uphold my law," stated the King.

"Your Majesty, please accept my apologies. I accept full responsibility for the error of this instance. My bailiffs were in error to think that as there were several witnesses who saw the murder, there was no need for a trial and knowing that the highwayman was an enemy of their King, having fought against you and your gracious Father, and knowing how dangerous this man was having threatened the life of their most gracious Lady Katherine, they took it as their duty to Your Majesty to rid England of this monster," said William feeling that his soul was in torment for having to grovel to the King.

"I gather that the man who was killed was a Jew. As you well know, it is my policy to rid my country of them. Did not they cause London to rise up against my father the King and myself? Did not my mother and sister have to flee along the Thames to escape from them and did not they shout abuse at them and throw stones? Was it not the highwayman doing service to England to rid us of a Jew?"

"Your Majesty, this Jew was a good man, popular in the community," said William pleading.

"William, there cannot be any good Jews. The wrath of God is upon them and will be forever more. They crucified the Son of God and the evil is now in their seed," stated the King. William had to think quickly how he should reply to the King's statement for he could end up in the Tower on a charge of heresy.

"As a Knight, Your Majesty, I took an oath to protect The Faith of Christ, to pledge my allegiance to my King. Have I not always done so? The instance was a mistake, the laws of the Crown have changed in much depth in a small space of time and some of your subjects are confused about the meaning and understanding of the new laws and need time to learn about them. The people in my Manor are most loyal and hold you with admiration and affection. On their behalf, I ask you My Gracious Majesty for your forgiveness."

"To make amends, William, you will while in your term of office as Sheriff commence on your return to Suffolk to expel all Jews and confiscate their wealth which belongs to the Crown of England and not Judaism. You will have the honour of being the first Shire to commence the expelling but the others will soon be following. Now that is enough of the affairs of the Crown. I wish you to come and take wine with me, for I wish to hear your news of your family. My wife will ask me questions about young Alice."

John had done most of the talking with the King for William was quite vexed with the request the King had made of him and was not feeling very comfortable in the King's company.

Chapter 24
TROUBLE AHEAD

When William and John arrived home, William was very quiet. I asked him what the King had said.

"Not now Katherine, I am very tired," he replied

William looked very drawn. He did not embrace me as he usually did, he had never been so stern with me when replying to my questions. He shut himself in his chamber and said he would eat in there as he had much work to do. I turned to John. "What has happened? What had the King to say? Have we been punished, John?" I asked. John took hold of both my hands affectionately and looked me straight in the eyes.

"Do not worry, Mother, it is nothing too bad. Father will speak to you when he is ready, it is best that he explains himself. William was in his chamber late into the night. Everyone had retired for the night, I knocked at the door of the chamber, telling him that I was now retiring. He just nodded in acknowledgement, not even looking up from his work.

I lay in bed waiting for William to join me, thinking about all the horrible ways the King could punish us. We could lose all our land and the Manor. I just hope that the King remembers that it was William and Osbert who helped him escape from Hereford Castle out of the clutches of Simon De Montfort. I wondered if William and I would ever have time to spend together, he will be away again for a great deal of time doing the King's work that William finds so disagreeable.

When I woke, William had not been to bed for any part of the night. I went to his chamber and he had fallen asleep with his quill still in his hand and his head dropped on to the parchments. I got him an apple and honey drink and gently woke him. I then got him to loosen his clothes and massaged his neck and shoulders with a lavender balm while speaking to him.

"William you must allow me to share your problems with you," I said.

"My punishment from King Edward was to clear all the Jews from Suffolk. They will be cleared from all over England as they will be in France, Spain and most countries with the blessing of the Christian Church who still blame them for the death of our Lord Jesus.

Most Kings, Barons and the Churches all owe the Jews money and will be pleased to see them go, then they will not have to pay back the money which they have borrowed. The Jews, because of their great success as money lenders and being the best trades people, have grown so rich and are envied. They are also better educated than the average Christians, speaking at least two languages. Besides having their own language, Yiddish, they also have their own rules and Judaism does not allow them to integrate in marriage. They manage to live outside the control of the Barons and Lords. The Jews are only answerable to the Jews. This is what is causing them the problem now.

However distasteful this job will be, I will have to do it. I am Sheriff of Suffolk and have to obey the King. I will not get problems with the Barons or the Bishops; most of them owe the Jews money and will rejoice in the King's decision to take the Jews' wealth and lands for the Crown. The holders of land and Manors will be responsible for rounding up the Jews on their lands. I will make the Burgesses and Aldermen responsible for collecting them in the Towns. I have made a list of the Castles where the Jews of each area will be taken, along with their wealth and plans of their land and the properties which they own. Having to travel around the castles and preside over the courts, the King will have his judges, Hengham and Britton, checking on me and the Barons to make sure that the King is getting all his dues of the wealth. The Jews will be held in the prisons at the castles till they can be banished. John will have to help me to inform the Barons and other holders of lands of the King's wishes and what they have to do."

"What about Mrs Calwe and her daughters? They are now part of our community taking part in the Saturday Market, they have many friends in our Manor, William," I stated, very worried.

"We will leave them for as long as possible but they are Jews so they must go. I also so feel very sad about it but I cannot show that I am treating any of them with favours," William said, not looking at me.

"John and I will not be able to get home very much, we will be away for months at a time, if not longer periods. When I have finished my term of office as Sheriff, I will ask the King if I might retire and not work for him any longer as I am getting old and so very tired.

I will make sure that the masons and builders get on with building our new Hall at speed now that they have finished Will's Hall. Katherine, we will be able to be together and entertain. I am looking forward to holding our own tournament and also having some time when we are not working and sorting out problems.

While I am away you can make plans of how you want your new home to look inside. Of course you must go with the Bailiff to make sure that everyone is working as they should. I am sorry that I am leaving you in charge of the Manor again but I do believe that you are better than I am of doing so.

I am now going to All Saints Church to pray for strength and guidance and of course forgiveness for what I am about to do. I feel in my heart that the Pope and the King are wrong in the clearing of the Jews. I took my Oath as a Knight to obey God and my King and that is what I must do," William informed me.

"I feel the same as you father. I will come with you to church, for I would rather go and fight in a war than have women and children rounded up like sheep," exclaimed John. "I will get my cloak and also come with you both," I said.

We all prayed for some three hours. Hugh was also at the church and prayed with us. He gave us God's blessing for what lies ahead. William embraced Hugh and said that he also forgave him and he may return to the family fold. I never once put pressure on William to forgive Hug; I knew William so well and that he would do so in his own time. We all felt so much better following our praying. That evening we had a lovely family meal with lots of laughter, something that we had not done for weeks. We were not too late in retiring to bed for William and John would leave early the next day, going in different directions.

That night while I was in our bed chamber brushing my hair before I went to bed, William came and took the brush from my hand and continued brushing my hair as he spoke to me.

"Katherine, you are so beautiful; not just to one's eye, you radiate beauty from within you. I have seen so many men look at you with envy, wishing that you belonged to them, but it is me that is so lucky, you are mine. I could not have coped with all I have had to do and what I need to do without you by my side, my beloved." With this, he put the brush down and gave me a little kiss upon my cheek, lifted me up in his arms and placed me on the bed where we spent a night of passion. It was so wonderful. William still had the ability to make our love melt as if we were as one; I felt that we were just touching on what heaven is like. I knew that there would be horrible times ahead of us and I knew

Chapter 24

that I would once again spend many lonely nights but I will have our lasting love to keep me warm.

Just before my men rode off, a messenger came with a letter from Will. It said that he had received a message from the King telling him to meet up with other Knights in the Welsh Marches to get ready to attack Llewellyn a Prince of part of Wales who had refused to pay homage to the King.

Will asked me if I would visit Amicia who was with child, while he was away.

"I wish that I could go with him," said John, looking very gloomy.

"Come now, we can not always do as we wish. We must now both be on our way," said William giving me a kiss goodbye.

I could not get Mrs Calwe out of my mind. I thought about her husband getting murdered and how brave she had been; she still came each Saturday to sell her wares at the market. I knew that Mrs Calwe was quite prosperous and I was sure that she would rather take a chance and hold on to some of her wealth. I could not bear to think about her being locked up in prison when she had not committed a crime. I kept turning the situation over in my mind and I thought about a plan which might work and could not get it out of my head. I also knew that I was the wife of the Sheriff and above all I could not go against him. I had never in all my married life deceived William and this is what I would have to do if I helped Mrs Calwe. It would also mean that I would be going against the King and, if found out, I would be a traitor making every member of my family one also. I would never be able to look William in the eye again and what would happen to him? I must clear my head of such thoughts of this plan. The thoughts stayed in my head both day and night.

Chapter 24

I confessed to Hugh about what I was thinking and that I just could not clear my mind. I asked Hugh if he thought that the Devil had entered my head.

"I don't think that it is the Devil. I think that it is Our Lord. We all know that it is wrong to clear the Jews. Tell me your plans, Mother."

I knew that I should not, Hugh had already got into William's bad books and William was sure that the King had heard that Hugh was behind the execution but I did ask him to take part in the plan.

"If you would go to Exning and collect Mrs Calwe and her daughters using her cart, take them to Denny Abbey where I am sure Berta would let them have habits to dress up as nuns. Then take them to Waterbeach where they could get a boat to take them up to Boston. The boat people are used to the nuns travelling up and down the river on their business. If they make towards Boston on the Fen Sea they could get a Norse trade ship to the other side of the North Sea. The Norse crew will not ask too many questions as long as they pay well. I think that this would work and no-one need know," I explained.

"Can you trust Mrs Calwe and her daughters not to tell anyone? You know what a chatty lady she is and there must not even be a whisper. We would all be in trouble if she does say anything. I am willing to do my part," said Hugh.

The next Saturday I told Mrs Calwe to follow me to the church as there was something that I wished to tell her and to do it discreetly. At the church I told her about what was going to happen to the Jews in England and that it was happening here first in Suffolk. I told her that she must not tell any other Jews what is going to happen even if she feels it is her duty to do so. If she wants to save her daughters and some of her wealth, no

Chapter 24

one must know.

    I said that she must pay the cost of the habits and the boat and ship so she should have gold coins ready. That she may take her valuables and some of her tools so that she will be able to start her trade elsewhere, but not too many of their possessions for she and her daughters will be nuns going about their business and must look the part. I told her to be ready on Monday at dawn. Hugh thought it best to do it as soon as possible before there was time to talk to any one. She was also told that, once she got home, she and her daughters must not leave the house. On the Monday when they are leaving they must have a dark cloth covering their heads and clothes so they can not be recognized in the local area.

    Hugh left on Monday morning. I could not concentrate on anything all day. Hugh got back on Tuesday evening. He said that everything had gone to plan. Berta thought that it would be better if Alice went with them as far as Boston, she would be able to help them find a ship. Also, as the boat people at Waterbeach knew Alice as being a nun, she would be able to do all the speaking if questions were asked. I did not feel very happy about this. Hugh said that he would return to Denny next week to make sure that Alice had returned. I told him that I would be going with him to see both Berta and Alice.

Chapter 25

ALICE

The following week Hugh and I were off to Denny. Mother had come to stay at the Hall as I like having a family member there when I am away. One of Poppy's daughters, Meg, is now Housekeeper for me. Poppy has raised her very well, she has beautiful manners and is very capable and is well educated, speaking French with much ease. Poppy always saw that her children attended the teachings at the church and they were all very sensible and capable to do most jobs.

Meg lives with her elderly husband who is a Freeman, in Poppy's old home next to the Hall as Richard had built Poppy a new home - a fine building containing four chambers and a separate kitchen. Richard had built it from timber as he now had control of the timber business following the death of his father, Will Sommers. Poppy now has Richard's mother living with them which caused them to need more accommodation. She now looks after both families and helps Richard to run the business, so she decided that she no longer wanted to work at the Hall, although when I need her she will act as lady's maid for me.

Meg and Hugh have been very good friends since childhood and are still the best of friends. Hugh often visits Meg and her husband for some of Meg's ale which she brews and it is said to be the best in the Manor. William does not like Hugh spending so much time with the Manor folk; he says that being on such friendly terms makes for bad discipline. Hugh's argument is that, as a priest, it is his duty to make God available to everyone. William forgets that when Hugh was a child his brothers were away training as Knights so were not there for companionship and, being a confident young child, sought company of whoever was available, He often

Chapter 25

accompanied me and Mother when we taught at the church and this is where he made friends and has remained loyal to them.

Arriving at Denny, Alice was in the court yard waiting for us. Seeing Alice's smiling face, I was full of pride. The habit which she wore framed her fair skin, the glow from the sun caught the pinkness of her cheeks, setting off her dancing eyes. She was indeed so beautiful. Alice embraced me and her brother.

"Alice, was your trip successful?" I asked.

"Yes Mother, very," she replied.

I did not mention it again. I knew that she would speak of it in her own time.

Alice took my hand and led me to Berta's study with Hugh following. Hugh would be returning to Barewe after he had eaten. I was going to stay for three days, then the Captain who William had left to protect us and the Manor while he was away would come and escort me home.

Berta stood to greet us, she now looked so frail. I then turned and looked at dear Clover's face which wore such a large smile stretching across her face with such a large beam that it sort of looked as if she had closed her eyes. I had not seen her for many years and was quite shocked at how old she looked. The skin on her face was like the inside of a walnut, all crinkled and the same colour; little tears ran down her cheeks with happiness as I hugged her.

"Katherine, dearest girl, how wonderful to see you! I have been waiting a long while for this day," she said, trying to pour the wine with her outstretched hand shaking. Her hand was covered with lots of little broken veins. I knew it would not be wise to help her. I knew from old times how proud she was to be in control and I would not want her to think that she could not even pour the wine now.

"Sit down now," said Berta sharply, looking at the pools of spilt wine on the table.

"Will and Amicia - how are they in their married life together?" she asked, wanting to know if Amicia was with child as yet for they had been married some six months and it would be expected that she should be.

"Yes, she is with child, Berta," I said smiling.

"How wonderful," said Clover.

"Let's hope that it is a son," said Berta thoughtfully.

"It is not all good news I am afraid. For Will has to join the King to move against Prince Llewellyn," I said, knowing that Berta knew what was going on in England. Even though she lived in a Convent, she would have her finger on the pulse and have all the news of what was going on in the country.

"Well, Llewellyn has quarrelled with his two brothers Prince Davydd and Prince Gruffydd and driven them out of Wales. He also keeps all the taxes which he collects to himself and does not pay any to the Crown. Also he refuses to pay homage to Edward and Edward is not as tolerant as his father. He is lion and will not stand for those who disobey him. That is what the problem is with the Jews; they go about their business with each other, paying little attention to the King's plans. The King wishes for trade to grow especially with other countries. He wishes for all the towns to grow and produce merchandise; the King is very interested in the wool trade and wishes for many more people to keep sheep and expand the spinning and weaving. They need money to expand and you know who controls the wealth and purse strings. It is the Jews and they fix high interest between them, growing rich through others' work. I do feel sorry for them in their troubles. Well that is enough about the Kings affairs," said Berta.

We had been some time eating our meal and when we had finished Hugh took his leave from us all. Alice helped me settle into my chamber and then suggested that the two of us should go for a stroll in the Spinney. I was quite excited for, as you know, the Spinney was one of my favourite places. It had not changed over the past years, it was still full of all the different herbs, the fragrance was so sweet and wonderful. The strong aroma of rosemary and lavender as our skirts brushed against them as we walked; we trod on thyme and camomile, both of them rendering up their perfumes.

"Mrs Calwe and her daughters?" I asked. "They are fine, Mother, everything went according to plan. I enjoyed the adventure," she replied.

I took Alice's hand and led her to my magical oak tree. I climbed inside the hollow in the tree and looked out through the peep hole as I had done in the past. I climbed out and looked up at its large strong branches moving in the light breeze as if to say "Welcome back Katherine." I then caressed its boughs and I felt the warmth of passion as it was on the day when I first cast my eyes on my William.

I sat down on a large log, I was deep in thought. Now, being an mature woman, I was wondering how I could have fallen in love with a person I did not know, who I had not seen before and knew nothing about, just through their appearance. It is not the appearance of a person which makes them what they are, it is their character, what they have within them. I am sure that it was God who helped me see William's soul as I had looked into his eyes.

"Mother, are you ill? What is the matter with you?" asked Alice loudly.

"No, my dearest I am not ill, just in love," I said as Alice sat down on the log next to me.

"This is where I first set eyes upon your father." Then I told her my story.

"Oh Mother, I know that it was the work of God that made you fall in love with my father. For Mother, God has also given my heart away."

I interrupted Alice. "He has given your heart to Our Lord Jesus you mean?"

"No, Mother. Of course Jesus is in my heart but I have fallen in love with a Scottish man called Gideon. He is a Healer who comes to the Convent when we have a very sick Templar Knight there. I have seen him heal people when we were sure that they would die. He is so clever. I have worked with him when sometimes he had to cut a limb off a Templar when it was so full of poison it would have poisoned his whole body and he would have died." She was so excited when she spoke.

I was so shocked. As I looked at her I knew now why her beauty was so radiant: she was indeed very much in love.

She continued. "Gideon has to return to the island of Malta soon and he wishes to marry me and for me to go with him to help him in his work. He is not a Knight Templar but wears the Cross of our Lord on his back."

"What about your final vows to become a nun and what has Berta got to say?" I asked.

"I have spoken to Berta and she knows about Gideon and has given her blessing. She says that I have far too much spirit to remain happy at the Convent also that I am a wonderful nurse, just like my mother was and she is sure that it is God's wish for me to go to the East and do God's work."

"I give my blessings also, Alice, but I do not know if your father will agree and of course he must."

Chapter 25

Alice took hold of my hands and gave me a kiss. "I knew that you would agree with me getting married. If I could have picked my mother from all the mothers in the world, I would have picked you, Mother."

"How beautiful, Alice. You have made me feel so very proud. Is Gideon in the infirmary for I wish to meet him?" I asked.

"No, he has had to travel to the Convent at Abington near Oxford where there are two very ill Knight Templar. He will then come back here and then he must leave for Malta and I hope that I will be going with him," was her answer.

After three most enjoyable days, I returned home. I told the Captain that I must find out at which castle William was now. I informed Hugh of Alice's news. He then rode off to the Abbey in Bury St. Edmunds for they had travellers who were passing through the town staying there from whom they gathered news and, of course, the matter about the Jews was the current topic. While he was gone, I wrote a very detailed letter to William about Alice's situation.

Hugh returned with the news that William was due at Framlingham Castle to hold court. I quickly dispatched the Captain to Framlingham. The Captain returned within the week with a letter from William. William's letter stated that he must leave the decision of Alice's marriage to me as I had stated that Berta had given her blessing. This Gideon must be of good character for not much gets past Berta who has the gift to read into one's soul. That he does wish for Alice's happiness and, as you well know, Alice will have her way, come what may. He stated he would return in about two weeks so Berta and Alice will be able to make arrangements following that date for the wedding.

Alice had made her plans to have a simple

wedding at the Convent. She would get married in her habit. Hugh would marry Gideon and herself and just close family would attend. Alice was aware that Will was away fighting the Welsh and would not be able to be at the marriage. I will inform Amicia but she is due to give birth shortly so will not be able to see Alice marry. I had informed Mother about Alice's news on arriving back at home. William will inform our people of the Manor at church. I must go to visit Poppy at her Petite Hall, I had been promising to visit her for some time but have not done so but now I must go and visit her to give her our news before it is local knowledge.

I rode to Will Sommers Woods for Poppy's home was quite a distance in the depth of the woods. On approaching Poppy's home I felt quite proud about the influences I had on the developing of Poppy's character for her Petite Hall was a delight upon the eye. The structure was built from wood for Richard had plenty of this material. It had a fast running stream which flowed into a large pond. It was surrounded with flowers and herbs which was also a play area for fowls and ducks, watched by sleeping cats with one eye opening always aware of the current situation, scattering off as I rode my mare Sparkle, the foal of Crystal who had long gone to her maker.

I took refreshment with Poppy while I told her of Alice's news while moving my eyes discreetly around her delightful chamber. It was like stepping back in time, for most of Poppy's artefacts were objects given to Poppy over the years which Mother and myself no longer needed. Poppy had laid the table so prettily with a large selection of sweetmeats displayed between the flowers which she had lovingly displayed.

"The sweetmeats are delicious and you have taken so much trouble, Poppy," I said.

Chapter 25

"I am so pleased with Alice's news, Lady Katherine, but it is very dangerous and she will be such a long way from her family and all of us," she said very thoughtfully.

"Well, we will have to pray for her and her husband and put our trust in God to look after them," I replied.

"My Lady, there is something which I must tell you before you hear this matter from gossip of others. My daughter Meg is with child," announced Poppy, standing up while she spoke and was very flushed.

"Well how lovely, another grandchild," I said, very surprised for Meg's husband was very old and it was said that he had the old age sickness in his head.

"My Lady, what I need to say is that Meg has never shared her husband's bed. Meg had made the arrangement with her husband before she married him and it was with his blessing. He needed Meg to look after him and he said that he got very lonely and enjoyed Meg's company because she was so bright. I know that she should not have married him for this reason but now it is done," she stated, being quite ashamed and dropping her head while she spoke. "That is not all, My Lady, for the father of the baby is your Hugh," she mumbled quite quickly.

There was silence as Poppy took her seat again awaiting my reply. I was very shocked. I knew that Hugh had been very close to Meg from his childhood. How would I ever be able to tell poor William who is so full of worries and this would be adding to them? I would not be able to tell him about this matter till after Alice's marriage. William frowns on Hugh and blames me for being too soft on him while he was growing up. It is not against the Pope's rules for his priests to beget children as long as they do not take the marriage vows. I knew that it would have been Hugh's idea for Meg to marry this old man, protecting her reputation. I think that he had always planned to have a family with her and may indeed love her, but it was very wrong of him. There will be much gossip within the Manor and, I expect, elsewhere

"Poppy, I will not tell His Lordship about this matter till after Alice's wedding. Try to keep it quiet about Hugh for the time being, till we get things worked out," I said, taking my leave.

William arrived home. He looked so tired and drawn. I could see from his appearance that he was not in the best of health. Over our meal he told me how terrible it was banishing the Jews, watching families being split up, men being taken to the male dungeons while their wives, holding tight to their screaming children's hands, dragging them to the women's dungeons. All they were guilty of was being Jews. The really very rich Jews had already left the country in haste, taking their wealth with them.

"What happens to the Jews then, William," I asked.

"They are taken to London under escort on carts and then put on ships to Den Haag or Bruges. I do try to make sure that the families are together again and travel first. I do allow them to keep some monies. This is very difficult when the King's Judges Hengham and Burnell are about; they are watching them and me like a hawk," he said.

"William, please try to take your mind off this terrible time. Everyone who knows you knows that you are a good man. You are just obeying the Pope and your King. God is aware and he has not stopped it. When I was at the Convent I read from many of the oldest scrolls and they all said that the Jews had been

Chapter 25

wandering for hundred of years because they had disobeyed God and really vexed him. Please relax and talk about Alice and our family."

We left for Denny - William, myself, John, Hugh, Mother and Poppy. Poppy was so close to our family and was so very fond of Alice and Alice of her that I thought it was right that she should be at the wedding. Although Mother was getting really old and had lots of stiffness in her bones, she said that she would ride on horseback as it was better than having her bones all shaken up by riding in the carriage. The roads have not been repaired for years because of all the wars and the cost and are indeed in a very bad state.

We arrived at the Convent and were greeted in the court yard by Ruth who supervised the nuns taking us to our chambers. William's and my chamber was the same one that I shared with Isabelle all those years ago. I am sure that this would have been Clover's idea for she was such a romantic. The chamber had not changed; it was as if it was in a time-warp. The same picture, the same bed.

There was a knock on the door. William opened the door and there stood Alice.

"I have just heard that you had arrived," she said, embracing her father. "When you have both refreshed yourselves, Gideon would like to meet you both in the library," she stated.

"I think it best that I am introduced on my own at first then he can be introduced to your mother," said William

"Yes, that will be for the best. It will be easier for your father to get to know Gideon when it is just the two of them in conversation," I replied as Alice's expression had changed, knowing how her father was plain speaking and would be firing many questions at Gideon.

Chapter 25

William commenced eating some of the sweetmeats and fudge which Berta had left for him knowing about his sweet tooth.

"Mother, would you like to come to the chapel with me, where Berta and Clover and some of the nuns are putting the finishing touches to the flowers and decorations? Father, when you are refreshed, if you go to the library Gideon will be waiting there for you."

The chapel looked very pretty and you could see how the nuns were really enjoying decorating it. Berta and Clover greeted me.

"Well, that's just about finished, you may clear up now," directed Berta to the nuns.

"It looks so wonderful, thank you all so very much," I said.

"I have to check that the arrangements in the rest of the Convent are going according to plan," said Berta.

"I must go to the infirmary to say my farewells to the sick and the frail," said Alice.

"While you are there, make sure that you get some comfrey cream to protect your skin against the sun, so that you don't get burnt, Alice. I will not come with you, I will help the nuns clear up and when we have finished I will stay to pray," I explained.

Once Berta had taken her leave, the atmosphere had changed; it was like having a vow released. There was giggling and merriment amongst the nuns who were mostly novices. Some of then had been at the Convent since they were ten and had had their childhood cut short and now again had hearts of children. I was picking up some of the unwanted branches when one of the nuns went to fetch the barrow to put the refuse into. Then a nun named Annie lifted up her gown and sat herself in the barrow, while the first nun raced down the aisle with her much to the other nuns' delight. They were all so happy for Alice, some I am sure wishing that it could have been them who were getting married.

If I had not been in my tree and cast my eyes on William, I may have taken my vows. Before I fell in love with William, I thought that there was no greater an honour than becoming a Bride of Christ. I would have indeed missed so much. I can make my own decisions, whether right or wrong, my days are not mundane like theirs. Theirs are disciplined by bells and prayers and their duties whilst with mine each day is different. They will never know the feeling of loving a man and having that love returned. Then they will not know the wonder of carrying a child and giving birth to it, holding it to the breast for the first time, looking at its perfect little fingers and seeing its blue eyes gaze up into yours. It is true on the whole that their lives would be safe and free of worries and sometime sadness but their spirit is not their own, they have given it to God and the Church and they are not free. They are indeed most holy to give so much. I am pleased that Alice is now to marry and will live her life come what may. I had not really thought before how difficult it would have been for Alice.

The nuns left and I asked God to forgive me for what I had just had in my mind. I told Him that I do love Him and that I think that I have done His wishes in most things. I asked Him for His protection for Alice and Gideon in their life head and to give them guidance.

Alice came to collect me. "Father and Gideon are waiting for you to take a walk in the grounds before our meal is served," she said, taking hold of my hand. "I do hope that Gideon melts your heart as he has mine."

As we approached the two men, I observed Gideon to be in his late twenties - older than I thought he would be. He had long dark hair, tied neatly into the nape of his neck. He wore a beard not too long. His eyes were lively and kind, the amount of facial skin that could be seen was fair but very weathered from the sun. Alice's eyes smiled as she introduced me to Gideon.

"My Lady Katherine, I am so honoured that you and Sir William have given your blessing to mine and Alice's marriage," he said as I held my hand out to him. He took my hand and lowered his head and kissed the back of it.

"I promise you and Sir William that I will love and cherish Alice and with the best of my ability I will see that no harm befalls her."

"Your parents. What of your parents, are they able to attend the wedding?" I asked quietly.

"My parents send their blessings for the marriage and hope that they will be able to meet Alice in the future. They live on an island off the west side of Scotland. There my Father is an Elder and does not get off the island very often. They will not be able to make the wedding. Father is responsible for the community there which consists of twenty-eight families. We live off the land and the sea. We do a little trade with mainland Scotland, selling and bartering objects made from seal skin and shells and we grow a strong flax which is made into a strong rope. The people lead a simple but happy life. I have two grown up brothers, James and David, who work the land and have a boat to fish and make trips to the mainland and two younger sisters - Mary fifteen years old and Martha ten years. I do not know them very well because I have not spent much time at home. My mother is in charge of the healing on the island, she has a cure for each ailment with her herbs and potions, this where I got my interest in health and healing. I do often feel guilty for not getting home as much as I should," said Gideon.

"When you are both in Malta, will there be any

ladies there for company for Alice?" I asked.

"The women who are there are mostly from the Island; we do sometimes have ladies who are on the Crusade with their husbands stay with us. I do work away from the Island in Acre and Sicily and other places where I am needed. I do intend to take Alice to the Holy Shrine. Alice is aware that we will have no home of our own, we will have to live in tents or monasteries, wherever we are needed."

John appeared. "We are all waiting for you in the refectory to start the meal. You had better come now if you do not want to vex Berta."

We enjoyed our meal, then we all retired early for we were very tired. I told William that I quite liked Gideon and that he seemed sincere. William said that it was early days as yet. Berta has faith in him and she is wise, I will put my trust in her.

Next morning William, Alice and I went for a walk together; we sat on the log, gazing up into my tree. Alice explained to her father that this tree was a very important tree for it was the tree where Mother peeped through a little hole when she was hiding from him.

"I always knew that your mother had magical powers. I now know that I was bewitched by this beautiful wood nymph," he said, laughing and giving me a hug and Alice and I laughed with him.

"Alice, we are going to miss you so much. This is because we are being selfish and thinking of our own feelings. It is your life, we just want you to be happy and fulfil your dreams," I said with a lump in my throat.

Alice threw her arms around William and myself embracing us. "I love you so much and my brothers and there will not be a day goes by that I shall not think of you all."

"Come now, I think that it is time we all got ready

Chapter 25

for the wedding," said William.

The little chapel was full, most of the nuns chose to attend; there were also four Knights Templar there. Berta proceeded down the aisle carrying a large wooden cross, followed by four nuns chanting. Then came Alice, wearing her habit and carrying the Holy Book decorated in white blossom and with roses trailing from the book. William wore a silk tunic bearing the family Coat of Arms. Behind them walked Ruth carrying a Tiger Lily. Ruth was now a very senior nun and was a great help to Berta, assisting with the administration of the Abbey. The nuns sang their own arrangement accompanied by a nun on the harp and two nuns playing the lute. Gideon was waiting at the altar with Hugh. Hugh said the normal vows for Alice and Gideon to agree with.

Once they were married, Berta gave Hugh a cloak to bless at the altar and sprinkle it with Holy Water. Then Berta took it and helped Alice put it on. On the back of the cloak was a large silk cross which was sewn by some of the nuns. When Alice had the cloak on, Hugh christened Alice as 'Daughter of the Cross' and sprinkled her with the Holy Water. Then the nuns sang again as Alice and Gideon left the chapel followed by the rest of us.

Alice cut a cake which she had made herself, this was handed around accompanied with a glass of wine. Following this, Alice and Gideon took their leave. For they had been invited to Guilford Castle to say their farewells to Queen Eleanor who was very experienced in the way of ladies taking part in the Crusades and I am sure that she wished to give Alice advice. Alice was looking forward to the visit to Queen Eleanor for she had not visited the Queen since she left her service when the Queen went off to the Crusades.

William and the rest of our family would also be

taking our leave to return to the Manor.

Chapter 26
UNSETTLED TIMES

When we got home there was a message from William's brother Walter saying that their brother Godfrey was very ill and that he really needed someone from the family to take care of Godfrey. As John was Godfrey's heir, Walter thought that John should be the one to go and William agreed with the suggestion.

"The clearance of the Jews is nearly concluded now, John. If you inform me what is left to be done in the area which you have been handling I, with the help of my Squire will bring this matter with the Jews to an end," said William.

"The Barons and Earls have banished the Jews under their control and the Bishops and the Churches were the first to get rid of theirs, for they were in great debt to the Jews. The main problems are in the towns. The problem there lies with the Aldermen and the Burgesses. For many of the rich Jews are their friends and of course there is a problem where a Jew is an Alderman or a Burgess," answered John.

"You will be free to travel to Boyton tomorrow. I will get to see Godfrey as soon as I can inform King Edward that there are no longer any Jews left in Suffolk and give the King account of how much land and wealth has been returned to the Crown," stated William.

"John, I will send with you some Holy Water and potions along with herbs to keep Godfrey comfortable. Walter did not say what sort illness his brother has," I said thoughtfully.

"When I see the King I will ask him to release me from being Sheriff of Suffolk and appoint some other Lord. I will tell him that I am now getting old and have aching limbs. That I would like to spend my remaining years with my beautiful Lady for, over the years, I have

Chapter 26

spent so much time away from her. I cannot think how the King could have much argument with my retirement for I have always been a good loyal servant to both him and his father," said William most strongly.

"I have another message here from Will to say that they have defeated Llewellyn and that he should be back at Hollymead Hall before their child is born," said William, passing me the note.

"How wonderful! I must visit Amicia as soon as possible, for I should have visited many days ago but the Wedding has taken up so much time, it must be done with much haste," I said, feeling very guilty.

"Tomorrow, Katherine, we will go to our new home together now the new Hall is just about completed and you, my sweet, can see what finishing touches you would like to have made so that it will be as grand and modern as any in society."

The next day John left early and William and I walked to the new Hall which was north from the old Hall, quite close to the Church. It was set amongst some very fine oak trees of a large size. I got very excited as we approached the trees, for it would not be long and we would be living there. There was a ripple on the moat which was very deep surrounded by steep banks. As we walked across the drawbridge I glanced back and looked at the track which approached the drawbridge. "We must have the track edged with holly bushes to ward off evil spirits," I said as William glanced behind him. We approached the very strong oak door which led into the main hall which was very large. It had stone fireplaces with the hearth set into the walls at both ends of the hall. The fireplaces had a projecting funnel to collect the smoke and there was a semi-circular arch. The walls were thickened by an external buttress and the flue was connected at roof level to the air. The roof was thatched with shingle tiles around the inflammable areas; these fireplaces were indeed very modern. William would hold his courts in this hall and we would use it when we had many guests, for banquets and entertainment.

We had an internal staircase to the chambers above which were for the family's use and sleeping chambers for guests. At the end areas of the floor were smaller chambers for the servants and storage. The upper chambers had plastered walls and floors whereas the lower floor was clay and stone. The lighting was candles in brackets high on the wall and at a lower level there were bowls full of goose oil with wicks floating in the oil.

Our kitchen was a detached building in case it caught on fire as kitchens often did. Being on its own, the fire would be able to be contained and would not spread to the main building. In the kitchen there was a centre hearth, large enough to have a spike capable to take a whole ox. There were two fire ovens set into the wall for baking the breads and other items. At the top of the building were louvres to get rid of the smoke and smells. The servants also had a chamber off the kitchen and there was a chamber where we had two large tubs to bathe in. I had already had new chopping blocks, work tables, cooking pots and storage vats. There were brackets on the wall to hold the large frying pans which had long handles so the cook did not get burnt by the fire when she was frying for she would use a lot of fat and often the pan would catch fire.

The court yard was surrounded by many outbuildings. There was the dairy, brewery, brine and curing building and I had taken a building to dry my herbs and have potions made and stored. At the far end of the courtyard were new stables for William wanted the horses kept close to the Hall.

Chapter 26

In the kitchen garden we would grow basic foods: pulses, beans, onions, garlic, leeks, cabbage and kale. A large pond was between the Hall and the Church which William said he would have stocked with different kinds of fish. The men were clearing a path to make a walkway to the Church which would be lined with apple trees which would add blossom in the spring, make shade in the summer and give fruit in the fall.

Following William giving his instructions to the Bailiff, we started on our walk home.

"William, the Hall is wonderful, it as near to perfect as it can be. I just cannot wait for us to start to live there and have guests to stay and to be able to show our new home off. I am so proud of it," I said with a smile and squeezing William's hand.

"It has been worth waiting many years for then, Katherine," William replied.

"The only thing which will complete my happiness will be that we will be able to spend most of our future days together," I answered.

When we arrived home William informed me that he will have to leave early the next day and that he would make a list of jobs he wanted completed at the new 'Barewe Hall'. He had already spoken to the men about them and I must give the list to the Bailiff to see that the work is completed with haste.

While William was making his list I went out to find Hugh. I thought that as William was in such a good mood that it would be a good time for us to tell William about Hugh and Meg. I went straight to Meg's home as I thought that I would find Hugh there, as I did. I asked him if it was true what Poppy had told me about Meg expecting his child. "Yes, it is and I have nothing to hide. I love Meg as she does me and I am not ashamed," he said. I asked him to return to the Hall at once and that he could inform his father of the situation when we had finished our evening meal.

William was still in a jolly mood and made jokes with Hugh and, though I laughed, my stomach was turning over and over for I knew that William would be most vexed with Hugh.

"Well, once again that was a wonderful meal. I can see when I am able to spend more time at home my stomach will grow outwards with such fine food and I will look like the Duke of Bedford," he said as once again we all laughed. "Please take good care of your mother while I am away, Hugh."

"Father I have something to explain to you."

"What is it Hugh?" asked William, somehow knowing that it was not good news.

"Well, Father, as you know it was never my ambition to become a Priest, I want to be a Knight the same as my brothers. I became a Priest because I love you and Mother so much and wanted to make you happy. I have been brought up in a loving home and in my training as a Priest I have learnt to love and care for my fellow humans. I watched my brothers fall in love and take beautiful gentle wives and I was full of envy. I had always been close to Meg since being a young child. As a man, I fell in love with her and she with me. I prayed and prayed to God to give me strength for I did not want to sin, for Meg was already married. Meg had told me that her marriage had never been consummated. She cried and said that she had married her husband out of kindness as she thought that she could live without having babies but as she watched other members of the family having children she became very sad. I took her in my arms just to give her comfort and tell that there were other things in life which would give her fulfillment. Instead of speaking to her, I kissed her lips and then I sinned. I love Meg and am so thrilled about my coming child," said Hugh sticking his chest out and raising his head proudly, showing no remorse.

William turned to me. "Did you know about this?" he questioned.

"Yes, I knew about Meg just before Alice's wedding, Poppy told me about the coming child."

"You could not bother to tell me but kept it a secret from me?" said William crossly.

"Only because I did not want it to spoil Alice's special day. I knew that you would be cross and that you and Hugh would both have your minds on the problem and that it would not be fair to Alice. That's why I did not tell you," I said with my voice being louder than usual because I was becoming more upset.

"Pour me a tumbler of wine," he said, not saying 'please' which was most unusual for William.

I gave him the wine and he drunk it in one swallow then picked up the flagon. As he was leaving the chamber, he turned to Hugh and said "Once again you have betrayed me and have made me look a fool in everyone's eyes, it is best that you leave the Hall, you are no longer my son. As for you, Katherine you have put your pride and everyone else before me." He slammed the door as he left for his study.

"Go," I said to Hugh with tears in my eyes.

"I will not go," said Hugh, following his Father into his study.

"All my life, Father, I have watched from afar as your eyes sparkle with love and pride as you look at both Will and John. Never have you looked at me like that. With envy I watched as you and your other two sons rode off together to hunt, never including me. I listened to the jollity and laughter when you spoke about the fun you had on the hunt. How I wished I had been included.

In your eyes, I was my mother's son; I felt that I was not anything to do with you. I had to turn to Richard to teach me the things that a boy needs to know to grow into a man. Richard's sons acted more like brothers towards me than my own brothers did. I thought that when I became a Priest I would earn your pride but it was not so. I was just part of the Manor like the bailiffs, needed to make the Manor function. Not once did you ask me "Hugh, what do you want from life? Will I miss not being your son? No, I will not because I have never been so."

William did not say a word to Hugh or to myself, he just left the study and rode off into the night.

"I will move out and go and stay with Grandmother at Heigham until I have decided what I will be doing," said Hugh with tears in his eyes.

I just sat on the stairs outside William's study staring into the empty chamber. I did not cry. My mind was in a whirl, it was telling me that William would never come back to me. I sat there for hours as the servants tried to get me to move. I did not hear them or see them. They sent for Mother and Poppy. I did not see them either. I did not remember any of this and only know what I have been told since. They took me to my chamber and put me to bed. They could not get me to talk or eat and had to force fluid into my mouth and stroke it down my throat. I was like this for days. Mother sent for Will who had returned from the war to his home.

When Will arrived, Mother told him that evil spirits had entered my mind as she had seen this illness before. To cure the mind and bring it back to the soul they must be quite cruel to me.

Mother got Poppy to get a large container of the coldest water.

"We must pull Katherine to her feet and you must hold her there Will while I throw the water over her. Then

Chapter 26

you must shout at her in a large voice and shake her at the same time and tell her to return to her God and her family that love her so," Mother informed Will. Mother threw the water and Will shouted and said what Mother had told him to say but added "Mother, do you not want to see your new Grandson?"

"It has worked!" shouted Mother as I fell into Will's arms and gave him a hug. I slowly lifted my head and looked at Mother and Poppy, both of them with their eyes fixed on myself and Will. I let go of Will and turned and sat on the bed, putting my head between my hands.

"Oh what have I done? Was it my pride that has driven William away? Have I lost William's love forever, will he ever forgive me?" I said between my sobs. Mother came and sat on the bed next to me, taking hold of my hand.

"Katherine my dear, of course William still loves you. He would not give up something that you both shared that meant so much to you both. It is his pride that is hurt and he is vexed with Hugh and some of his anger brushed off on you as well as anyone else who gets in his way while he bares this anger. You must give him time to heal and to think the whole situation through. He will remember what young love is like and forgive Hugh and he will realise that you were trying to do your best for the whole family. Now let us help you get dried and changed because I want to hear about the new member of our family - don't you?" said Mother as she looked at Will.

Mother went with Will downstairs, while Poppy helped me get dressed.

"My Lady, you are in no way to blame for this situation, it is down to Meg and Hugh - mostly Meg for she should have known better than to tempt a celibate young man in such a way. Believe me, she knew what she was doing, she desperately wanted a child of her own. I have seen it in her eyes each time her sisters and brother have a new child in their family. All this trouble she has caused and shame she has brought upon both our families. Meg must be punished, My Lady," said Poppy with anger in her eyes.

"I must go and speak to Will and apologize for having to see his mother in the state of turmoil and despair, a condition that no Knight should see his mother in," I said quickly, hurrying down the stairs.

"Will I have a new grandson? How is Amicia? I am so sorry that I should cause a problem at a time like this when you should be at home with your wife and son. I ask your forgiveness."

"There is nothing to forgive. You travel back with me tomorrow to Waldingfield and you will be able to see what your grandson is like yourself. Amicia is fine and is very keen to show our little William off to you. You will stay a few days with us and I will not take no for an answer."

I tried my best to sound enthusiastic about the coming visit although in my heart I did not feel so. I left with Will to return to his home to visit Amicia and my new grandson. I had given the list that William had left about the finishing touches to the Hall to the Bailiff before we left. Mother said that she would find a new home in Heigham for Meg and her husband so she will be away from us when we return. Mother also said that she would try to calm Hugh while he is staying with her they are very close and she feels that she might help him get rid of some of his hostile feelings which he has towards his father.

Poppy was not travelling with us, I can manage to take care of myself for the short time I will be away. Poppy will take care of the running of the Hall while I am

Chapter 26

away. I will not stay as long as Will wants me to for I have decided that when I return home I will start the move into our new Hall, whether it is finished or not. Then William and I can make a new start in a new home when he returns.

I just hope that while William is away from us he will be able to sort out his feelings. To understand that everyone in life makes mistakes and that his family are just people and not perfect as he seems to think that they are. To just remember what it is like to be young and in love. I think that it will toil in his mind how we did not understand how Hugh felt different from his brothers when he was growing up. Hugh thinking that he was not as precious or loved as much by us as the rest of the family. William was away so much while Hugh was growing up and they did not get to know each other. Because of Hugh's breathing problems as a child, I did not allow him to develop and encounter the problems a boy does and solve them for himself as I was over-protective and perhaps made him look weak in William's eyes.

I must put all these problems out of my mind now because we have arrived at Hollymead Hall and I will not have anything spoil this visit for me. I just removed my cloak and did not bother to refresh myself although I had been riding for over four hours. I went straight to see my grandson; he was just so beautiful, so much like his father when he was a baby. The mass of fair hair, fair skin covered with down over his face, violet blue eyes. I picked William up from his crib and he looked at me as if he knew me. I cradled him and rained kisses on his brow.

"Not too many kisses, Mother, he must learn discipline now even while he is in his crib, for when he grows up he will carry a lot of responsibility on his shoulders," said William, looking with admiration at his son.

"No, William, your mother may bathe our son with kisses if she so wishes for he must also learn while he is in his crib that he is loved and that he belongs," Amicia said strongly.

I spent seven wonderful days at Hollymead which really lifted my spirits and I was in a great mood as I rode home escorted by Will's Squire and two of his men.

It took me over seven days to get our possessions moved from the old Hall to the new. I was working making a herb garden helping to replant the herbs I had brought from the old hall when William appeared. He took hold of my hand and led me into the Hall where he kissed me passionately.

"I am so sorry, Katherine, I should not have been so cross with you. I am sure you thought that you did the best for everyone. I was tired and this problem with the Jews has really got to my soul. It has now come to finish and I have seen the King and he has now released me from the King's work. He said that he understands and that he wishes he could spend more time with his wife."

So we will be able to spend more of our days together.

Chapter 27
CHANGES AHEAD

It is now summer of 1284. The King has released William from his duties to the Crown. William still has to supply 1.5 knights for service to the Crown for the holding of Barewe. This means we have to find the money to pay for the Knight's keep and expenses. We also need to find extra money for the upkeep of our beautiful new Hall.

Our Manor for the whole of Barewe is some 2550 acres now. William will still be working the land and will continue with his fine stud of horses which are sought after by the Knights. He has decided to lease out our old Hall along with arable land of 240 acres, 1.5 acres of meadow, 0.5 acres of pastures, 23 acres of woodland and one windmill.

It is to be leased to Sir Adam Creting jointly with his wife Nicola. I was not very happy about the lease at first because it would mean that we would be sharing the heart of Barewe; also the villeins who worked and lived on the Creting's holdings would have a new master and they will not be too happy. We will need to share All Saints Church between the two Lords. Hugh suggested that there should be two services on the Sabbath, each Lord attending his own service with his people, for the Lord and his Bailiffs speak about the Manor and the work for the coming week at the services. Sir Adam can then contribute to Hugh's living; he needs money to contribute towards his child.

There is still a problem between William and Hugh who only talk together about affairs of the Manor and the Church; there are no courtesies or family matters spoken about. I pray to God that William may treat Hugh as a son again and forgive him. This is the only blot on my happiness now; I have my husband at home with me most of the time and we live in harmony and my highlights are still cuddling up in William's arms at night and becoming as one.

I do not see as much of my children as I would like to. Alice is still in the Holy Land, I get very warm written notes from her saying how happy she is and how much she and Gideon still love each other. How she has become nearly as good a healer as Gideon. Every day is so different and that her life is so exciting and that God has been so good to her. But she does miss her family back in England as she loves us so much. Sometimes in the quiet of night when she looks up at the stars she feels very close to us all. I find that I read her news time and time again and each time I get a tear in my eye.

Son William is very busy with his family and, with encouragement from the King, is building up large sheep herds and training his villeins to learn to spin and make cloth. William is still in the King's service and spends a good deal of time in Scotland trying to woo the Scottish King for King Edward would like to become heir to the Scottish Throne

John has made his home at Boyden with his uncle Godfrey who is so very frail that John has had to take over the running of the whole of his Manors and lands. John is also a very fine warrior and has built up a large troop of men; many of the men have been transferred from his great uncle Osbert's forces. Osbert is now very old and although he still has duties in the Welsh Marches, it is usually John who puts the flame out there with the rebels who dare to raise arms against the King.

To display the grandeur of our new Hall, William has decided that we shall hold a Tournament in the Manor on the Feast of John the Baptist which will be the 24th of June. We will also be holding a fair which was

Chapter 27

granted by the Crown back in 1267. There will be musicians, acrobats, jugglers and other entertainers who will all be descending on Barewe.

We will invite all the local Gentry who will not need to stay at the Hall and will be able to return to their own homes each night. Then there will be Knights and their Ladies who will erect their own pavilions, all displayed with their Coat of Arms and pennons. If King Edward and the Queen should honour us with attending the Tournament they will, of course, stay at the Hall. Although King Edward loves Tournaments as he is so good at jousting, it is unlikely that they will attend as they are in Gascony where the King is trying to sort out some trouble that has arisen.

Isabelle will be leaving her Chateau and will be travelling to Suffolk. I am so looking forward to seeing her. It has been some time since we were last together, there will be so much news to catch up on. I will be so proud to have her as a guest in my beautiful home.

Amicia and her mother Lady Wimpole will be coming to stay some days before the Tournament as Lady Wimpole has great experience of holding large functions at her Hall and will help with sorting out accommodation for the dignitaries' servants.

Food will not be a problem as the Manor is flourishing with livestock. William has already selected the oxen and rams to be killed and will be holding some hunts for boars and stags. The cooks at the Hall have already started to prepare jellies, sweetmeats and delicacies. We will be able to keep them cool in watertight vats which we can store in the moat until we are ready to use them.

It was just days before the Tournament and everything was going to plan. Lady Wimpole had arrived with Amicia and my grandson William who is just adorable with golden curls and the same violet eyes as his grandfather.

Isabelle was one of the first guests to arrive; she made a spectacular entrance seated on a beautiful white charger which was adorned in golden silk and wearing plumage on its head. She had a large escort of guards and, ahead of them carrying her Coat of Arms, was a French Knight Errant and his Squire who would be competing in the Tournament for Isabelle. Her ladies in waiting came next followed by many carts overloaded with trunks and goods. William and I and Lady Wimpole and Amicia were in the court yard to greet her.

"William! Oh, where will we put the rest of the guests if they arrive with such a large entourage?" I asked with much alarm.

"A very good question indeed," he answered without solving the problem.

The Knight Errant and his Squire approached us and the Squire dipped Isabelle's colours to William to pay homage. He then proceeded towards Isabelle to help her dismount; she needed little help as she could not contain herself and was halfway dismounted when they offered help. We both hurried towards each other. We greeted with a hug with Isabelle taking my face between her hands and kissing my forehead and cheeks.

"Katherine my dearest, it has been so long and I have missed you so much," she said as she kissed me again.

"I think of you every day Isabelle, wondering what you have been up to and what sort of troubles you have got yourself in to," I said as I looked towards her Knight Errant as she dismissed him.

I took her hand and led her to where Lady Wimpole and Amicia were standing. Isabelle paid her

Chapter 27

courtesies in a reserved sort of way as there was no love lost between the Wimpoles and the De Clares.

"The Hall is spectacular, William, very grand but has much charm. Well done both of you, it reflects both of your characters," she said enthusiastically.

Poppy directed Isabelle's ladies to the chambers while the Bailiff saw to the escort and carts. It was not until the next day that Isabelle and I had some time to be on our own and catch up with our more intimate news. I explained about what had happened with Hugh and Meg and how it was the only time in our life together that William had been vexed with me and how I thought that I would never see him again.

"How foolish you were, Katherine. William could not survive with out you," she laughed.

"Well, and you Isabelle, have you turned France upside down yet?" I questioned.

She laughed again "Not quite. I have been invited quite a few times to Paris to stay with King Philippe III and his Queen Margaret. As you know, I am not into Court life but I thought that I should keep in with the French Crown when I own so much property in France and with the country being so unsettled between the English and the French.

I like Philippe very much; on the whole, he is liked by his subjects. He is quite a weak man and a little foolish sometimes. He had this man friend who was his barber called Peter who became one of his favourites. Philippe let Peter have good deal of power which the Nobles did not like; he also made trouble between Philippe and Margaret. She had Peter watched at length and had him condemned as a traitor for treason. He was hanged which got rid of him.

Philippe at the moment has taken an army to Sicily to support his uncle Charles who is King of Naples and Sicily. Charles is a harsh man and has been cruel to the Sicilians. They have risen up against him and have offered the crown of Sicily to Pedro the King of Aragon if he helps them get rid of Charles and Pedro has accepted. So you see that the French get as many problems as the English."

"Speaking about the English, in the summer King Edward and Eleanor came and stayed at the Chateau I have on the coast. I am so very fond of Eleanor she is such a wonderful, kind, sweet woman, I have never heard her say anything bad about anyone. Everyone who meets her falls in love with her. I do worry over her as she is so frail she looks as if you blew hard at her she would break. For she is always with child; she has already given birth to fourteen babies but six of her children have died. She does not have a wet nurse and fed them all herself which takes all her nourishment from her. Eleanor says how God has smiled on her and Edward to make them so fertile."

"There is no doubt that Edward worships her and she him. They are always together, Eleanor is a fine horsewoman and even accompanies Edward when he rides into battles and is always close to the scene of the action. When on the beach, he carries Eleanor in his arms out to where the sea is quite deep and floats her so that she gets the goodness of the sea into her body. He does not trust anyone else to take her. He then brings her back to where he has had a place made on the beach which has been made into a bed covered with petals, then lays her down for the hot sun to dry her and he then lays next to her as they hold hands. They spend any social time they have in a simple way, usually with their children, when they are not into Royal Courts. Their marriage was certainly a gift from Heaven," said Isabelle with admiration.

Chapter 27

"I am surprised that you have not got married again yet, Isabelle. You must have had many suitors from both countries?" I asked.

"Of course I have, I am very rich which is widely known. But I am like your mother, I do not wish to lose control of my money or my land. I like my own way and will not answer to any man. I have had enough trouble with my brothers over the years who feel they know better than me how to control my wealth, encouraged by their greedy wives. I do like the company of men but have become a master of flirting and can keep myself from becoming too involved with then. I get my excitement by playing games with them. I race against them into the sea on horse back; we race until the horses have to swim and then dive off into the sea. You see Katherine, I have never really grown up. I do admire a fit young male's body as I admire a fine horse but they do not share my bed," she answered me firmly.

"I do hope that you and William, now you have more time, will come and stay in my Chateau. You could both do with some sun and I think that it is about time that you both had some fun in your life."

Chapter 28
FEAST OF JOHN THE BAPTIST

June 20th - the Knights and their Ladies have started to arrive. They will have their pavilions erected on the sites which have been allocated to them at the front of the Hall on the meadows called Great Hay and Little Hay. The hay on the meadows has been cut and stored for the winter and the area made smooth for the Tournament. The fair and the entertainers will be accommodated on the green which is near to our old Hall.

Hugh has organized the ceremony of The Feast of John the Baptist which needs to be held prior to our Festival and Tournament. This is a ceremony to pray for the souls of the deceased. Many of the deceased have paid money before their demise to Secular Chaplains and the Friars of Babewell who will attend Barewe's All Saints Church to pray for the souls of those who have paid for such. Just a prayer usually costs eight marks; for a cross or lantern with a stem of silver or gilt to be carried before the procession on the principal day would cost as much as forty shillings.

Hugh will lead the procession, carrying the cross of Jesus followed by the Friars and Chaplains who will be carrying the lanterns and crosses, chanting the prayers. William and I will follow on horseback; behind us will be the Knights and their Ladies then our honoured guests, followed by the mourners of the deceased. The procession circles the complete Manor finishing back at All Saints.

William and I will take our seats in the main pavilion along with our family and honoured guests. The Knights will come and pay homage to us and then the Tournament can commence. The Knights taking part in the Tournament are, of course, mostly young men who rode with Will and John in King Edward's elite squad of knights.

Bearing the names of De Clare will be the sons of Richard - Gilbert and Thomas, the Gifford's kin of ours from the West of England, the grandsons of the old Duke of Bedford. There will also be Knight Errants who make their income from tournaments. William has put up a pouch of gold and one of precious jewels that he had saved from the bounty he obtained while fighting in the East. He is also giving a stallion for a prize.

The feast for the Lords and their Ladies will be served in the Hall and the grounds of the Hall. For others, there will be food served on the green and in the grounds of the Church. This includes everyone in the Manor - guest and villeins. William has put guards around the Manor to stop the poor and undesirables who have already set off from Bury to descend on Barewe for free food. I said to William that the guards should give them some food before turning them away but he said 'No' for that would just encourage more of them.

We had finished the procession and had taken our seats ready for the Tournament to commence when an elderly Knight rode in with his escort. This was Sir William de Valence who was made overseer of the tournaments on behalf of King Edward. He rode up to William and paid his courtesies to him.

"My Lords, Ladies, Honoured Guests and others." Everyone looked at Sir Valence, who indeed had a very loud voice. Our most gracious Queen Eleanor had given birth to a new Prince to be named Edward after his father. "Our most Brave and Honoured King has given a pouch of gold as a prize for the Broad Sword competition to honour the new Prince."

The crowed all stood and cheered. The Knights who were already mounted placed the tips of their lances to the ground to pay homage to the New Prince.

"The King has set up a code of rules for all tournaments that were first drawn up in 1267. The King's 'Statute of Arms' was influence of chivalric values and Arthurian romance. Our King Edward has preference for single combat between two champions separated by a tilt rather than a group of Knights doing combat," said Valence.

My William had to have a discussion with Sir William de Valence for it had been arranged to have a group combat. Sir William de Valence said that the King frowns on group combats as he feels that it causes bad feeling amongst his Knights. Sir de Valence said that as the combat would be between the De Clares and the Giffords and, as there has always been friendly competition between them, Sir de Valence would allow it to take place this time. He then examined the lances to make sure that there were no sharp points and that the swords were blunt.

The Home Knights were my sons Will and John, John's friend Sir Robert de Vere, Amicia's brother Sir Edward Wimpole and Sir Thomas Gifford from Stoke by Nayland. The challengers were the four young De Clares and Isabelle's French Knight. The spectators were so pleased that the group combat would be allowed to go ahead for it causes so much excitement and colour. It brings the spectators to their feet as they try to participate with their spirit in supporting their squad.

The trumpets sounded and the Knights went to their ends of the meadow. Sir William de Valence stood in the middle of the meadow and dropped his hand and the Knights rode towards each other with their lances at the ready. The first to be unseated was Amicia's brother, Edward, by Isabelle's French Knight. Isabelle, who was seated next to me, got so excited and stood up making squeals of delight. Lady Wimpole was seated behind her and was cross with Isabelle's response which was not the way for a Lady to behave. Lady Wimpole left the pavilion.

"Isabelle, you should follow Lady Wimpole and apologize for your reaction," I said crossly.

"No, there is no point in apologizing, she will know that I do not mean it," said Isabelle with her eyes still fixed on the Tournament. I felt that I should apologize on Isabelle's behalf but, with second thoughts, I felt that I might make the matter worse.

John brought Gilbert de Clare down. John jumped off his mount, gave Gilbert time to get to his feet and then they both drew their broad swords and commenced fencing in a friendly way. Neither squad retired in the time given for the combat and Sir Valence had the trumpets sound to mark the end of the combat; he then declared the combat to be equal. The supporters were not too happy with the decision and made unfriendly noises.

Next came the archery tournament which gave the Knights a rest. Many of the Ladies left the tournament and went to the Hall to take refreshments and socialize with other Ladies. Following the archery, was the single jousting combat. This tournament was won by an unknown Flemish Knight who scored two extra points in the final against our young Will which was quite a shock to the English Knights. We learnt that this Flemish Knight was Count Pierre de Latilly. He did not win in the broad sword combat; this was won by our John. I don't think that there would be a Knight who could beat John with the sword except for King Edward who is so skilful with the sword and was mentor to our John a few years back when Edward was the Prince and

Chapter 28

John a young Knight.

We concluded for the day following the sword combat as our great feast was ready. There were two large boars that had been roasted in the Hall's kitchen and many spits had been erected over fires in the Hall grounds to roast the pigs, sheep and stags and many of our rabbits from the warren which were quite a delicacy. Our cooks had made hot pasties of venison which were very popular and there were countless custards and jellies and sweetmeats.

Following the feast, we had arranged a Corpus Christi play performed by the travelling minstrels about the life of John the Baptist. There was also music in the grounds for those who did not want to watch the play. There were also fools and entertainers on the green where the fair was.

The next day was a quieter day. Falconry took place in the meadows; there were four falcons and their owners taking part in the competition. Captured wild birds were let loose and the falcons were released; the falcon that brought back the most birds was declared the winner. William also had rabbits released from the warren and the points worked the same. William gave a pouch of coins to the winner.

In the latter part of the day there were stallion races in the meadow. William took part in this competition for he wanted to show off the Arab stallions he had bred for speed. Many Knights took part but they were no match for William's horses and the foreign Knights were most interested in the horses and wished to buy their choice of the stallions.

We again had a great feast. The minstrel once again performed a play, this time it was about King Arthur. It told how Arthur was born the son of Uther Pendragon and Ygerna the Duchess of Cornwall. He

Chapter 28

was Crowned King of Britain at Silchester at the age of fifteen years in the sixth century. It tells how Arthur defeated the Saxons at Bath and Lincoln. He then crossed the channel to subdue the French. While there, news came that his nephew Mordred had seized the crown. Returning to Britain, he defeated Mordred and killed him at the battle of Camblan but Arthur was mortally wounded. He was carried away by his knights to Avalon where he had ordered Gifflet to hurl the sword Excalibur into the lake. A hand rose up from out of the water and grasped the weapon. Then a boat drifted along carrying Morgan and her ladies who took Arthur on board and sailed off again into the distance. It is said that crown passed to Arthur's cousin Constantine in the year 542. The minstrels played very sad music at the end of the play and most of the ladies had tears in their eyes. They all stated what a beautiful play it was and I was most pleased and explained that it was King Edward's favourite play.

    The next day, most of the Lords and Ladies left; Isabelle stayed a little longer. The festival was now given over to the people of the Manor. Will and John had organized the men into teams with the villeins against men from the army. In this game they had to kick a stuffed pig's bladder from one end of the meadow to the other, with each team having to guard their area only with their feet, which was marked by two rocks. Then they played games of club ball, it was most enjoyable to watch. Following these games, the Manor people were allowed to eat the food which was left over from the feast and take some of it away for another day if they so wished to.

    When the guests had all left I had time to spend with Isabelle before she returned to France. William did say to her that we would try to visit her at one of her

Chateaux in France in the near future.

"Katherine, your festival was perfect and it will be the talk of society for months to come. I am so proud of you and William," said Isabelle giving me a big hug.

"I am so sad that our Alice could not be with us. I know that Alice is so happy but I miss her so much Isabelle," I said.

"You must not be sad for Alice is happy and you must find your happiness with William, for had it not always been your wish to have time to spend with him? You are funny, Katherine, you should spend more time thinking about yourself, be a little more like me!" said Isabelle with a great big laugh. "Not a lot like me though!" We both laughed while saying our goodbyes with lots of hugs. I then watched her ride off in her grand manner in a way that only Isabelle could, which brought a smile to my lips. I then wondered how much in monies the festival had cost us. I would not ask William, he will tell me if he so wishes to. I did feel very proud of myself.

Chapter 29
DARK DAYS

For the next six years England remained quite calm. William and I were most happy having time to spend together. We spent a great deal of time riding and I even went hunting with William. We now had three grandchildren: two belonging to Will and Amicia also Hugh had a daughter who was named Maud after my Mother. Little Maud spent a great deal of time with her great grandmother and brightened up Mother's days. Mother now had to be cared for and it was Maud's mother Meg who did most of the caring. Little Maud spends a great deal of time with her father as Hugh still lives at Heigham.

Hugh was still not happy. When we had the festival, Hugh did not bother to watch the Tournament. I believe that he was envious of his brothers as they took part. I feel heavy in my heart and guilty that I was not able to help Hugh lead the type of life he would have liked to have led. He now drinks too much for the good of his health. He spends a good deal of time with Sir Adam and Nicola de Creting. William has tried to be more friendly towards Hugh, more for my sake than William having true affection for him.

Our son Will works hard at Waldingfield and has managed to do good trading with the wool that they have produced. He still has his duties to do for King Edward. As for John, we see very little of him as he still has duties in the Welsh Marches keeping the peace. His uncle Godfrey is now deceased so John has the responsibility of the Manors and their people in the shires of Cornwall, Wiltshire and Suffolk. He also rides quite often with the King when the King is about his business.

King Alexander of Scotland died in the year 1287

and before he died he made his granddaughter his heir to the Scottish Throne. So in 1287 John rode with the King to Scotland to make an arrangement with the Scottish Nobles for a marriage between Queen Margaret, known as the Maid of Norway, who was four years old and Prince Edward who was three years old at the time. The marriage was intended to unite England and Scotland under one crown. The Nobles agreed but in 1290 Queen Margaret died in Orkney on her journey from Bergen where she had been living with her Father King Eric II of Norway and her Mother Margaret, daughter of the late King Alexander.

King Edward went with great speed to Scotland for he could see his dreams of uniting Scotland and England were about to be crushed. Queen Eleanor had just given birth to her fifteenth child Princess Blanche who did not survive. Eleanor was still very weak following the birth and the loss of her daughter but she wanted to go north with Edward. So she followed at a more leisurely pace. On her arrival at Hardy in Nottinghamshire, she was taken ill with a fever; she did not improve and the King was sent for but she died on 24th November before he arrived. Edward was heartbroken and never really recovered. The cortège took twelve days to get to Westminster Abbey for King Edward had a cross erected at each place the procession rested overnight. Queen Eleanor was so loved by her subjects that all the streets were lined all the way from Lincoln to Westminster with people paying their homage and praying for her soul. William and I rode to Woburn to pay our last respects to Eleanor. Will and John both rode to Westminster both carrying much grief for they both grew close to Eleanor when they were at Guilford. How will our dear Alice will feel when she hears about the Queen's demise? What shock and sadness she would feel when she does hear for she dearly loved the Queen and the Queen returned her love, for the Queen named one of her daughters after Alice which was a great honour.

    King Edward was so grief-stricken that it was said that he could barely speak or walk and could not look anyone in the eye for he was afraid that he would shed tears. This must have been the only time in the King's life that he had been afraid of anything. To add to Edward's grief, in 1291 his mother, Queen Eleanor of the Provence who had become a nun at Amesbury Abbey died. Her death was followed by that of the young Princess Alice. The whole of England was thrust into mourning, some saying that the King had brought this upon himself and was being punished by God for all the killings he had taken part in and also for banishing the Jews. The little bit of joy brought to the King was that he had as prior condition the recognition of himself becoming Overlord of Scotland agreed by the Scottish Nobles.

    The year seemed to reap nothing but death, for within our own family we had sadness when Mother died. William's father also died. Though my mother was old and I knew that she would not always be with us, I was quite shocked and will miss her greatly.

    In 1293 England was at war with France. King Philippe was asserting himself in King Edward's affairs in Gascony. This meant that both Will and John had to go and fight in France. Prior to John going to war, he sent a message to his father to say that if anything should happen to him or if he should be detained for a long period of time, would he go to his Manor in Cornwall to check on a guest that was staying there. It seems that John had rescued a Welsh Princess from some mercenaries that King Edward had paid to patrol the Welsh Marches. John had to pay and buy the Princess's freedom from the mercenaries. The Princess was called Deirdie and belonged to the Gruffydd Family. John took her to Beyton in Cornwall for he felt that she would be accepted and would feel more comfortable amongst the Celt Bretons people who are of the same culture as herself. Meanwhile, John would try to find some of her family to whom he could return her and she would be safe but, as yet, has not been able to find them.

The war did not go well in France for Edward and he lost Gascony to Philippe's army. While he was there, the Welsh took their opportunity and rose up in rebellion. Edward returned to England in great haste and, with a very tired small army, he continued on to Wales. He moved through Wales which he had previously divided into counties. He intended to put the rebellion down one county at a time, but the Welsh united and things did not go as well for Edward as he had planned. He and what was left of his army then had to take refuge in his Castle Beaumans, owing mostly to the extreme severity of the winter and shortness of supplies.

Edward had this castle built in an unusual way. The castle had access to the sea so the King was able to have equipment, supplies and more troops brought into the castle by sea and, because it had been built with increased security, they were able to sit out the worst of the severe winter. So John was away many months and William once again had to leave me and Barewe on his travels. He would be away for some time for Cornwall is a great distance and, being winter, William will be travelling more slowly. He will be taking some of his army with him. The army is now only small, mostly made up with local men, and he also felt that he had to leave some of the men for the security of Barewe.

Chapter 29

William had only been gone two days when we had a very heavy snow blizzard with the largest snow flakes that I have ever seen. This blizzard went on for three days and even then the weather was so cold that there was no sign of a thaw. I summoned everyone who was in charge of livestock: the shepherds and the grooms along with the bailiffs. I told them to make a plan to section off Barewe into six areas and to put a reliable man in charge of each area and the bailiffs to oversee them. They will need to clear the roads, droves and tracks so that we can get access into the fields with the carts to feed the livestock and dig them out where needed. I told them that if there was stock which was dead they must put them in the carts and bring them back as they would only have died by freezing and we would be able to use them for food. The Manor was cut off by snow; this is a problem which happens when there has been heavy snow. It is because we are at the top of a hill and our fields are much higher than our roads and the snow blows off the fields on to the roads and gets very deep at the bottom of the hill. The deepest snow being at Needles Eye, this is an area where two hills meet, it is called so because it is like an eye of a needle. The snow also builds up at Barewe Bottom which is the main way to get access on to the Icknield way. The Bury Road will also be cut off at the Sheep Dip just before one gets to Little Saxham. I just hoped that the hay and turnips that we harvested in the summer will last the winter out as we will have to use a great deal now.

I had the cooks at the Hall make great pots of soup for all the men that had been working out in the freezing weather. They could call at the Hall to get some soup and hot ale before they went off duty.

With young Will being away at war, I was wondering how they were coping at Will's Manor at

Waldingfield for he has put a great deal of money and time in building up large sheep flocks and would not be able to afford to lose them. I just hope that he has good livestock men on his Manor. I was also very worried about my husband and his men for he could not have got any further than Buckinghamshire - if they got that far before the blizzard - and of course they would need shelter. They may even have got cut off somewhere because of blocked roads. These thoughts were not out of my mind when William's foot soldiers appeared on their way back to Denham. One of the Captains came to see me and told me it was very difficult and that Lord Gifford said that it was too much for the foot men and that they were slowing down the travelling through no fault of their own and that they should return home while they can. He told me that the Master just continued with some of his cavalry and had told the Captain to tell me that he is in good spirits.

    The snow had now stopped but there was still no thaw. We had got control of the situation but we were having to use more hay than I wanted to and I was wondering if there would be enough for the rest of winter.

    We were all feeling very tired and cold and things got worse as the winter illness swept through the Manor. There was hardly anyone who escaped it and we had three infants die and five of the old people. It was an illness where food would not stay in people's insides and was thrown up or discharged too often through the normal functions and those who had it grew very weak. This illness nearly always came with the snow.

    I had sage and tarragon infused together in large pots at the Hall and then had it distributed at the church to the villeins who brought their containers to put it in. They were told to only take the tonic and hot ale and not

Chapter 29

eat any food till the condition improved.

William had been away for six weeks and the weather had started to improve and it looked as though spring would not be too long now. To my great joy, William returned home looking very drawn and tired.

Over our meal, William said that his journey to Cornwall had been very difficult and very cold. I asked William what Deirdie was like.

"She is a typical Welsh young woman. In appearance, she is much shorter than most English ladies in stature, she is quite rounded in her body but is not fat and has a good deportment and carries her head with much pride. She has a lovely sunny face with big dark brown eyes and a beautiful smile and very thick dark curly hair, much like Isabelle's hair. Her fingers are much shorter than yours and Alice's. Her hands are not soft as you would think a Princess's would be; in fact you can see that they have been used in many practical events. Deirdie is very confident and well-educated and quite worldly and I like her very much.

The Manor and the Hall are in a neglected state. My brother Godfrey could not have been there for some time; perhaps it may have been as long as a year. On arriving, I found the chief Bailiff drunk in the kitchen which was in a terrible mess. Deirdie told me that he had been drunk most of the time since she had been there and that he had been given a warning by John when they arrived. So I had my men throw him out and told him that he no longer had the position of a Bailiff. I had all the servants who worked at the Hall line up and I told them that no one leaves the Hall till it is cleaned up. The next day I rode around the Manor with my squire Zac and Deirdie. What livestock there was, I found to be in very poor condition and I could see that they had not been fed or cared for properly. I came across a man who

Deirdie said John had spoken well about and, after speaking to him and asking him many question, I liked his answers. I made him Chief Bailiff. I then told him to go and let all the male villeins know that they must all be at the church at dawn in the morning where they will meet with me. I then went and found the priest and from the amount of wine and fine food I found in his home, I could see that he was having a wonderful quality of life at John's expense. I told him that he was to do penance for two days in the church without food, that he may have a drink of water and that I will send one of my men to see that he does not leave the church and that he should consider himself lucky that he still has his position and a home.

The next day in the church I had every man say what his work was and his name. I had Dierdie write all the facts down for me. In a very assertive way I told them how they had let their Lord down and that it would not do. I told the stockmen that unless they looked after the animals much better they would also lose their homes. I informed them that I would leave Zac as overseer and that they must treat him as if he was their Lord till their master returned.

I found Dierdie to be very capable. She told me that she belonged to Prince Gruffydd's family, a second cousin. I am sure that she hopes that John will be able to contact her family for her. Through her conversation, I can see that she is very fond of our son and her feelings may be a little more. Most of the time she was asking questions about John, in fact she asked so many that I think she could write a book about him. Dierdie had only the one gown that she was wearing when she was taken prisoner by the mercenaries. So we rode to the town of Launcester to buy her some material and have some gowns made and a cloak and other attire a lady needs.

Chapter 29

She is a fine horse woman and rides astride. I told her that in England it was not the way that a young lady should ride and that they should just ride side-saddle. With this, she just kicked her heels into the horse and galloped off at great speed in a very wild way. She did apologize to me about her behaviour later. I could see John having great fun in trying to tame her and train her in the ways of a young English lady if he is as fond of her as she is of him.

I really think that it would be better for John to sell the Manor in Cornwall, it is very difficult for him to keep control of all three Manors when there are so many miles in between them and he has so little time. It made me think about our Manors and on my journey back home I called in to see Gilbert de Clare. I made a transaction with him that I would give him our Manor in Gloucester for him making over the Manors of Brockly and Hartest in Suffolk and then I will not have to travel so much. They are quite close to Will and we may be able to work them together."

William then said how tired he was and that he should retire to his bed which he has missed so much, for in his bed he has this beautiful Lady who keeps him warm. He then went to swing his arms around me to catch hold of me but managed to knock the wine over. I then escaped, fleeing at speed up to our chamber, with William chasing me.

Chapter 30
CRUMBLED ANGEL

Spring was here and everything looked brighter. I am glad that William was here to take care of the stock for they had not been fed as well as they should, because we were so short of supplies. Now that it is spring, he will have to make sure that they do not eat too many of the new spring shoots for they must be feeling quite hungry as we had to cut their feeds right back. Although the winter had been hard, it has done some good to the fields and the soil for now every thing is blossoming at a rapid rate.

Will is now back home safely from the war and he has paid us a visit. We also had word from John saying that he is in good health and is returning to Cornwall to collect Dierdie and to take her with him to Wales to try to find what is left of her family.

Will said that he had heard from other Knights that John has lost his heart to a Welsh Princess and that, once they find her family, John will ask for her hand in Marriage.

William said that he had noted that the fact that Dierdie speaks about John whenever there is an opportunity to do so and that he is sure that her reply will be 'Yes.' I was very happy with that situation and hoped that everything goes according to plan.

I asked Will how young Maud was getting on for she had gone to live at Hollymead Hall following the death of my Mother. There she is being educated along with Will's daughter Katherine (Kate) and also is a companion to Kate. Maud is already known as Lady Maud and Will has made sure that this will continue. Will said that Maud has settled in well and is as bright as a sparkling gem and that Kate just adores her.

He said that he did lose quite a few sheep

Chapter 30

because his men could not get to them but good use was made of the dead sheep. The whole of the Manor lived on mutton stew for weeks and the dogs had never been fed as well. So they were happy, but my purse is not. They did manage to save some of the fleeces. The rams are all in good health so they must work much harder this spring so that we can build up the flocks again. Will seemed very happy when he left us to travel home.

We then received a message from Alice saying that she is very happy for they would be returning home soon for they were both very tired and Gideon thought that it was time for him to retire. They were to visit the Temple in Loure to give information to the younger Healer who would be taking Gideon's place.

William and I had heard that there was much trouble in France caused by difficulty between Pope Boniface and King Phillipi IV. The King is a cruel man and has been taking the Templar's wealth from their Temple. He has also thrown some of them into prison. Alice and Gideon may not be aware that there is trouble and may have been taken by surprise as they will not be on their guard. I hope that it will not be too long and they will be home. I am so looking forward to seeing them both and I can barely wait.

I thought, as William did, that this was going to be a good year but, as the time went and we did not hear any more from Alice, I felt in my bones that something was not right and I began to worry. I could not sleep at night and had no appetite to eat. I knew that William was also worried but he got vexed with me because I had Alice on my mind all the time.

There was some happy news when we heard from John that he had found Deirdie's kin and obtained their blessing. He also said that had he married Deirdie while with her family in Wales and that he and Deirdie would be visiting us as soon as they could. John also said "King Edward has given me duties to tidy up some pockets of resistance in Wales. I have written to Edward to say that I would like a little time to myself to tidy my affairs but as yet have had no reply. Deirdie will be staying with her family while I am away."

It was not long after John's message that the Scottish nobles repudiated Edward as their King. I think that it was because of the large taxes which King Edward wanted them to pay. We have also had our taxes increased a great deal to pay for the wars and all the castles which Edward is having built along the Welsh Marches. Most of the English Nobles are also not very happy about the tax increases.

So King Edward is once again riding against Scotland and our sons are both away fighting in wars. Will is not very happy to do so as he needs some time to spend on his Manor. King Edward will not have the war all his own way as the Scottish have made alliance with the French. The Scots have crowned John de Baliol as their King.

The war with Scotland did not last long and went in favour of King Edward. John de Baliol was captured. Edward had Baliol put into honourable confinement at one of the King's castles in the Welsh Marches. Above all, Edward was a most honourable King and behaved with chivalry when at war, not like that tyrant King of France.

Following the war in Scotland commencing, we had a parchment from Isabelle saying that she would be returning to England as soon as possible for she needed to sell her chateaux and collect as much of her wealth as possible. For the tyrant King Phillipi has made things quite uncomfortable for the English Nobles who are

Chapter 30

living in France; he has put great taxes upon them.

King Phillipi is nothing like his father who was an honourable man. The King is not an honest man and spreads false testimonies to stir up the feelings of his people telling dark tales. He tells how the Knight Templar "Trample and spit on the crucifix and do many horrible deeds." King Phillipi has formed his own Knights who are not of noble birth nor even bear a Coat of Arms. They have obtained their positions by their own efforts of dishonesty and are without any honour. As long as their service and loyalty is to the King, the King favours them and gives them a high position in the government.

"My dearest friends who I love dearly, I find this next piece of news difficult to write. The gossip amongst the English here is most sad. A youngish English Noble woman has been found shocked and injured laying next to a dead Knight Templar in woodlands in Compiegne. The Lady and the body have been taken to the Abbey of St. Jacques. It is said that the assault had been committed by the Knights of King Phillipi. People here call them the Knights of Satan.

My dearest friends, I hope for all our sakes that this is not our Alice and Gideon. There is so much trouble in both countries at the moment. I hope that it will not be too long before I meet with you. Love and much hope and prayers. Isabelle."

I was not shocked and I did not shed a tear. I knew that there was no time for tears. I had known in my heart for some time that something had happened to Alice. It is something that a mother feels in her bones. I have grieved for Alice every day.

"I will ride with you to France, William," I said as William was already getting ready to leave for France.

"No, Katherine, if you ride with me I shall have my mind on your care. I must keep a very clear head and have all my wits about me. I will travel with two of my best Captains and at great speed. We will take spare stallions. With us also I will take several pouches of gold just in case I have to pay a ransom to get Alice back." William kissed me on the forehead and was away to get supplies and to send the groom to Denham Castle to fetch the Captains.

Following William leaving, I just could not concentrate and spent most of my time unable to cope with the simplest of jobs. I tried spending time working in my herb garden which usually seemed to comfort me. This did not clear my head which was full of worries about Alice. Then there were my two sons fighting in the war and, of course, my beloved William who is not growing younger and is beginning to feel his age. He may be called upon to fight as France considers England her enemy at the moment.

I have such a beautiful home but that does not bring happiness. We seem as a family to travel from one trauma to another. I think about the nuns at Denny who live with calm heads. The only worry that they get is that they did not hear the early morning gong to go to prayers. Then I have known love that I have shared with a man and having one's child which is put into your arms following their birth. The pride of watching ones children grow and develop. I have had all this; they have not.

I asked Hugh if he would come and stay with me, at least I would have one member of my family with me. Over the years, Hugh and I have grown closer together. I feel for Hugh. I know that his pride is hurt, he is not a Knight but he rides well and I wish that William would understand him and treat him as a son. William could have asked Hugh to ride to France with him to find his sister. Hugh preached a service the next day with all the people of the Manor attending church to pray for the safety of our family.

I replied to Isabelle thanking her for sending the news, even though it was not good news. I informed her that William had left for the Abbey of St. Jacques.

"Please, Isabelle, do take good care of yourself and get back to England away from that tyrant King," I pleaded.

I asked Hugh to go to Hollymead Hall to let Amicia know what has happened so she could tell Will when he gets back from the war. Then I suggested that Hugh should spend a few days there with his daughter Maud. Hugh thought that this was a good idea.

It took William just over three weeks to find Alice and return home with her. Being summer, we had the doors of the Hall open. I heard William arrive and quickly went out into the court yard. I just stared with shock when I saw this crumbled person sitting next to William on a horse. This was my beautiful daughter Alice.

I moved towards her as the groom did the same to help her down from her horse.

"Leave her," said William in a loud voice. He dismounted and lifted Alice from the horse and, cradling her in his arms, took into the Hall, then upstairs to our day chamber, gently putting her down on the chaise longue.

Alice did not look at me or her surroundings. Her head was still tucked into her neck, with eyes looking downwards towards the ground. I knelt on the floor next to her, taking her hand in mine which felt so rough and dry, her skin so dark with blisters that had been covered with hard skin. I removed her head cover; there were just little stumps of hair growing from her scalp. I gently put her face between my hands and lifted her head so we made eye contact.

"My dearest daughter, you are home now. I am

your mother. What ever you have suffered your family will not let anything else happen to you. This we promise you, Alice".

She moved her eyes away from me and still did not speak. I tried to put my arms around her shoulders but she shrugged away. I stood up as tears rushed down my cheeks and turned to William just closing my eyes. He took me in his arms and then I saw that he had shed a tear, something I had not seen him do before. I looked up at him and said "What has happened to her? She is so afraid. When I took hold of her hand I could feel her heart beating so fast. Alice is like a drooping flower just waiting to die," I said with a lump in my throat.

"I will speak to you later. She needs food; she has not eaten all the way back from France. I did offer her food but she refused to take it. She just had a little fluid, enough to moisten her mouth, that's all," said William with a shrug of his head.

"I will get the cook to warm some goat's milk for her. It will be best. William, if you take Alice to her chamber I may be able to bathe her."

William took Alice to her chamber. Alice would not take the goat's milk but held her lips tightly closed.

"Alice, you must eat. For my sake and the sake of your brothers Will, John and Hugh and your dear father who loves you so much, as we all do."

I picked the milk up again and at first she turned her head away from me. Then she slowly turned it back. This time I spooned a little of the milk into her mouth which she swallowed with much difficulty. I then knew that she must have a sore mouth or throat which I must treat.

I finished feeding her the milk then commenced to wash her face. I removed her gown. I went to remove her under garments but this she would not allow and held tightly on to them. I then gave her the washing cloth, which she took. I noticed how bruised her arms and shoulders were and her neck was covered in bites. I had brought a clean dark gown and some under garments which I gave to her. Then I left the chamber hoping that she would wash herself.

    I went to find William and told him about the bruising on Alice. He said that the men who attacked had beaten her and had their wicked way with her. I will not have them called Knights. They are lower than animals; their soul is that of the lowest beast. They will pay with their lives for what they have done to our daughter and her husband. The time is not right just yet but it will not be too long. On the way back from France on the ship, I was speaking with a French Nobleman. He told me that he had heard that, following the defeat of Scotland, King Edward and King Phillipi had made a treaty. Now that the war with Scotland has been concluded, Will should be home soon and I will get him to go and see King Edward and tell the King what has happened to Alice. The King is aware of how fond his Queen Eleanor was of Alice and I am sure he will want to see the wrong put right as much as it can be.

    I will tell Will to ask the King for advice. The King I hope should then say "Leave it to me to find out who was responsible for the attack on Alice and her husband. For I have many spies in Phillipi's Court. When I have learnt their names, I will tell you so that you may take revenge." This way the King will think that the revenge was his idea and will not rebuff us.

    "I must return to Alice now to make sure that she has settled." I collected some healing lotions for her skin: comfrey cream and marigold cream, for her throat sage and Alder Flower rinse. Alice was sleeping peacefully when I returned. She had washed herself and put the clean gowns on. I was much happier now that she is slowly improving.

Over the next few days there was not much improvement. I could now take her hand and lead her into the day chamber. I would spend a great deal of time trying to build up her confidence. I spoke about what we did when she was a young child. I would speak about happy times in our life and ask her if she remembered the event but I got no reply. I knew that she was listening to me and sometimes even lifted her head to make eye contact. She did take broths which I offered her but would not eat them while anyone was in the chamber with her. She would eat it when alone.

Chapter 31
REVENGE IS NOT SWEET

The years have been passing and William and I are still as much in love as when we first met. We visit Alice quite often and she seems to be happy. I don't think that she has quite forgotten what happened to her and I don't think that she ever will. Alice says that she feels really close to Gideon living at that Abbey. That she is able to communicate with him through prayers and dreams

Alice had been made responsible for the Abbey garden and has made it very beautiful. I take with me when we visit different herbs from the Hall and she has built up quite a large herb garden. When William and I visit, we walk with Alice in the garden and then we will all sit and relax. Alice is also in charge of the vegetable garden and, with the help of the junior nuns, she can supply the Abbey with all its vegetable needs, and then have some left to sell at the local market. We are very proud of the life she has made for herself.

Alice did not want to return to her healing as she finds it very emotional as she always worked so closely with Gideon. The nuns who work in the infirmary often ask her for advice when they have a difficult problem, which she is pleased to give.

At home William and Hugh are busy drawing up plans for All Saint's Church. The Church needs structural work done. There has not been any work done to the church since my ancestor Sir Ralph de Passelewe rebuilt the wooden Anglo-Saxon Church into one of stone.

Since King Henry had built Westminster Abbey, King Edward has encouraged the land owners to reconstruct their churches where the need be and beautify them to the glory of God and to honour their deceased Queen Eleanor. William in his plans would start with reconstructing the tower and doing work on the outside of the Church where it is needed most. He then had plans for a new chancel and south aisle.

Isabelle is now back living in Gloucester now that she has had a new Hall built. Her two daughters still remain in France for they have married French Noblemen. William and I paid her a visit there and stayed just over a week. Although we enjoyed ourselves, William is still not one to socialise and says that he prefers Isabelle to visit us in Barewe.

John and Deirdie have visited us. Deirdie is a different young lady to what we are used to, but I do like her very much. She speaks with a blunt tongue and is very honest and expresses her feelings when she does speak. We can see that she and John are very much in love. They tell us that Deirdie is now with child.

William spoke to John about taking his chattels and wealth, which we had been keeping. He took some of the jewels and some gold and asked us to keep the rest in safe keeping for him for he is away from his home such a lot and they would be best with us.

William then spoke to John about himself and Will going to France to seek revenge for what happened to Alice and Gideon. He told John that Will has already had a word with King Edward and the King will be contacting loyal people in the service of his new wife-to-be. For he is to marry Marguerite de France in September this year, 1299. She is the daughter of the deceased King Phillipi III and sister to Phillipi IV. Marguerite does not get on with her brother and is quite happy to help us with the information that we need. Those in her service will be able to obtain the information from the government of the Legist which caused Gideon's death and that which happened to Alice.

Chapter 31

King Edward told Will that in no way would he be able to plead for us if anything went wrong with our plans and that we will be on our own. He gave his blessing and he said that he remembers how fond his beloved Queen Eleanor was of our Alice.

"I have also been to Denny Abbey to contact a Templar Knight who has just returned from France. He has given me names of safe places where the Knights Templar stay and a note which he has signed saying that we can be trusted. He tells me that there is a Legist who is a favourite with the French King called Guillaume de Nogaret who has deceived King Phillipi by giving false testimony against the Templars and several of the Templars have been burnt at the stake as being witches.

"I understand, Father, of course I will ride with you and Will. For is not for Alice's revenge but for the sake of the Gifford's honour," answered John proudly.

I begged William not to go after revenge for my sake and that Alice doesn't want revenge and would not want any of those that she holds so dear killed or hurt in any way. I expressed this strongly.

"It is nothing to do with Alice now. It is as John said: a question of family pride and honour. I will hear no more," said William firmly

"Do you have to go, William? Why, you are an old man of some eighty years. Let just Will and John go, they may do better without you with them," I pleaded.

"Enough. I will hear no more about this matter," was his reply being very vexed with me.

The day had come for them to leave for France. They were just taking their squires with them. William had not had a squire for many years for he is as old as William and has been retired some time. He would be taking one of his bright young Captains. They were also taking spare stallions. William had had tunics made for all the group; a copy of the French Legisti with a white cross on the back which made them look like the Knights Templar. William, Will and John each had a pouch of gold as they may have to pay for information.

"We will fight my deceased uncle Osbert's way. Let his name be our war cry when we attack. When we attack we will wear the tunic with the Gifford's Coat of Arms on it," said William to the party.

My loved ones left and although we had not spoken to our people in the Manor, they seemed to know that there was something important about to happen. For they lined the streets to wave goodbye to William's party and wish them good luck. I was so pleased to see how much affection our people had for my family. I then went straight to the church to pray for them. Hugh was already there praying. He did love his brothers, even if he thought that they were given the best chances in life. To me Hugh was a good son and his life did not hold much happiness for him.

My days were long and full of worry. I have known these days before many times. I knew that I would have to keep occupied. I would ride to Thetford to see Alice and we would pray together. Often I would fall asleep on the seat in the herb garden there with the help of the beautiful aroma. For I did not sleep at night; I could not calm my mind.

It was some six weeks when there was noise in the court yard of the Hall. There I could see six figures on horses at the far side of the yard. As I hurried over, I thanked God for their safe return.

Will came towards me. "Mother, I do not wish to alarm you. I do not think that there is much wrong."

I knew from these words that there was indeed something wrong. I watched as they gently took William down from his horse.

Chapter 31

"Take him straight to his bed chamber," directed Will.

I followed as they carried William up the stairs and into the chamber and laid him upon the bed.

As I looked at him where he lay, he was so drawn and tired looking. I put my hand upon his brow, it was wet and clammy. As I did so, he opened his eyes and just said "Katherine", closing his eyes again.

I looked at Will and John and asked "What is wrong?"

"We do not know, Mother," was the reply.

"I have already sent a messenger to the Abbey in Bury for a Healer," said John.

"We really do not know what happened to Father. We had been very successful obtaining our revenge and had just commenced our last assault which had gone very well for us but had taken a great deal of time for us to make a mark on the combat. One of our opponents had fled the battle and John and I rode after him. Our men followed us, leaving Father to check the dead. When we returned, Father was still on his horse but slumped over it. There didn't seem to be any movement in his right arm and his speech came out all wrong and muddled," said Will.

I had seen William's condition before, it is most serious. Some say that it is the work of the Devil; others say that it is a punishment from God for action which God does not approve of.

I sent for some warm water and John and I bathed William for he was very dirty from his travels. While we made him comfortable, his limb just hung down. I tried speaking to him; he did understand but when he tried to answer his speech came out muddled.

The Healer arrived, it was Father Nicholas whom I had known for many years, for he often came and obtained herbs from us for his healing. I had great confidence in his healing ability. Father Nicholas examined William and then continued to put sharp needles into William's right arm to see if there was any pain and feeling but there was not any. The Healer then put the needles into William's right leg and William drew his leg away from the Healer trying to say something to him.

The Healer looked at me, and said "That's good, his right leg is not affected. Now I must look into Sir William's mouth." Father Nicholas opened William's mouth and peered down his throat and then he proceeded to pull his tongue with much force. William's response was to push the Father away with great force with his left hand. So great was the force that he would have fallen to the ground but John managed to catch him.

"Yes," said Father Nicholas. "He is not weak, that is a good sign. The problem is that his brain is just worn out. Not completely worn out, it is crying out for rest. What must happen is that we must shut the brain down to give it chance to recover. It means that he must sleep for at least three days. In that time he must not be woken to eat or drink or anything else. To make sure that this happens, I must administer to him a large dose of Opium which I have with me. Most of the time it works and there are complete recoveries but, there again, sometimes there is no recovery. The decision is yours, Lady Katherine."

I knew that William could understand what I was saying even though he could not speak. I told him what Father Nicholas had said and asked him if he wanted this treatment. He said "Yes" with a nod of his head. The Healer then had some ale heated and put the Opium into it and we got William to drink it.

Chapter 31

"That is a good sign," said the Healer, "he can swallow. That is a very good sign indeed. Yes, a very good sign. I am sure we will have success here."

Father Nicholas had the evening meal with us. Hugh had also joined us. My sons and Father Nicholas ate the meal with great lust for Will and John needed a good meal following their travels and one could see that Father Nicholas had a liking for fine food and wine. Myself, I was unable to eat and had to take my leave. I went and sat with William who was already asleep and his breathing was very shallow which Father Nicholas has said it would be. I just sat and held William's hand and gazed at the tired lines on his brow. He was still very handsome. His eye brows and lashes were now white, as was his hair. I moistened his lips and spoke to him, although I knew he could not hear me.

"My dearest husband, I do hope that I have been able to make you happy during the short time which we have had together. Your life has been very hard with all the fighting and things which were not of your taste which you had to do in the name of God and the King."

I fell asleep in the chair and woke at dawn. William was still asleep so things were going to plan. I moistened his mouth and put cool cloths containing lavender water on his brow and made him as comfortable as I could. On returning to the day chamber, I found that Will and John had already left. I was told by the staff that Father Nicholas was still in his chamber and that he had drunk so much wine the evening before that Hugh had to put him into a bed for the night. I thought to myself that it must be something to do with being a priest that they drink so much.

Three days had gone and Hugh had stayed with me to help me nurse his father. William had started to stir, we were waiting for Father Nicholas to return.

Chapter 31

William had woken up before he made his return. So Hugh sat William up in bed and I gave him some goat's milk which he drank and he returned the tumbler back for some more milk. Father Nicholas did return later in the day. He examined the right arm with his sharp needles and this time William pulled it away.

"Well, Sir William is much improved. The right arm will need to be exercised by moving it t three or four times day. As for speech, encourage him to talk and if the words do not come out in the correct order, tell him how to say what it is he wants to say and make him say it several times. This way the brain will learn the order of things again. It is just a matter of time now. Goodness, it is getting late in the day; by the time I have ridden back to the Abbey I will have missed my meal," said Father Nicholas with such a pleading smile.

"Father would be very honoured if you would take your meal with us and I will have a chamber prepared so you don't have to leave in the dark," I said as I smiled back.

The weeks passed and William made a good recovery. He was able to hold objects in his right hand - not a sword, thank goodness. His speech was making improvement each day. He got very frustrated sometimes and I would tell him how well he was doing. We went riding together quite often and he could walk to the church to oversee the construction work.

Chapter 32
WILLIAM'S LAST JOURNEY

We didn't see much of our sons. Will and John had gone with King Edward to fight in Scotland, this time against William Wallace. William Wallace was defeated in 1305 and was captured and executed.

King Edward has now established a government in Scotland and we all hope that now Edward would be satisfied and spend some peaceful years away from war for he is now getting quite old. My sons, like Edward, are also getting on in years and would like a little less of war and some time to spend with their families and Manors. The wars cost everyone so much in taxes.

The peace was not for very long - only two years - and it was back to Scotland for the Scots had revolted again. They crowned a man called Robert Bruce as the King of Scotland which did not please King Edward.

My sons and grandsons were off again to try to subdue the Scots. This time King Edward did not make it for he died from dysentery en route, at Burgh-on-Sea, Cumberland and had to be taken back to Westminster for burial.

His son Prince Edward was crowned King in February 1308 under King Edward III. Conditions in the country did not improve. He was not liked by his subjects and failed to appease the Barons. He followed in his grandmother's footsteps and preferred foreigners as his favourites and gave them positions in the government. Among his favourites were Peter de Gavescton and Hugh de Despensers.

William and I were often visited by our grandchildren and we are now also great-grandparents. Hugh was now also a grand-parent, Maud had married a Captain in duty with the De Clares and is very happy with three children. I have made the Manor of Heigham over to Hugh when I am deceased. Of course Will, being the eldest son, will inherit Barewe when William has gone and John has already inherited from his uncle.

The work being done on All Saints is now nearly completed; it is just the south chancel to be finished.

William has had a beautiful tomb built. It is decorated with a frieze of knights in combat in the Holy War. Also at the top of the tomb there is a painting of two angels flying up to Heaven holding a baby between them. This is meant to be William's son Walter. The tomb bears the Gifford Coat of Arms and next to it is a smaller Passelewe Arms in honour of myself.

I manage much of the Manor now for William sleeps a great deal. He is now very forgetful. I just say to him when I think that something needs doing. "William, I thought that you were going to get (what ever needed doing) done?" Then he replies "Yes. I must remind them, they must have forgotten." For he is still a man of great pride and would not consider that it could be him who was forgetful. This has all happened since his illness but I think that he is quite a happy man.

It was only a few weeks later that William had gone to the church to see if the chancel was now finished. He had not been gone very long when Hugh returned to the Hall with others pushing his father in a hand cart. As they entered the Hall, Hugh called out "Mother, Father has collapsed."

Hugh, with the help of the servants got William to the bed chamber.

"William, my dearest," I said as I put my hand upon his brow which was all clammy. His lips had turned mauve and his face was tinged with that colour, he was also clasping his left arm.

"Katherine, I have such pains in my chest," he said, letting go of his arm and taking hold of my hand. "It

Chapter 32

is time for me to leave you, Katherine," he said, gasping for breath. "I do not want you to grieve for me, Katherine, when I have gone. I will still be with you in spirit."

"Rest, my dearest," I said, putting my cheek next to his. I then felt the last three thuds of his heart upon my face and, as I did so, I said "In the name of the Father, the Son and the Holy Spirit." I then closed his eyes with my fingers and Hugh prayed for his soul.

William was now with Bea and Walter and our dear family that had already left us. I stood up straight and held my head up full of pride as Berta had taught me.

"Hugh, you must ride at once to let Will know what has happened. Then he must ride and find John and let him know of his father's demise."

"Mother, I will let Will know but there is not time for Will to find John for Father needs to be buried. It will take too long to ride all that way and back again."

"I would like all the family at the service, Hugh. King Edward kept Queen Eleanor for two weeks before she got to Westminster for her burial."

"She was embalmed and her viscera were removed in Lincolnshire before she started her long journey back," Hugh said gently to me.

"Just let Will know. You go now Hugh. I will send for the carpenter to direct him how to make a coffin fit for a Knight. I will have a Captain take a message to let Isabelle know, she may not be able to make it for the service either. Then there is Alice; someone must go to Thetford to fetch her home."

"Shall I call into the Abbey and ask the Archbishop to call on you so that you can make arrangements with him for the burial service?" asked Hugh.

"No. I know that your Father, because of his

position, should have a Bishop to take the service but we have always lead a simple life and I could not think of anyone better that you, Hugh, to take it. For you love and know your father and that is what I want." Hugh then rode off with some haste.

Hugh was back by the next day along with Will. They then started to prepare their father's body. They dressed William in his tunic which bore the Coat of Arms on it. Also they put his gilded spurs of a Knight on him and the Knight's sword belt and placed his sword in his hand. His amour would stand next to the tomb. Then the coffin was taken to All Saints where it would be put on display with the lid off so the rest of the family and friends and people from our Manor could come and pay homage to him and say their farewells.

The Knights in the family would take it in turn to stand vigil both day and night till the lid is put on the coffin and the coffin placed in the tomb and closed.

I put on my widow's robes. I will remain in them for the rest of my days on earth. This way I will show that I have no interest in remarrying. I made sure that I was kept busy so that I stopped the sadness which I felt entering my head. For my husband had asked me not to grieve for him. Also I am the Lady of the Manor and a Gifford and Passelwe and must always be seen holding my head high with pride and not weeping.

I had to direct the servants about the sort of food that the guests would require and to get the bed chambers ready for them. I did not know how many guests would be attending the service. Will had let people know about his father's death and had also been to fetch his sister home.

The day of entombing had arrived and I had all my family around me except for John. There were representatives of all the Suffolk Nobility, the De Clares,

Chapter 32

the Dukes of Norfolk and Bedford, William's old friend Sir Thomas Gifford from Stoke by Nayland and the town Burgesses and Alderman. The church was full and our people from the Manor who could not get in the church had to stand outside and there was a large crowd. All these people came to pay their respects to my husband I was so honoured. Just as Hugh and Will were going to close the coffin there was the noise of some cheers from outside the church. Everyone looked at the church door then in came John, covered in dust from his long ride. I was so pleased. He went straight to the altar and paid homage to his father. Then John and his brothers and my oldest grandson William lifted the coffin upon their shoulders and took it to the tomb where they lowered the coffin into its place and put the lid on.

For the next years, the days were long for me. Isabelle visited me several times, usually bringing her favourite grand-daughter Elizabeth with her. Although she was now an old lady, she was still as colourful as ever, riding with her large retinue. She now had a Knight Errant who had dusty brown skin and was indeed very handsome. He was known as Leonard and caused a great deal of interest. My sons frowned on Isabelle but I loved her visits; she brought colour into my life which was usually very dull.

It was always "Katherine do you remember?" and we would reminisce on the time we were growing up together which caused much laughter together. She would bring me all the sort of news ladies like to hear about which my sons either don't want to know or don't bother to tell me. I was always quite sad when she left for we still had the bonding for each other which came from our early childhood.

In 1314 King Edward II led an army once again against Scotland and was defeated by Robert Bruce at

Chapter 32

Bannock Burn and was unable to defend the North of England. This brought great sadness for my John's youngest son David was killed. The Barons and Earls were angered by the King and held little respect for him. The whole of England was suffering from increased taxes which caused all the King's subjects much hardship.

In the following seven years the harvests were very poor each year and there was near famine everywhere. My son Will was looking for money for he had expanded his sheep farms greatly over the years, mostly on land that was leased. The owners of the land were the De Clares who also needed money and said that Will must buy the land or vacate it.

So a Transaction was made between the Countess of Gloucester (Isabelle) that freed land which Will required in Waldingfield for his sheep. He should give the Manor of Barewe, including the Hall and the Church, to Isabelle's grand-daughter Elizabeth who was married to Bartholmew Badlesmere. My husband, of course, left Barewe to William his eldest son with the condition that I should live at the Hall for the rest of my remaining days. Will really needed this Transaction to be done so I released him and I will go and live at Heigham, although it really hurt deep down to give the Hall up which William built for us.

My grandson William had also married into the De Walpole family and now owns the Manors of Brockley, Whepstead, Whelnetham, Lawshall and Hartest in Suffolk. Hugh would inherit Heigham when I died and of course John has already inherited his uncle's Manors.

Part of the agreement was that Isabelle would keep Hugh in gowns and give him £100.00 a year while I live and that he could remain as Rector and also clerk for her.

Chapter 32

I moved to Heigham and was very sad for it felt as if I had sold my people as well. I no longer had control over their well-being. Hugh helped me remove my personal belongings. I also had to remove John's trunk of treasures and money which was still in my safe keeping. Will had already taken his father's stallions and was continuing with the breeding of them.

Lady Elizabeth only lived at the Hall and held the Manor for one year. For her husband Sir Badlesmere joined the King's cousin Sir Thomas of Lancaster in a revolt against King Edward caused by a territorial ambition of the Despensers, father and son, in Wales. Badlesmere and Thomas of Lancaster were defeated at Boroughbridge in Yorkshire in March 1322 and were executed. The King took Barewe for the Crown, the punishment for a revolt against the King. The King then gave it to Hugh Despenser who was also married into the Clare family. For he married Eleanor, niece to the King and sister to the young Earl Gilbert de Clare. This really vexed Isabelle to think that her grand-daughter had her Manor taken away by the family.

Sir Hugh Despenser was a bad Lord of the Manor and treated the villeins badly. He also made me when I attended All Saints to sit in a pew at the back of the Church with the villeins. He did not bother about the crops or the animals in the Manor and the Manor began to get run down. He just took from it for his own needs. Also Hugh had problems getting payment from him for being Rector of the church.

This made Hugh's drinking problem worse. He spent much of his time in Bury in the taverns. He was often brought home just before dawn on a Sunday morning and I would have the job of making him sober so he could take the services at the church. Fortunately Hugh Despenser and Lady Eleanor were away a great deal at Court with the King and did not get to know of Hugh's habits.

It all came to a head when John came to visit me at Heigham in 1325.

"I will take my chattels and treasures with me as I will be returning home following my visit here."

John and I went to collect them and when we opened the trunk we were both shocked for there were lots of items missing. John confronted his brother Hugh who said that he had taken them and had meant to replace them but, since Despenser had lived at the Hall, he was unable to get the money to buy them back.

"Mother I will not say anything for your sake. I will now no longer consider Hugh as my blood brother. I do so for is he not a man of the cloth, to do such a terrible thing?" said John, so vexed and sad. John cut short his visit; he said that he could not now stay in the same place as Hugh.

Somehow Sir Despenser got to hear about our troubles and, with great delight, told Hugh that he could no longer be Reverend of All Saints Church as "he was no man of God but had sold his soul to the Devil."

I was so unhappy I could not go to church in Barewe. I could not hold my head up high amongst those who were once my people. Hugh no loner stayed at Barewe and I only got news about him now and again. I did visit Alice sometimes but I was getting to be a very old lady and found riding very difficult.

It was only the following year that I felt a little happy for Sir Despenser was executed. The wife of King Edward, Queen Isabelle, returned from France with the King's young son, also Edward. She was with Sir Rodger Mortimer, said to be the Queen's lover, and with them a rebel army. They landed at Orwell in Suffolk. When the government heard that she had young Prince

Chapter 32

Edward with her, there was no war. The government just collapsed and executed Hugh Despenser.

Barewe was returned to Elizabeth Badlesmere and her young son Giles who now owned the Manor. A young man called John de Bereton took care of the Manor for Elizabeth and the villeins were much happier. Hugh started to visit Heigham again and did not drink so much now. He was on good terms with John de Bereton and they spent a great deal of time together. Hugh could not return to being the priest at the Church for there was now a Rector called Joes de Felton.

Chapter 33
THE RISING AT BURY ST EDMUNDS

It had been another poor harvest all over England. It was January 1327 and, as always in January, food to feed the town and country people is nearly always short. This year seems worse than others for there is near famine. Hugh has told me that at a tavern in Bury where Hugh does most of his socializing there gathers a large group of townsmen of some importance with leading men like John Frauncy and others who are encouraged by London agitators to do something about the situation.

I asked Hugh, "What could be done if there is not enough food?"

"It is so terrible in the town, people are starving so near to death. I saw a young mother carrying her young child in her arms. The child was dead and she did not know what to do with it. I followed her to see if I could be of some comfort to her. She just took the dead child to the cemetery and lay it on a grave and just lay down beside it, waiting to die. I could not persuade her to come with me. So I just had to leave her," he told me.

"Hugh, that was terrible. Could you not get any help for her?" I asked.

"No, there many like her, there is no one to help them except those greedy abbots and monks who still have a great deal of food and wine and they will not help. They just keep on growing fat and rounder from all their gluttony. The Alderman went to the Abbey to beg for help for the starving people. Abbott Richard told the Alderman that they could not help. That they needed all the food they have and that it is time that townsfolk paid the money that is owed in taxes to the Abbey. For the Monks have no choice but to let the Sheriff know that the people of Bury St. Edmunds are refusing to pay their

Chapter 33

taxes," said Hugh.

"There is no way I can help. We have so little here for the few people who live in Heigham. I have already had most of the livestock killed off. I would send food if I could, Hugh," I said.

"It would not help. I think that it would make things worse. We must do something else altogether. The people in the town they must stand together against the Monks. That will be the only way," said Hugh.

"That will not help, it will just make trouble," I said, very worried.

"I must go now, Mother. I will not be seeing you for a few days or so. Please do not worry. Perhaps it may be good for you to go and stay with Alice for a while," said Hugh, taking his leave.

I would not be going to stay with Alice for I have a feeling that it important that I stay here.

It all started on the 14th January. The Tollhouse bell was rung and some three thousand armed people assembled having forced entrance at the great gate of the Abbey. They roughly handled the monks and servants. They took a register and accounts which showed that the monks had been falsifying the accounts which led to the Abbotts getting in trouble with the Baron of the Exchequer.

January 15th. Nine monks were taken prisoner and compelled to sign with common seal not to take action against the rebels and to pay debts due to the town of £2,000 and fifty barrels of wine. The leading Burgesses devoted themselves to taking over the government of the borough and its profits. Rent due to the Abbey was collected for the use of the Aldermen. A new Alderman was made, John de Breton the same who held Barewe for Giles Baslemere.

On January 28th Abbott Richard returned from

Chapter 33

London hoping to restore peace. Abbott Richard was forced to sign a charter prepared for him, containing a restatement of the ancient borough privileges and new demands for the townspeoples' freedom from monastic rule. The Abbott was allowed to return to London to get the charter royally confirmed.

On advice of the Barons, the Abbott was told to ignore the charter as he had signed under duress. On February 16th the townspeople, hearing of treason, started to riot again, joined this time by the villeins of the countryside who also wanted freedom from toll and customary work.

By March, the disturbed conditions of the town led to a Royal Mandate to the Abbott and to the Bailiffs and the Townsmen of Bury St. Edmunds forbidding them to fight each other and to make peace with each or to forfeit their wealth. On May the 26th the Abbey was taken into the King's protection. On August 1st the King sent a letter to the town's Burgesses saying that he was going to proceed with vigour against them, because they had imprisoned and beat the Abbott while the King was in Scotland.

In June the following year, Thomas Earl of Norfolk and his army marched on Bury to imprison the rebels. Thirty cart loads of prisoners - over four hundred people -were taken to Norwich for trial. I just do not know what had happened to Hugh. I do know that he did take part in the rising up against the Abbotts and monks. I did hear that Hugh spoke up for the prisoners and that he was thrown into a cart along with them and was taken off to Norwich prison.

Will did ride to Norwich to plea for Hugh but could not find any trace of him. Will said that some people said that Hugh was riding to London with a few others so they could come back at a later date and revolt again. Others

Chapter 33

said that Hugh had taken off to Scotland.

Will asked "What are you going to do now, Mother? Are you going to stay here at Heigham or are you coming back home with me to live with Amicia and myself? You could go and live with Alice at the Abbey at Thetford or even go and live with Isabelle. I am sure that she would welcome you and be pleased with your company." I knew what I wanted to do, I was going to stay at Heigham and keep the home going in case Hugh came home. I said to Will that I would give thought to the options for I did not discuss the situation with Will. Will returned to Waldingfield without me. The following day I had my bailiffs visit most of the villages in Suffolk to see if Hugh was in hiding anywhere.

I was now old and lonely and seemed to have lost interest in most things. I did sometimes walk to All Saints Church to pray to God and talk to William and I would say that I hoped that it would not be too long till I was with William. I would hurry to the main door of the Hall if I heard the sound of a horse arriving at Heigham, just hoping that it would be Hugh. It was never Hugh, though. I could not sleep at night; I always had things on my mind. I would think about Hugh and would feel full of guilt thinking that it was my fault that Hugh had such an unhappy life. Then I would think what would happen when I died for, if God should choose for me to go to Heaven, William would already be there with his young son Walter and William's beautiful wife Bea. I have heard that one remains at the age that they were when they died. Bea was young and beautiful and I am all old with a crinkly face and white hair. What man would want to be with an old lady when he could be with a young one? I don't think that I would be able to function each day with Bea being young and myself being old. I would then call out to William asking what I should do. Then the servants would come into my bed chamber and say that I must be quiet for Sir William is dead and cannot hear me and that it is best for me to go to sleep. Who do they think they are to tell me what is best for me?

    Then one night I thought that I would show these people at the Hall what I can do. I shall go to the Church in Barewe and speak to William. I waited till they had all gone to bed and could not hear them any more. Then I put on my cloak and let myself quietly out the main door. It was very dark and cold and I stumbled and fell over once or twice but I would not give up. I will go to All Saints Church and ask William if he was happy with Bea and ask him what I shall do. I know he would tell me even if it is in my next dream. For he would not let me down; he would tell me what I should do.

    I know that I went to the church, I can remember that. I then thought that I would go and sit in Barewe Hall's herb garden. The Hall was built for me and I love it and it should still be mine. Then I don't know what happened. I remember standing at the large fish pond and throwing stones in like William and I used to do. That is the last thing that I can remember. I do not know what happened or how I died.

    Well, here I am. I have been walking around the Herb Garden and the Moat and Hall and sometimes the Manor if there is something I want to see. For hundreds of years, I have watched people come and go and watched the demise of my beautiful home. There is no time or period of time - I can go and come in any period of history. I am not aware of the length of the many hundreds of years I have been in Barewe. I am not free, something holds me here. I want to be with my husband wherever he is.

I ask you, Pat, to tell my story. Then perhaps whatever holds me here will release me, Katherine Spirit of the

Chapter 33

Dell.

ISBN 1412090061-X